Gender Equality
Striving for Justice in an Unequal World

UNITED NATIONS RESEARCH INSTITUTE FOR SOCIAL DEVELOPMENT

Printed in France
GE.05-00187-February 2005-4,500
UNRISD/GPR/05/1

ISBN 92-9085-052-3
Sales No. E.05.III.Y.1

Contents

Tables

Figures

Boxes

Acknowledgements

In preparing this report, UNRISD has benefited immensely from the valuable contributions of a large number of individuals and organizations.

Background research was carried out on four broad thematic areas: macroeconomics, well-being and gender equality; women, work and social policy; women in politics and public life; and gender, armed conflict and the search for peace. The research was carried out under the general direction of Shahra Razavi; the research under the four thematic areas was coordinated by Ann Zammit (Section 1), Shahra Razavi (Section 2), Anne Marie Goetz (Section 3) and Urvashi Butalia (Section 4). The chapters were written by Urvashi Butalia, Anne Marie Goetz, Maxine Molyneux, Donna Pankhurst, Nicola Piper, Shahra Razavi, Stephanie Seguino and Ann Zammit.

The report was edited by Maggie Black. Susana Franco supervised the analysis of the data and the construction of the tables and figures of the report, with the collaboration of Hanny Cueva for Section 3. Research assistance was provided by Alessandra Dal Secco, Constanza Tabbush, Naomi Alfini, Zohra Moosa and Jaya Bhattacharji.

At UNRISD, Caroline Danloy coordinated the production and translation of the report. Susan Curran copyedited the text. Latitude designed the cover and the inside layout of the report.

The following authors prepared background papers for the report: Brooke Ackerly, Cecile Ambert, Paola Aznar, Amrita Basu, Rasil Basu, Jo Beall, Günseli Berik, Savitri Bisnath, Virginia Bouvier, Monica Boyd, Elissa Braunstein, Rosalia Cortes, Bina D'Costa, Carmen Diana Deere, Ngoné Diop, Tanja Djuric-Kuzmanovic, Anita Doraisami, Rada Drezgic, Sokari Ekine, Alma Espino, Rosalind Eyben, Goran Fejic, Eva Fodor, Dan Gallin, Jayati Ghosh, Meghna Guhathakurta, Chandra Hardy, Pat Horn, Rada Ivekovic, Cecile Jackson, Du Jie, Deniz Kandiyoti, Ratna Kapur, Eleonore Kofman, Teréz Laky, Marnia Lazreg, Ching Kwan Lee, Zongmin Li, Ilja Luciak, Frances Lund, Maureen Mackintosh, Rashida Manjoo, Alejandra Massolo, Valentine Moghadam, Sisonke Msimang, Binaifer Nowrojee, Celestine Nyamu-Musembi, Le Anh Tu Packard, Ito Peng, Deanna Pikkov, Nicola Piper, Nitya Rao, Rita Reddy, Teresa Sacchet, Kumudini Samuel, Stephanie Seguino, Onalenna Selolwane, Gita Sen, Sunanda Sen, Carolyn Israel Sobritchea, Fatou Sow, Silke Steinhilber, Ramya Subrahmanian, Paula Tibandebage, Rosalba Todaro, Dzodzi Tsikata, Martha Walsh, Ann Whitehead, Keiko Yamanaka and Dubravka Žarkov.

The report benefited greatly from the intellectual guidance provided by the members of the Advisory Group: Jan Breman, Diane Elson, Maria del Carmen Feijoo, Marnia Lazreg, Maxine Molyneux, Gita Sen, Fatou Sow, Julia Szalai and Paul Tiyambe Zeleza.

The following organizations generously shared their data series and research materials: the United Nations Population Fund (UNFPA) provided information for the construction of the table on women's rights, gender-based violence and reproductive rights in Chapter 1; the Statistical Division of the Office of the United Nations High Commissioner for Refugees (UNHCR) supplied detailed information for the preparation of the figures in Chapter 13 on refugees and other people of concern; and the Department of Peace and Conflict Research,

Uppsala University, Sweden, provided valuable assistance in analysing data on armed conflict worldwide.

Naila Kabeer and Georgina Waylen as external referees provided valuable comments on the draft report. Useful comments and inputs were also received from the following individuals: Purshottam Agarwal, Debbie Budlender, Stephanie Barrientos, Damini Butalia, Monica Das Gupta, Diane Elson, Yakin Ertürk, Vrinda Grover, Shireen Hassim, Sahba Husain, Elizabeth Jelin, Rob Jenkins, Satyakam Joshi, Jamal Kidwai, Frances Lund, Maureen Mackintosh, Amina Mama, Kavita Punjabi, Dzodzi Tsikata, Dilip Simeon, Richa Singh, Amanda Sloat, Martha Walsh and Ann Whitehead.

At UNRISD, the research staff provided valuable comments and feedback. Special thanks are due to Yusuf Bangura, Thandika Mkandawire and Peter Utting for their extensive intellectual engagement with the report. Jenifer Freedman provided useful input on the production and dissemination of the report. Thanks are also due to Josephine Grin-Yates, Sylvie Brenninkmeijer-Liu and Wendy Salvo, who provided administrative support throughout the project.

UNRISD would like to thank the European Union, the Department for Research Co-operation of the Swedish International Development Agency (Sida/SAREC), the International Development Research Centre (IDRC, Ottawa, Canada) and the government of the Netherlands for their financial support for the preparation of this report.

Preface

The Fourth World Conference on Women, held in Beijing in September 1995, was a high point in international efforts to advance women's human rights in all dimensions. Ten years on, many actors around the world will be reflecting on the achievements of the past decade.

The impetus for this report was the recognition that the mainstream international policy debates on some of the most pressing and contested issues of our time—economic liberalization, democratization and governance reforms, and identity and conflict—are not being systematically informed by the knowledge that is being generated through gender research and scholarship. At a time when organizations and researchers concerned about global progress in gender equality—both within the UN system and outside it—were preparing the "Beijing Plus Ten" assessment requested for 2005 by the UN General Assembly in June 2000, a research-based report that set out to fill this lacuna appeared appropriate.

As an autonomous research institute within the UN system with an ongoing programme of research on the gender dimensions of development, UNRISD seemed well placed to make a useful research-based contribution to this process of reflection and debate, tackling difficult and controversial issues that currently preoccupy many people around the world. While drawing on the Institute's past and ongoing research programme on gender, a wide range of feminist scholars from diverse countries and regions, particularly in the South, were commissioned to prepare background papers. Their work has immensely enriched the substantive content of this report.

Economic and political reforms of the 1990s play a central role in the analysis that is presented here. If most of these reforms did not directly address gender equality, they nevertheless received considerable scrutiny from a gender perspective. One reason was that whatever their design and intentions, the reforms had enormous implications for gender relations and women's well-being.

While the task of evaluating progress in gender equality poses many challenges, there is no doubt that there have been significant improvements in the social and economic status of women. One of the most outstanding developments of the past decade is the growing presence of women in the public sphere—whether as political actors in national legislatures, civil society organizations and social movements, or as economic agents increasingly visible in the paid workforce and in migrant streams. There has also been much progress in the enrolment of girls in primary and secondary education. Women in the state and legislature in many countries, building on political pressures brought to bear by women's movements, have worked hard to make national laws more responsive to women's rights.

Yet as the report argues, progress has been uneven, and the positive outcomes must be qualified in the light of continuing gender inequalities and a less than favourable economic and political environment.

Recent years have seen some reassessment of the role of the state, a rediscovery of social policies, and a new faith in institutions and "good governance" as necessary to foster growth and a vibrant private sector. However, while this may have rendered the "Washington Consensus" more palatable, the now more eclectic policy reform package retains some of the core elements of economic orthodoxy—trade and financial liberalization, and tight monetary and fiscal policies—while adding the "good governance" agenda onto it.

Orthodox economic policies have produced disappointing outcomes, even in the estimate of their designers. Rural livelihoods have become more insecure in contexts where cutbacks in state support to domestic agriculture have coincided with increasing exposure to competition from large subsidized producers. Insecurity is also on the increase across the world with the growth of informal economies, in which women are overwhelmingly concentrated. This has meant the increasing precariousness of jobs and a greater insecurity of livelihoods. With weak public health and welfare programmes, and underfunded and fragile infrastructures, the provision of unpaid care by women and girls has intensified, reaching intolerable levels, for example, in sub-Saharan Africa, where the HIV/AIDS epidemic is taking a staggering toll of lives.

For the vast majority of women, gender equality will remain a distant dream as long as the market continues to be the principal arbiter of policy. Attaining gender equality requires the strengthening of publicly accountable and universal systems of social provisioning. This means investing in well-functioning and accessible public health and education services, labour standards and rights that protect women's employment and conditions of work, and investment in the public provision of a range of complementary services that support the care economy.

The task of democratizing the state, and building its capacity and accountability to its citizens has long been emphasized by scholars and activists from the South. The difficulties that women have experienced in promoting gender-equity legislation, and in seeing it passed into law and implemented, indicates that women have a keen interest in seeing the capacity and accountability of the state strengthened. Yet the danger in much of the current good governance reforms is that they impose highly abstract and uniform institutional blueprints on developing countries that many fear will not even produce a vibrant private sector, let alone enhance social equality.

In recent decades, virtually all countries have witnessed a deepening of inequality as neoliberal macroeconomic policies have tightened their hold, and previously accepted values such as equality and redistribution have been sidelined. Many of the prevailing policies—trade and financial liberalization, tight monetary and fiscal policies, market-based entitlements to welfare—operate as obstacles to meeting the objectives that were agreed upon in the global conferences of the 1990s, including in Beijing. Indeed, as the title of this report alludes, achieving gender equality and gender justice will be very difficult in a world that is increasingly unequal.

On the tenth anniversary of the Beijing Conference, women's movements will be considering not only the continued dominance of ideologies and policies oblivious to both developmental concerns and inequality, but the challenges thrown up by the recent shifts in geopolitics and the new forms of religious-identity politics. Many fear that women's ambitions for social change risk taking a back seat to concerns about security. The multilateral framework within which transnational feminist networks painstakingly nurtured a global women's rights regime over the years appears fragile today. There is the danger that in a polarized ideological climate where security concerns loom large and internal dissent is discouraged, it will be difficult to sustain the autonomous spaces that have been so essential for the vibrancy of women's movements.

Three overarching messages emerge from this report. The first highlights the dangers of an axiomatic mode of thinking in which policy implications are simply derived from first principles. Actual outcomes are, however, deeply conditioned by multiple factors so that a similar set of policies can have dramatically different outcomes in different settings. Thus, for instance, the assumption that liberalization of labour markets would automatically benefit social groups disadvantaged by extant labour market regimes is not borne out by evidence. In virtually every case where there have been improvements, these have been due to a whole range of complementary policies, including affirmative action, and special investments in human development and social infrastructure.

The second key lesson is the importance of attending to issues of redistribution, social protection, production and reproduction simultaneously. Today, social policy remains largely detached from economic policy and continues to be seen as a way of mitigating the social costs of unfettered economic liberalization. What is needed is a major rethinking of economic policies and a much more serious attempt to integrate social and economic policy.

Third, success in the economic and social domains determines the "quality" of democracies. The report clearly suggests that the considerable political gains that women have made in the last decade have been compromised by failures in the social

and economic policy arena that have rendered the lives of most women and their dependents insecure. The challenge thus remains in using women's gains in terms of political presence to render state policies, practices and spending patterns more responsive to the interests of all women.

Thandika Mkandawire
Director
December 2004

Overview

After Beijing:
Uneven progress in an unequal world

Ten years after the Fourth World Conference on Women in Beijing an important question that many women's organizations around the world will be asking is how much has been achieved in the past decade? For those interested in the quest for gender equality, the answers are difficult to find as well as being ambiguous.

There have clearly been some notable gains for women over the period: increased visibility in elected assemblies and state institutions; some closing of gender gaps in primary, and to a lesser extent secondary, school enrolment; a larger female presence in the labour market and in labour flows that cross international borders; and lower fertility rates.

Such changes in women's lives are associated with the social transformations that attend economic development, but they are not simply the by-product of economic growth. In many instances change in women's social position has been instigated or accelerated by state reforms and social movements. Women's movements, both national and transnational, took advantage of the changed political context of the 1990s to advance women's rights. One of the remarkable achievements was in bringing issues of sexual and reproductive health and rights, violence against women, and inequality of power in gender relations to the centre of global and national debates.

The persistence of gender inequalities

Such positive outcomes must be qualified in the light of continuing gender inequalities, and a less than favourable economic and political environment.

Despite women's greater numerical presence in the world of work and in the domain of politics, the narrowing of these broadly defined gender gaps conceals marked gender asymmetries and segmentation, which place limits on women's access to income, authority and power. Declining fertility continues to improve women's life chances in their reproductive years in many countries, but in some countries it has also been associated with an increase in artificially high ratios of males to females in the population, because of discriminatory behaviour towards females. At a more general level, the ambivalent nature of women's achievements is illustrated in the "feminization" of the labour force, whereby women's access to paid work has increased in most countries, but coincided with a deterioration in the terms and conditions of work for many.

There is no single explanation for these various outcomes. Gender inequalities are deeply entrenched in all societies, and are reproduced through a variety of practices and institutions, including policy interventions. A question posed in this report is: what contribution does development policy make to bringing about favourable or unfavourable conditions for achieving greater gender equality?

The disabling policy environment

The neoliberal economic agenda, which rose to dominance in the early 1980s, was centred on fiscal austerity, and the strengthening of private property rights and profit-driven markets, and called for the "rollback" of the state. While inflation was brought under control in many countries, price stability was achieved at the expense of growth and job creation. Financial crises and economic volatility became more frequent, and income inequalities widened all over the world.

In the absence of adequate safety nets, economic liberalization placed the livelihoods of low-income households under severe stress. Under conditions of economic hardship, low-income women became increasingly visible as economic actors outside the household sphere, as casual agricultural labourers, in the overcrowded urban informal economy, and as migrants. Meanwhile, the creeping commercialization of welfare services, particularly in the context of the HIV/AIDS pandemic, meant that poorer households had to adjust by shifting more of the care into the household and onto the shoulders of women and girls.

The social crisis that has continued to hit many parts of the world has been expressed most dramatically in civil unrest and political turmoil, including outbreaks and continuations of civil wars, in which underlying economic and social distress are among the causal dynamics. In such zones of insecurity and pervasive violence, few escape the disastrous impacts of warfare, whether or not they are actively involved as combatants.

Bringing gender back in

The analytical approach advanced in this report assumes that societies, their social relations, economies and power structures contain deeply etched gender divisions, in the same way that they reflect class, ethnic and racial divisions. Inequalities based on sex are a pervasive feature of all societies; they are the product of socially constructed power relations, norms and practices.

While there is increasing concern with gender inequalities in some arenas—at the intrahousehold level in particular, as well as in the legal domain where "traditions" and "customs" have an important role to play—the attention paid to gender

in public policy is often selective. The resulting silences and omissions are revealing: for example, markets and macroeconomic flows (trade, capital) are not always subjected to gender analysis, the implicit assumption being that they are essentially benign and gender-neutral. However, the report finds that this is true neither of the economy nor of the family; nor do states, communities, political parties or "progressive" social movements necessarily operate in gender-neutral ways.

The analysis undertaken by the report is largely of social relations, and particularly gender relations, across a wide spectrum of institutions. The primary focus, however, is on women, understood as differentiated by class, race, ethnicity and caste. It is important to keep the spotlight on women, in view of the recent shifts in thinking (and language) both in development bureaucracies and in some strands of academic research, which have sometimes inadvertently overlooked the continuing significance of women's subordination. This does not imply that men are invariably advantaged, even if they might be, in relation to women. Masculinist cultures can be counter-productive or even destructive for men, and while men are the main perpetrators of violence, both domestic and public, they are also the main victims of violence outside the domestic sphere. Nor does the emphasis on women's subordination imply a static picture of unchanging gender relations: rather, it is important to acknowledge that gender hierarchies constantly change as old forms dissolve and are recreated.

Current policy agendas:
Implications for gender equality

The political and policy context of recent years has presented some new opportunities, as well as challenges, for the attainment of gender equality and women's rights. The fact that social policies and "good governance" reforms are now high on the development policy agenda seems to offer an important entry point for addressing gender-based inequalities in access to resources and services, and gender-specific capacity and accountability failures on the part of the state.

The now dominant policy package—known as the "post-Washington consensus"—does however retain some of the core elements of economic orthodoxy, supplemented by the "good governance" agenda of democracy, "participation" and "community ownership". Behind the apparent consensus forged by a shared vocabulary of "poverty" and "social protection", conflicting understandings of social policy vie for attention, based on different values, priorities and understandings of state responsibility. Similarly, while a broad understanding of the "good governance" agenda would embrace political liberalization, human rights, and address the problems of social inequality as part of a fundamental commitment to democracy, critics contend that such governance reforms have in fact been dominated by the imposition of undifferentiated and abstract blueprints for institutional reform. This has tended to exclude gender equality. However some governance reforms, in particular the decentralization of political power to local government bodies and municipalities, seem to have facilitated women's political representation at the local level, with the potential to impact favourably on policy. Such positive outcomes may be difficult to achieve where traditional patriarchal systems at local levels resist women's active presence in local power structures.

Indeed, a phenomenon to emerge with particular force in recent years is that of "identity politics", especially in the form of movements that mobilize around ethnic, racial and religious identities. While there have been tensions between some versions of identity-based claims and notions of gender equality, these are not necessarily irreconcilable. But some radical attacks on human rights and women's rights agendas have resulted from the resurgence of religious identities that include the assertion of "traditional" gender roles and systems of authority. The "traditions" and religious doctrines typically invoked by some of these movements may be neither traditional nor authentic, but instead have been recently coined to serve political ends.

Forging links between economic policy and gender equality

A world in which the dominant policy model tends to deepen social and economic inequality and reinforce marginalization, in which redistribution has no place, and in which

governments compromise the interests of their citizens to accommodate global forces, is unlikely to be a world that secures gender equality. For this reason, women's rights activists have increasingly been devoting more of their attention and energies to the larger structures of global power, and the evolution of problems of global injustice relating to macroeconomic trends. Global economic justice is also central to the achievement of women's sexual and reproductive health and rights. Yet bringing the interdependence between global economic justice and gender justice into sharper focus for policy makers is no easy task, and once achieved, requires considerable effort to bring about gender-sensitive policy change.

Moreover, the global political environment in which economic justice and gender justice have to be negotiated has been less favourable in recent years. Human rights and women's agendas, and the entire multilateral framework within which the gains of the 1990s were made, have been weakened by the current global political crisis occasioned by terrorism, militarism, war and unilateralism. If gender justice is not to slip yet further down the agenda, women's movements will require new alliances with governmental institutions, social movements and political parties.

SECTION 1: MACROECONOMICS, WELL-BEING AND GENDER EQUALITY

Liberalization and deregulation: The route to gender equality?

Neoliberal macroeconomic policies and associated policies of domestic deregulation have been pursued widely in the developing world in recent decades. They are rooted in the belief that minimal government intervention in the economy and greater reliance on the profit motive and free play of markets lead to a more efficient allocation of economic resources, higher rates of economic growth, widespread development, more rapidly rising income, and a resulting decline in poverty and inequality. The inference is that women will be equal beneficiaries, and that increased access to jobs, income and education can lead to greater gender equality.

However, analytical insights and mounting empirical evidence provide scant support for such a prospect. This policy approach has not provided a supportive environment for improving women's well-being, overcoming gender biases and eroding gender gaps in basic capacities, opportunities and access to resources. Nor has it brought about a fairer sharing between women and men of the unpaid work and the costs involved in caring for the family and raising children.

Indeed, neoliberalism has proved largely unsuccessful, even in its own terms. Tight monetary and fiscal policies have generally curbed inflation, but this has been at the cost of reduced growth rates in most regions (and particularly the poorest countries), limited structural change, and slow or negative growth in employment. The liberalization of international capital flows has resulted in rising financial and economic volatility, and more frequent and severe financial crises. Many countries have been subject to fiscal squeeze, resulting from reductions in trade and finance-related taxes and from declining tax rates on capital. These have often contributed to a reduction in government expenditures as a share of GDP. In several instances, expenditure cuts have been concentrated in capital expenditures affecting infrastructure, and in others, expenditures on health, education, welfare and social safety nets have been eroded.

Moreover, in most countries there has been little reduction in internal income inequality, and there has been a widespread increase in poverty. Trends in human development, poverty and inequality indicators question the capacity of neoliberal policies to generate social development, in terms of either steady increases in GDP, or improved standards of health and human security.

In sum, the predicted benefits of higher economic growth and poverty reduction have not materialized, and precisely at a time when effective social protection is most needed, the capacity of governments to provide public services and social protection has been widely eroded.

In contrast, however, a number of Asian countries that pursued policies to manage markets rather than to fully liberalize them in pursuit of industrial development have achieved significant success with regard to economic growth, development and poverty reduction. Yet while they have been significantly more successful in advancing some aspects of women's well-being than countries pursuing the neoliberal path, they have not achieved significant all-round advances in gender equality.

Liberalization, labour markets and women's gains: A mixed picture

In an increasingly competitive world economic environment under liberalization, a development strategy that places emphasis on labour-intensive export-oriented production, whether in industry, agriculture or more recently in services, has intensified firms' efforts to hire least-cost labour. Women's relatively lower wages have made them an attractive source of labour, and the result has been an increase in the level and share of female paid employment in many developing countries, often directly or indirectly associated with multinational enterprises.

Nevertheless, evidence regarding improvements in women's well-being and in gender equality deriving from the liberalization of trade and FDI suggests a mixed picture. Indeed, analysis points to a coincidence between gender roles (related to norms that relegate women's paid work to secondary importance after their domestic and care responsibilities), job segregation by industry, and the needs of enterprises in a highly competitive international environment.

In some cases women's pay and conditions are better in export-sector formal jobs than elsewhere in the economy, but many jobs are insecure and dead-end. Women's subcontracted work, including home-based work, is equally if not more precarious, and subject to extremely poor conditions. Nor are women's employment gains always permanent, as is evidenced by declines in the female share of paid employment in the manufacturing sector in many countries. Women who lose jobs in internationally mobile labour-intensive industries face difficulty in obtaining employment in the more capital-intensive manufacturing industries that may replace them. In addition, competition from cheap imports has led to declines in local manufacturing jobs.

Furthermore, the deflationary bias in macroeconomic policies, leading to slow growth and recessions, has had more serious repercussions for women than for men; for example, unemployment levels are often higher for women than men. Moreover, greater numbers of women than men are to be found in self-employment or wage work in the informal economy.

These employment conditions facing the majority of women make it structurally difficult to raise women's wages and to close gender wage gaps. Indeed, studies of the more rapidly growing Asian economies suggest that the growth of exports of labour-intensive manufactures and economic growth have been most rapid in those countries that had the widest gender wage gaps. Even in some of the most rapidly growing Asian economies, discriminatory portions of wage gaps have not been reduced during the era of globalization.

The financial and economic crises resulting from policies promoting unfettered capital flows have been found to have a differential impact on female and male workers. During the 1997 East Asian crisis, women were often the first to lose their jobs, due to their less secure employment conditions and also to discrimination based on "male breadwinner bias".

Public spending: A lifeline for women?

Constraints on public spending as a result of fiscal squeeze have particularly negative effects on women. Static or reduced government expenditure on infrastructure and public services places a particularly heavy burden on women, as it is they who are principally responsible for household management and unpaid care work. During normal times, the family functions as the surrogate safety net or refuge of last resort, with women bearing the greatest burden in stretching their time and energies between paid and unpaid work; this situation is aggravated in times of economic crisis. This has both short- and long-run costs for women as well as for micro- and macro-efficiency.

If female capabilities that would give them access to wider segments of the labour market are to be raised, higher levels of state spending on health and education are essential. There is also need for higher government expenditure on mechanisms for social protection that also cover the female labour force, as this is particularly affected by the insecurity of employment caused by economic volatility, the high labour turnover rates in increasingly flexible labour markets, and women's preponderance in informal work. In sum, the need for the state to protect all its citizens, women and men, from the vagaries of the market is critical in an open, competitive environment.

The privatization of services for fiscal and other reasons also has considerable short-term and potential long-term costs for women. The introduction of user fees by the government has not provided a socially satisfactory solution, particularly from the perspective of women; they frequently bear the burden of managing household budgets on less income and with fewer essential services, and exemption schemes have generally not been found to work in practice.

Consolidating women's gains: The need for a broader policy agenda

In addition to tracking trends in women's absolute status regarding well-being, it is essential to evaluate changes in their status relative to men. This is because gaps both affect and reflect power dynamics, which themselves have the potential for positive change in the processes of resource and capabilities distribution. It is important to assess whether gender gaps in well-being have changed in both fast and slow-growing economies, using a wide range of indicators rather than just the money metric of income per capita.

While there has been some narrowing of gender gaps, there are noticeable exceptions and also reversals, indicating that positive changes are not necessarily stable or enduring. Similarly, the narrowing of gaps also requires careful examination, as this may reflect a reduction in male attainments. Positive trends in female capabilities do not, however, always translate automatically into greater opportunities for women. For example, in slow-growing economies where jobs are scarce, gender norms play an important part in ensuring that men have a greater claim on job slots than women.

Gender equity is unlikely to be achieved without the empowerment of women. But the mere presence of women in legislatures does not necessarily translate into women-friendly economic policies. The introduction of the ostensibly more participatory approach to formulating development strategies through Poverty Reduction Strategy Papers (PRSPs), involving consultation with a wide range of civil society representatives, has not proved to be a highly effective vehicle for women's empowerment. The most pertinent failings include a low level of consultation with women's groups, and a frequent lack of integration of gender analysis into the diagnosis of poverty. Generally gender has not featured as an issue in the macroeconomic and development policy analysis, or in the sections of PRSPs concerning the recommended poverty reduction strategy, resource allocation, or monitoring and evaluation.

Which macroeconomic strategies would best promote gender-equitable development that, in addition to enhancing women's capabilities and opportunities to provide for themselves and their families and improve their well-being relative to men, also improved their bargaining power within the household and in other social institutions? In principle, it would be reasonable to expect that such improvements would most likely be achieved when there are relatively rapid economic growth, macroeconomic stability, a favourable external economic environment, expanding formal employment opportunities, redistributive taxation and public spending, and social policies that also embrace women.

Feminist economists have joined heterodox economists in identifying the components of an alternative macroeconomic policy package, and associated policies that would provide developing countries with a wider range of policy instruments, and give them greater scope for tailoring policies to their particular circumstances. However they recognize that, though necessary, changes in macroeconomic policy are not sufficient.

The extent to which macroeconomic policies promote gender equality does not only depend on their ability to enhance economic growth. The effects of economic growth are gender-differentiated, as growth operates through various types of markets, through intrafamily and intrahousehold resource distribution, and through public spending. Each of these last elements are subject to the pervasive influence of social norms regarding the roles and rights of women. Hence women's and men's capabilities, their access to resources such as time, land, credit and income, and their ability to obtain social insurance, differ. For example, in relation to earned income, the effect of macroeconomic policies is mediated through a system of gendered job segregation, even when there is an otherwise level playing field between men and women in terms of educational qualifications, skills and control over assets. This implies that economic policy alone is unlikely to bring about gender equality.

Therefore, to effect substantial improvement in key aspects of women's well-being and greater gender equity, measures specifically designed to address gender-based inequalities and constraints are also essential. Concerted efforts are also needed to erode the norms and remove the discriminations that account for the persistence of gender segmentation in labour markets. Specific policies are required to remove the structural constraints on women's ability to take up widening labour market opportunities, especially their relative lack of education and appropriate skills, and importantly, their relatively greater responsibility for the provision of unpaid care.

Also, if economic growth is to be widely shared, there is a need for labour market policies and related interventions that affect working conditions in both formal and informal employment situations, and that rectify gender imbalances and discriminatory practices. The solution would also involve the improvement of core labour standards (which include the prohibition of all forms of discrimination and the principle of equal pay for work of equal value) and the creation of decent conditions of work, including the right to social protection for all workers, formal and informal, as well as the evolution of "family-friendly" workplace practices. Other necessary policy measures include gender policy objectives for public expenditures, and mechanisms such as gender-responsive budget audits to monitor implementation.

Finally, these changes depend largely on the mobilization of women themselves, whose case needs to be built on rigorous analysis and a clear vision of where appropriate policy interventions are most needed.

SECTION 2: WOMEN, WORK AND SOCIAL POLICY

The feminization and informalization of labour

Over the past three decades women's economic activity rates have been rising in most parts of the world, with the exception of Eastern and Central Europe (since 1989) and the Middle East and North Africa, where women's economic activity rates remain low by international standards. Despite the increase in work for pay by women, labour markets continue to be segmented by gender. Even in the Organization for Economic Co-operation and Development (OECD) countries, where women's labour-force participation has been rising, there is continuing gender difference in labour markets, which is nowadays largely based on time, with men working full-time and women working part-time (given their disproportionate share of unpaid care work). There is also a substantial earnings gap between men and women, in part because many women work part-time; but there are also earnings gaps among full-time workers, which reflect occupational segregation and the fact that "women's jobs" earn lower wages.

Furthermore, the intensification of women's paid work over the past decades has been paralleled by a deterioration in the terms and conditions of much of the work on offer.

The new concept of "informal employment" defines it as employment without secure contracts, worker benefits or social protection. According to recent International Labour Organization (ILO) statistical evidence, informal employment constitutes one half to three-quarters of non-agricultural employment in developing countries, and tends to be a larger source of employment for women than for men in all developing regions except North Africa.

Rural impoverishment has historically contributed to migration into urban areas, and continues to do so. A large contingent of young rural migrant women can be found on the lowest, least visible, rung of the informal employment ladder. Many lack the skills and connections needed to secure more stable jobs with decent pay. They are typically engaged in small-scale domestic production, increasingly under competitive pressure from cheaper imported goods. Others engage in a variety of service occupations and in petty trading.

In many parts of the world, types of employment relationship are emerging that are purposely disguised to avoid labour legislation and deny social benefits. In other cases there may be a contract, but the relationship is deliberately disguised as a commercial transaction. Often the employment relationship is ambiguous: for example, workers operate at home on an exploitative piece-rate basis outside the purview of labour legislation. Many female homeworkers process products in the global value chain, while others work on articles destined for the domestic market. The payment they receive is extremely low; many also use their children as subsidiary workers. These areas are untouched by labour laws and social welfare.

Patterns of informalization differ from region to region, but the overall trend is discouraging in terms of prospects for realizing women's rights and well-being. A promising development of the 1990s, however, has been the emergence of new forms of organizing among women workers in the informal economy, both domestically and internationally. However, many of the new trade unions, as well as non-governmental organizations (NGOs) and community-based organizations (CBOs) responding to women workers' rights, face difficulties in expanding their reach and becoming sustainable. Trade unions and NGOs also face challenges in alliance-building to broaden the scope and reach of their efforts beyond the more visible "traded" sectors.

Collective action through democratic organizational routes presents the only practicable avenue for regulating and improving the conditions of work of informal women workers. The idea that the formalization of property rights constitutes the solution to the problems of the informal economy—a view that is being endorsed by some international organizations—

has no validity as far as working women are concerned. Most of these women have no "property" to be registered, and engage in the informal economy because they cannot find work in the formal sector.

The changing terms of rural living

During the 1980s, many African and Latin American countries suffered economic crisis, and this was diagnosed by the international financial institutions (IFIs) as stemming directly from heavy state involvement in the economy. The agricultural sector was seen as a prime victim of state-directed regimes.

In truth, most developing country states were heavily involved in the economy, due to the widespread belief that markets on their own were inadequate for building a strong economy. Agricultural prices were artificially depressed by overvalued exchange rates and export taxes; but this was to some extent redressed through positive resource transfers into the sector via public investment, subsidized credit and inputs, and agricultural services and marketing. Such public provision has come under attack.

Subsequent reforms, however, have not adequately addressed some of the long-standing problems afflicting the agrarian economy. In Latin America the economic reforms have tended to reinforce, rather than redress, existing divides between regions and producers. One of the downsides of liberalization in the region has been the rise in agricultural imports, with an often severely detrimental impact on rural livelihoods. In sub-Saharan Africa food crop production has not increased, while the performance of export crops has been very uneven; the problems of food insecurity remain dire in many countries. In many contexts credit systems have collapsed, and there has been a sharp decline in input use, especially among smallholders.

Rural livelihoods have become more insecure, as well as more diversified, in contexts where cutbacks in state support to domestic agriculture have coincided with increasing exposure to competition from large subsidized producers. Volatile and depressed commodity prices have trapped large numbers of rural people in poverty, hunger and even famine.

Gender-differentiated examination of the implications of economic reform for rural livelihoods is difficult. National agricultural statistics are inadequate in a number of key respects, some of which stem from using either the individual holder, or the holding, as the unit of analysis. This means that the relationships between the members of farming households cannot be assessed. Case studies of changing gender relations under the unfolding impact of liberalization are few and far between.

Where they can, smallholders have moved out of traditional cash crop production and into the production of more lucrative crops. How has this affected male and female household producers? A view which gained currency in the 1990s was that the weak "supply response" of African agriculture to liberalization could be ascribed to the inflexibility of gender roles within households and women's unwillingness to contribute unpaid labour to cash crops controlled by their husbands. But these intrahousehold gender constraints and conflicts of interest have been exaggerated. There are significant areas of common interest between husbands and wives in smallholder households, and considerable evidence of flexibility in gender roles in agriculture. If liberalization has failed to enhance agricultural production, it has much more to do with the broader constraints on smallholders that liberalization itself has exacerbated, rather than the economic consequences of intrahousehold gender roles and conflicts.

Several overlapping processes over the past 30 years have contributed to changes in the gender division of labour among Latin American smallholders, sometimes described as a tendency towards the "feminization of agriculture". During the recent liberalization era, women's participation in agriculture appears to have changed: they are no longer merely "secondary" workers. Women are emerging as farm managers, providing the bulk of family farm labour as men migrate in search of alternative sources of income. By withdrawing direct state support to domestic food production, agricultural reform has galvanized this process. In addition, exports of traditional agricultural products such as coffee have declined as a result of global trade liberalization and depressed commodity markets. The "feminization of agriculture" is therefore a phenomenon associated with the lack of viability of smallholder agricultural production in the current era.

Besides the changes in smallholder farming, two other important trends have emerged as companions to liberalization. The first and most directly attributable is the growth of large-scale corporate export farming, particularly of high-value horticultural products such as flowers, fruits and vegetables. This is a significant new source of employment for rural women in many parts of the world (especially Latin America), even though women are overwhelmingly employed in more insecure, less well-paid, and lower-skilled activities, without opportunities for advancement. The second is the more general diversification of smallholder livelihoods, with men, women and child household members being increasingly propelled into off-farm activities to avert poverty. In some cases, the incomes earned are so poor that diversification in fact contributes to a cycle of impoverishment. Women tend to be overwhelmingly clustered in low-return activities to which they are driven by survival needs.

One of the major lessons of the experience of economic reform and liberalization is that the resource poverty of farmers prevents them from taking up new opportunities. A critical asset in the rural economy remains land. In many countries women's rights activists have been closely involved in policy debates on land tenure, often alongside other civil-society groups. Such efforts led to significant progress in the passing of more gender-equitable land tenure laws during the 1990s.

Even where women's rights are formally recognized, there continues to be a substantial gap between the legal recognition of their right to own or hold land, and their effective access to land. The reasons for this gap are complex and varied. But two significant policy trends require attention if poorer women in particular are to have access to land on a secure basis: the emphasis on developing markets in land (which are likely to exclude poorer women), and the resurgence of policy interest in various local and informal mechanisms and institutions for land management (where it may be difficult for women's interests to find a clear articulation and be acted upon).

Cross-border migration of workers

The movement of people from countryside to town or across international borders has become an established feature of many people's livelihoods, entailing both positive and negative manifestations and opportunities for the countries and individuals involved. The contemporary patterns and nature of cross-border flows are characterized by three broad trends: an increasing shift toward temporary migration (of the highly skilled and semi or unskilled), rising numbers of undocumented migrants, and the feminization of migration. Despite continuing differences in migration regimes between different clusters of countries, there is an emerging convergence towards selective migration, where highly skilled workers are welcomed, based on the belief that they will integrate more easily and contribute more to the economy, whereas low-skilled immigrants are regarded as hard on the public purse, and their numbers therefore ostensibly need to be controlled. Such stratifications are also gendered, given men's preponderance among the highly skilled strata.

Women's position on the bottom rung of the labour market, the low value accorded to domestic and caring work which many migrant women undertake in industrialized societies, and the lack of social protection in irregular occupations, especially in the "entertainment and hospitality" industries, mean that many women are vulnerable to exploitation. The fact that many highly educated women from developing countries undertake unskilled or semi-skilled jobs raises the issue of deskilling, which is rarely addressed in policy.

In North America and Europe, the principal framework within which women migrate continues to be as spouses or dependants of male principal applicants. Only where labour flows are destined for female-typed jobs, such as nurses and domestics, do women predominate as economic migrants. In some European countries, women in the caring professions are increasingly sought to fill gaps in health, social and care services and as domestics, at wages or under terms only acceptable to migrant women. Their remittances are nonetheless highly significant to the household economy from which they come.

Women from Eastern and Southeast Asia are increasingly migrating to neighbouring countries or further afield in search of opportunities. The more positive side of the picture is some female entry into information technology and other upwardly mobile employment. The downside is the overwhelming presence of women in the "entertainment" sector and the private sphere as domestic helpers: two areas of employment not covered by labour laws and thus prone to high levels of abuse.

Discrimination against immigrants, combined with racial and gender inequalities, makes migrant women "triply disadvantaged" and likely to be over-represented in marginal, unregulated and poorly paid jobs. At the same time, the experience of migration—whether by women on their own or jointly with men—has the potential to reconfigure gender relations and power inequalities. Opportunities emerge to improve lives and escape previously oppressive situations.

The search for a new social policy agenda

Livelihoods in today's world are subject to a range of insecurities. Formal social protection mechanisms are missing in many developing countries for the millions of women and men who work in the informal economy (as well as for some even in the formal economy). Contingencies such as ill-health, childbirth and old age are themselves powerful drivers of impoverishment, as earnings fall and assets are depleted to purchase health care in increasingly commercialized contexts.

There has recently been more recognition of these realities. The 1990s saw a shift in global policy pronouncements, acknowledging the vital role of social policy in the development process. However, considerable tension exists between different policy approaches regarding the scope and institutional mechanisms of social policy. The IFIs champion an approach in which the state only fills gaps and provides safety nets for the truly indigent, while the non-poor seek social provision through the market. The underlying assumption is that targeted public provision is the way to achieve greater social inclusion. This assumption, however, is open to question.

Means testing and targeting are often the last resort of unequal societies; they can trap people in poverty, generate social exclusion and entrench inequality, rather than deal with inequality through redistribution; they are also very demanding as far as the administrative capacity of the state is concerned.

An alternative view holds that social objectives have to be integrated within development strategies, and that the state has to be a major player in providing resources to ensure social protection inclusively. Social policies founded on principles of universalism and redistribution, with strong cross-subsidies from the better-off, tend to be more sustainable, both financially and politically.

Both the process of social policy reform and its outcomes are inescapably gendered. The early efforts to provide formal social protection in many developing countries were biased towards men, who were over-represented in the formal sector. However, while efforts could have been made to cover a much wider range of people, there has in fact been a reversal over the past two decades. In many regions there has been a strong thrust towards the commodification of social services and social protection by imposing various "user charges" for public services and expanding market-based provision. Hence, the "male breadwinner model" is being eroded not by gender-equitable reform of state-based entitlements, but by their drastic reduction.

The impacts of commodification are likely to be felt most strongly by women, given the gender ordering and stratification across private and public institutions. These include intra-household resource allocations (where girls are likely to receive a smaller proportion of household investments in health and education than boys); market institutions (where women tend to be more cash-constrained than men, given their disadvantages in labour and credit markets), in the unpaid care economy (where a disproportionate share of unpaid care is provided by women and girls when formal social provision remains out of reach); and the public social care sector (where working pressures generated during public-sector reforms are likely to fall most heavily on women workers, given that they are predominantly located at the lowest rungs of skill, authority and remuneration). Yet debates on social policy have failed to engage with how men and women will be differently affected or involved.

Health care reforms, with a focus on the marketization of care and drugs, have been built on a number of hidden gendered assumptions, including that women—the principal clients—will be able to procure money for fees, and also be able to take on more unpaid care responsibilities. This has come at a time when the HIV/AIDS epidemic has imposed severe economic and social strains on families, especially in Africa. Evidence on reform outcomes points to patient exclusion; rises in maternal and newborn morbidity; and increasing gaps in wages and working conditions between senior clinicians and the nursing work mainly performed by women.

In the case of pension reforms, the move towards privatization has major gender implications. The fact that pension benefits in privatized systems are strictly determined by the overall amount of money contributed by the insured person, and that women typically earn less money and work for fewer years than men (given their care responsibilities), means that women receive considerably lower benefits. Since women's higher life expectancy is taken into account in most private systems, women's benefits are further comparatively depressed. In public systems with defined benefits, some of the disadvantages faced by women can be mitigated by generous minimum pensions, by the fact that life expectancy does not affect benefit levels, and by credits sometimes given for years spent caring for children.

By extending the coverage of existing social protection programmes (health insurance and pension provision) to new groups of informal workers, and by facilitating cross-subsidies, some important efforts are being made, in a diverse range of countries, to extend the reach of existing social protection mechanisms. These more inclusive social systems are being forged in contexts where there has been a great deal of contestation and debate concerning social responsibility, and where there is an ideological commitment to social equality.

SECTION 3: WOMEN IN POLITICS AND PUBLIC LIFE

Women in public office: A rising tide

Since 1995 women's visibility in, and impact on, public life has grown. Although the average number of women in national assemblies has only increased from 9 per cent to almost 16 per cent, in 16 countries the proportion has reached 30 per cent or more. This is the critical threshold at which it is thought that women in office can change the culture, practice and outcomes of politics to respond better to gender equality concerns.

Women of course voice their interests in a wide variety of political and civic associations, so women's political participation cannot be measured in terms of numbers and proportions of women in national assemblies alone. However, enabling more women to succeed in competitive politics remains an important challenge for women's movements around the world, as does the project of building their effectiveness, once in office, in advancing women's rights. Contemporary women's movements are particularly concerned to identify the determinants of higher rates of women's access to formal politics, as well as the features of political systems that support a progressive gender-equality legislative agenda.

Cultural, educational and other differences affect women's participation in civil society, but do not easily explain their presence or absence in elected assemblies. Electoral systems are the best predictor of the numbers of women in formal politics. Those with electoral systems based on proportional representation (PR) tend to return assemblies with a higher average of women politicians than those with plurality/majority systems or semi-proportional systems. But electoral systems alone do not determine numbers of women in politics. Other determinant factors include the presence and type of affirmative action system, party systems and ideologies, the presence of women in the executive, and the responsiveness of the bureaucracy to women's interests.

During the last 10 years, there has been considerable experimentation with the use of affirmative action in order to meet the goal of gender parity in representative politics. Quotas on party electoral lists are the most common means; today they are in use in over 80 countries. They are most effective where there are large electoral districts, and requirements that women are spaced evenly on lists: a "zipped" list, or a "zebra" list in southern Africa, contains alternating women and men. Where there are penalties for non-compliance, such as withholding of campaign subsidies, co-operation is better assured. In simple plurality systems, measures to reserve seats for women have been preferred over quotas for women candidates. However, reserved seats have sometimes been a way of boosting government majorities, undermining the perceived legitimacy of their occupants, and sometimes making it difficult for women politicians to build credible relationships with the women's movement.

Parties on the ideological left, or willing to commit the public sector to compensate for inequalities in the private sphere, have been more responsive to gender equality concerns and supportive of women in politics.

Despite women's greater prominence in political life, they have in many cases yet to translate their visibility into leadership positions and influence over the decision-making process: there are still many instances where they are simply used as an extension of male power structures. The transition from a heightened presence of women in politics to actual advance for gender equality issues and women-friendly policies takes time, and will depend upon the effectiveness of women's movements in holding governments to account, and on the capacity of public sector agencies to translate ambitious gender-equity policy agendas into effective implementation. This is a matter of good governance in women's favour.

Women mobilizing to reshape democracy

A strong and autonomous women's movement can greatly magnify the influence of women in representative politics, and indeed of national advocacy bureaucracies (such as an equal opportunities commission), providing an external base of support and legitimacy. Although a unified agenda is difficult to discern in the great variety of women's associational activity, women are well mobilized in civil society almost everywhere. The globalization of communications has created new opportunities, enabling women to experiment with new means for holding key actors—governments, corporations and international organizations—to account for their actions in relation to women's rights. Global conferences have enabled women to network internationally, and conferred legitimacy on their participation in global policy debates. Female mobilization and solidarity also occur in trades unions, political parties, mass organizations, and civil society groups vocal on behalf of women members.

A notable feature of women's associational activity in the past decade has been the central role women have played in many democratization struggles. Recent transitions to democratic forms of government in Latin America and South Africa have offered opportunities to women to claim space for gender equality in newly emerging or reformed institutions. Although women's positions tend to be profoundly divergent on many issues, there has been a patch of common ground on which many converge: the demand for gender parity in public office. Since the late 1990s, civil society campaigns for equal representation with men have gathered momentum, backing reforms to electoral systems, including through constitutional revision, that support women's ability to run for office.

While political liberalization has enabled some women's movements to flourish, in some contexts it has been accompanied by loss of momentum in feminist politics. In Eastern Europe, for instance, where feminism has been associated with a repressive state, it has taken most of the decade for women's movements to regroup. In other contexts, where political liberalization has been only partial, disillusionment with states that fail to deliver either development or democracy appears to have contributed to the growing appeal to women of conservative ethnic and religious movements.

Some of these identity-based forms of mobilization assert the superiority of "traditional" gender roles along with systems of patriarchal authority, particularly where "women's liberation" is seen as part of unwelcome modernization. Women's deportment, mobility, dress and roles within the family are often central to the cultural revival or pious society the groups proclaim; women's behaviour is upheld as a marker of authenticity and moral integrity. Although women are rarely given access to institutional power within these groups, they are encouraged to engage in their political activities, and even to become highly militant and visible activists because of their great symbolic impact.

Gender and "good governance"

Programmes of governance reform have recently attracted considerable international and national attention. Good governance is seen as the essential condition enabling economic reform programmes to function effectively, and is at the core of the current emerging "post-Washington consensus". The concept of "good governance", however, is given different meanings by different policy actors. Although IFI reform packages address issues of government legitimacy and the public participation of socially excluded groups, critics believe they are dominated by a narrower preoccupation: the use of "governance" reforms to expand market activity and its supporting institutions, especially private property rights. In such circumstances, governance reform is not sympathetic to gender concerns and may even undermine them. To tackle gender equity, programmes of reform must take into account from the outset the way in which formal and informal institutions are shaped by unequal gender relations. These institutions will tend to reproduce gender-based inequality unless they are appropriately redesigned during the reform process.

The gendered dimensions of current governance reforms have not been given appropriate consideration except in discussions on decentralization. Yet there are gender-specific capacity failures in all public institutions targeted for reform. Public expenditure management systems fail to acknowledge women's needs, or distribute budgetary resources equally. The civil service and judiciary may be dominated by men. Women workers clustered at the bottom of state bureaucracies may be the first to be fired when cost-cutting efficiencies are introduced. "Rule of law" reforms may limit women's scope to profit from informal private enterprise, or fail to secure assets over which they previously enjoyed customary rights. Legislative committees may

be ill-equipped to conduct a gender analysis of the bills they review. Some policy makers do advocate women's greater participation in politics and the public sector—on the instrumental basis that they may be less corrupt than men. Whether this is indeed the case (the evidence for it is uneven), it is not the appropriate starting point for a gender-sensitive consideration of capacity and accountability problems in the public sector.

Women's associations have prioritized several areas for gender-sensitive public sector reform. These include recruitment quotas to ensure a stronger presence of women in the bureaucracy; the introduction of gender-equity concerns in performance measurement; consultation with women clients of public services, and measures to respond to their complaints; and reforms to legal frameworks and judicial systems to improve women's access to justice. A tool increasingly used for monitoring government spending is the "gender budget" method pioneered in Australia and South Africa. Gender budgets analyse the likely impacts of planned spending, and supply parliamentarians with gender-aware budgetary information in the hope that they will goad the executive into more appropriate spending. In some places they have been effective in exposing the gap between government commitments to certain social policies, and actual spending.

Decentralization and gender equality

The part of the governance agenda that is focused on the decentralization of authority to local entities has been more sympathetic to gender concerns. Women's participation has actively been encouraged, and women generally, as well as low-income and other socially marginal groups, are expected to benefit from the accountability and service delivery improvements that government in close proximity should provide. Indeed, local government positions are expected to be particularly open to women, because they do not face the mobility and financial constraints at local levels that they face in striving for national public office. A comparison of available statistics on women's engagement at national and local levels, however, shows that this is not consistently the case: sometimes there are more women in national than in local politics. This alerts us to the significance of resistance to women from traditional patriarchal systems at local levels, and also to the importance of gender-sensitive institutional engineering to improve women's access to local government forums and services.

Various systems of affirmative action have been tried. These include the reservation of a proportion of seats on local councils for women, as in India, and the creation of special electoral wards for women, as in Uganda. However, women face the resistance of entrenched male hierarchies accustomed to control, and hence the likelihood that decentralization may reinforce male sway over local power structures, and their influence over the informal social institutions governing marital relations, conflict resolution, and property rights. As with the case of women in national politics, the situation can change over time. Although experience is mixed, there are signs that women in local government are having a tangible impact on local spending patterns and building social acceptance of women's political authority. NGOs have offered training in capacity-building and women's assertion of their own voice. In some settings, spending patterns have been influenced in the direction of services and amenities favoured by women, such as water supplies and public health. Local government remains a key arena to watch over the next decade, as more and more women assert their leadership ambitions and challenge patriarchal systems at this level.

SECTION 4: GENDER, ARMED CONFLICT AND THE SEARCH FOR PEACE

The impacts of conflict on women

Ten years after the Beijing Conference, the world is still enduring an epidemic of armed violence, with 19 major conflicts and many smaller confrontations ongoing in different parts of the globe. Although the number of major conflicts appears to be declining, incursions into Afghanistan and Iraq, ongoing wars

in Sudan, Kashmir and the Democratic Republic of Congo, and failure to end struggles in the Middle East, Colombia, the Chechen Republic and Sri Lanka, present a picture of violence and insecurity affecting millions of people worldwide. Most of these wars are internal, and fighting is not confined to battlefields and "war fronts" but pervades whole populations. Women are caught up in a number of roles, including to some degree as combatants; more importantly, they may become a direct target of attack; and they have to assume extra caring and provider roles for their families in an environment where economic life, formal systems of protection and the rule of law have collapsed.

At stake in today's wars are not only territories, but ethnic and religious identities, control over natural resources, and over lucrative and sometimes illicit trade, such as in drugs and arms. Tensions have been exacerbated by economic crises and their accompanying social distress, and the weakness of state institutions in the face of impoverishment and civil unrest. In a world in which the balance of power is lopsided, and where many people feel economically or politically vulnerable, bonds of common identity (based on religion or ethnicity) often provide a powerful mobilizing force.

During the recent past, women's visibility in war has become especially marked in certain connections. The war in Bosnia and Herzegovina, and the Rwandan genocide brought to world attention the use of sexual assault as a systematic means of terrorizing populations, and rape has since become internationally recognized as a weapon of war. Thus the full ramifications of conflict borne by women personally have become better appreciated, and some mechanisms of response have been put in place, even while the impacts on women's socially constructed roles as carers and providers have been less well appreciated.

Women have also been given greater credibility in their assumption of peace-making and conflict resolution roles; in some cases they have helped reduce hostilities or bring them to an end. Their life-saving roles in care and refuge provision, and their conduct of humanitarian relief programmes at considerable personal risk, have been less widely noticed; but they are beginning to claim, and win, places at the peace table and in the negotiation of a "gender-friendly" peace.

Although armed violence is commonly regarded as a male preserve, women have long taken on active military roles in wars and revolutions. For some women combatants, military participation stems from their experience as victims; others are coerced into carrying arms or working for military commanders. Yet many women are inspired by identification with the cause in which war is being waged by kin and identity groups. Their participation is not limited to revolutionary and radical causes; chauvinist or nationalistic movements include women among their principal cheerleaders. Women's agency in conflict situations can grow in a variety of different political contexts—democratic, revolutionary and authoritarian—and in strong as well as weak states.

After conflict: Women, peace building and development

In the context of today's wars, where a peace settlement rarely signals the end of physical insecurity, the postconflict environment cannot be characterized as one in which life for women invariably returns to "normal". The upheaval of war, in which societies and gender relations have been transformed and livelihood systems disrupted, has its own impact on intrapersonal relationships and societal expectations.

Women commonly find their contributions to the war and peace efforts marginalized or disregarded in both official and popular accounts of war (as happened in Europe after the Second World War). Moreover, there seems to be a denial of the fact that shifts in gender relations were required for women to take on their wartime roles. The ideological rhetoric is often about "restoring" or "returning" to a state of gender relations resembling those perceived to have been associated with peace in the past, even though the proposed "restoration of normality" may further undermine women's rights. The challenge to gender relations experienced during war seems to become too great for patriarchal societies to maintain in times of peace.

There are, however, also significant openings for positive change in postwar circumstances. Some wars end in an atmosphere imbued with the desire to build a new type of society;

where the situation of women received a lot of attention during the conflict, it may be possible to push for legal or policy changes to improve the fulfilment of their rights. Where international peacekeeping or reconstruction is involved, there may be external pressure for policies that support women, and funds may be directly available to women's organizations. However, women need to be agile and strategic in the initiatives they adopt: the bodies responsible for devising new institutions of government will tend to disregard gender claims unless these are represented persuasively. Where they are not, livelihood opportunities may be deliberately removed, and other discriminations introduced. In such postconflict actions as sorting out land claims, women may lose rights they had previously asserted. Speedy service reconstruction, especially health care and education, is especially important for women.

In the immediate postwar setting, special measures are often put in place to provide support for ex-combatants before, during and after the processes of "demobilization, development and reintegration". It is still common for women (and child, especially girl) ex-combatants to be relatively marginalized, if not completely neglected, in such programmes, in spite of attention having been drawn to this unsatisfactory state of affairs for nearly a decade.

Nevertheless women have made inroads, even if fewer than they would wish. In recognition of their vulnerability in all stages of war, the UN Security Council's landmark Resolution 1325 in 2000 urges member states to ensure representation of women at all levels of decision making in mechanisms for the prevention, management and resolution of conflict, in order to promote actions necessary for the protection and support of women. This is one helpful sign that women are gaining ground in postconflict activity. A further indication comprised the first ever prosecutions of perpetrators of violence against women in wartime by the tribunals dealing with war crimes in former Yugoslavia and in Rwanda. In the case of Rwanda, a Women's Caucus for Gender Justice was formed in 1997 within the International Criminal Court (ICC), thereby helping to ensure that a gender perspective was central to the functioning of the court.

Despite this progress, the majority of sexual crimes against women during wartime still go unpunished. What is more, wartime prosecutions tend to be painfully slow. Women survivors of such abuse are still stigmatized to a far greater degree than male survivors of human rights abuses. It is therefore not surprising that most women find it very difficult to take legal action and give evidence.

"Truth and reconciliation" procedures have been used to address women's cases and gain their participation, notably in Rwanda where the traditional Gacaca system has been revived to handle postgenocide disputes. However, the issue of amnesty and truth-telling remains controversial; where amnesty is offered in return for truth-telling, the sense of being deprived of justice could provoke further violence.

The most common abuses under-reported to Truth and Reconciliation Commissions (TRCs) are those suffered by women, as indeed are those least prosecuted. Although women sometimes constitute the majority of those giving witness in court regarding acts of violence committed against others, only few speak out regarding acts of sexual violence committed against themselves, unless a strategy of proactive engagement with women and the broader community is put in place (as in the case of the TRC of 2001 in Peru).

Chapter 1
After Beijing: Uneven progress in an unequal world

Ten years on from the Fourth World Conference on Women in Beijing, the question being posed by many women's organizations across the world is how much has been achieved in the past decade? For those involved in the search for gender equality this is an important question to ask, but by no means an easy one to answer.

The task of evaluating progress in gender equality poses many challenges. The standard indicators of income and well-being offer some guidance, but a proper and grounded assessment demands much more than they alone can provide. The challenge lies not only in developing an adequate analytical approach, but in understanding that the terms of engagement may themselves be questioned. What counts as progress is often a contested field in which there are competing visions of "the good society", and of women's place within it. The concept of progress has itself undergone revision and qualification, along with the realization that the complex process of social change does not follow a uniform path and offers few guaranteed outcomes. Social and economic development may not always enlarge the realm of human freedom, nor is the idea of "development" always, or simply, associated with one version of modernity.

These caveats notwithstanding, there can be little doubt that since the first World Conference on Women in 1975 there have been significant changes, many of them positive, in the social and economic status of women. Girls' enrolment in primary and secondary education has increased rapidly the world over, sharply reducing or closing, and in some cases reversing, the gender gap in school attendance. The decline in fertility in many developing countries has both reduced the risk of maternal mortality and eased the burden of unpaid care work which

invariably falls to women and girls. The presence of women in public life has also grown, whether in politics, in the workforce, or in the migrant streams that cross international borders.

Such changes in women's lives are associated with the social transformations that attend economic development, but they are not simply a by-product of economic growth. In many instances change in women's social position has been instigated or accelerated by state reforms and social movements. In this respect, the last decade of the 20th century was particularly significant. The period was marked by a series of political transformations that included the transition from authoritarian rule in many parts of the world, the collapse of "state socialism" in Eastern and Central Europe, and in the major industrialized countries the presence in power of administrations that were supportive of some elements of the women's agenda. This context helped to promote shifts in the international policy agenda towards a greater emphasis on the importance of democracy and human rights for the development process.

Women's movements, both national and transnational, took advantage of the changed political context, which they themselves had helped reshape, to advance women's rights, working both inside and outside state machineries for legislative and policy reforms. Faced with a window of opportunity they were able to forge effective alliances with other political forces of all kinds: popular movements, parties and governments. Perhaps the most remarkable achievement of the 1990s was in bringing issues of sexual and reproductive health and rights, violence against women, and inequality of power in gender relations to the centre of global and national debates on human rights and human development. The transnational mobilization of women had a noticeable impact on global rule-making, as is evident from table 1.1. Indeed, some observers of long-term social change argue that the body of UN Conventions, especially the Convention on the Elimination of All Forms of Discrimination against Women (CEDAW), and other international and regional legal instruments promoting gender equality, have undermined the legitimacy of patriarchy, while the social effects of female education, later marriages and labour market openings are combining to erode its remaining pillars.[1]

THE PERSISTENCE OF GENDER INEQUALITIES

If the 1990s saw women achieve some of their historic demands, and if there was progress in education, employment and political representation, these positive outcomes must be qualified in the light of continuing gender inequalities and a less than favourable economic environment. In education for example, despite the advance in many countries towards

Table 1.1 Key international and regional legal instruments promoting gender equality (1990–2004)

Area of commitment	Convention on the Rights of the Child (CRC) Adopted – 1989 Came into force – 1990	International Convention on the Protection of the Rights of All Migrant Workers and Members of Their Families Adopted – 1990 Came into force – 2003	Inter-American Convention on the Prevention, Punishment and Eradication of Violence against Women Adopted – 1994 Came into force – 1995
Non-discrimination based on sex	Art. 2: "States Parties shall respect and ensure the rights set forth in the present Convention to each child within their jurisdiction without discrimination of any kind" (including gender).		Art. 6.a: "The right of women to be free from all forms of discrimination"
Elimination of violence against women	Art. 19.1: "States parties shall (…) protect the child from all forms of physical and mental violence (…) including sexual abuse" Protocol [1] Art. 1: "States Parties shall prohibit the sale of children, child prostitution and child pornography"	Art. 10: "No migrant worker or member of his or her family shall be subjected to torture or to cruel, inhuman or degrading treatment or punishment"	Art. 1: "(…) violence against women shall be understood as any act or conduct, based on gender, which causes death or physical, sexual or psychological harm or suffering to women, whether in the public or the private sphere" Art. 3: "Every woman has the right to be free from violence in both the public and private spheres"
Economic and social rights		Migrant workers (including migrant women) shall enjoy equality of treatment with nationals of the state concerned in relation to condition and terms of work (arts 25 and 54), social security (art. 27), access to education, health and social services (art. 43) courts and tribunals (art. 18).	Art. 5: "Every woman is entitled to the free and full exercise of her (…) economic, social and cultural rights, and may rely on the full protection of those rights as embodied in regional and international instruments on human rights"
Civil and political rights		Art. 26.1a: "States Parties recognizes the right of migrant workers and members of their families to take part in meetings (…) of trade unions and of any other associations (…) in the view to protecting their economic, social, cultural and other interests"	Art. 4.j: "The right to have equal access to the public service of her country and to take part in the conduct of public affairs, including decision-making"

Sources: United Nations Treaty Collection 2001; ILO 2002a; OAS 2000.

gender parity, notably at primary level, progress has been far slower than expected. At higher levels of education too, the gender balance in many developing countries still heavily favours boys, despite some change (see figure 1.1).[2]

Despite the greater numerical presence of women in the world of work and in the domain of politics (see figures 1.2 and 1.3), the narrowing gender gap conceals marked gender asymmetries in pay and status. Women continued to be concentrated in jobs with low pay and authority levels, placing limits on their overall access to income, status and power.

Table 1.1 (cont.) Key international and regional legal instruments promoting gender equality (1990–2004)

Home Work Convention	Rome Statute of the International Criminal Court	United Nations Convention against Organized Crime and its Protocols	Area of commitment
Adopted – 1996 Came into force – 2000	Adopted – 1998 Came into force – 2002	Adopted – 2000 Came into force – 2003	
Art 4.1: "The national policy on home work shall promote (…) equality of treatment between homeworkers and other wage earners"			Non-discrimination based on sex
	Arts. 7 and 8 define rape, sexual slavery, enforced prostitution, forced pregnancy, enforced sterilization, or any other form of sexual violence of comparable gravity as crimes against humanity and war crimes.	Protocol[2] Art. 2.a: "The purpose of this Protocol (…) to prevent and combat trafficking in persons, paying particular attention to women and children" Protocol[3] Art. 2: "The purpose of this Protocol is to prevent and combat the smuggling of migrants (…) while protecting the rights of the smuggled migrants" (including women).	Elimination of violence against women
Art. 4 promotes equality of treatment in relation to: protection against discrimination in employment and occupation; in the field of occupational safety and health; remuneration; statutory social security protection; access to training; minimum age for admission to employment or work; and maternity protection.			Economic and social rights
Art. 4 (2a): "Equality of treatment shall be promoted (…) in relation to the homeworkers' right to establish or join organizations of their own choosing and to participate in the activities of such organizations."			Civil and political rights

Notes: (1) Optional Protocol to the Convention on the Rights of the Child on the sale of children, child prostitution and child pornography (adopted in 2000); (2) Protocol to prevent, suppress and punish trafficking in persons, especially women and children, supplementing the United Nations Convention against Transnational Organized Crime (adopted in 2000); (3) Protocol against the smuggling of migrants by land, sea and air, supplementing the United Nations Convention against Transnational Organized Crime (adopted in 2000).

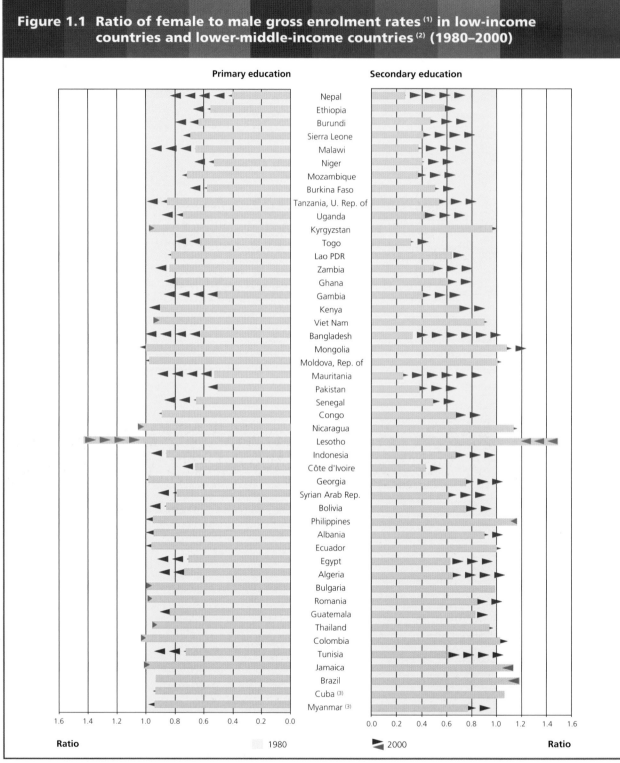

Figure 1.1 Ratio of female to male gross enrolment rates [1] in low-income countries and lower-middle-income countries [2] (1980–2000)

Notes: (1) A value of 1 for the ratio indicates equal enrolment ratios of females and males. A value below 1 indicates that the rates of female enrolment are lower than male enrolment rates. (2) Only countries for which data on secondary education was available for 1980 and 2000 are included. Countries are ordered in ascending order according to their 2000 gross national income (GNI) per capita (Atlas method, US$). (3) Data for GNI per capita not available.

Source: Calculated from World Bank 2004b.

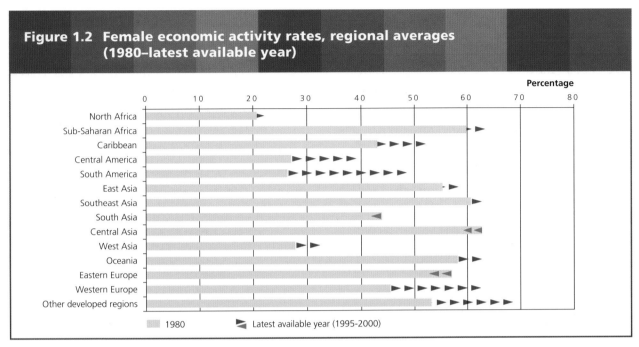

Figure 1.2 Female economic activity rates, regional averages (1980–latest available year)

Source: Calculated from ILO 2003.

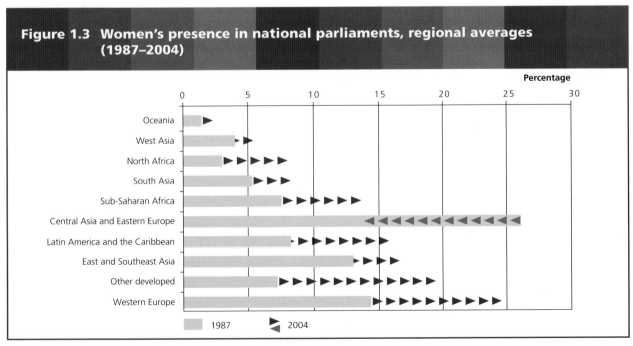

Figure 1.3 Women's presence in national parliaments, regional averages (1987–2004)

Source: Calculated from IPU 2004; UN Statistical Division 2004; UN 2003.

In many countries, both developed and developing, the gap between rich and poor households has been growing,[3] which also means that there are increasing inequalities among women. While the World Bank claims that the global poverty rate has fallen from 32 to 25 per cent between 1990 and 1999, decreasing the number of poor from 1.3 billion to 1.1 billion, there are major controversies about the Bank's methods of measuring poverty. In particular, distortion is produced by including the special case of China, which offsets trends of constant or increasing poverty in a number of other regions.[4] Although it is difficult to estimate gender differences in the incidence of poverty, given that income is most often measured at the household level (which ignores how resources are distributed within the household), it is reasonable to assume that women constitute a disproportionate share of the world's poor given their constrained access to capital and land, their lower labour market status, and their disproportionate responsibility for the provision of unpaid domestic and care work.

This, however, is not to deny the fact that some women are among the elite and have benefited enormously from the same policies that have been very adverse for the majority of the population.

Declining fertility continues to improve women's life chances in their reproductive years in most countries of the world, but in some it has also been associated with an increase in artificially high ratios of males to females (sex ratios) in the population.[5] Sex ratio imbalances have deepened in societies with marked "son preference" in tandem with rapid fertility decline, as infant daughters are subjected to maltreatment, neglect and abandonment, and new technologies allow sex-selective biases against females. Table 1.2 presents the most recent estimates of "missing women"[6]—those missing as a result of the unequal treatment of males and females—in countries where the problem is considered to be acute. Figure 1.4 presents data on juvenile sex ratios and fertility rates for China and India, the two countries that account for nearly 80 per cent

Table 1.2 Estimates of "missing women"

Country	Year	Actual number of women	Actual sex ratio	Expected sex ratio at birth	Expected sex ratio	Expected number of women	Number of missing women	% of missing women [(1)]
China	2000	612.3	1.067	1.050	1.001	653.2	40.9	6.7
Taiwan, P. of China	1999	10.8	1.049	1.052	1.002	11.3	0.5	4.7
Korea, Rep. of	1995	22.2	1.008	1.047	1.000	22.4	0.2	0.7
India	2001	495.7	1.072	1.039	0.993	534.8	39.1	7.9
Pakistan	1998	62.7	1.081	1.042	1.003	67.6	4.9	7.8
Bangladesh	2001	63.4	1.038	1.040	0.996	66.1	2.7	4.2
Nepal	2001	11.6	0.997	1.037	0.992	11.7	0.1	0.5
Sri Lanka	1991	8.6	1.005	1.052	1.006	8.6	0.0	0.0
West Asia	2000	92.0	1.043	1.042	1.002	95.8	3.8	4.2
Afghanistan	2000	11.1	1.054	1.024	0.964	12.1	1.0	9.3
Iran, Isl. Rep. of	1996	29.5	1.033	1.039	0.996	30.6	1.1	3.7
Egypt	1996	29.0	1.048	1.044	1.003	30.3	1.3	4.5
Algeria	1998	14.5	1.018	1.043	1.005	14.7	0.2	1.2
Tunisia	1994	4.3	1.021	1.043	1.000	4.4	0.1	2.1
Sub-Saharan Africa	2000	30.7	0.987	1.017	0.970	312.5	5.5	1.8
World		**1774.8**					**101.3**	**5.7**

Note: (1) The percentage missing is arrived at by dividing the number of "missing women" by the actual number of women alive.
Source: Klasen and Wink 2003.

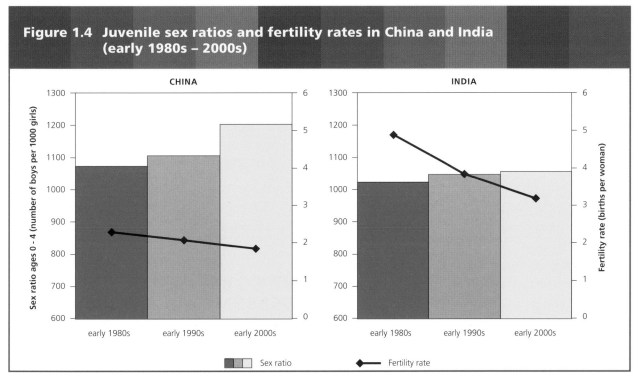

Figure 1.4 Juvenile sex ratios and fertility rates in China and India (early 1980s – 2000s)

Notes: China's sex ratios and fertility rates for 1982, 1990 and 2000. India's sex ratios for 1981, 1991 and 2001. India's fertility rates for 1980, 1990 and 2000.
Sources: Fertility rates from World Bank 2004b; sex ratios calculated from UN 2004 (for early 1980s and 1990s) and UNDESA 2001 (for early 2000s).

of all "missing women" in the world. The fact that these two countries have also produced some of the fastest rates of economic growth over the past decade or so only serves to underline the point that there is no guarantee that growth will enhance gender equality.

At a more general level the ambivalent nature of women's achievements is perhaps illustrated most strikingly in the "feminization" of the labour force. In the past two decades women's access to paid work has increased in most countries, but at the same time a deterioration has occurred in the terms and conditions of much of the work on offer. The growth of informal work across the world, along with the informalization or casualization of formal sector employment, has allowed employers to lower labour costs. However for ordinary women and men the outcome has been an increasing precariousness of jobs, and greater insecurity of livelihoods. Recent

International Labour Organization (ILO) estimates suggest that informal employment tends to be a larger source of employment for women than for men in all developing regions (except North Africa).[7]

These various outcomes do not have one single cause. Gender inequalities are deeply entrenched in all societies and are reproduced through a variety of practices and institutions, including policy interventions. A question posed in this report is what contribution does development policy make to bringing about favourable or unfavourable conditions for achieving greater gender equality? Has the policy model that has prevailed in recent decades, preoccupied as it is with balanced budgets and free markets, made it easier or more difficult to promote social equality, in particular in redressing inequalities between women and men?

THE DISABLING POLICY ENVIRONMENT

If the record of the policy model in reducing poverty and promoting growth is the subject of ongoing debate, most analysts agree that it has been associated in most parts of the world with deepening inequality.[8] Moreover in the 1980s and 1990s, structural adjustment left many millions unemployed and in acute poverty, creating a widespread distrust of market fundamentalism. The policies responsible for deepening inequality and for the social crisis had specific gender effects, shifting the burden of adjustment onto women in particular as "shock absorbers" and carers of last resort for households on the edge of survival.[9]

The neoliberal economic agenda, also known as the Washington Consensus, which rose to predominance in the early 1980s, centred on the strengthening of private property rights and profit-driven markets, and called for the "rollback of the state". To give full reign to the "invisible hand" of the market, primary emphasis was to be placed on price stability and governments were urged to restrict public spending. At the same time, state-centric strategies and policies were widely discredited, often justly, for fostering clientelism and corruption, authoritarianism, and a lack of state accountability to citizens. With earlier policy models having lost much of their appeal, and in the absence of adequate debate about the reform agenda, neoliberal ideas quickly took hold while critical voices were sidelined. It took the "lost decade" of the 1980s to reveal the severe limitations, risks and human costs of market fundamentalism.

Adjustment policies without adequate safety nets placed the livelihoods of low-income households in both rural and urban contexts under severe stress. Insecurity became a widespread feature of daily life even for the most protected public sector workers such as teachers, nurses and civil servants, many of whom were now forced to make regular forays into the informal economy to supplement their dwindling incomes.[10] In the "scramble for cash"[11] and under conditions of economic hardship, low-income women became increasingly visible both as casual agricultural labourers and in the over-crowded urban informal economy; and as migrants from countryside to town and across international borders.

Meanwhile, the creeping commercialization of welfare services meant that poorer households had to adjust by shifting more of the care into the household and onto the shoulders of women and girls; while the increased monetary cost of health services meant that women could less frequently afford to use such services for themselves and their children. Markets—not as they are hypothesized to function in neoliberal economics, but as they are "substantiated"[12] or made operative through the interaction of real social groups[13]—were powerful drivers of inequality, social exclusion and discrimination against women, whose unpaid care work held the social fabric together without recognition or reward.

THE SOBERING ASSESSMENTS OF 2000

As researchers documented the social costs of macroeconomic policies, more sober accounts of global developments emerged, especially after the Russian and Asian financial crisis of 1997 which underscored the fragility of an international order based on unregulated financial flows. By 2000, when the "Plus Five" reviews of the global conferences of 1995 took place, there was much less certainty that neoliberal globalization was going to improve people's lives.

While inflation was brought under control in many countries, price stability was achieved at the expense of growth and job creation. The new market orthodoxy was not delivering even on its own terms: growth rates were disappointing (see section 1). Financial crises and economic volatility were more frequent, with predictable economic and social consequences. Income inequalities widened all over the world, and fiscal deficits continued as governments faced severe difficulties in raising revenues to finance infrastructure, social services and other redistributive measures to compensate for the severe exclusions and failures of markets.

The social crisis that has continued to hit many parts of the world has perhaps been expressed most dramatically in the civil unrest and political turmoil, including outbreaks and continuations of civil wars, in which underlying economic and social distress are among the causal dynamics. In such zones of insecurity and pervasive violence, few escape the disastrous impacts of warfare whether or not they are actively involved as combatants. Women's particular vulnerabilities during war and conflict were drawn to world attention by women's rights activists, especially in connection with the war in Bosnia and Herzegovina and the genocide in Rwanda; these two events were mainly responsible for revealing to the world the extent of crimes of sexual violence and their systematic use as weapons of war.[14] However, women are also profoundly affected by war and violence in their socially constructed gender roles as family carers and providers.

Even where conflict has ceased, crime rates have typically soared, as have incidents of gender-based and sexual violence. To the trauma of conflict with its detrimental impact on interpersonal relations and community networks have been added breakdowns in law and order, of police and judicial systems, of health and education services, and a weakening of social and ethical norms.[15] In "normal" times too, crime and violence have seemed to be on the increase. Urban populations have been witnessing a growth in the use of private security services, the rise of walled compounds and separated areas within cities, and a widespread lack of confidence in the police and justice system.[16]

THE UNRISD REPORT

The impetus for this report was the recognition that in the maelstrom of ideas and events associated with the recent past, there has been some loss of gender perspective among the many issues vying for attention in international policy debates. While liberalization and governance reform programmes have received critical attention and generated considerable debate, there has been a lack of systematic appraisal from the point of view of gender equality. At a time when organizations and researchers concerned about the progress of women in the world, within the UN system and beyond, are preparing the "Beijing Plus Ten" assessment requested for 2005 by the UN General Assembly in June 2000, an UNRISD Report which set out to redeem this omission appeared appropriate.

The report aims to reestablish the centrality of gender equality in ongoing efforts to reorient the development agenda to meet some of the key challenges that are integral to the development process: economic growth and structural transformation; equality and social protection; and democratization. These objectives resonate with those elaborated in the United Nations Charter more than 50 years ago, and have been reinforced through key international conventions that numerous countries have signed and ratified in the subsequent period. They were also at the heart of the United Nations Conferences of the 1990s.

In the past few years several major policy reports from organizations within and outside the UN system have underlined the salience of gender issues to development processes, in different ways and from diverse points of view.[17] This report adds fresh perspectives and its own distinctive analysis to the debate.

Rather than attempt to review all potential areas of concern to women identified in the Beijing Platform for Action, UNRISD determined to focus on a more limited range of issues, essentially those areas of policy and institutional reform critical for the substantiation of women's rights and the search for gender equality in an unequal world. In reflecting on the recent achievements of the post-Beijing agenda, and in exploring the reasons for the ambivalent outcomes, the report addresses directly or indirectly eight of the 12 key areas of concern articulated in the Beijing Platform for Action. These are: Women and Poverty; Women and Health; Violence against Women; Women and Armed Conflict; Women and the Economy; Women in Power and Decision-Making; Institutional Mechanisms for the Advancement of Women; and Human Rights of Women. These topics are addressed within the following four key thematic areas the report has singled out for analysis.

Macroeconomics, well-being and gender equality

This analysis of macroeconomic policies from a gender perspective begins by reviewing the many areas of contention thrown up by the neoliberal agenda, the currently dominant economic policy model. There has been a tendency by mainstream analysts to treat macroeconomic policy as a gender-free or gender-neutral zone, and to ignore the gender impacts of policy choices; yet all outcomes in terms of growth, structural transformation, equality, poverty and social protection have implications for gender equality or for lessening gender inequality. This review, contained in the next three chapters (chapters 2, 3 and 4), also examines whether heterodox macroeconomic policies have performed any better than neoliberal models in achieving growth and social equity, and if so whether they have served the goal of gender equality any more effectively.

Women, work and social policy

The next section (chapters 5 through 8) considers how policy reforms associated with the liberalization of the economy have transformed the world of work and people's access to social security more broadly, and the implications for low-income women in particular. The past decade has seen the emergence of women as the dominant workforce in various sectors of the economy, with many potentially positive implications. However, much depends on what kind of work is available to them, and the degree to which seeking paid work represents a distress strategy to sustain family livelihood. At the same time women have been facing additional burdens in their domestic management and care roles. The key question posed is whether some of the opportunities that have recently opened up for women compensate adequately for the burdens and risks that the same policy agenda has thrust upon society, and particularly upon women. While numerous innovative initiatives by civil-society organizations, social movements and government bodies address the insecurity of livelihoods confronted by informal women workers, the standard reforms in social security (such as pensions) and service provision (such as health sector reforms) have tended to widen gender gaps. Gender analysis rarely informs social policy, and tends to remain a "silent term", marginalized from policy debates.

Women in politics and public life

The section on women in politics and public life (chapters 9 through 12) strikes a different note: in these contexts, women's increased visibility is conspicuous. The section begins by holding a magnifying glass to one of the great achievements of the last decade, women's increased prominence in formal political institutions and elected assemblies. Enthusiasm for the greater show of female hands in representative bodies, however, needs to be tempered by the recognition that entrenched male biases and hierarchies still exist, and there is a long way to go before anything resembling parity is reached in most political environments. Another focus of this section is women's activism within civil society, especially in the light of political movements which mobilize around faith, ethnic identity or nationalism, and which have their own reverberations concerning femininity and women's rights. Female visibility in this context has ambivalent characteristics. On the institutional side, the current enthusiasm for "good governance" and the associated institutional reform agenda, especially the decentralization of decision-making structures, comes under scrutiny; are women making real or superficial gains by such devices as quotas and "reservations"?

Gender, armed conflict and the search for peace

The proliferation since the end of the Cold War of internal or civil wars, the holdover conflicts from the postcolonial era, and the major military incursions associated with the contemporary "war on terror" have important implications for women. The 1990s saw widespread recognition that rape was commonly used as a weapon of war, and that sexual assault was a feature of any setting engulfed by turmoil and armed violence; but the implications of modern forms of war for women in their socially constructed and livelihood roles have not been given similar attention. Women have been noticed as programmed for peace—as instigators of peace initiatives or conflict resolution; this chimes with the idea of the quintessentially pacifying female presence. But they are often ignored in the formal negotiations which bring postconflict institutions into being, and therefore lose out from peace settlements. Two chapters (chapters 13 and 14) inspect the gendered battlefield during war, during the search for peace, and in the postconflict environment. The limited extent to which peace secures women's interests is another example of the convenient oblivion to which gender considerations are so often confined.

BRINGING GENDER BACK IN

The analytic approach advanced in the report assumes that societies, their social relations, economies and power structures contain deeply etched gender divisions, in the same way that they reflect class, ethnic and racial divisions. Inequalities based on sex are a pervasive feature of all societies; they are the product of socially constructed power relations, norms and practices.

Feminist research has revealed persistent inequalities in the intrahousehold allocation of resources, rights and power, exploding the myth of family altruism and equality represented in the idea that the private sphere is always a "haven in a heartless world".[18] Documenting the dark side of family life has not meant that the injustices committed against girls and women within the private domain—in terms of either severe resource deprivation, or physical and sexual abuse—are being adequately addressed and remedied. Indeed, the domestic arena remains one of the most difficult and controversial of policy contexts. Even where progressive laws have been put in place to protect the victims of domestic violence, weak implementation—through elitist and sometimes corrupt judicial and police systems—means that those who need protection against violence and abuse in the domestic domain often remain vulnerable and at risk. Nevertheless, within policy debates on gender, the family and the household have come under increasing scrutiny over the past decade. There are some interesting shifts in policy that reflect the findings of intrahousehold research: anti-poverty programmes, whether in the form of micro-credit or cash transfers to poor households, increasingly target women on the grounds that they will spend the resources under their control in ways that enhance family and child welfare.

While institutions such as the World Bank now concern themselves with gender inequalities in some institutional arenas—at the intrahousehold level in particular, as well as in the legal domain where traditions and customs have an important role to play—the attention to gender is selective and uneven.[19] The silences and omissions in such frameworks are particularly revealing: significantly, markets and macroeconomic flows (trade, capital) are not subjected to the same gender analysis, the implicit assumption being that they are essentially benign and gender-neutral. However, the report finds that this is true neither of the economy nor of the family; nor do states, communities, political parties or "progressive" social movements necessarily operate in gender-neutral ways. Indeed the reverse is more common. The evidence presented by the report reveals gender inequality to be a persistent and integral feature of the modern world, even though some of the modalities through which it is expressed have undergone change in recent times.

Gender and men

The analysis undertaken by the report is largely of social relations, and particularly gender relations, across a wide spectrum of institutions in both private and public life. The primary focus, however, is on women (differentiated by class, race, ethnicity and caste) even though full recognition is given in the analysis to the complex web of social/gender relations in which they are involved. It is important to keep the spotlight on women, in view of the recent shifts in thinking (and language) in development bureaucracies as well as in some strands of academic research, which have sometimes inadvertently blunted the significance of women's subordination.[20]

Feminist researchers have raised concerns at the shift that has occurred away from a focus on women, towards women and men, and then back to men. Activists from the Caribbean have described how this has resulted in an emphasis on "men at risk". Women in this region score higher than men on a variety of indicators, including education and health. Yet women also face unemployment rates which are twice those of men. When coupled with the prevalence of female-headed households (over 35 per cent in a number of Caribbean countries), women's job exclusion undermines the case for considering women to be "better off than men".[21] Moreover, despite justified concern about low male educational attainment, society clearly has different expectations of males and females. Male educational underachievement has not led to parallel underachievements in wealth and politics. Women need higher levels of attainment than men to compete for jobs, decision-making positions, and access to an equal share of productive resources.[22]

However, if gender hierarchies are not disappearing and if the subordination of women continues to be a significant social issue, this does not invariably mean that men are advantaged. Masculinist cultures can be counter-productive or even destructive for men, reinforcing the point that men too have gender identities which expose them to risks. This is shown by the excess mortality of adult males under conditions in which economic stress undermines the norm of the "male breadwinner", a role closely interwoven with men's sense of identity across many cultures. One example is provided by the high rates of suicide among male cotton farmers in Andhra Pradesh, India, in 2001 as a result of indebtedness.[23] Another is the excess mortality of adult males in Central and Eastern Europe after 1989 due to stress-related health risks and alcoholism associated with unemployment and other adverse labour market changes.[24] While men are the main perpetrators of violence, both domestic and public, they are also the main victims of violence outside the domestic sphere.

The emphasis on women's subordination does not imply a static picture of unchanging gender relations: rather, it is important to acknowledge that gender hierarchies constantly change. Current processes of social change and their intersections with policies show that while some forms of gender inequality have dissolved and women have been able to enjoy new opportunities and freedoms, other forms of subordination and new constraints have emerged. As women have gained access to education and paid work, won the right to vote and stand for political office, and have achieved some control over their sexuality and fertility, they have also had to contend with segmented labour markets,

exposure to workplace discrimination, greater personal insecurity, and increasingly commercialized sexuality. In the same vein, anthropological research on youth cultures demonstrates the ways in which gender roles are constantly recreated by simultaneously breaking with past models and reproducing some traditional attributes of these roles, such as male aggressiveness.

CURRENT POLICY AGENDAS: IMPLICATIONS FOR GENDER EQUALITY

The rediscovery of "the social"

The political and policy context of recent years has presented some new opportunities and challenges for those concerned with gender equality and women's rights. In response to escalating popular discontent, as well as internal and external criticism from leading economists, international financial institutions (IFIs) have shown themselves willing to give social and political concerns renewed attention. The rediscovery of these areas of policy concern is expressed under indicative conceptual headings such as "participation", "social capital" and "good governance". The change of direction was particularly evident in the World Bank's 2001 **World Development Report: Attacking Poverty,** which identified "social risk management" as the most sustainable basis for poverty reduction.[25] The "good governance" agenda ostensibly seeks to make development more participatory and more responsive to the needs of marginalized groups, including women.

However, while this may have led to a degree of mutual accommodation between the IFIs and their critics and rendered the Washington Consensus more palatable, many of its central policy tenets remain in place. The dominant policy package—known as the "post-Washington Consensus"—retains the core elements of economic orthodoxy: trade and financial liberalization, and tight monetary and fiscal policies, while adding the "good governance" agenda of democracy, participation, decentralization and community ownership. It would be more accurate to speak of a new "moment" in the neoliberal agenda than of a new paradigm.[26]

There are therefore important continuities, as well as some innovations in the current policy agenda, and it is in this light that some of the recent policy responses to social distress, such as the World Bank's Poverty Reduction Strategy Papers (PRSPs), need to be seen. Behind the apparent consensus forged by a shared vocabulary of "poverty" and "social protection", conflicting understandings of social policy continue to vie for attention. These are based on different values, priorities, and understandings of state responsibility and of the responsibilities of different individuals and social groups to each other. In the social risk management framework, the state is charged only with providing social safety nets for risk coping, as well as risk management instruments where the private sector fails. This approach is effectively a continuation of the earlier policy of minimal safety nets, and overrides equality agendas.

An alternative view of social policy is premised on the centrality of redistribution, equality and universal social provision. This is not merely an abstract proposition but is grounded in the historical experiences of building the welfare state in many European countries. Recent adaptations and reforms may have diluted those principles but they have not fundamentally overturned them. The goals of inclusion and universal social provision are also being pursued in some developing countries, where there has been considerable public debate about social responsibility and where an ideological commitment to social equality remains intact. Despite glaring social inequalities in countries like Brazil, South Africa and Chile, efforts are being made to extend social protection mechanisms to people in rural areas and in informal work situations.

"Good governance" reforms and the democratic deficit

An emphasis on "good governance" has been an integral part of the Washington and the post-Washington Consensus. But the governance agenda has had both a mixed reception and a mixed record in those countries where it has driven donor and government policy. The existence of formal democratic rules and the protection of civil and political rights are preconditions of virtually any kind of critical engagement with the state by social forces pressing for reform. Women's movements are no exception. Women's mobilization has been essential to the success of many pro-democracy movements, especially when conventional channels for popular expression (political parties, trade unions) have been closed to political activists. However, mobilization in opposition to authoritarian rule has not always secured women representation in formal institutional politics after the transition, especially where transitions have been sudden, or are the outcome of negotiations between exclusive or elite groups.

While many countries have now formally become democracies with established institutions of representative government, the degree to which democracy has been consolidated varies, along with its institutional forms. Even where elections have been held, political parties often remain elitist and weakly institutionalized; mechanisms for popular participation are not embedded in society, and the implementation of law and order rarely succeeds in protecting the civil rights accorded to citizens, especially those who are socially marginalized. There are increasing concerns about the resurgence of semi-authoritarian states, "soft dictatorships" and "masculine democracies".[27] Even where high-level political commitment to women's rights exists—in terms of constitutional provisions and key policy statements— the translation of these provisions into actual government policy, targeted spending, and effective procedures for bureaucrats and service delivery agents is far from guaranteed.

The connection between political commitments and effective policy implementation defines what is meant by "governance". The difficulties that women have experienced in promoting gender-equity legislation, and in seeing it passed into law and implemented, would indicate that women have a keen interest in seeing the capacity and accountability of the state strengthened. The fact that governance reforms are now high on the agenda of many multilateral and bilateral donor agencies therefore seems to offer an important entry point for addressing gender-specific capacity and accountability failures. Ways of doing this include addressing gender biases in public expenditure management systems, enhancing gender equality in the staffing of public institutions such as the civil service or the judiciary, and facilitating rule of law reforms that secure women's access to assets and ensure that instances of abuse and violence against them can be prosecuted.

Contrasting and contested interpretations

A broad understanding of a "good governance" agenda would embrace political liberalization, participation and human rights, and address problems of social inequality as part of a fundamental commitment to democracy. Such an agenda would encompass the kinds of issues of state legitimacy, capacity and accountability that social movements and women's movements have confronted for decades. With such an agenda in mind, governance reforms with their aim of enhancing the capacity of the state and making it more accountable to its citizens have been welcomed in many parts of the world. Critics, however, point out that although governance reforms can and should address issues of government legitimacy and the public participation of socially excluded groups, they have in fact been dominated by a much narrower preoccupation. This centres on the "sound" management of the economy along neoliberal lines, and on expanding private property rights in order to support economic activity. When these are the main parameters of "good governance", gender equality has typically been excluded from the concerns of the reformers and from their reforms.

Some of the reforms may indeed have very adverse implications for women. The case of land tenure reform, which is of critical importance both to the investment environment and to the livelihoods of rural people, illustrates the problem. In much of sub-Saharan Africa, for example, land is held and used under plural legal arrangements. The fixation with the market advantages of formal titling and individual ownership rights, however, risks eroding women's socially sanctioned claims to land, as historical evidence from countries such as Kenya illustrates.[28]

Decentralization as a forward and backward step

Good governance reforms have also encouraged the decentralization of political power to local government bodies, municipalities and village councils. The emphasis on bringing government "closer to people" resonates with the "local democracy" initiatives that many non-governmental organizations (NGOs) and social movements have long championed. In some countries women's representation in local government has been facilitated through quotas, which have given large numbers of women their first experience of political office: the 30 per cent quota for women in the Panchayati Raj institutions in India is the best-known example.

Once in office, however, the willingness and capacity of women representatives to press for gender-equality initiatives is critically dependent on the support that they receive from women's movements and NGOs. In very unequal societies, there is always the risk that elites, usually men, will "capture" the available power in replacement or new institutions, reducing the prospect that women's presence in political office will significantly influence programmes and spending patterns. Where decentralization additionally involves conferring power on "traditional" authorities such as tribal elders or religious councils, the invocation of tradition and custom may be deeply inimical to women's interests. This raises fundamental questions about the extent to which local government bodies will be based on democratic principles and practices, and will themselves contribute to the consolidation of democracy or its reverse.

Hence, while the recent donor attention to the question of "good governance" is to be welcomed, much depends on how it is interpreted. A great deal depends on whether the democratization of politics and the participation of marginalized social groups are seen as integral to reform objectives and are embraced in institutional change; and on whether reducing social and gender inequalities are among the core principles guiding the programme of state institutional transformation.

The resurgence of identity politics

A phenomenon to emerge with particular force in recent years is that of "identity politics". The term refers to those movements that mobilize around ethnic, racial and religious identities, and often contest long-standing histories of marginalization and discrimination by mainstream institutions and cultures. In response to such claims many states have put in place constitutional and legal provisions and institutional mechanisms to accommodate ethnic, racial and other diversities.

While there have been tensions between some versions of identity-based claims and notions of gender equality (the latter based on universalist principles), these are not necessarily irreconcilable, at least in principle.[29] For example, international legislation granting rights to indigenous peoples and their cultures (ILO Convention 169) stipulates that customary law should be respected when it does not conflict with universal human rights. This formulation has been incorporated into a number of state constitutions, especially in Latin America in the 1990s. In practice, however, women who are active in these movements often find it difficult to get a hearing for gender equality concerns, an experience that resonates with women who have been active in nationalist movements.[30]

More radical attacks on human rights and women's rights agendas have also resulted from the resurgence of religious identities that include the assertion of "traditional" gender roles and systems of authority that intrinsically violate women's rights. The most extreme example of women's oppression, designated "gender cleansing" by some commentators, was by the Taliban regime in Afghanistan. This is not the only case of its kind: the Islamist movement in Iran that captured state power in 1979 based its grievances against the monarchy and the United States, and its own system of government (the "governance of the jurisprudence" or *velayat faqih*), on a highly patriarchal interpretation of Islam. Subsequent social and gender restructuring led to state and domestic violence against women, violated women's rights with impunity, and had a lasting impact on gender relations and society.[31] However, since women are a visible political force in the country, both as individuals and as a social group, doctrinaire positions on women's rights and many early Islamization measures have been renegotiated or reformed through the efforts of women's rights advocates both inside and outside parliament.

Some of these faith-based movements gather members from among those feeling humiliated and powerless in the face of unacceptable behaviour by their own state or by foreign powers. Grievances and dislocations are also fuelled by development policies and outcomes that exacerbate people's experience of poverty, inequality and social exclusion. A deeper analysis of these movements would include a critique of "modernity" and an examination of backlashes against Western, consumerist and libertarian ideas which contribute to their ideological predispositions. From a gender perspective, their appeal to women also needs to be probed: women are visible among both the membership and the leadership of many such movements even though they are not incorporated into formal power structures.[32] Women have been publicly active in some of them, and have assumed roles that violate traditional gender norms, for example the militant Hindu nationalist women involved in inciting anti-Muslim pogroms in Gujarat, India, in 2002. Along with their conspicuous public engagement, a feature of women's involvement in these movements is their support for reforms that restrict women's rights and subjugate them to men in the name of religion and tradition.

The "traditions" and religious doctrines typically invoked by some of these movements may be neither traditional nor authentic, but instead have been recently coined to serve political ends. Some women's rights advocates have therefore set out to provide alternative readings of religious texts supportive of gender-egalitarian practices. This has been one of the main thrusts of feminist activism in the Muslim world, where examining the rights of women under *Shari'a* law has been an acceptable terrain for discussion in some settings. However, when religious authorities become the spokespeople for nations and ethnic communities, and where no guarantees exist for equality, democracy or human rights protection within the political context, there is very little scope for contestation and dialogue.[33]

As is the case with Christianity and other religions, belief in Islam has been associated with a range of state forms and legal interpretations; modern Islamist movements are not uniformly hostile to women's rights. The moderate Justice and Development Party of Turkey is a case in point. In November 2002, the party acceded to power amidst fears that this would herald a retreat to conservative religious politics. However, the new government seems to have embraced secular democracy and rejected the orthodox interpretations of Islam practised by some of its supporters. In a move that was welcomed by many women's rights advocates in Turkey, the government's Directorate of Religious Affairs instructed the nation's imams (spiritual leaders) to turn their spiritual guidance to the arena of human rights and women's rights. Worshippers in different parts of the country are being told that "honour killings", in which men murder female relatives suspected of tarnishing the family name, are a sin as well as against the law.[34] Such messages conveyed by the imams can "reach people the human rights advocates often cannot—the 15 million men in Turkey who attend services every Friday".[35]

FORGING LINKS BETWEEN ECONOMIC POLICY AND GENDER EQUALITY

Securing livelihoods and creating an enabling economic environment are necessary preconditions for attaining gender equality and women's rights. But what is an "enabling economic environment"? To a significant degree, women's ability to achieve parity with men in access to resources and influence, and in well-being, depends on the macroeconomic policies and development strategies on which their livelihoods and ways of life, and those of their families and communities, ultimately depend. As emerges from the evidence presented in the following chapters of this report, policies aimed at trade and financial liberalization and global economic integration have profound impacts on the lives of women, and on those of their

partners and other family members. A world in which the dominant policy model tends to deepen social and economic inequality and reinforce marginalization; in which redistribution has no place; and in which governments compromise the interests of their citizens to accommodate global forces, is not going to be a world that secures gender equality.

For this reason, women's rights activists have increasingly been devoting more of their attention and energies to the larger structures of global power, and the evolution of problems of global injustice relating to macroeconomic trends: the implications for socially disadvantaged and discriminated groups of unregulated transnational capital flows, debt service payments, trade liberalization, inequitable trade patterns and the shrinkage of public resource expenditures on welfare needs. One example is the attempt to influence trade negotiations at the global level, which has required transnational feminist solidarity and organizing, as a complement to women's collective action at the national level.[36]

These links between global economic justice and women's rights have been central to women's global campaigns for sexual and reproductive health and rights. Transnational activism has been given impetus by the continuing concern over the harsh social impacts of neoliberal policies; the emergence of large transnational coalitions demonstrating against the WTO, and at G-8 summits and IFI gatherings; and the leadership of Southern women's groups whose work for sexual and reproductive health and rights has consistently been linked to a strong economic justice platform as set out in box 1.1.[37]

Box 1.1   Sexual and reproductive health are human rights

Rights cannot be divorced from needs. Reproductive and sexual health and other basic human needs—education, sanitation, clean water, nutrition—are equally important and interdependent; all are human rights. Especially for women, good pre-natal and obstetric care, safe contraception, and other aspects of health are inseparable from such basic amenities as reliable transportation, hygienic conditions and clean water. At the same time, their rights to liberty, security of the person and development are unattainable without comprehensive, accessible and affordable reproductive and sexual health services and the freedom to make decisions about their fertility and sexuality. These rights form a seamless web, and all are grounded in basic human needs. To rank them denies the basic realities of women's lives, especially for poor women.

Source: Excerpt from flier, circulated at the UNGASS for ICPD+5, March 1999, by Women's Coalition for ICPD, made up of 80 NGOs from around the world, cited in Petchesky 2003:15.

Yet creating the political alliances—with governments, NGOs and social movements—to help bring the interdependence between global economic justice and gender justice to the awareness of policy makers, and then actually to realize gender-sensitive policy change, is no easy task. In attempting to make an impact on global rule-making, feminist activists need not only to bring on board those governments and global institutions that are redesigning the architecture of the international political economy, but also to enlist the support of mainstream activists who are not always attentive to gender equality concerns.[38]

Moreover, the global political environment in which economic justice and gender justice have to be negotiated has been less favourable in recent years. In the mid-1990s the Vatican and some Islamic country delegations united against the adoption of the International Conference on Population and Development (ICPD) Programme of Action, and maintained persistent opposition to gender-equality proposals through succeeding conferences. While conservative religious groups were most vehement in their opposition to abortion and same sex partnership, these positions were symptomatic of their core objection to gender equality itself. These tensions came to the fore in the "Plus Five" reviews for the Cairo and Beijing conferences.[39] Despite such tensions over women's rights, considerable advances were nevertheless possible on sexual and reproductive health and rights during the 1990s because of the limited control over state power by religious fundamentalists. Both the Cairo Plus Five and Beijing Plus Five reviews ended with the gains of Cairo and Beijing intact, and with further progress on some key fronts.

Confronting complex realities

Such positive outcomes were however hard won, and many women's organizations consider that in the current international climate, many of the gains won in the UN conferences, summits and special sessions of the 1990s look fragile. Human rights and women's agendas and the entire multilateral framework within which the gains of the 1990s were made have been weakened by the current global political crisis occasioned by terrorism, militarism, the war on Iraq and hostility to unilateralism. Human rights agendas have come under pressure not only in countries where democratic institutions remain weak, but also in the heartlands of democracy. In both North America and Europe there are concerns about the rights of ethnic minorities and immigrants, especially Muslim minorities. Fundamentalist extremism and terrorist acts have served to reinforce suspicion of Muslim populations in particular, who may be simplistically and erroneously branded as uniformly hostile to the West and to democratic values, especially in regard to gender issues.

There is, however, no "clash of civilizations" on women's rights and gender issues between the "neoconservatives" and religious conservatives.[40] The last few years have seen the most powerful nation in the world join, even at times replace, the Vatican in global negotiations as the key strategist against the women's agenda on sexual and reproductive health and rights. Under the 2000-2004 administration, the United States slashed aid budgets supporting contraception, and promoted abstinence and greater parental control over adolescents as the way to contain sexual freedom and the HIV/AIDS pandemic.

Governments have not, in the main, caved in to such pressures, as emerged in regional and subregional discussions around ICPD Plus Ten and Beijing Plus Ten. But there are fissures and tensions among those who have resisted such pressures. The attempt to create a strong bloc out of Southern governments to confront the economic North in trade negotiations gives hope of greater global economic justice; but within the new alliance there is no common ground on sexual and reproductive health and rights, and indeed positions vary considerably. Women's organizations recognize that it is only by keeping up the pressure and by participating in the largely gender-blind arenas where global economic justice is debated that they have any chance of forging links between the issues of economic justice and gender justice.

WOMEN'S MOVEMENTS: WALKING A TIGHTROPE TO CHANGE

If gender justice is not to slip down the agenda yet again, women's movements will require new alliances with both governmental institutions and social movements. Working with governments means enlarging the scope for representing women's interests in all areas of policy making, including economic policy. While gender analysis reveals the ways in which economic policies are gendered, and women's movements can demand that policies that disadvantage women be changed, the arenas in which these policies are debated have rarely included significant representation of women's interests. Getting recognition of the need for a gender perspective in fora where macroeconomic discussion takes place is difficult, but a first step has been taken with the successful lobbying for gender budgets.

Alliances with new and old social movements are also essential, but require careful negotiation. One of the promising developments of the 1990s was the emergence of new forms of organizing among women workers in the informal economy, as well as greater responsiveness among some older trade unions to women informal workers. Not all organizations in the movement for global economic justice, however, are sensitive, interested and attentive to the gender-related aspects of the issues they address.[41] For their part, women's movements that have not considered broader social or economic justice issues may be limited in their efficacy. If progress towards the goal of gender equality has been uneven, this is partly because some of the obstacles to achieving it lie in the character and tactics of the forces that seek it, even while others lie in the structures and practices through which gender inequalities are reproduced. The key question on the table for discussion is how can women's organizations simultaneously tackle women's subordination and unequal access to resources, and confront the broader processes and policies that entrench inequalities between and within nation states?

UNRISD hopes that this report will help provide some answers to this question by casting light on some of the processes—economic, political and social—that link gender and economic justice. In this way it should contribute to the debate over how gender equality might best be advanced. In recent decades, the world has become more unequal as neoliberal macroeconomic policies have tightened their hold, and previously accepted values such as equality and redistribution have systematically been sidelined. Many observers see prevailing policies—trade and financial liberalization, tight monetary and fiscal policies, market-based entitlements to welfare—as the main obstacles in meeting the objectives that were agreed upon in the global conferences of the 1990s, including Beijing. Placing the various elements of the neoliberal reform programme under a gender lens, and examining their implications for equality and justice, is the task set out for subsequent chapters in this report.

Notes

1   Therborn 2004.

2   UNESCO 2003; Jha and Subrahmanian 2004.

3   Milanovic 2003; Cornia et al. 2004.

4   The case of China is controversial because its high rates of economic growth and decline in poverty have been the outcome of heterodox macroeconomic policies (for example, China maintains a non-convertible currency and state control over its banking system) rather than the standard prescriptions of the international financial institutions. It is problematic therefore to use global evidence on poverty that is biased by poverty reduction in China to defend the orthodox macroeconomic policy agenda.

5   Because the female human being is more biologically robust, there should be a higher number of women than men in any population. However, in certain societies where son preference is marked, human intervention in the form of girl neglect favours the survival of males (Klasen and Wink 2003; Das Gupta and Bhat 1998; Jackson and Rao 2004).

6   Sen 1989, 1990.

7   ILO 2002b.

8   Milanovic 2003; Wade 2001; Cornia et al. 2004.

9   Elson 2002.

10 Bangura 1994.

11 Bryceson 1999b.

12 Polanyi 1957.

13 Hewitt de Alcántara 1993.

14 UN Secretary-General 2002.

15 UN Secretary-General 2002; Rehn and Sirleaf 2002; Commission on Human Security 2003.

16 Caldeira 2000.

17 UNDESA produced **The World Survey on the Role of Women in Development** in 1985, 1989, 1994 and 1999; the UN General Assembly has requested that this continue to be updated on a quinquennial basis. The Human Development Report Office of the UNDP devoted its 1995 **Human Development Report** to gender issues. UNIFEM produced **Progress of the World's Women** in 2000 and in 2002 (volumes I and II), and the World Bank brought out a Policy Research Report entitled **Engendering Development** in 2001.

18 Whitehead 1981; Folbre 1986; Dwyer and Bruce 1988; Sen 1990; Agarwal 1990; Kabeer 1994; Hart 1995.

19 World Bank 2001a.

20 Baden and Goetz 1998; Razavi and Miller 1995.

21 Seguino 2003b.

22 Bailey 2003.

23 Patnaik 2003.

24 Cornia 1996.

25 World Bank 2001c; Holzmann and Jorgensen 2000.

26 Molyneux 2002.

27 O'Donnell 1993, 1998; Eisenstein 1993.

28 Whitehead and Tsikata 2003.

29 Phillips 2002; Molyneux and Razavi 2002b.

30 Hernandez Castillo 2002.

31 Paidar 2002.

32 Basu 2004.

33 Molyneux and Razavi 2002b.

34 WLUML 2004.

35 Ertürk 2004, quoted in Collins 2004.

36 Mohanty 2003.

37 Petchesky 2003.

38 Liebowitz 2004.

39 Sen and Correa 1999.

40 Sen 2004.

41 Sen 2004; Liebowitz 2004.

Section 1
Macroeconomics, well-being and gender equality

In the last two decades economic policies have reflected a drive for accelerated global economic integration ("globalization"), which is usually associated with greater economic liberalization, both internationally and within national economies. Policy institutions favouring economic liberalization—the international financial institutions (IFIs) and the World Trade Organization (WTO)—are often inspired by neoliberal and market-oriented thinking, and consider the extension and deepening of global markets, and the "rollback" of the state, to be on the whole desirable from the point of view of economic efficiency, growth, and even human welfare. Heterodox economists favour a much stronger degree of state involvement to govern markets and achieve economic growth, structural transformation and human welfare. For some, the East Asian experience, characterized by rapid economic growth, industrialization, and relatively egalitarian income distribution, underscores the need for strong public policy interventions, and industrial policies in particular. What have the implications of these different development models—liberalization as prescribed by the IFIs, and "governed markets" as they have been substantiated in East Asia—been for women and for gender equality?

The first chapter in this section, "Liberalization and deregulation: The route to gender equality?", starts by examining the general parameters of macroeconomic policy in the current era of global economic integration. It then goes on to examine the various components of the agenda: trade and financial liberalization, deflationary macroeconomic policies, fiscal restraint and privatization. This is followed, in the second chapter, "Liberalization, labour markets and women's gains: A mixed picture", by an assessment of the principal effects of these policies on women and the search for gender equality. The third chapter, "Consolidating women's gains: The need for a broader policy agenda", looks at how women have fared according to a range of indicators broader than measures of income and wages. It ends by considering what kind of changes in the macroeconomic policy agenda would help to improve women's well-being and promote gender equality.

Chapter 2
Liberalization and deregulation:
The route to gender equality?

The macroeconomic terrain, and the degree to which economic liberalization—both international and domestic—should be pursued, rather than some degree of state intervention and market management, have been hotly contested issues over the last 20 years. The effects of liberalization on economic growth have been disappointing, and it has exposed millions of people to poverty and unemployment in the absence of effective social provisions and safety nets. There have therefore been increasing calls for interventionist and redistributive action, both to repair social distress and to reinstall equality in the policy equation.

In the debates on international trade and financial capital flows, restrictive monetary and fiscal policies, and in other critical areas such as privatization of welfare services, little attention has been paid to gender concerns. Feminist economists have, however, produced a thorough gender analysis of current macroeconomic trends and policies, identifying specific impacts on women and on gender equality. Before their findings are examined in the following two chapters, a broad-ranging description of the key areas of macroeconomic policy concern is presented as a starting point.

LIBERALIZATION AND GLOBALIZATION

The neoliberal agenda which became dominant in the early 1980s centres on the view that the best way to pursue human welfare is to reduce the role of the state, liberate entrepreneurial energy, in order to achieve economic efficiency and promote faster economic growth. Some governments, notably the US government led by President Ronald Reagan and the UK government led by Prime Minister Margaret Thatcher, embraced this agenda of their own volition. But many governments in the South had it thrust upon them as the condition for more loans from the International Monetary Fund (IMF) and World Bank in the context of the debt crisis of the early 1980s.

The debt crisis itself was a result of the neoliberal agenda. The roots of the debt crisis lie in the decisions taken in the 1970s about how to adjust to the dramatic increase in oil prices in 1973 and 1979. One possibility was to recycle the massive additional dollar earnings of oil-exporting countries to oil-importing countries via a low-conditionality facility at the IMF. However, much of the recycling of petrodollars took place via the emerging private international financial market. This was of enormous benefit to US, European and Japanese banks. But this international market turned out to be very different from the competitive market depicted in neoclassical economics textbooks. The over-selling of loans by private banks to sovereign governments was widespread. The debt burden of these dollar-denominated loans exploded in the early 1980s, when Paul Volker, the Chair of the Federal Reserve Bank, sharply increased interest rates as a means to control inflation in the United States. High interest rates coupled with the heavy loan burdens combined to produce the debt crisis.[1] There were always critics pointing out that the oil price rises and the debt crisis were collective problems and needed internationally equitable solutions, but their warnings went unheeded. The debt crisis of the early 1980s thus provided a critical opening for Washington to try to impose a succession of new international economic policy regimes through the Bretton Woods institutions, reinforced since 1994 by the Uruguay Round Agreements under the World Trade Organization (WTO).

Neoliberal macroeconomic policies

A key feature of neoliberal policy regimes is the deregulation of financial and labour markets. As far as labour markets are concerned, in the neoliberal perspective they need to be highly flexible to allow transnational and national companies maximum manoeuvrability in a trading and manufacturing environment in which product demand is subject to rapid change. However, it would be a mistake to think of this process as one in which regulation is entirely removed: the complete absence of regulations would give rise to anarchy.[2] On the contrary, and in contrast to neoliberal claims, the deregulation or liberalization of markets has actually involved new regulations or re-regulation conducive to a particular international financial institution (IFI)-led strategy for global economic integration. These new forms of regulation tend to enhance the power of private corporations, and downgrade the relative importance attached to the interests of society at large.

Recent globalization has involved liberalization of international trade in goods and services on the one hand, and the flows of international capital (direct foreign investment, portfolio equity investment, bank lending) on the other; and it has involved new, often standardized, regulation, ostensibly to bring about level playing fields. One area of re-regulation designed in such a way as to confer advantage on corporate interests is the new regime of intellectual property rights. WTO agreements reinforce corporate rights in such areas as pharmaceuticals, thereby guaranteeing monopoly power to multinational manufacturers, leading to high prices for life-saving drugs. This has been particularly pertinent, for example, in the context of treatments for HIV/AIDS, and has a special bearing on women in sub-Saharan Africa who suffer high rates of infection and whose lives, and offspring's lives, are especially at risk.

Monetary and fiscal restraint are also considered centre-pieces of neoliberal policies; they are deemed necessary to control inflation, and thus help to attract mobile financial capital. This is because inflation erodes the yield on financial investments, and high rates of inflation are likely to repel, rather than attract, financial investors. Budget deficits are seen as inflationary, and thus reduced public spending is seen as crucial to attracting such flows.

While there has been a move to liberalize external economic relations as indicated above, there has been no corresponding push to liberalize international labour flows. Proponents argue that poverty can be reduced via a liberalized trade regime that generates employment, coupled with specialization in labour-intensive goods.

Neoliberal proponents acknowledge that greater domestic competition and the opening up of economies to international trade and capital flows might subject developing countries to internal and external shocks, and result in a degree of financial and economic volatility. However, they argue that this is compensated for by the resulting higher growth that generates new jobs in place of those destroyed, and that minimal social safety nets are sufficient to cope with the casualties.

As far as the situation of women is concerned, the neoliberal view, as espoused by the World Bank in particular, is that the promotion of the neoliberal macroeconomic agenda is conducive to bringing about gender equality.[3] This case rests on the idea that market liberalization promotes higher levels of gross domestic product (GDP), that there is a correlation between higher incomes and improved female access to education and employment, and that this access leads to greater gender equality; therefore market liberalization itself promotes gender equality. This thesis is open to question, and much of this and the next chapter indicates the inadequacy of evidence to support it.

"Managed-market" approaches

While neoliberals emphasize the role of liberalization in promoting growth and thus improved well-being, a number of countries have achieved economic growth and development without following neoliberal prescriptions. These "managed market" exceptions include several Asian economies, notably Republic of Korea, Taiwan Province of China, China, and to a lesser extent India and Malaysia. Their macroeconomic approaches can be described as "heterodox": that is, governments exhibit a willingness to intervene strategically and regulate markets in order to promote development and growth. Although there is no "one size fits all" policy, these countries have to varying degrees selectively intervened to regulate exchange rates, financial flows, trade and foreign direct investment in order to promote technology acquisition and learning on the part of domestic industries.[4]

Although these countries industrialized and attained high economic performance before the era of globalization, their achievements are being claimed to be supportive of the neoliberal agenda.[5] These reinterpretations after the event of successful development models ignore the central role played by state intervention and market management. The countries in question used state intervention to help domestic industries "catch up" with those in industrialized countries, generating a strong internal growth dynamic. To this end, strategic controls on foreign direct investment (FDI) have been used as a means to increase productivity and competitiveness, and to maximize spillovers to other domestic industries, thereby helping move the country up the industrial ladder, but without ceding the government's ability to shape the industrialization process. A case in point is provided by the Republic of Korea during the late 1970s, where multinational enterprises were permitted to invest in the electronics industry, but barred from other sectors.[6] When domestic technological capability had been sufficiently expanded in that industry, FDI was again restricted. Similarly in China currently, FDI is limited to targeted industries where the government desires to attain capability.

In many of these countries, moreover, trade was only liberalized strategically. In some cases limits were imposed on imports of consumer goods, particularly luxury items. This both saved on foreign exchange, and boosted demand for domestically produced goods. While neoliberals have labelled such policies protectionist and inefficient, in fact there was often a quid pro quo: domestic firms were required to meet export and investment targets in return for subsidies and import protection.[7] As a result, protective industrial policy did not end up blocking structural change as it did in other countries. Such policies were also used to cushion the effects of structural change, with protectionism allowing firms an acceptable level of income while they retooled. They also indirectly protected workers' wages, and thus stand in sharp contrast to the experience in economies that have adopted full-fledged neoliberal policies, where structural change can be accompanied by significant economic disruption and income losses for workers.

Asian economies have also placed limits on financial liberalization, to varying degrees. For example, China continues to maintain the inconvertibility of its currency, protecting the yuan from rapid fluctuations that might negatively affect the stability of the domestic economy, while maintaining a favourable exchange rate to promote exports. Malaysia, too has intervened, most notably directly after the Asian financial crisis, at which time capital controls were temporarily reinstituted as a way to protect the value of the domestic currency and reduce the necessity of raising interest rates. Those controls are widely believed to have helped Malaysia weather, and then recover from, the financial crisis more rapidly than countries that did not introduce such controls.[8]

Thus these countries have been willing to avail themselves of a broader set of policy tools as a way to promote domestic growth, to achieve competitiveness in a global economy, and to smooth economic fluctuations. They can be characterized as pursuing strategic economic openness—that is, managed economic openness, tailored to achieving the domestic goals of promoting industrialization and stable economic growth, while at the same time pursuing the means to acquire advanced technologies. As a result, many of these countries have managed to nurture more capital and skill-intensive goods production, and thus achieve higher per capita incomes. As for the earlier industrializers in this group—Republic of Korea, Taiwan Province of China and Singapore—such policies have allowed them to escape the negative effects of increased competition among low-wage export producers for a limited market share. Instead these countries have moved up the industrial ladder to compete in markets for more sophisticated goods.

Each of these countries represents a different and flexible approach to achieving growth and development, but they share a common feature with those countries that have adopted neoliberal policies: they are increasingly integrated economically with the rest of the world. This integration is indeed a key mechanism by which to raise domestic productivity. The outward orientation in many of these countries, especially Taiwan Province of China and the Republic of Korea, has however been strategically determined rather than the result of across-the-board liberalization. It is nevertheless notable that many of these countries have been increasingly adopting the neoliberal model, either voluntarily or due to pressures induced by the Asian financial crisis and other political tensions. For example, the IMF pushed the Republic of Korea to adopt the model of an independent central bank after the crisis, thus limiting the extent to which targeting of loans and subsidized credit could be used as a tool to promote industrialization and growth. China is currently under a great deal of pressure from the United States to revalue its currency, while Taiwan Province of China has moved to liberalize FDI flows.

Although these governments have exhibited a willingness to intervene to promote productivity growth, resulting in robust GDP growth, they have not adopted the same enthusiasm for the pursuit of equity. However, there are cases in which equity was pursued because redistribution was viewed as necessary to promote growth. For example, in the Republic of Korea wage guidelines were a tool to raise the wages of workers who otherwise possessed little leverage to bargain for increases commensurate with their productivity growth. In some cases, this provided the necessary incentive for workers to "exercise their intelligence on the shop floor", thus accelerating the adoption of new imported technologies and raising productivity growth.[9] This suggests that growth with equity is possible, and that the conditions under which this is pursued differ by country, economic structure and historical circumstances. In both the Republic of Korea and Taiwan Province of China male workers at least experienced wage-led growth, with higher wages spurring productivity and economic growth, generating funds to finance social expenditures that promoted equity.

For a variety of reasons, however, growth alone has been insufficient to close gender gaps in income and well-being.[10] In part, this is because women are typically excluded from technologically advanced industries, and instead are confined to types of work in which they are less able to improve their terms of employment and access to social provision. This has ramifications for women's ability to bargain for a better distribution of resources and labour effort within the household. Indeed, the experience of East Asia underscores the fact that, while growth can raise living standards in an absolute sense, it does not automatically lead to a reduction of inequality, and in particular gender inequality (see chapters 3 and 4).

MACROECONOMIC EFFECTS OF GLOBALIZATION

Policies that have contributed to globalization have led to several important shifts in macroeconomic variables over the last 20 years. Cross-border transactions, measured as FDI, portfolio flows, and traded goods and services as a share of GDP, have increased, in some cases dramatically.[11] Although difficult to estimate precisely, financial flows have also seen a spectacular rate of increase. Even by 1994, gross financial flows to developing countries had increased by 1200 per cent over a decade earlier.[12] FDI has also increased. Although the bulk of such flows still go to developed economies, the developing economy share has been rising. The flows are relatively concentrated, however, with just four countries—China, Brazil, Hong Kong (SAR China) and Mexico—accounting for roughly 60 per cent of all FDI flows to developing and transition countries in 2001.[13]

Perhaps more importantly, FDI as a share of developing countries' investment has been rising, as is shown in figure 2.1, which gives the sum of inward and outward FDI as a percentage of gross fixed capital formation (in other words, investment). This ratio provides an approximation of the degree of firm mobility (as opposed to financial mobility). That is, the sum of FDI flows between one country and another gives an indication of the ability of firms to relocate, should local conditions challenge the firm's profit goals. As the figure shows,

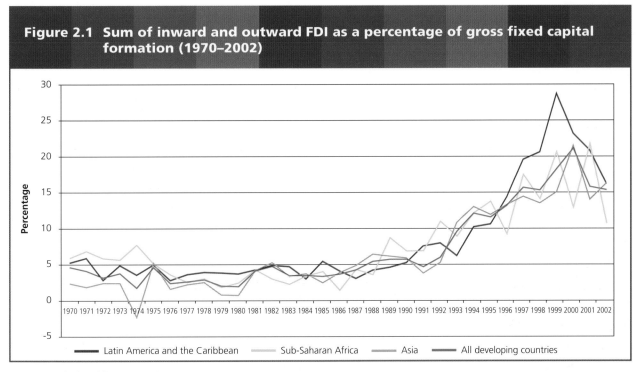

Figure 2.1 **Sum of inward and outward FDI as a percentage of gross fixed capital formation (1970–2002)**

Source: Calculated from UNCTAD 2004.

the ease with which firms can relocate has increased dramatically. In part this is due to declining communication and transportation costs, which make it more feasible to shift segments or the entire production process to another country. It is also due to the liberalization of financial capital flows. Deregulation of national rules on foreign investment has facilitated this trend. In terms of effects on workers, one way to interpret these data is as a measure of trends in corporate bargaining power relative to local governments, workers and citizens. The fluctuations in this measure are significant, since they reflect the real potential for capital to relocate, and underscore the credibility of that threat to workers and governments.

A notable effect of the pursuit of neoliberal policies, in particular monetary and fiscal restraint, has been a decline in inflation rates. In the case of a number of developing countries, the decline has been dramatic (see table 2.1). Lower inflation is expected to produce a macroeconomic stimulus because it induces more investment. It is argued that this, coupled with the

reorientation of production to tradeables as well as a reduced role for the state, should raise productivity, output and growth. These policies have been a central plank of neoliberalism. Reducing inflation (through fiscal and monetary restraint) can however have a negative impact on aggregate demand, output and growth, and this could offset the benefits of low rates of inflation.

The evidence suggests that the costs have been substantial, and have resulted in slower rates of economic growth in most regions (see table 2.2). With the exception of East and South Asia, growth rates for 1981–2000 are below those of the 1961–1980 period. The growth effects of liberalization are thus disappointing at best, particularly for the poorest countries. The slowdown in growth has serious implications for countries' ability to improve incomes and well-being.

Table 2.1 Inflation (Consumer prices, 10-year averages)

	1986–1995	1996–2005
Advanced economies	3.6	1.8
Developing countries	58.0	8.8
Africa	27.4	12.2
Developing Asia	11.2	4.0
Middle East	17.7	9.5
Latin America and the Caribbean	194.7	9.0

Note: This table uses the geographical grouping of countries that the IMF uses in *World Economic Outlook* (Latin America and the Caribbean = IMF's Western Hemisphere).

Source: IMF 2004.

Table 2.2 Trends in per capita GDP growth, average annual percentage growth (1961–2000)

	1961–1980 (%)	1981–2000 (%)	Percentage point change
Africa	1.7	0.3	-1.4
North Africa	3.3	1.7	-1.6
Sub-Saharan Africa	1.1	-0.4	-1.5
Latin America and the Caribbean	3.0	0.6	-2.4
Caribbean	3.2	2.2	-1.0
Central America	3.1	0.6	-2.5
South America	3.0	0.5	-2.5
Asia	2.7	4.4	1.7
East Asia	3.1	6.1	3.0
Southeast Asia	3.7	2.9	-0.8
South Asia	1.7	3.5	1.8
Central and West Asia	2.8	1.1	-1.7
Oceania	2.0	0.0	-2.0
Developed regions	3.2	1.4	-1.8
Eastern Europe	10.7	1.7	-9.0
Western Europe	3.4	1.9	-1.5
Other developed regions	3.4	2.3	-1.1
World	2.8	1.9	-0.9

Source: Calculated from Heston et al. 2002.
Note: GDP growth rates by region are population weighted.

Not surprisingly, slow growth has resulted in limited employment options. Formal-sector job opportunities are insufficient, as evidenced by the growth of casual work and self-employment where workers lack protection and security.[14] Moreover efforts to make labour markets more flexible have increased the tenuousness even of formal-sector jobs. Recorded unemployment rates remain high, even staggering, in a number of developing countries. They have also risen in Europe and Japan. In the United States too, average unemployment rates in the 1990s exceeded those of the 1950s and 1960s, and there has been an increase in the rate of involuntary part-time employment. In general, paid work continues to be scarce and is increasingly precarious.

Other serious macroeconomic problems have emerged as a result of the process of liberalization and economic integration. Policies to liberalize financial flows have contributed to growing financial volatility. As a result, financial crises are occurring with increasing regularity and severity, particularly in middle-income countries, which have been major recipients of cross-border capital flows. Such crises have extensive costs in terms of lost growth, and contribute to a more unequal income distribution at the country level.[15]

Revenues, taxes and public expenditures

There is evidence of a fiscal squeeze in recent years, due to a reduction of revenues resulting from trade liberalization and tariff reductions. Over the period 1970 to 1998, for example, trade taxes as a share of total taxes declined from an average of 40 per cent to 35 per cent in low-income countries.[16] As a result, the ratio of tax revenues to GDP declined by an average of 3 per cent in low and upper middle-income groups of countries in the wake of trade reform over the period 1985–9 to 1995–8. Domestic financial deregulation, the liberalization of capital markets, the phasing out of multiple exchange rates, and currency devaluations have also deprived developing country governments of other sources of revenue.[17] Moreover, the emphasis on private investment and attracting FDI has resulted in declining tax rates on capital, with countries forced to offset the revenue loss by raising taxes on labour.[18] There has thus been a redistribution of the tax burden from owners of capital to workers. However, given the small size of formal-sector employment and the scale of the informal economy in many developing countries, most have had to resort to sales and value-added taxes, which are generally regressive.

The pressures on government revenues, due to lost sources of revenue, has contributed to a reduction in government expenditures as a share of GDP in a number of countries. While in some cases cuts in spending have been concentrated in capital expenditures—that is, infrastructure—social expenditures (on health, education, welfare and social safety nets) have also suffered in some regions, such as in Latin America and Africa.[19]

Human development, poverty and income distribution

Although trends in the basic macroeconomic magnitudes are not much disputed, the question of whether liberalization policies have led to an improvement in well-being is more contentious. The debate is fuelled in part by differing conceptualizations of well-being. Neoliberals have tended to define well-being and poverty in income terms, relying on monetary measures of poverty as a yardstick to evaluate liberalization policies. Recent years have seen more willingness to consider trends in inequality, and a major debate is under way among economists as to the extent to which the goal of equity should be pursued. Some have argued that equality (particularly in education) is a prerequisite to growth. Others argue that it leads to greater political stability and less dysfunctional macroeconomic policy. The emphasis on equality then tends to be instrumental, related to its potential effects on market outcomes.[20]

Those who stress human development, informed by a human rights focus, offer a different yardstick by which to measure progress.[21] This latter approach emphasizes that the goals of development do not only comprise per capita incomes, but should also take into account "capabilities" and "functionings" (such as life expectancy and education) as well as power relations, inequality, dignity, and opportunities and rights of self-expression.[22] All of these influence human freedoms and the ability to make meaningful life choices.[23]

Even using a money metric, the effect of globalization policies on poverty rates is much debated. The World Bank's estimates of global poverty rely on an absolute poverty threshold of one US dollar a day, adjusted for country differences in purchasing power.[24] Using this poverty threshold, the global poverty rate has fallen from 32 to 25 per cent between 1990 and 1999, decreasing the number of poor from 1.3 billion to 1.1 billion. However this threshold has been contested, and is regarded by a number of scholars as an underestimation of global poverty.

The challenges to the World Bank data are based on its method of converting local currency to international dollars, the choice of a poverty threshold, and the distortion provided in particular by China, which offsets trends of constant or increasing poverty in a number of regions: sub-Saharan Africa, Latin America and the Caribbean, and the Middle East and North Africa.[25] Further, the Bank's poverty threshold of one US dollar a day fails to capture poverty trends in developed economies, where income insufficiency induces social exclusion and thus deprivation.

A human development perspective expands the information on which to base an evaluation of trends in well-being. Evidence that emphasizes capabilities and functionings suggests a more problematic effect of macroeconomics trends over the last 20 years. For the period 1980–2000 compared with 1960–1980, for example, the rate of progress on a number of social indicators—infant mortality, literacy, life expectancy and education—has slowed.[26] Globalization appears therefore to be correlated with, if not causally linked to, a slowdown in progress in human development.

In addition to basic capabilities measures, human development approaches emphasize the importance of inequality as a measure of well-being, since this influences power relations, which can determine the distribution of output in markets, by the state, and within the household. This emphasis has led to intensive scrutiny of the relationship between growth, inequality and poverty in recent years. There is substantial evidence of persistent and even widening income and resource gaps within countries, including a number of rapidly growing economies (table 2.3). The growth of inequality has been noted in a heterogeneous set of countries, including China, the United States, a number of Latin American countries, including those in the Southern Cone, and several Eastern European countries.[27] This evidence may provide a partial explanation for the slowdown in progress in closing other human development variables. Much recent empirical evidence on trends in inequality suggests that income gaps between countries are also widening, although some controversy remains on data definitions and measurement.[28]

Table 2.3	Trends in income inequality in 73 countries, from the 1950s to the 1990s					
	Countries				Share of	
	Developed	Developing	Transitional	Total	World population	World GDP-PPP
Rising inequality	12: Australia, Denmark, Finland, Italy, Japan, Netherlands, New Zealand, Portugal, Spain, Sweden, United Kingdom, United States.	16: Argentina, Chile, China, Colombia, Costa Rica, Guatemala, Hong Kong (SAR China), Mexico, Pakistan, Panama, Puerto Rico, South Africa, Sri Lanka, Taiwan Prov. of China, Thailand, Venezuela.	20: Armenia, Azerbaijan, Bulgaria, Croatia, Czech Rep., Estonia, Georgia, Hungary, Kazakhstan, Kyrgyzstan, Latvia, Lithuania, Macedonia TFYR, Rep. of Moldova, Poland, Romania, Russian Fed., Serbia and Montenegro, Slovakia, Ukraine.	48	47	71
Constant inequality	4: Austria, Belgium, Canada, France.	10: Bangladesh, Brazil, Côte d'Ivoire, Dominican Rep., El Salvador, India, Indonesia, Senegal, Singapore, U. Rep. of Tanzania.	2: Belarus, Slovenia.	16	29	12
Declining inequality	2: Germany, Norway.	7: Bahamas, Honduras, Jamaica, Rep. of Korea, Malaysia, Philippines, Tunisia.	0	9	4	8

Note: The 73 countries included in the sample account for 80% of world's population and 91% of world's GDP–PPP.
Source: Adapted from Cornia et al. 2004, tables 2.7 and 2.8.

In sum, the evidence presented highlights the slowdown in rates of growth and increased firm mobility, accompanied by an exacerbation of financial and economic volatility. Further, consideration of human development, poverty and inequality indicators raises serious questions regarding whether neoliberal and globalization policies more generally are able to generate social development, in terms of either steady increases in GDP, or improved standards of health, education and human security.

Negative human development outcomes of the neoliberal agenda have been linked to the reduced ability of the state to provide a social safety net and promote human development goals, the destabilizing and disempowering effect of mobile capital, and the negative employment effects of slow growth. These trends imply that neoliberalism may not be necessary, or even good, for economic growth, and that a more heterodox set of policies, individually tailored to country-specific conditions, are a viable alternative, at least for promoting growth. Some countries that have had more rapid growth rates based on heterodox policies have not, however, done significantly better in promoting an important aspect of human development: that is, gender equality. Growth, adequate government revenues, and limits on capital mobility may provide a better foundation for the pursuit of well-being and equity but they are not sufficient, any more than neoliberal policies suffice.

Notes

1   Loxley 1997; Elson 2002.

2   Jomo 2003.

3   World Bank 2001a; Dollar and Gatti 1999.

4   Amsden 1989; Wade 1990.

5   World Bank 1993a.

6   Amsden 1989.

7   Jomo 2003.

8   Stiglitz 2002.

9   Amsden 1989.

10   Hsiung 1996; Seguino 1997.

11   Data on these trends can be found in UNCTAD's Trade and Development Report for various years and World Investment Report for various years (see UNCTAD 2004). For detailed data on FDI trends, see Braunstein 2004.

12   Eichengreen and Mussa 1998.

13   Braunstein 2004; South Centre 1997; UNCTAD 2004.

14   Heinz and Pollin 2003; ILO 2002b.

15   Kirkpatrick 2002; Blecker 1998; Bhagwati 2002/3; Singh 2002.

16   Khattry and Rao 2002.

17   Grunberg 1998.

18   ILO 2004a.

19   Khattry 2003.

20   Solimano 1998; Persson and Tabellini 1994.

21   See UNDP 2003; Elson 2002; Cagatay and Ertürk 2003.

22   The terms "capabilities" and "functionings" were first coined by Amartya Sen (1985) and are now widely used.

23   Sen 1999.

24   World Bank 2002; Chen and Ravallion 2001.

25   See for example Reddy and Pogge 2003; Vandemoortele 2002.

26   Weisbrot et al. 2001.

27   Cornia et al. 2003; Khan and Riskin 1998.

28   See Milanovic 2003; Wade 2001.

Chapter 3
Liberalization, labour markets and women's gains:
A mixed picture

Women's ability to achieve parity in well-being with men depends on the type of macroeconomic policies and development strategies undertaken. This is because women's and men's capabilities, and their access to resources such as time, land and credit, differ. Those differing starting points influence women's ability to generate income and obtain social insurance. Macroeconomic policies are mediated through a system of gendered job segregation: an important factor, even where there is an otherwise level playing field between women and men in terms of qualifications, skills and control over assets. While there is some variation in country-specific conditions, job segregation between paid and unpaid labour, and within paid labour markets—by occupation as well as industry—continues to be globally pervasive, a tendency that has shown little sign of abating.[1]

There are differences in women's and men's capabilities and possibilities for generating a livelihood, resulting from differential treatment in important markets such as labour, land and credit. The ability of macroeconomic policies to promote gender equality thus depends first on the degree to which economic growth is enhanced, and second, on the gender distributional effects of growth: via public expenditure, through intrafamily/household resource distribution, and through various markets.

This chapter considers the pathways by which liberalization policies produce gendered outcomes, emphasizing measurable labour market changes. This focus is in part due to the emphasis that globalization proponents place on the beneficial effects of liberalization on women's employment and income. The evidence presented questions the validity of this claim.

Of course, women's livelihoods, especially in developing countries, are affected more broadly than merely through employment. Liberalization policies affect agriculturally based economies via the impact on the types of goods a country produces, the extension and reach of markets (through commercialization), and the degree of integration with the international economy. As a consequence, women's ability to provide for their families in the agricultural sector, either through subsistence production or through production of cash crops for domestic markets and commodities for export, is deeply affected by liberalization policies. Further, such policies have an impact on the degree of informalization of work. These issues are elaborated in greater detail in section 2 of this report.

LIBERALIZED TRADE AND INVESTMENT FLOWS

Employment effects

Trade and investment flows have increased in recent years, as noted in the previous chapter, whether this is a result of neoliberal policies or of state-guided efforts to promote an outward orientation in the economy. Changes in these policies can have important employment effects, which are gendered due to labour market segmentation.

Proponents argue that liberalization of trade in particular is a gender-equalizing strategy. More flexible exchange rate policies and lowering trade barriers (that is, reducing quotas and tariffs) permit countries to expand exports of goods they can produce most cheaply, stimulating export demand. Countries are also able to import cheaper intermediate and capital goods, potentially reducing the costs of production and raising productivity. For developing countries, trade liberalization is expected to stimulate foreign demand for labour-intensive manufactured goods and high-value agricultural export crops (HVAE). With firms pressured to hire least-cost labour as a result of international competition, women's relatively lower wages make them an attractive source of labour, and this should give rise to increased female employment.

The liberalization of foreign direct investment (FDI), it is argued, should also improve women's access to paid work. FDI acts as foreign savings that stimulate investment above what would be possible if countries had only domestic sources of saving and investment to rely on. FDI should therefore act as an employment generator. Women in developing countries are likely to benefit differentially, since FDI to those countries is often directed to labour-intensive industries that seek out low-cost production sites. FDI-induced employment growth may also result in women's indirect employment by multinational enterprises (MNEs). They may, for example, work for local firms that are subcontractors for larger offshore corporations, with local employment dependent upon contracts from MNEs.

Some evidence exists to suggest that over the last three decades, women's employment and share of paid employment have risen as a result of liberalized FDI and trade. It is increasingly difficult however to distinguish the gender effects of trade liberalization from those of investment liberalization, since the two partly coincide, sometimes because MNEs that employ women are largely concentrated in the production of low-cost exports. Quite similar gendered employment trends are observed across diverse regions and countries, and by level of per capita income. This has led to the notion that employment

Box 3.1 High tech and high heels in the global economy: Women, work and pink-collar identities

In the early 1990s, Barbados saw a sharp increase in female employment in the informatics industry. Women employed in these jobs perform work until recently unheard of on this small island in the eastern Caribbean, representing vast changes in labour patterns and technology use in the global arena. As offshore data processors, they are linked with service workers in such disparate places as Ireland, the Dominican Republic, Jamaica, Mauritius, and the United States, as the informatics age signals intensification of transnational production and consumption of labour, capital, goods, services and styles.

This (pink-collar) work is gendered not only because it recruits women workers almost exclusively, but also because the work process itself is imbued with notions of appropriate femininity, which include a quiet responsible demeanour along with meticulous attention to detail and a quick and accurate keyboard technique.

Globally, the new pink-collar informatics worker represents both a reconfiguration and a cheapening of white-collar service work. What was once considered skilled information-based computer work can now be performed offshore without compromising the product or the speed with which it is produced.

The pay received for such work is sometimes less than could be earned in the cane fields, but the clean office atmosphere is attractive to women. Despite the image of prosperity and professionalism portrayed by pink-collar workers, a street scene between Christine, an informatics worker, and her former boyfriend Paul tells a different story. As the worker emerged from the building with her friends, Paul began shouting and motioning wildly for everyone around to look closely. 'You see she? You see she?' he exclaimed. 'Don' mind she dress so. When Friday come, she only carryin' home 98 dollar.' What this outburst conveyed was, 'In case you people might mistake her for a middle-class woman with a good office job, let me tell you, she is really just a village girl with a factory wage.' By exposing the reality of Christine's meagre wage in contrast to her impressive appearance, the disgruntled former boyfriend threatened to undermine a powerful image conscientiously created and enforced by women workers and the informatics industry that employs them.

Source: Freeman 2000.

has become "feminized" or female-intensive in the developing world, induced by a shift to an outward orientation. The trend extends to the service sector, and encompasses a diverse set of jobs, including tourism, informatics and data processing, all of which generate foreign exchange. Service-sector employment—at least, in the sense of office jobs—is sometimes viewed as more desirable than manufacturing jobs since these jobs are seen to have higher status. They may not, however, provide significantly more in terms of pay and security (see box 3.1).

Female employment in the agricultural sector, where trade liberalization has created seasonal employment in the area of agricultural exports, has also risen.[2] In the case of Chilean and South African export grape industries, for example, women are the preferred source of temporary labour and hold a small share of permanent jobs. This phenomenon is visible in a number of sub-Saharan countries. Such work opportunities can be viewed as a means for women to diversify their income sources, but livelihoods earned under these conditions are inherently precarious, a topic that is covered in greater deal in chapter 6.

The quality of employment

The benefits of employment resulting from trade and FDI liberalization depend on a variety of factors, including wages (discussed in the next section), the conditions of work, and the security of work. Using these criteria, the benefits of trade and FDI for gender employment equality are questionable. In part, this is because those jobs that women can find lack stability to a greater extent than jobs in male-dominated sectors. Data suggest, for example, that women's employment gains are not always permanent. Declines in the female share of paid employment are evident in the manufacturing sector of a diverse set of countries. In some cases, it appears that as developing countries "mature" industrially, shedding labour-intensive manufacturing jobs, women lose employment in declining industries but face difficulty in obtaining slots in the more capital-intensive manufacturing industries. This is particularly evident in the first-tier East Asian economies, such as Taiwan Province of China,

Singapore, Hong Kong (SAR China), and Republic of Korea (table 3.1).[3] In those cases, as wages rose and lower-wage sites emerged, firms relocated labour-intensive operations to Southeast Asian countries as well as Central America. In some of these countries, declines in the female share of manufacturing employment are in part due to competition from even lower-wage sites (such as China), underscoring the precariousness of employment in labour-intensive export-oriented industries.

Table 3.1	Female share of paid employment in manufacturing, selected Asian economies (1991-2000)		
	1991 (%)	2000 (%)	Percentage point change
China	42 [(1)]	46	+4
Hong Kong (SAR China) [(3)]	47	43	–4
Korea, Rep. of	41 [(2)]	36	–5
Singapore	45	41 [(3)]	–4
Taiwan, Prov. of China	45	42	–3
Thailand [(4)]	50	49	–1

Notes: (1) Data for 1990; (2) Data for 1992; (3) Data for 1999; (4) Data refer to total employment in manufacturing.
Source: Data are from ILO 2004b except for Taiwan Prov. of China, which are from Directorate General of Budget and Statistics 2003, and China, which are from National Bureau of Statistics 2004.

In a number of African countries, female employment in manufacturing has declined as a result of import competition from cheap manufactured goods from other developing countries—the other side of trade liberalization. The decline of textile manufacturing in Zimbabwe and Tanzania, for example, resulted in employment losses in female-dominated industries, due to the flood of cheaper imports from Asia after tariffs were reduced. Similar trends were evident in Côte d'Ivoire, Nigeria, Kenya, Ghana and South Africa.[4] In many developed countries, too, increased trade has led to a disproportionate loss of female employment in many industries with large concentrations of women (textiles, wearing apparel, footwear and leather goods).[5]

GENDER EQUALITY: STRIVING FOR JUSTICE IN AN UNEQUAL WORLD

The precariousness of female jobs resulting from FDI in labour-intensive industries, and also through subcontracting, is linked to firm mobility. Firms in these sectors have an easier time shifting production to other locations to meet their profit targets than do firms in more capital-intensive industries. Men, on the other hand, are more intensively hired in MNEs which tend to generate more stable employment, due to the sunk costs of training in capital and skill-intensive industries. Layoffs thus tend to be less likely.

The attractiveness of women as workers in labour-intensive export industries, whether they be domestically or foreign-owned, is related to the ease of shedding these workers, based in part on gender norms that relegate women's paid work to secondary importance after their domestic and care responsibilities. This neatly fits with the desire of employers to reduce labour costs by also shifting the burden of uncertainty over product demand to workers, whose conditions of employment are increasingly flexible and intermittent. The flexibility of employment is more accentuated the more labour-intensive the industry. This is feasible because less investment in worker training is needed in such industries. Competitive pressures amongst firms to lower costs in the context of an increasing number of suppliers vying for access to developed country markets (such as those from China, and Mexico since the North Atlantic Free Trade Agreement (NAFTA)) also mean that firms have little incentive to train workers to upgrade their skills. Workers are thus seen primarily as a cost, rather than an asset. Their job trajectory in such firms is often short and precarious, with little chance for movement up the job ladder or acquisition of such skills as would enable them to move to more secure employment in other sectors. These are in other words dead-end jobs.

There is thus a coincidence between gender roles, job segregation by industry, and firm needs in a competitive international environment. The segregation of men and women into different types of jobs, due to gender norms that reserve higher-paying more stable work for men, suggests that FDI and trade liberalization may reinforce the tendency toward job segregation. Indeed, as noted, there is little evidence of a decline in job segregation by gender with liberalization.

The work conditions in the jobs women can obtain also place in question whether such employment is gender-enabling. In cases where women have gained formal-sector export jobs, such as in East Asia, for example, the conditions of work are often harsh, hazardous, and in some cases women work longer hours than men employed in non-tradable industries. Whether they are directly employed by MNEs or employed by local firms hired as subcontractors to larger firms in global commodity chains, female workers in the export sector have little bargaining power for better work conditions, partly because of the mobility of firms. Thus demands for better work conditions, shorter hours or more secure employment can lead firms to relocate or outsource to cheaper production sites, causing job losses. Because women are concentrated in such jobs, they face greater challenges than men in improving their conditions of work.

Even where beneficial employment effects are noted, such as the increase in female garment-sector employment in Bangladesh, competition between low-wage countries makes workers vulnerable if lower-cost producers emerge. In Bangladesh, for example, job opportunities are expected to diminish in the near future due to the planned phase-out of the Multi-Fibre Agreement (MFA) in 2005. That agreement had defined quotas for textile imports to developed economies. A number of countries with guaranteed access to developed country markets can expect to be squeezed out by lower-cost producers with well-developed textile industries, for example China.[6] In other words, a redistribution of global garment employment among developing countries is anticipated, with countries with the lowest unit labour costs being well positioned to gain. This highlights the problem of a growth strategy predicated on exports to developed-country markets. Export-oriented growth based on labour-intensive goods is difficult to sustain in the context of competition from many other low-cost producers. This is exacerbated by overproduction in the face of insufficient demand for goods from developed countries, due to slow growth. Given women's concentration in the production of such goods, the limits to employment and wage growth are evident, as are the constraints on achieving gender equity via this growth strategy.

In sum, there are clearly beneficial effects of globalization via women's increased access to employment. In some cases, pay and conditions are better in formal export sector jobs than in domestic enterprises and the informal economy.[7] This gain is not to be underestimated. Women who have taken up such employment, particularly in the more patriarchal societies, tell poignant stories of their increased ability to provide for their families and children. These are frequently short-term gains, however, as a result of the precariousness of such work. Further, it should be born in mind when evaluating the gender effects of globalization that women so employed are only one segment of the global commodity chain. These outcomes must be compared with those of the larger segment of "invisible" workers in home-based production, many of whom work under terms and conditions far inferior to those in formal-sector jobs. Indeed, there is evidence of an accelerated move to informalize many formerly formal-sector jobs since the Asian financial crisis.[8]

There are other concerns that should be borne in mind. Although such employment can raise women's absolute status, and can provide some escape from oppressive patriarchal relations, the potential to erode unequal gender relations is limited. Overcoming patriarchal structures of power, including social norms that result in gender inequality, requires sustained improvements in female livelihoods and the stability of those livelihoods. Such income-generating opportunities as have been created through globalization do not meet that criterion, since the jobs many women can get are insecure and often dead-end. That is, they do not provide a ladder to higher-paying and more prestigious types of employment. To attain equity requires an approach that generates access to livelihoods that are stable, and that provide a clear mechanism for increasing female incomes. The strategy of globalization in and of itself would not seem to yield the requisite conditions.

Gender wage gap effects

According to advocates, trade and investment liberalization should lead to improved wage prospects for women, and a narrowing of the gender wage gap as women's wages are bid up more rapidly than men's. This will occur if women's job opportunities expand relatively more rapidly than men's, and if women are in a position to translate increasingly tight female labour markets into higher wages. This should produce spillover effects onto wages in other sectors, since higher manufacturing wages set a floor beneath which female wages would not fall. Thus, theoretically women employed in all sectors of the economy should benefit, including those in less formal types of employment. FDI is also often thought to raise wages, both by stimulating employment growth and because it is often argued that foreign firms pay higher wages than local firms, thus pushing average wages higher. Some thus claim that female wages will benefit from liberalized FDI. Of course, women's relative wages can also rise as they attain higher levels of education, or due to changes in wage-setting institutions that affect wage bargaining.

But as noted above, there are a number of counteracting factors that reduce women's ability to bargain for higher wages. First, the process of "crowding" women into some sectors of the labour market, particularly the labour-intensive export-oriented parts, artificially induces an "oversupply" of female labour for these jobs. Second, in these industries there is intense pressure to keep costs low, and firms can relocate relatively easily. The result is that employment conditions make it structurally difficult to raise women's wages and to close gender wage gaps.

Nevertheless, simple wage ratios (average female wages as a percentage of average male wages) indicate that wage gaps have narrowed in a number of developing countries. The most extensive internationally comparable data are for the manufacturing sector and, as the data in table 3.2 show, the ratio of female to male wages has risen in a number of developing countries. This data is likely to overstate this ratio, since labour surveys that generate these data are often limited to firms of five or more workers. Thus women who work in small enterprises that subcontract are excluded from surveys, and their wages tend to be much lower than those of women working in larger firms. Nevertheless on the basis of this information, declines are evident in some Latin American countries as well as in Hong Kong (SAR China).[9] A central question is to what degree these trends are attributable to trade and investment liberalization, rather than to other factors that influence wages, such as increased female educational attainment relative to men.

Table 3.2	Female to male manufacturing wage ratios (in percentages), selected countries (1990–1999)		
	1990	**1995**	**1999**
Africa			
Egypt	67.9	73.6	75.2
Kenya	73.3	92.8	-
Swaziland	87.7	86.6	62.8[1]
Latin America			
Brazil	53.6	56.9	61.7
Costa Rica	74.3	70.9	73.1
El Salvador	94.1	96.6	62.0
Mexico	-	68.7	69.7
Panama	-	-	93.2
Paraguay	66.5	79.5	54.6
Asia			
Cyprus	57.6	60.1	54.2
Hong Kong (SAR China)[2]	69.5	60.9	57.3
Korea, Rep. of	50.3	54.1	55.6
Malaysia	50.1	57.9	62.9[1]
Philippines	-	74.3	79.9
Thailand	-	61.6	64.8

Notes: The female to male wage ratios are calculated as the ratio of the average female manufacturing wage (across all subindustries, such as textiles, electronics and shipbuilding, and all occupations), relative to the average male wage, similarly measured. The ratio can vary because women are paid less than men in the same occupation and industry, but also because women's employment is concentrated in substantially different occupations and industries than men, with consequent effects on wages. Thus, job segregation, education or other productivity-related factors, or simple discrimination can influence wage ratios. None of this is reflected in the raw gender wage ratio.
(1) 1997.
(2) Non-agricultural wages.
Source: Calculated from ILO 2004b.

Explaining gender wage gaps

In order to isolate the effects of trade and FDI liberalization, numerous studies have carefully controlled for alternative factors that might affect female and male wages. Several have found that increasing international trade (measured as export orientation) tends to widen gender wage gaps.[10] It is particularly interesting that these negative effects are evident in several rapidly growing East Asian economies. This implies that although increased female education relative to men's could potentially lead to a narrowing gender wage gap, the downward pressure on female wages—resulting from women's lower

bargaining power under trade and investment liberalization—works in the opposite direction, thus expanding the gender wage gap. The downward pressure of liberalization on female relative wages is often construed as discriminatory: women fail to be paid a wage commensurate to their productivity.

Examples from Asia are illustrative. One study of Taiwan Province of China and the Republic of Korea found an inverse relationship between trade shares (the ratio of imports and exports to GDP) and the ratio of female to male wages, adjusted to take account of gendered skill differences.[11] In China, the data indicate that inequality between men's and women's wages increased.[12] The proportion of the gap between male and female wages that is unexplained by skill differences is larger in the most deregulated sectors of the economy, and smallest in the least deregulated (the public sector).[13] Thus the private sector shows evidence of greater wage discrimination against women than the public sector. In Viet Nam, there has been only a slight change in the economy-wide gender wage gap. An increased return to skills has helped women, but there is a larger negative effect of discrimination that holds down women's wages.[14]

As the data in table 3.2 show, wage gaps appear to have increased in some Latin American countries as well as in Hong Kong (SAR China). In a number of cases both male and female wages declined, but the decrease in women's wages was greater, partly because of their concentration in the hard-hit apparel sector.[15] In Uruguay, an otherwise gender-equitable economy with a fair macroeconomic performance in the 1980s and 1990s, gender gaps have narrowed, although this is primarily due to declining wages for men rather than rising wages for women. Statistical analysis shows the portion of the wage gap that is due to discrimination has risen in Uruguay, and that gender gaps are wider in the private than the public sector. In Chile also, while the economy-wide gender wage ratio has improved, the portion of the wage gap attributable to discrimination has increased.[16] By way of contrast, in Brazil there is evidence of a decline in the discriminatory component of the gender wage gap in the 1990s, although in part this was the result of a decline in male wages resulting from stringent austerity policies.[17] Brazil is also much less export-dependent than many of the Asian economies, and thus the pressures to hold down female wages may be attenuated.

With regard to FDI, there is little evidence that investment liberalization can contribute to narrowing of gender wage gaps. One study showed that the positive effect of FDI on the wages of both men and women ended in the late 1980s when capital became more mobile.[18] A number of more recent studies show a negative effect of capital mobility on wages due to the "threat effect" of firm mobility, and among those, several indicate that FDI has widened the gender wage gap.[19] In Taiwan Province of China, which witnessed rapid growth of female employment in the 1970s and 1980s, FDI rules were later liberalized. The resulting shift abroad of labour-intensive industries caused a fall in relative female wages. This stands in contrast to the Republic of Korea's experience. There, FDI rules remained rigid for a longer period of time, with consequent immobility of firms and a continued narrowing of the gender wage gaps.

Another example of the negative effects of FDI on gender wage gaps is Mexico where, in the period 2001–2, there was a massive relocation of "maquila" firms mainly to China, with the loss of 160,000 jobs in labour-intensive industries. Wage differentials between China and Mexico were one of the major considerations in this shift, and these pressures may explain the widening gender wage gap that has emerged in Mexico.[20]

Firm mobility also makes it easier for firms to appropriate the gains of productivity growth, thus making the distribution of income between capital and labour more unequal. In the case of Bangladesh's female-dominated garment industry, profit margins increased from 13 per cent to 24 per cent in the early 1990s as productivity rose, with the wage share of value-added falling, which signifies women's lack of bargaining power vis-à-vis employers.[21]

As is evident from this discussion, trade and investment liberalization are two differing but complementary aspects of the current period of globalization, although most studies analyse their effects separately. What is clear, however, is that the employment and wage effects of globalization imply a tendency for greater inclusion of women in the paid economy but under exploitative conditions, related to the intense competition amongst countries for labour-intensive export market share. Not surprisingly, there is evidence that the growth of exports of labour-intensive goods and economic growth has been most rapid in those countries that have the widest gender wage gaps.[22] It is particularly significant that even in some of the most rapidly growing Asian economies, the discriminatory portions of wage gaps have not been reduced during this era of globalization. Indeed, part of the success of the East Asian "tigers" can be attributed to such gaps.[23]

The benefits of women's increased access to paid work are thus attenuated by the insecurity of such jobs and the limited power women possess in the jobs into which they are segregated to demand higher wages and better working conditions. While some women may experience improved bargaining power at home, as a result of their improved status as wage earners, for others, the insecurity and low wages do not translate into improved ability to renegotiate the distribution of labour and resources in the household.[24]

SLOW GROWTH AND ECONOMIC VOLATILITY EFFECTS

While rapidly growing economies have witnessed an increase in female employment and thus women's inclusion in the paid economy, there are also gendered implications in slow-growing economies, with women often at the back of the job queue. Slow growth has been linked to deflationary macroeconomic policies. These include monetary policy designed to rein in aggregate spending as a means to control inflation; cuts in public-sector spending to reduce budget deficits (which are perceived as inflationary); and increases in interest rates. In all cases, a major goal is to establish credibility with financial markets in order to attract financial capital, which is interested in receiving high rates of return on investment.

There is the danger, however, that the goal of attracting financial capital can come into conflict with development objectives, due to the negative effect such policies have on aggregate demand and GDP growth. There is some evidence that the deflationary bias of these policies outweighs the possible benefits of lower inflation, financial liberalization, and low public-sector deficits. Further, financial liberalization tends to contribute to the volatility of capital inflows and outflows, which may amplify the ups and downs of the business cycle. The financial crises that have occurred over the past decade in Mexico, Asia, Russia, Brazil, Turkey and Argentina, with contagion effects on countries not initially implicated in the crises, have been linked to such volatility.

Gendered effects of deflationary macroeconomic policies

The deflationary bias in macroeconomic policy has direct implications for progress towards gender equality. The evidence from diverse regions is that slow growth and recessions have more serious negative effects on women than men.

In the Caribbean region, for example, which began liberalizing in the late 1970s, growth rates have been inadequate to provide sufficient employment. As a result, despite women's high levels of education and the attractiveness of lower-cost female labour in export-intensive small open economies, women continue to face greater exclusion from employment than men.[25] In most countries of the region, female unemployment rates exceed those of men, and in some cases they are almost double.

In Latin America, unemployment rose steadily in the 1990s, even though GDP growth rates improved.[26] With regard to Uruguay, there is clear evidence of gender effects. The onset of inflation and crisis after the adoption of liberalization policies led to the emergence of unemployment as a significant problem, and the negative effect on women was greater than on men. Women's unemployment rate almost doubled between the early 1970s and the 1980s, while men's increased by half that amount. The gender effects of slow growth are masked when those who cannot find work take up self-employment or wage work in the informal economy, a phenomenon that affects women in particular, given that they constitute a higher share of informal-sector work despite their much lower share of the labour force. This trend is evident in Latin America (as elsewhere); the decline in formal-sector employment has been paralleled by the spread of informal employment.[27]

In the transition economies, which formerly had high rates of female labour force participation, recent slow or negative rates of growth have resulted in particularly adverse implications for women. In Central Europe, for example, female labour-force participation rates have fallen absolutely, and in some countries, more than men's. For example, in Hungary from 1990 to 2001, men's participation rates declined 16 percentage points, compared with women's decline of 23.5 percentage points. Unemployment rates for women exceed those of men by several percentage points in the Czech Republic and Poland, although not in Hungary. In the latter case, the female unemployment rate may be artificially low since women have withdrawn from the labour force by a greater margin than men (see chapter 5).[28] Even in developed economies, and in particular in Western Europe, slow growth has resulted in increased unemployment that has affected women more than men.

Financial crisis, economic instability and gender

Mounting evidence indicates that women bear the brunt of financial and economic crises, both in the short and the longer term, as research-based evidence from the 1997 Asian crisis attests.[29]

While the gendered employment effects of crises depend in the first instance on the particular sectors affected and the degree to which they constitute "women's" or "men's" work, women workers in general are particularly vulnerable to dismissal in times of economic downturn. They are often the first to lose their jobs, due to their less secure employment conditions and also due to discrimination based on the "male bread-winner bias".[30] During the Asian financial crisis, for example, women in the Republic of Korea were laid off at a rate twice that of men. The decline in total female employment was almost three percentage points greater than that of men (–6.9 per cent compared with –4.1 per cent). Among the category "regular workers", the negative effects on women were even more evident. The numbers of female regular workers fell by 18.8 per cent, while the number of male regular workers fell by 6.6 per cent.[31] Similarly in Thailand, women suffered greater job losses due to the economic downturn induced by the financial crisis.[32]

The societal calamity that these financial crises produced was seen as highly gendered, for public expressions focused mainly on the woes of male workers, while women, who suffered a disproportionate share of job losses, were perceived mainly in their role as "carers". This speaks to the tenuousness of the movement toward gender equity via liberalization. If employment gains are not secure and long-term, highly gendered job perceptions reassert themselves and turn back the clock on gender equality.

Further, the very considerable reversals in poverty reduction achieved in preceding years in some Asian countries were undermined, affecting women in particular. Reductions in women's incomes were more sharply felt, owing to falling real wages or lower earnings when shifting to informal-sector work in efforts to maintain a livelihood, in the absence of public welfare benefits and widespread unemployment benefit schemes.

Other impacts of such crises include the withdrawal of children, often young females, from education to assist with household tasks while the mother seeks income to make up for the household's decline in earnings. Frequently this withdrawal is permanent, especially when educational charges are introduced to deal with budget deficits resulting from economic crisis. Gender gaps in educational enrolments are therefore reinforced, preventing the accumulation of female human capital and thus prejudicing women's future earnings potential and keeping their economic productivity lower than it otherwise might be.[33]

It is at times of economic crisis that women's unpaid labour and the "care" economy become both more obvious and more crucial, particularly in developing countries where the family functions as the surrogate social safety net or refuge of last resort.[34] Under the prevailing gendered division of household labour, women have the main responsibility for the provision of family food security, health care, basic services such as water and energy and also "affective" care. While even during normal times in developing countries, the burden on women of stretching their energies between paid and the unpaid work is substantial, in times of economic crisis it becomes severe.[35] The cost is not only in terms of women's health and well-being but also in terms of micro and macroeconomic efficiency.[36]

FISCAL RETRENCHMENT

The ability of low-income developing-country governments to fund public expenditure depends on domestic macroeconomic policy, and also on the cost of borrowing and the proportion of Official Development Assistance (ODA) given for budget support. Government ability to spend has come under increasing pressure from the international financial institutions as well as liberalized financial markets, which encourage tight fiscal policies involving the reduction of budget deficits to keep inflation low. Hence governments have to tailor expenditures to their ability to raise revenue, principally from domestic sources.

Government tax revenues have been subject to contradictory pressures. In the context of trade liberalization, countries are encouraged to reduce trade taxes (tariffs and export duties), which in developing countries constitute on average one-third of government tax revenues.[37] A second revenue-weakening effect of liberalization is tax competition. Global competitive pressures make governments wary of raising income and capital taxes for fear that foreign, or even national, capital will flee elsewhere. The tax base is also constrained by the increasing informalization of the economy. Hence, over and above the reduction of state revenues derived from international trade, tax reforms have included a reduction of income and capital taxes. Efforts to expand the tax base (to collect taxes from those previously not taxed or in compliance with tax laws) have also been made, although these have not been particularly successful partly due to the weak capacity of tax authorities.[38] As a result many governments have increased sales and value-added taxes, regressive taxes which tend to hit the poor hardest.

The combined effect has often been a reduction in government resources for infrastructure spending, and for expenditures on social programmes and safety nets. There is also pressure to privatize government-owned enterprises, including those that provide public goods, such as water, electricity and telecommunications, with a concomitant reduction in public-sector employment. The gender effects of such policies are significant because the state is an important agent in redistributing resources and income.

The contradictory effects of globalization

While government fiscal capacity is constrained, globalization enhances the need for the development of infrastructure, investment in human capital, and mechanisms for social protection. Increased economic volatility and the reduced security of employment increase the turnover rate of labour, and thus the number of workers who are in transition, and women figure predominantly in this group. To cushion these negative effects, interim and in some cases long-term expenditures for unemployment insurance are required, as well as other forms of income support to ensure access to health care and adequate housing.

In addition to social protection, globalization also increases the need to invest in education and training to make sure that a country's labour force is sufficiently adaptable to changing conditions of competition in a global environment. Because most workers do not have the resources to finance their own training and education, there is an increasing need for the state to provide the resources necessary for human capital investment.

Moreover, to make their country an attractive location for investment, governments must also invest in physical infrastructure. These public expenditures are in general complementary to private investment because they raise the productivity and thus the profitability of private firms. The East Asian economies of Taiwan Province of China and the Republic of Korea are examples of developing countries that have made significant investments in education (beyond the primary level), while Singapore, noted for a more hands-off approach to development, nevertheless made substantial public infrastructure investments, which led to substantial MNE investment.[39]

Paradoxically, then, the viability of a growth strategy that relies on openness and market liberalization increasingly depends on the extent to which the state can afford to protect its citizens from the vagaries of the market. Further, an expanded role for the state is critical in an open, competitive environment since businesses cannot take on the costs of providing social protection if they are to remain competitive.

Gender effects of fiscal retrenchment

The gender effects of fiscal retrenchment operate mainly through the following four channels: (1) the distributional effects of tax reform; (2) the net effect of fiscal spending cuts on social safety nets and social welfare, with implications for women's unpaid labour burden and their security of income; (3) the effect of fiscal retrenchment on female and male employment; and (4) the privatization of public utilities, enterprises, services and common property resources.

As mentioned earlier, financial liberalization places pressure on states to lower income taxes on corporations, as well as on the wealthy as a means to reduce capital flight and attract foreign capital. The result has been a shift of the tax burden from capital to labour. Further, the move to user fees and indirect taxes as a way to supplement tax shortfalls results in a more regressive tax structure, which demands that low-income households provide a disproportionate (to their income) share of the revenues raised through taxation.

Given the lower labour-force participation rates and lower earnings of employed women, the low rates of direct taxes clearly favour males, because they are higher income earners and more likely to be owners of companies or shares in corporations than women. Men constitute a stronger tax base and would have to pay more if the rate structure was more progressive and exemptions lower, and—most of all—if the laws were enforced. The same is true for the low share of total taxes coming from property taxes. The gendered effect of the shift to greater reliance on indirect taxes such as sales taxes is difficult to assess. To the extent that indirect taxes are regressive, which they clearly are in many countries, we can assume that women as lower income earners are more disadvantaged. Where the degree to which they are regressive is tempered through exclusions focused on basic goods and services in health and education, as in Costa Rica and Jamaica, the incidence is presumably more gender-neutral.[40]

Under conditions of globalization and market liberalization, it appears that the limits on the state's ability to provide social expenditures and investment in infrastructure have become more pronounced. While the 1980s saw severe pressures on public spending due to rising interest rates and costs of servicing external debt, there has been a lessening of those pressures in the 1990s. Still, total government expenditures as a share of GDP (which includes capital or infrastructure spending) increased only marginally (0.45 per cent) in low-income countries, while declining significantly in lower-middle-income countries (–12.8 per cent) and in upper-middle-income countries (–5.5 per cent). While there have been improvements in per capita social expenditures (education, health, social security and welfare) in the late 1990s, as the data in table 3.3 show, these expenditures as a share of GDP have declined in a number of developing countries. These negative trends are most pronounced in sub-Saharan Africa and in Eastern and Central Europe. Moreover, given the need for expanded social expenditures, some of the increases in expenditure noted here are insufficient.

Table 3.3 Social expenditure per capita in constant international prices, five-year averages (1975–1999)

Country	1975-1979	1980-1984	1985-1989	1990-1994	1995-1999
Low income					
Cameroon	93	94	136	**96**	**43**
Ethiopia	26	29	29	**24**	-
Indonesia	35	50	53	71	96
Nepal	19	24	30	30	46
Zimbabwe	187	308	**292**	**245**	380
Lower-middle income					
Colombia	-	280	291	**224**	368
Dominican Republic	121	142	**116**	119	202
Egypt	214	279	**278**	307	**262**
Iran, Islamic Rep. of	395	**391**	**323**	401	517
Morocco	232	264	**254**	291	305
Paraguay	140	207	**153**	225	-
Sri Lanka	191	**151**	178	238	246
Syrian Arab Republic	154	209	**126**	**105**	159
Thailand	116	163	191	279	417
Tunisia	480	**464**	575	659	813
Upper-middle income					
Argentina	724	**539**	**525**	689	1028
Chile	690	947	**779**	854	1270
Costa Rica	659	**648**	671	691	759
Mauritius	737	740	**705**	916	1303
Mexico	481	492	**371**	505	539
Panama	569	660	773	805	916
Uruguay	932	1137	**1065**	1550	2138
High income					
Korea, Republic of	156	251	337	564	800
Singapore	437	759	970	1096	1372

Note: Social expenditure comprises public expenditure on education, health, and social security and welfare. Income groups are based on World Bank 2004b. Some countries lack some years on the averages due to unavailability of the data. Numbers in bold indicate decreases in average per capita expenditures compared with the previous five-year average. Base year for constant prices is 1996.
Sources: Calculated from IMF *Government Finance Statistics* (several years); Heston et al. 2002.

Governments have responded to fiscal pressures in various ways. In some instances social expenditures have been protected, but infrastructure spending has been forced to bear the brunt of revenue shortfalls. In others, social spending has also declined. This has impaired the ability of developing countries to promote human development, exacerbating the growing problem of inequality.

The need for public expenditure is even more pressing if the objective of achieving gender equality is to be taken seriously, with both the level and composition of public spending playing a crucial role. Women are often disadvantaged in labour and credit markets, making them more cash-constrained than men. Where women are responsible for financing their own and their children's health and education (as in many parts of sub-Saharan Africa), when access to these services requires cash payment, the result can be particularly detrimental for women and children. If there are also gender biases in the intrahousehold distribution of resources, due to the gender-biased social norms that value boys more than girls, the result can be particularly disadvantageous for girls. State spending on education and health aiming to achieve gender equity in access to these services is an important means of improving female capabilities (see chapter 8).

Evidence from gender budget initiatives, designed to evaluate the effects on women and men of government expenditures, thus far suggest that cuts in public infrastructure spending have especially negative effects on women. Lack of access to clean water, for example, impacts more heavily on women, who are largely responsible for household management and care. Reduced government expenditures on health care, such as rural clinics and public hospitals, means that women's unpaid care work increases. Negative health effects of excessive work can result (see chapter 8).

Downsizing of the government sector also negatively affects employment, and some studies indicate that women have been more negatively affected than men, though systematic evidence across countries and regions is lacking.[41] In many cases women shift to service-sector work, frequently in the informal economy where the terms and conditions of work are adverse.

There has also been pressure to reduce social safety nets. And yet women even more than men are in need of social safety nets, due to their heavier representation in insecure jobs as well as their care responsibilities. Of course most social safety nets provide broader coverage to formal-sector full-time paid workers, thus excluding most women from coverage. To the extent that pressures to reduce budget deficits erode the coverage of such schemes, there is less protection for men, which reduces differences in coverage between men and women, but through "downward harmonization". Nevertheless, and perhaps more importantly, as work becomes more insecure the state is less able to afford to smooth the income flows of its citizenry, and given the preponderance of women in informal and insecure work as well as in unpaid work, fiscal constraint acts as a major impediment to gender equality through "upward harmonization".

Privatization

Privatization of services and the introduction of user fees for state services have been major thrusts of neoliberal agendas. Privatization is argued to promote economic efficiency, and can result in lower costs and higher quality for essential goods such as electricity and water, health care and education, while user fees are seen as a mechanism for financing state services.

The benefits of privatization for low-income groups and in particular women are, however, disputed for a variety of reasons. Through privatization, public-sector providers are replaced by private monopolies. The result has been lack of competition, evidenced by inflated prices, under-investment, intermittent supplies and exclusion of consumers unable to pay.[42] Privatization may not even save public finance, when public money is spent on improving the efficiency of public-sector enterprises to make them more attractive to private buyers. The low rate of corporate taxation together with evidence of tax avoidance suggest that privatized entities are not likely to make much of a contribution to the public coffers.

The implications of privatization for the macro economy can only be assessed for each specific country, taking into account which state assets are privatized, the terms and conditions of privatization, and the national and international economic climate.[43] However there is widespread evidence of considerable short-term costs, and reason to think that the cost for women may be long-term. In Africa and Latin America, privatization has been more detrimental to women's employment prospects. Experience shows that the poor are not effectively protected from user fees, as exemption systems rarely work in practice. Moreover in the area of public services, because the anticipated expansion of services has often not materialized, nor have fees fallen—in many cases they are higher—women frequently bear the burden of managing household budgets on less income and with fewer essential services.

GLOBAL ECONOMIC INTEGRATION AND WOMEN'S PARTICIPATION IN DECISION MAKING

The period of global economic integration has coincided with processes of democratization as well as decentralization of decision making. Such political transformations, to which women's movements have contributed, can both increase the space for women in decision making and improve the accountability of governments to female constituents. Women's greater access to political decision-making bodies in local political institutions, or as participants in advocacy groups, can thus improve their ability to effect gender-equitable change (see section 3). There is clear evidence of such changes in recent years, as numerous countries have passed legislation that can improve women's lives, including laws against domestic violence as well as reform of family law. While these changes have indeed been beneficial, one area that has not seen improvement is women's ability to influence economic policy. This is because advances in women's access to decision-making bodies have coincided with a diminished opportunity for parliaments in particular to influence macroeconomic policy.[44]

Noteworthy in the reduced control of national governments over economic policy is the enlarged role of the international financial institutions in setting macroeconomic policies in economies that confront serious balance of payments difficulties due to adverse trade balances or capital flows. In such contexts these organizations directly influence, and often set, policy by influencing exchange rates, public-sector spending levels, and rules that affect liberalization of trade and capital flows. They are able to enforce their policy programmes by withholding needed balance of payments support and other aid, subjecting developing countries to pariah status in international markets should their governments default on their external debts. The irony is that the shift in power to these global institutions tends to subvert national control at a time when women are making noteworthy advances in gaining access to parliamentary seats.

In addition to their influence over national macroeconomic variables, these organizations have also pushed for central bank independence—that is, giving central banks the ability to maintain the value and stability of the domestic currency, free from pressure from the central government to pursue other goals such as full employment or industrial development. Independent central banks have increasingly pursued inflation targeting as the primary, even single, focus to the exclusion of other goals that might promote development and well-being. The independence of central banks can weaken democratic accountability by insulating critical centres of policy decision making from participatory processes and public debates over the ideal inflation target and other critical policy choices.[45]

Debate over targets can be contentious, with many economists arguing for example that the goal of low inflation produces costs that far outweigh the benefits.[46] While monetary restraint may keep inflation low, which can be beneficial to consumers and to financial investors who desire higher real rates of return on investment, the costs are felt in higher unemployment rates. Indeed, even World Bank economists note that there is little empirical evidence that inflation under 40 per cent annually has a negative effect on growth.[47] And yet central banks often pursue inflation targets that are close to zero, with negative effects in terms of lost employment and income. In the absence of greater public debate and decision making on these matters, a second-best option would be for the governing bodies of independent central banks to embrace a more diverse set of social interests, including those of women.

Notes

1 Anker et al. 2003.

2 UN 1999; Deere 2004.

3 Berik 2000; Ghosh 2004a; Jomo 2001.

4 Malhotra 2003; Hart 2002.

5 Kucera and Milberg 2000.

6 Siegemann 2004.

7 Kabeer and Mahmud 2004.

8 Balakrishnan 2002.

9 Seguino 1997.

10 Gupta 2002; Oostendorp 2004.

11 Berik 2004.

12 Maurer-Fazio et al. 1997; Liu 1998.

13 Maurer-Fazio and Hughes 2002.

14 Packard 2004.

15 World Bank 1995b:107.

16 Montenegro and Paredes 1999.

17 Arabsheibani et al. 2003.

18 Paus and Robinson 1998.

19 Busse and Spielmann 2003.

20 Palma 2003.

21 Bhattacharya and Rahman 1999.

22 Seguino 2000b.

23 Seguino 2000a.

24 Acero 1995.

25 Seguino 2003b.

26 Weeks 1998.

27 Standing 1997; ILO 2002b.

28 Fodor, E. 2004b; UNIFEM 2002.

29 Singh and Zammit 2000; Lim 2000; Floro and Dymski 2000; van Staveren 2002; Baden 1996.

30 Cho et al. 2004; Singh and Zammit 2000; van Staveren 2002.

31 Cho et al. 2004.

32 Zhiqin 2000.

33 Elson 1998.

34 Elson and Cagatay 2000.

35 Bakker 1994; Elson 1995.

36 Ertürk and Cagatay 1995; van Staveren 2002.

37 UNRISD 2000:33.

38 Huber 2004; Cagatay and Ertürk 2003.

39 Jomo 2003.

40 Huber 2004.

41 Packard 2004; Lee 2004.

42 Zammit 2003.

43 Van der Hoeven 2000.

44 Bangura 2004.

45 Boylan 1998a, 1998b; Elgie 1998; for a different perspective see Goodman 1991.

46 Epstein 2002.

47 Bruno and Easterly 1996.

Chapter 4
Consolidating women's gains: The need for a broader policy agenda

The preceding chapters underscore that neoliberal policies and globalization produce contradictory effects on individual well-being. While under current rules of liberalization, capital becomes increasingly less encumbered by national rules and constraints, there are contradictory effects on productivity growth and standards of living. Although competition might stimulate productivity, this is not guaranteed since increased firm bargaining power can allow firms to rely on low wages to reduce costs instead of embarking on innovation. Furthermore the public sector's ability to manage the process of growth and development can become more limited. In this process, women can benefit from employment possibilities that heretofore had not existed, but at the same time they are confronted with a macroeconomic environment that is more volatile than before, and there is little social protection. How have gender gaps in well-being changed during the era of liberalization and outward-oriented growth? Further, do those countries that grow more rapidly do better in closing gender gaps?

To answer these questions requires a method of evaluating gendered well-being. Measures of average income are inadequate because they most often use the household as the unit of analysis, and assume equal sharing of household resources between males and females; they are not therefore a good measure for tracking changes in women's access to household income. Furthermore, macroeconomic aggregates such as gross domestic product (GDP) per capita do not take into account unpaid labour, which is largely undertaken by women. In any case well-being is more extensive than can be measured by a money metric. These concerns have resulted in a profound transformation in the way that gendered well-being is conceptualized.

The newer frameworks for evaluating trends in gender well-being bear some similarity to the human development approach. In that approach, development is conceptualized as the broadening of people's choices, created by expanding "capabilities". Central to the notion of capability is the ability to live a long and healthy life, to be well nourished and clothed, to be knowledgeable, to have access to the resources and opportunities that ensure an adequate standard of living. Other less quantifiable capabilities include the ability to have self-esteem, to be treated with dignity, to be able to be connected—that is to be able to care, to be cared for, and to be free of systematic social exclusion due to discrimination or other factors. It includes too the freedom to have a voice in economic, social and political arenas: to be empowered and to exhibit agency. In this approach inequality is seen as an "unfreedom" because it contributes to social exclusion and can lead to disempowerment, lack of political and economic voice, and possibly to a degradation of other basic capabilities.[1] This concept of well-being is complex, extending beyond the material realm, which makes translation into measurable indicators a challenging prospect.

Most gendered analyses of well-being evaluate not only women's absolute status, but also their status relative to men: that is, the degree of gender inequality in well-being. Measures of female well-being relative to men's are useful because the gaps both affect and reflect power dynamics that influence the process of resource distribution. Gender wage inequality, for example, can contribute to unequal bargaining power within the household and thus an unequal distribution of family resources, and this condition, as a result, can affect women's absolute level of well-being. This implies that measures of both absolute and relative well-being are necessary, not only to capture status at a point in time, but also to illuminate the potential for change in a positive direction over time.

Research on gender equity in well-being focuses assessments on three distinct but interrelated domains: capabilities, access to resources and opportunities, and empowerment. In empirical research to date, capabilities are more narrowly defined than in the human development literature, and capture basic human abilities as measured through indicators of health, education and nutrition. The second domain refers to equality of access to resources (such as credit, land and property) and to opportunities for generating income (such as through participation in labour markets). Finally, empowerment refers to the ability to make choices from a meaningful set of alternatives that can alter outcomes, and is meant to reflect the degree of participation relative to men in deliberative bodies as agents of change.[2]

INDICATORS AND MEASUREMENT

In practice the selection of indicators is shaped by data availability, although in some instances this difficulty can be overcome by using more easily quantifiable proxies. In the category of capabilities, educational attainment and enrolment ratios are important indicators, along with measures of life expectancy and sex ratios in the population. Additionally, measures of maternal mortality may be used: this is narrower because it captures women's absolute status, rather than gender inequality. Indicators of heath and education are markers of capabilities that have intrinsic value and are also the preconditions for participation in provisioning and decision making.

There are many serious concerns about the existing data sets. For example, the ratio of girls to boys in schools reflects educational inputs into children, but this is not strongly correlated with completion rates, and does not reflect the quality of education and student learning.[3] Completion rates are not, however, as widely available as enrolment ratios. While overall life expectancy is useful as a measure of well-being, the use of male and female life expectancy to capture gender differentials in well-being masks age-specific differentials in mortality. In India, for example, the higher life expectancy of women is largely the consequence of the greater survival chance of older women, which "more than compensates (mathematically speaking) for the lower survival of younger females".[4]

Data problems to do with reliability and comparability are as limiting in the area of social indicators as they are in the case of economic data. Very few developing countries, for example, have comprehensive and reliable systems, for registering vital statistics (that is, births and deaths) from which demographic profiles can be obtained, India being perhaps an exception. And even for those with complete registration systems the estimates of mortality and life expectancy produced by international agencies may not be accurate because of the overuse of model life tables.[5] Many of the statistics used for estimating under-five mortality are based on mathematical models rather than on up-to-date data.[6]

Data challenges also make it difficult to assess gender equality in access to resources and opportunities. The measures most frequently relied on are labour market data, including labour-force participation rates and employment rates. The scarcity of data on unemployment, hours of paid and unpaid work, security of employment and wages makes it difficult to gain a complete and reliable picture of income-generating opportunities in labour markets. Ideally, such data would be combined with information on job segregation to paint a more complete portrait of gender gaps in opportunities. Of all of these variables, what are most needed are improved data on gender wage gaps in different industries and occupational categories, and on unemployment, for measuring status in labour markets. For countries in which income is generated by other means, such as through smallholder farming, information on the extent of women's access to, and control over, land, labour, capital and crops would be useful but is not widely available. All of this suggests that we only have a partial picture from which to infer trends in access to resources and opportunities.

Empowerment reflects a dynamic process, with power exercised in a variety of settings, including in the household, in the economic, legal and political arenas, and in cultural institutions (such as religious bodies).[7] As yet, the development of measures of empowerment is at an early stage, rendering difficult the quantitative analysis of trends. It is also intrinsically difficult to capture processes of social change, such as empowerment, through indicators. Measurement of empowerment cross-nationally and over time therefore has to rely on innovative proxies to capture the ability of women to make meaningful choices and to influence decision making. It is most frequently tracked as the female share of parliamentary seats, one of the few measures for which global data are available. The indicator is imperfect since it says little about whether women in parliament can make an impact on the shape and content of policies. However, as noted earlier, the economic power of national political bodies has, in some countries at least, been circumscribed in the period of global economic integration.

Other measures of empowerment have been used, though less broadly. For example, the age of women and men at first marriage reflects bargaining power in the household, and this has implications for resource distribution and opportunities. This indicator is salient in a number of developing countries that tend to be agriculturally based, but may not be broadly relevant for global comparisons of trends in well-being. Women's economic empowerment is also sometimes represented by their share of executive and managerial positions. There is limited data on this variable, however, and it may be more relevant in countries with extensive labour markets, than in countries with large agricultural sectors. Violence against women is also now recognized as a measure of dis-empowerment.[8] Such violence is a barrier to women's use of capabilities or access to opportunities. Worldwide, it has been estimated that violence against women is as serious a cause of death as cancer among women of reproductive age.[9] While accurate data on violence against women could tell us a good deal about women's status and well-being, efforts to measure this variable are constrained by serious under-reporting, as well as difficulties in disaggregating acts of violence into specific acts. Thus while little comparable cross-national data is available, efforts are being made to address this gap.

PROGRESS IN CLOSING GENDER GAPS IN WELL-BEING

Analyses of well-being have to take into account that, while there may be progress in one domain, there may be lags or setbacks in others. Thus, assessments of well-being need to evaluate progress not only on individual indicators, but also across a wide spectrum of measures in the three domains, in order to achieve a more comprehensive picture of women's relative status. It is, however, useful to review the evidence on the three domains separately before turning to an analysis of the composite state of gender equality of well-being.

Trends in capability gaps

Several UN reports have assessed trends in life expectancy and education and observed the narrowing of gender gaps.[10] There are notable exceptions. Female to male secondary enrolment ratios have declined in a number of countries in recent years, including in Central and West Asia (seven countries), sub-Saharan Africa (10 countries), Eastern Europe (six countries), Latin America and the Caribbean (six countries), and Asia and the Pacific (two countries).[11] This is a disturbing and perplexing finding, contradicting the notion that progress toward gender equity is a positive though slow-moving process due to change in social norms and institutional rules that disadvantage women. That there are substantial reversals in a short period of time suggests that positive changes are not stable or enduring. These reversals require scrutiny to understand more fully the dynamics that can undermine progress.

As further evidence of the persistence of gender inequality, several recent studies have found that the ratio of females to males in the population has declined in a number countries, including in several with rising per capita GDP—China, India and the Republic of Korea—as well as in several Latin American countries.[12] The causes for the declines are varied. Low sex ratios often reflect excess female infant and child mortality, primarily due to sex bias in access to health care. But, in some countries at least, they seem to reflect sex-selective abortion, especially of higher-order daughters.[13] This underscores the notion that growth is not sufficient to improve women's status, and indeed that, in spite of growth, women's relative status can worsen.

Further, dismal statistics from Africa and Asia on death, disablements and chronic illness related to preventable complications during pregnancy or childbirth underscore that women continue to lack access to essential and emergency obstetric care, as well as more comprehensive reproductive health services.[14] In addition to these problems, HIV/AIDS has developed into a serious health threat in Africa, with women's infection rate exceeding that of men: they comprise 55 per cent of infected persons.[15] This underscores the continued power differential between women and men, with women frequently unable to protect themselves from sexual encounters or to ensure that those encounters are safe. The epidemic puts heavy costs on women in terms of care work. Increasingly, older female family members are left to care for orphaned children.

In contrast to these statistics, there are numerous cases in which women have surpassed men in various categories of capability. The most frequently discussed are cases where female enrolment rates in educational establishments now exceed those of men. One analysis showed that 72 of 191 countries in 1999/2000 had female to male secondary enrolment ratios of one or greater, implying gender parity or a reverse gap in favour of females at the secondary level.[16] On its own, this statistic might suggest greater gender equality and improvements in female absolute well-being. Other data, however, belie that interpretation. For example, of these 72 countries, only one-third have high rates of female enrolment (above 90 per cent). Further, in a number of countries, particularly in the Caribbean, ratios of greater than 1 reflect male departure from schooling at an earlier age, for different reasons including the availability of lucrative income-earning activities—for some at least.

In sum, while there is evidence of progress towards closing gender gaps, especially in education, it is noteworthy that in a number of countries, gender gaps in secondary school enrolments have widened over the last decade. Evidence of widening gaps in female to male population ratios likewise signals that progress is uneven and indeed reversible.

Trends in gender differences in access to opportunities and resources

The translation of capabilities into access to opportunities is not automatic, especially in slow-growth economies where social tensions may emerge over a small and sometimes shrinking economic pie. Gender norms in those cases can play an important part in influencing the distribution of resources and jobs. Data from the 1995–7 World Values Surveys, for example, showed a significant percentage of men (40 per cent compared with 32 per cent for women) agreeing that when jobs are scarce, men have more right to existing job slots than women.

Such gender norms are apparent in Latin America and the Caribbean, where from 1990 to 2002, of 18 countries for which data are available, 13 experienced increases in unemployment. In all but three of those countries, women bore the brunt, with unemployment rates rising by a larger margin for women than for men.[17]

Unemployment data do not suffice to evaluate gender gaps in access to opportunities. This is in part because unemployment data are scarce, but it is also because women's constrained access to paid work often results in their withdrawing from the labour force, leading to artificially low female unemployment rates. Further, women may move into informal work as "self-employed" workers. In reality, much of this type of work is disguised unemployment, although data are lacking to estimate the extent of the problem. We may infer, though, that the existing unemployment data are a minimum estimate of lack of access to reasonably remunerated work. Women's real unemployment rates are likely to be higher, given their greater representation in poorly remunerated, makeshift work in the informal economy.

Another measure of women's relative access to opportunities is the female share of paid employment. This measure does not completely overcome the data weaknesses just noted. Nevertheless, it does capture those who work for a wage (in contrast to the self-employed). Here, there are strong indications that women's relative access to paid work has increased in a number of countries, although progress is not even, and there are again some reversals. A report on progress towards meeting Goal 3 of the Millennium Development Goals—to promote

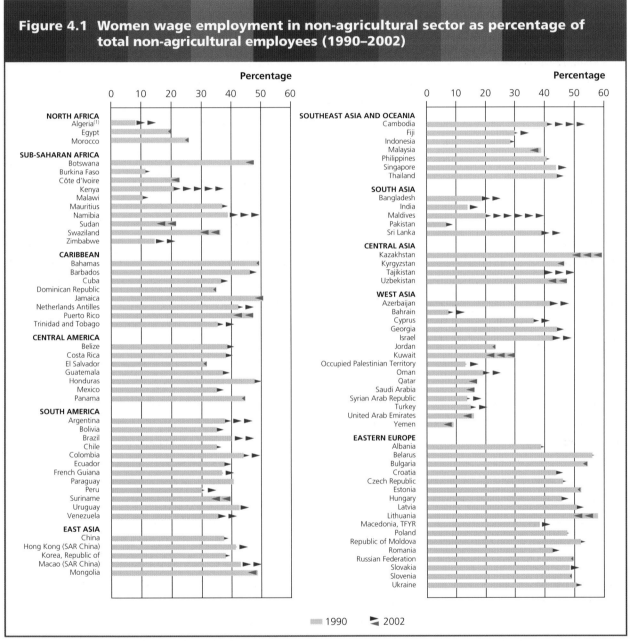

Figure 4.1 Women wage employment in non-agricultural sector as percentage of total non-agricultural employees (1990–2002)

Notes: The figure does not include countries in the Western Europe or Other Developed geographical groupings. None of the countries
          for which data was available in those areas have experienced gender reversals in wage employment in non-agricultural sector.
          (1) Data for 2001 rather than 2002.
Source: ILO 2004c.

gender equality and empower women—found, for example, that of 124 countries that have data for 1990 and 2002, 81 had increases in the female share of non-agricultural employment and 30 had declines.[18] Figure 4.1 provides data on women's share of waged work for 1990 and 2002. Particularly notable are those regions in which women's share of non-agricultural wage employment lies below 25 per cent, a challenge that is particularly evident still in some countries of South Asia, West Asia, and Africa.

As noted in chapter 3, declines in the female share of manufacturing jobs are also apparent in mature semi-industrialized economies, starting around the early 1990s.[19] Slow growth or a decline in the female share of job openings in the manufacturing sector has led women to either withdraw from the labour force or move into service-sector work. The degree to which the shift to service-sector employment provides decent work remains unclear, however. In some cases, well-educated women have moved into financial services employment, where work conditions tend to be favourable. Employment has also expanded in export service-sector jobs, such as informatics, data possessing and call centres. While work conditions sometimes appear more favourable than in export manufacturing, the downward pressure on wages in these jobs is similar to export manufacturing-sector jobs, insofar as competition amongst developing countries places serious limits on women's bargaining power and wages.[20]

Another export service-sector industry—tourism—has begun to absorb significant numbers of female workers. While conditions may be favourable in formal-sector jobs, work is often seasonal and insecure. Still other women, particularly those with a secondary education or less who cannot find manufacturing employment, take up informal work in the services sector, which in some cases is precarious and badly paid, or depends on "self-employment" on any terms.

Data on agricultural employment is sparse, but there is some evidence that the female share of employment in that sector has increased. In part, this may be due to the expansion of high-value agricultural export crops in different regions, including Asia, sub-Saharan Africa and especially Latin America, with women frequently serving as temporary wage labourers (see chapter 6).[21] In other countries, including in Central America and some African countries, male migration has increased the number of female household heads and female participation in agriculture (see chapter 6). The impact on women's overall labour burden in such cases is likely to be severe. This underlines the fact that a simple increase in female share of employment is not a sure indicator of improvement in women's situation.

While wage-gap data would be useful in assessing women's relative opportunities, the scarcity of such data makes a complete analysis impossible. From the data that do exist, there is evidence of a narrowing of gender wage gaps in a large number of countries as noted in the previous chapter, with notable exceptions. However, given the closure of education gaps, the reduction in the gap between female and male wages is not necessarily a result of a decline in discrimination. Indeed, simple female-to-male wage ratios can mask an increase in female exploitation. As the previous chapter indicated, country-level studies that isolate the effects of trade liberalization find that the discriminatory portion of wage gaps is rising in a number of countries. The evidence of greater gender wage exploitation in some rapidly growing economies, including China and Viet Nam as well as wider gaps in Chile, tells a cautionary tale about the benefits of trade liberalization for women's relative well-being.

Table 4.1 provides data on selected indicators of well-being for Latin America, the Caribbean and Asia. This is a useful comparison as the Latin America region has been plagued by slow growth over the last two decades while Asian economies, with few exceptions, have had rapid growth, and many of these countries have chosen to follow the managed-market rather than the neoliberal model. The data indicate that in two areas—fertility and labour-force participation—there have been improvements in gender equity in well-being. For all other indicators, however, there have been reversals in both slow and in rapidly growing economies. For example, in 8 out of 21 countries, female-to-male population ratios fell. Secondary school enrolment ratios also declined in several countries. Particularly noteworthy is the worsening gap between female and male unemployment rates, observed in 14 countries in this group. This contrasts with the rising ratio of female-to-male labour-force participation rates, and suggests that while more women may be seeking employment, a smaller proportion of women than men are able to find employment.

Empowerment trends

Most of the indicators used to measure empowerment are proxies, often imperfect ones, that can lend some insight into the degree of change in women's ability to influence decision making on matters that have an impact on their own lives as well as those of others. The most frequently used is female share of parliamentary seats

Table 4.1   Changes in indicators of gender equality in well–being (1970–1999)

	F/M population ratio[1]	Fertility	Ratio F/M secondary school enrolment	Ratio F/M total yrs. educational attainment	Female share of labour force	Female share of non-agricultural employment[2]	Ratio F/M unemployment rate[3]
Argentina	0.05	–0.6	–0.06	0.06	7.84	3.69	0.11
Bahamas	0.01	–1.3	–0.10	0.10	7.16	–1.74	0.61
Barbados	–0.06	–1.3	0.03	–0.04	6.02	1.97	0.08
Belize	–0.03	–3.8	–0.08	–0.08	3.16	–7.44	0.43[4]
Bolivia	–0.02	–2.6	0.15	0.18	5.90	2.05	0.35
Brazil	0.02	–2.8	0.14	–0.08	11.74	3.04	0.66
Chile	–0.01	–1.8	–0.13	0.03	10.84	0.73	–0.17
Colombia	0.01	–2.9	0.14	0.28	14.24	5.89	–0.06
Costa Rica	0.01	–2.4	0.05	0.00	12.70	–	0.13
Dominican Republic	0.00	–3.3	–0.11	0.08	8.24	–6.28	0.36
Ecuador	0.00	–3.2	0.19	0.09	9.18	2.64	–0.19
El Salvador	0.05	–3.2	0.08	0.32	15.42	2.98	–1.42
Honduras	0.00	–3.3	0.33	–0.20	9.10	2.37	–0.14
Jamaica	–0.03	–2.9	0.05	0.04	3.20	2.24	–0.13
Mexico	0.05	–4.1	0.39	0.27	13.80	1.66	–0.19
Panama	0.02	–2.7	–0.05	0.00	9.82	0.09	0.17
Paraguay	–0.04	–3.4	0.02	0.10	3.40	1.86	–0.06
Peru	0.03	–3.4	0.17	0.16	8.66	–	–
Trinidad and Tobago	–0.02	–1.8	0.01	0.11	4.50	4.25	0.05
Uruguay	0.05	–0.7	0.15	0.04	15.24	4.25	0.17
Venezuela	0.01	–2.5	0.35	0.04	13.96	4.60	0.43
Hong Kong (SAR China)	0.03	–2.4	0.28	0.24	2.30	5.76	–0.32
Indonesia	0.00	–2.9	0.44	0.21	10.38	–0.20	–
Korea, Rep. of	0.00	–2.7	0.35	0.21	9.10	1.08	0.09
Malaysia	–0.01	–2.4	0.42	0.34	6.68	0.68	–
Philippines	0.00	–2.2	0.07	0.03	4.78	0.17	–0.42
Singapore	0.04	–1.6	–0.02	0.22	13.16	–0.96	0.34
Sri Lanka	0.11	–2.1	0.00	0.04	11.40	–2.70	–0.88
Thailand	0.00	–3.5	0.16	0.11	–1.88	1.73	–0.14

Notes: Changes in indicators are calculated as the difference between the value of the indicator in 1999 and its value in 1970 (unless other dates are specified). For instance in Argentina, the ratio of females to males in the population increased by 0.05 points (from 0.99 in 1970 to 1.04 in 1999).
(1) Population ratio is defined in this case as number of females/number of males.
(2) Data for change in female share of non–agricultural employment are from 1990 to 2000 or closest year available.
(3) Data for change in ratio of female to male unemployment rates are from 1990 to 1999.
(4) Data are for change in ratio from 1993 to 1999.
Sources: Seguino 2003a, 2002; ECLAC 2004; World Bank 2004b; ILO 2004b.

(see section 3). We might expect that as women gain capabilities and opportunities in other domains, this will improve their status as well as their ability to move into decision-making bodies within economic and political institutions. There have been some other innovations in measuring empowerment across a broad range of countries, including contraceptive prevalence, and

various databases that assess women's political rights (measured as the right to vote and participate in the political system equally with men) and social rights (the right to equal inheritance, and equal power to enter into a relationship of choice with a partner).

Using the data that is widely available, a variety of UN reports find that female share of parliamentary seats has increased in many countries (see section 3). While this progress is gratifying, there have been numerous cases of reversals, emphasizing once again that progress towards gender equality is not necessarily permanent or stable, and that gains can be tenuous. The data further indicate that progress is unrelated to the level of per capita GDP of a country, which is a widely used indicator of growth and development. As a case in point, between 1995 and 2004 the female share of parliamentary seats declined marginally in China, despite its rapid rates of economic growth, while those in many sub-Saharan African countries rose considerably over the same period in the context of economic stagnation.

Given that multilateral financial institutions have considerable influence over national economic policies, the power of parliaments to determine these matters is often circumscribed, particularly now that many countries are committed to the legally binding Uruguay Round Agreements under the World Trade Organization (WTO) concerning trade-related matters.

The World Bank, however, has made efforts to improve participation in policy decision making through Poverty Reduction Strategy Papers (PRSPs). More specifically, in return for financial assistance developing country governments are expected to prepare a poverty reduction strategy, to specify the budgetary resources needed to implement it, and to establish a monitoring framework for assessing the achievement of strategic goals. This strategy is to be developed by the government in consultation with civil society.

Although the PRSPs are to be developed through a process of consultation, criticisms of the participatory nature of this process have been noted. Often national legislatures are not involved in decisions on the policy content of these strategies, and some observers argue that civil society participation does not translate into influence. It has been observed that generally there is a very low level of consultation with women's groups throughout the PRSP process, limiting women's agency in decision making. Rather than facilitating democratic debate on macroeconomic policies, these documents often incorporate the macroeconomic policies that the IMF has set for borrowing countries.[22]

A review by the World Bank's Gender Division of 15 Interim PRSPs (I-PRSPs) and three PRSPs completed by early 2001 found that less than half discussed gender issues in any detail in their diagnosis of poverty. Even fewer integrated gender analysis

into their poverty reduction strategy, resource allocation, and monitoring and evaluation sections. Gender issues were, however, better integrated into the health, nutrition and population sectors, and to some extent in education. But gender did not feature as an issue in macroeconomic and development policy. Similar findings are reported in independent evaluations of PRSPs.[23] Given the important effect of macroeconomic policy on gender outcomes and the limited space for negotiating the World Bank and IMF basic policy prescriptions, PRSPs do not at present appear to be a fruitful avenue for women's empowerment.

MACROECONOMIC STRATEGIES FOR GENDER-EQUITABLE DEVELOPMENT

Movement toward gender equity in well-being requires strategies that enhance women's capabilities and opportunities to provide for themselves and their families. In achieving both capability and livelihood goals, the aim is to raise both women's absolute well-being, and also their well-being relative to men, partly so as to improve their bargaining power in the household and in other social institutions.

It would be reasonable to expect that improvements in women's well-being and a reduction in various gender inequalities are most likely to be achieved when there are relatively rapid economic growth, macroeconomic stability, a favourable external economic environment, expanding formal employment opportunities, redistributive taxation and public spending, and social policies that favour women.

Improving women's well-being and reducing gender equality: Would faster economic growth be enough?

The significant progress that has been made in some domains of well-being, and the failure to achieve sufficient progress in others, make it imperative to understand the factors that have contributed to closure of gender gaps in well-being. In particular, have gender gaps closed as a result of globalization and employment trends, or have other factors, such as pro-equality political and social movements, been major factors? A number of studies have attempted to sort out the causal mechanisms that have led to changes in indicators of well-being.

With regard to the impact of globalization, advocates have argued that women's well-being is a beneficiary of the policy shift to liberalization and global economic integration. The primary effect, it is often argued, will be felt through increased female access to employment, as well as the more rapid growth experienced through letting markets "get prices right". The World Bank, a major proponent of this view, claims that countries with higher levels of per capita GDP have greater gender equality. The policy implication, according to the World Bank, is that the promotion of economic growth via liberalization is an important tool for closing gender gaps in well-being.

However, the World Bank's analysis does not take into account the fact that the recent period of global economic integration has not had a positive effect on economic growth (see chapter 2). Moreover, its argument is founded on a rather limited empirical base, namely that there is a positive relationship between improved gender ratios of secondary school enrolments and life expectancy on the one hand, and per capita GDP on the other. It does not evaluate the effects of economic development and growth on the more "economic" aspects of women's well-being, such as the female share of employment, gender wage gaps, or other variables that measure women's relative access to income.

In particular, the World Bank's analysis misses the point that most of the gains in per capita GDP (except for some Asian economies) occurred in the pre-globalization era.[24] As a result, the data merely show a relationship between growth in the pre-globalization era and gender equity in capabilities today, and tell us nothing about how current macro level policies are likely to affect well-being.

The information that can be derived from using a single indicator of well-being is clearly limited. Furthermore, taking one category of indicators for tracking progress in women's well-being over time is also limited. This is because, while there may be improvements in some domains of well-being,

this can coincide with reversals in others. Composite measures of well-being that sum across the three domains of capabilities, opportunities and empowerment have therefore been developed for this purpose, and to allow international comparisons. Several measures are currently in use.

The Gender Development Index (GDI) has been widely used, and is based on an adjustment to the Human Development Index (HDI), reflecting the degree of gender inequality. In particular, the HDI rankings—based on measures of life expectancy, education and per capita GDP—are "penalized", or adjusted downwards, for the degree of gender inequality in basic capabilities. In this sense, the GDI is not a measure of gender inequality as such, but rather a human development measure that takes into account gender gaps in well-being. The strong influence of GDP on the HDI and GDI dilutes the ability of the GDI to capture gender inequality; thus, this measure fails to escape the tyranny of GDP in evaluating well-being. A second composite measure, used by the United Nations Development Programme (UNDP), is the Gender Empowerment Measure (GEM), which captures the extent of gender equality in economic and political power. Although it is distinctive from the GDI (which is focused primarily on basic capabilities and living standards), the GEM is also weighted by per capita GDP, and thus open to the same criticisms as the GDI.

Newer approaches to composite indices have been developed, based exclusively on measures of gender gaps in capabilities, opportunities and empowerment. One such composite index, the Standardized Indicator of Gender Equality (SIGE), draws on five measures of relative well-being: (1) education, measured as literacy ratios and primary and secondary enrolment ratios; (2) ratio of female to male life expectancy; (3) relative labour force participation rates; (4) female share of technical and professional, and administrative and managerial, positions; and (5) female share of parliamentary seats.[25]

Using this more comprehensive composite measure of well-being , one study explores the relationship between the composite index of gender equality SIGE and GDP growth rates from 1975 to 1995 for 95 countries clustered into four groups (or quartiles), ranging from the poorest to the richest in terms of per capita income.[26] Generally speaking, the economic structure within each group is roughly similar and, as a rule of thumb, the higher the per capita GDP, the more industrialized the countries in the group. This method of clustering countries by per capita GDP is a useful way to gauge the relationship between gender and growth by level of development, because the role of women in the economy differs by economic structure, and so we can expect that the influence of growth on gender equity will also vary. Correlating GDP growth rates for the period 1975–95 and the composite well-being index in the respective groups of countries to ascertain the extent to which higher growth rates produce better performance in achieving greater gender equality, the study finds mixed results. There is a positive correlation only for the third-highest and the highest income countries, while there is a negative relationship between growth and gender equality in well-being in the lowest and the second-highest income groups. This suggests that in the latter two groups (that is, the poorest countries in terms of GDP per capita, largely comprising agricultural economies with a primary commodity export dependency, and the Asian and Latin American semi industrialized economies) the countries that grew the most rapidly from 1975 to 1995 during this period of increasing global economic integration had the worst performance in terms of gender equality.

Similar findings emerge from the few regional studies that have been recently undertaken on this subject. In Latin America and the Caribbean, while some gaps in well-being have narrowed, progress is uneven across a set of nine indicators, and in some cases conditions have worsened. Where it has occurred, economic growth has not exhibited a beneficial effect on gender equality, and instead appears to exert a negative effect on some indicators. Conversely, growth in government expenditures and female share of the labour force exert a positive effect. In Asia, there is evidence that those countries that have performed the best at closing gender gaps in well-being, measured with a composite index, had the slowest rates of economic growth during the period 1970 to 1990.[27]

All of these results need to be considered with caution, particularly bearing in mind the frail databases on which the indicators are based. Moreover, association between different phenomena (captured through correlations) does not necessarily infer causality, and may in fact be linked to some other unidentified third relationship. Nevertheless these results provide further evidence for the various arguments that suggest that economic growth and structural change are not sufficient in themselves to promote gender equality. Only better datasets and continuing research and analysis can provide a more definitive answer.

More policy instruments to improve gender equality

As in all successful macroeconomic policy formulation, the development of gender-equitable macroeconomic policy is in some sense an art, in that no simple recipe exists. The actual policy choices made, the intensity with which different parts of the same policy package are pursued, and their sequencing, will depend on a wide range of factors. These include the history of individual countries and the absorption of historical experience into political, social and economic structures; the position of individual counties in the global order; and the constellation of social and political forces. Any proposal for alternatives must therefore avoid the error of prescribing "one size fits all" remedies as orthodox approaches have sought to do.

Nevertheless, a report such as this can usefully focus attention on widely shared objectives, and reinforce the view that there is a wide range of policy instruments for different political actors to choose from, depending on their circumstances. Moreover, as a general principle, policies adopted must be sensitive to issues of production, distribution and social protection, and their gendered demands and implications. In thinking about policies in each of these spheres, it is important to bear in mind that an important determinant of success is the exploitation of affinities, so that policies work in the same direction, or at least do not work at cross-purposes.

This said, there are some clear guiding principles. At a minimum, effective policy requires that the number of policy instruments must be at least as many as the objectives being pursued. It demands a creative blend of strategies that ensure the benefits of regulation without undermining the potential gains of market liberalization. This is based on the recognition that, under the right conditions, liberalization can produce benefits in the form of increased efficiency and opportunities, but it also involves economic and social costs.

The role of regulation is to reduce those costs sufficiently that the net effect is a macroeconomic environment in which capital has the flexibility to produce higher standards of living, but without imposing costs on vulnerable groups. Moreover, where certain groups do not share in the benefits or find their situation considerably worsened, the state needs the necessary room to manoeuvre so as to provide effective mechanisms for social protection. As has been noted, the macroeconomic policies of the last two decades have not only reduced dramatically the number of policy instruments available to the state, they have also reduced the capacities of states and the instruments available to deal with the adverse social consequences.

Clearly, if a broad agenda that places gender equality at the core of policies of economic development and structural change is to be adopted, then there is a need for a wide range of instruments, including some that are specifically designed to address gender-based inequalities and constraints.

It is clear from the discussion in these first three chapters regarding macroeconomics and gender that the orthodox or neoliberal policy approach of tight monetary and fiscal policies, and free trade and capital flows, has not provided a conducive environment for either widespread development or extensive improvements in gender well-being and greater gender equality. There is growing body of support among economists for alternative macreconomic policies that, while aiming for macroeconomic stability, take more heed of development and social goals. Changes in policy direction would include monetary and fiscal policies that are more expansionary, taxation policies that provide governments with adequate revenues to fund social expenditures and repair the erosion of the protective capacity of the state, policies that pursue selective strategic liberalization of capital flows and trade, and regulation of capital flows so to avoid excessive volatility in employment and exchange rates. More precisely, trade and foreign direct investment (FDI) policy must serve as a tool of development, rather than to pursue the liberalization of trade and capital flows as ends in themselves.

Moreover, a variety of policy measures often referred to as "industrial policy" are essential to promote transition from an economy tied to the vagaries and limitations of over-emphasis on the production and export of commodities and labour-intensive low-value manufactures. Policy measures that help to overcome these constraints include market protection, selective promotion of goods which are likely to be in increasing as world's demand income rises, subsidizing research and development, selective credit allocation, measures to foster intersectoral linkages, labour market and other policies to enhance human capital formation.

If developing countries are to be able to choose from a wider box of policy tools, changes will be required in the trade and trade-related rules embodied in the Uruguay Round Agreements. The latter restrict the range of policy choice and prevent developing countries from employing a number of policy instruments that would promote their industrial development, when in fact what they most need is greater policy "space".

In addition, bearing in mind that the policies of advanced industrial countries exert a considerable influence over the development prospects of developing countries, the former also need to effect substantial changes in policy, including raising their rate of growth so to raise the level of world aggregate demand, and dismantling the protection of their markets and the heavy subsidization of agricultural products, which results in the "dumping" of these products in other markets, particularly to the detriment of developing countries.

Nevertheless, such changes in macro and meso policy, while more likely to foster growth, development and structural change, are not guaranteed in and of themselves to improve women's well-being or, more particularly, to promote rapid progress in gender equality. This can only come about if a thorough gender analysis penetrates all levels and branches of government policy making, in order both to detect the gender implications of strategies and policies, and to ascertain at what level or point gender-equitable policy interventions are feasible and effective.

That changes in the macroeconomic framework will not necessarily effect substantial improvement in key aspects of women's well-being becomes evident when one considers labour markets. Labour markets differ significantly from other markets, if only because the labour traded is that of sentient human beings with all their socially constructed identities. It is in this market that gender segmentation, reflecting social values and norms, is most vivid. In many societies the labour market is also the point of entry to many social rights, social integration, and sense of self-worth and dignity.

The extent to which economic growth, structural change and technological upgrading expand women's work opportunities and income-generating capacity depends on two crucial factors. First, it depends on the erosion of norms and removal of discriminations that account for the persistence of gender segmentation in labour markets. But is also depends on the removal of structural constraints on women's ability to take up widening labour market opportunities. Among the most important of these constraints are women's relative lack of education and appropriate skills, and their relatively greater responsibility for the provision of unpaid care. In sum, from a gender perspective, effective labour-market policies must involve more than simply creating more jobs.

If gender inequalities in labour markets are to be rectified, society as a whole has to seek specific means of both progressing towards a better balance between the provision of unpaid care and paid labour, and facilitating greater gender equality in both domains. As section 2 of this report shows, this remains a challenge even in many advanced industrialized countries.

Furthermore, if economic growth is to be broadly shared, it is necessary to introduce a set of labour market policies and related interventions that can affect working conditions in both the formal and informal employment situations. These should not only enhance the capabilities of workers to capture some of the gains, but also rectify gender imbalances and discriminatory practices. Such policies would involve the improvement of core labour standards (which include the prohibition of all forms of discrimination and the principle of equal pay for work of equal value), and the creation of decent conditions of work which include the right to social protection for all workers, formal and informal, and the evolution of "family-friendly" workplace practices. These issues are discussed in the next section of the report.

Government, at both the national and local level, represents a critical locus of resources with which to promote gender equity through expenditures that, for example, expand women's capabilities. Nevertheless, faster growth together with taxation policies that generate higher levels of government income (and are gender-sensitive to the extent possible) do not necessarily lead to a more gender-equitable use of these resources. To ensure that that there is greater gender parity in expenditures on education and health, for example, and that women benefit from mechanisms promoting social security, gender-policy objectives have to be set, and mechanisms put in place, to guarantee that public expenditures are targeted to these areas, and to the provision of infrastructure and services that contribute to a reduction in women's unpaid labour time.

An increased female presence in governmental bodies can contribute to greater government accountability to gender interests. Gender-responsive budget audits are also a means to promote equity. Budget audits can be used to review and analyse national budgets and expenditures to determine which groups benefit from fiscal policies, and whether there are inbuilt biases against women, especially those from low-income families. In these efforts, the ultimate objective is to make macroeconomic policy, and in particular public expenditures, responsive to the needs of women.

Gender budget audits can also examine the likely feedback effects of public expenditures on unpaid work. For example, health care expenditures may be found to redound on women's unpaid labour time. The implementation of user fees for essential goods such as water and electricity may have similar effects. Gender budget audits thus make more transparent the gender effects of such policies, permitting a broader social debate and awareness of the effects of such policy choices. As such, they can serve as an important tool to ensure that public expenditures promote gender equity.

Finally, these changes depend on women's mobilization in different circles and with different objectives. Pressing the ethical or human rights case is not enough, nor is presentation of empirical evidence of gender disparities in capabilities, opportunities and outcomes. In order to improve the prospects for improving women's well-being and achieving gender equality, women's case must be build on rigorous analysis, a clear vision of where appropriate policy interventions need to be made, and effective mobilization demanding states deliver on policy promises to do with gender equality.

Notes

1   Sen 1985, 1999; Nussbaum 2000; Agarwal et al. 2003; Razavi 2000b.

2   Kabeer 1999; Grown and Rao Gupta forthcoming.

3   Grown and Rao Gupta forthcoming; Saith and Harriss-White 1999.

4   Chatterjee 1990 cited in Saith and Harriss-White 1999.

5   Murray 1991.

6   UNICEF 1993:8.

7   Malhotra et al. 2002.

8   UNIFEM 2002.

9   Grown and Rao Gupta forthcoming.

10 UNIFEM 2000, 2002; United Nations 1986, 1989, 1990, 1994, 1995b, 1999, 2000b; UNDP 1995; World Bank 2001a.

11 UNIFEM 2002.

12 Klasen and Wink 2003; Seguino 2002.

13 Klasen and Wink 2003.

14 The Corner House 2004.

15 UNAIDS 2003.

16 Grown and Rao Gupta forthcoming.

17 ECLAC 2004.

18 Grown and Rao Gutpa forthcoming.

19 Cagatay and Ozler 1995; Razavi 2000a; Ghosh 2004b; Jomo 2001.

20 Freeman 2000.

21 Deere 2004.

22 McKinley 2004.

23 Whitehead 2003.

24 World Bank 2001a.

25 Dijkstra 2002.

26 Seguino, Stephanie 2004.

27 Seguino 2002, 2003a.

Section 2
Women, work and
social policy

DOGON WOMEN
LISTEN TO THE RADIO
AS THEY WORK.
DOUENTZA, MALI

Unequal gender relations shape the ways in which families and households allocate resources, influencing the distribution of entitlements and responsibilities, work and leisure, between male and female members. It is less well recognized, especially within mainstream economic analysis, that social hierarchies and gender orderings have similar effects within market institutions. These do not operate in gender-neutral ways despite neoliberal protestations. On the contrary: markets, with all their risks and variable performance, embody gender hierarchies as they are found in society and its institutions. Nor do market institutions recognize the economic value of goods and services that take place outside the cash nexus. Hence, much of the unpaid work women do remains invisible. Market-based entitlements are therefore inherently male-biased.

Unless qualifying measures are introduced which help redress the inbuilt discriminations and vulnerabilities to which liberalized markets expose them, women in the workplace and in their livelihood and caring roles will tend to lose out. The thrust of contemporary neoliberal economic policy, however, has been against the use of regulatory measures to compensate for social risks and redress inequalities, in the name of efficiency, growth and freedom.

Liberalization has certainly opened up new job opportunities for some women, but it has also imposed upon them new burdens and risks. The four chapters in this section examine the impacts on women in different contexts. The first, "The feminization and informalization of labour", reviews women's increasing presence in the non-agricultural work force, while the second, "The changing terms of rural living", examines impacts on agricultural livelihoods. The third, "Cross-border migration of workers", is concerned with the phenomenon of women's growing mobility in search of work; and the final chapter, "The search for a new social policy agenda", explores the insecurities women have suffered from the lack of social protections in the era of liberalization, and examines prospects for realising them.

Chapter 5
The feminization and informalization of labour

Over the past three decades women's economic activity rates have been rising in most parts of the world, as was shown in figure 1.2 and is shown in figure 5.1. There are exceptions to this general global trend, notably in the transitional economies which are part of Eastern Europe as well as Central and Western Asia where there have been notable reversals, and in the Middle East and North Africa (MENA) where they remain very low.[1] But the general trend is towards increasing female visibility in the economic domain, and in some countries women's activity rates are nearing men's. What does the apparent convergence in male and female economic activity rates actually mean? Does it signify the disappearance of gender from the labour market? In other words, is being a man, or a woman, no longer a significant attribute as far as one's entry into the labour force, pattern of employment, labour market status, and access to pay and welfare benefits are concerned? Another question that arises from the increase in female labour force participation is whether this has had an equalizing affect on the gender division of unpaid domestic and care work.

The evidence explored in chapter 3 suggests that, while there have been important changes in women's work patterns—notably the increase in work for pay—labour markets continue to be segmented by gender, as well as by factors such as race, caste and ethnicity which intersect with gender. Labour market segmentation does not disappear with modernization and growth, as the experience in the Organization for Economic Co-operation and Development (OECD) countries clearly illustrates. As labour markets restructure and modernize, there are invariably both changes and continuities. However, the recent intensification of women's paid work has been paralleled by processes of deregulation in the conditions of work, as well as outsourcing and fragmentation of international supply chains.

The first key issue concerning women's participation in the labour market is the way in which their employment has to accommodate their paramount role in the unpaid domestic and care economy. Even in industrialized countries where this type of work is shifting to institutions other than the family, the paid care undertaken in hospitals, crèches and homes for the elderly is a small part of all care work done in a society. The fact that this work is almost exclusively performed by women has repercussions for female employment; it tends to penalize working women and is key to their weak position in terms of earnings and occupational status.[2] Although many regard caring as a fulfilling occupation, in households where incomes are low and amenities few, women's caring load can be disproportionately high and, where it includes food and utility provision, costly. Policy concerns therefore include the need not only for more and better work opportunities for women, but to ease their domestic and care burden through better provision of basic services, and to encourage a fairer male–female distribution of unpaid work.

However, even when women are included in the labour market, women and men tend to be segregated into different occupations (what is often referred to as horizontal segregation). Women are also more likely than men to be in occupations with lower pay, poorer working conditions, and worse prospects for advancement (vertical segregation). This is one of the main reasons why labour market segregation is so pernicious. Authoritative research finds that, despite some improvements

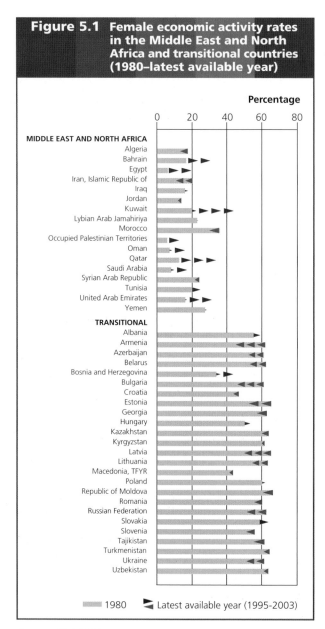

Figure 5.1 Female economic activity rates in the Middle East and North Africa and transitional countries (1980–latest available year)

Source: ILO 2003.

in the 1990s, levels of gender segregation in the labour market remain high throughout the world.[3] Women tend to congregate in relatively low-paid and low-status work at the bottom of the occupational hierarchy, and also to have little job security. Reducing gender segregation requires proactive state intervention in areas such as special training for women and anti-discrimination legislation; as well as the promotion of women

employees' needs and rights within authoritative workers' organizations capable of demanding accountability from governments and employers.

The final gender considerations related to women's workforce participation and earning are the potential repercussions on their personal relations at work and at home. Earning money in any amount for the first time may not alter certain characteristics of gender subordination, such as women's dependence on male protection; but it may reduce their dependence on male provision, and enhance their economic security and say in household decisions. For younger women it could mean greater mobility, the chance to postpone marriage, and a bit of discretionary income. Their new-found value can also affect how women are treated, as well as their feelings of self-worth.[4] These gains notwithstanding, there are reasons for caution in equating women's paid work with empowerment. As already noted, women may find their total workload increasing without any change in care responsibilities. There are also instances where men reduce their contribution to the household budget, especially in places where it is common for fathers not to live with their children, as in South Africa and some parts of the Caribbean.[5]

NORTH AND SOUTH: CONVERGING AND COMPETING?

The global economy, as pointed out in Chapter 2, is operating substantially below capacity and levels of unemployment are becoming more severe. Unemployment rates in most OECD countries are very high, as is open unemployment in developing countries. This marks a change: typically, developing countries have had lower open unemployment rates while disguised unemployment or underemployment has generally been more prevalent. The change therefore suggests that the problem of finding jobs has become so acute that it is now captured in such data.

Another common pattern is the global trend whereby work is becoming increasingly informal and casual, although the extent of convergence between patterns in North and South should not be exaggerated. The "informal economy" includes both self-employment in small and unregistered enterprises, and wage employment without secure contracts, benefits or legal protection; this economy is growing in importance worldwide, both in its proportion of total employment and in the number of informal enterprises.[6] Even in developed economies, fewer workers have secure contracts, and many in formal employment are losing work-related social benefits, such as health insurance and pension provision.[7] In much of sub-Saharan Africa and South Asia, and in such Latin American countries as Bolivia, Ecuador, Peru and Mexico, only a fraction of the workforce has ever been engaged in formal employment. But in countries such as Argentina and Chile whose labour markets had come to resemble those of the industrialized world, factories have closed, public sector employment has been cut, real wages have fallen, and increasing numbers of households have become dependent on the informal and unregulated economy.[8]

This trend was unforeseen. In the 1960s and 1970s, it was assumed that the worldwide development of the modern economy would shrink and absorb informal activity, as had happened historically in the industrialized countries. The subsequent extensive growth of the informal economy has reversed such expectations; instead, the global economy has shown a tendency to encourage precarious forms of work which do not bring in sufficient earnings to meet subsistence. In spite of this deepening phenomenon, work and employment currently receive relatively little attention internationally, except, importantly, from the International Labour Organization (ILO); this is even the case within the poverty reduction agenda of the last decade. Indeed, employment hardly features in the Millennium Development Goals.

Finally, while the effects of global integration on workers in the South have been regarded, by trade economists at least, as positive for developing countries, the available evidence is ambiguous.[9] For the vast majority of developing countries, manufacturing employment has actually stagnated or declined over the past decade, while the growth in manufacturing activities and employment has been confined to a handful of countries: China, Malaysia, Indonesia, Thailand and Chile. The rapid surge in imports associated with trade liberalization is responsible for manufactur-

ing's poor performance elsewhere, as cheap, newly deregulated imported goods have displaced those made by small-scale, employment-intensive domestic producers unable to compete in international markets. Job losses from import competition have been significant in some developing countries, and has not be compensated for by the opening up of export employment.[10]

Some advocates of trade liberalization argue that women in the South have emerged as winners in the new manufacturing employment scenario. But the picture is not straightforward. Wherever export-oriented manufacturing industries have grown (including in China, Malaysia, Bangladesh, Mexico and Thailand), women have been disproportionately absorbed into their workforces. And even though the working conditions and terms of pay in many of these factories are poor by international standards, they are usually better than in the urban and rural informal economy. However, these positive considerations concerning expanding female employment opportunities need to be qualified.

In the first place, as chapter 3 has shown, as these industries have upgraded, matured, and needed a higher skilled workforce, there has been a widespread defeminization of labour.[11] There has also been a strong tendency in industries with a largely female workforce, especially garment manufacturing, towards deregulation and subcontracting; this often leads to the extensive use of homeworkers, one of the most invisible groups in the informal economy (see below). Finally, jobs that are destroyed as a result of import liberalization are not only those occupied by the male "labour aristocracy" in state-owned or state-protected industries, but include jobs held by women. These may be in the state-owned sector as in China, or informal forms of work in small-scale and labour-intensive local enterprises.[12]

WOMEN'S EMPLOYMENT IN OECD COUNTRIES: CONTINUITY AND CHANGE [13]

In the OECD countries, women's labour force participation has been rising as industrialization and urbanization have drawn women into the formal workforce, albeit unevenly across countries.[14] In some, women's employment rates are nearing men's.

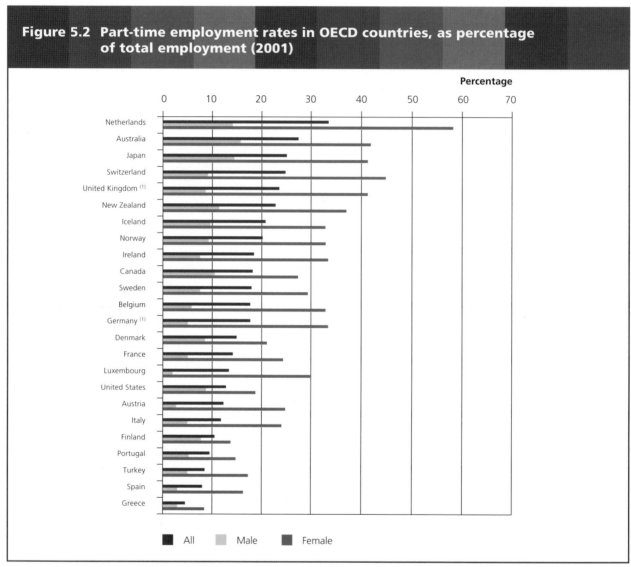

Figure 5.2 Part-time employment rates in OECD countries, as percentage of total employment (2001)

Note: (1) Data for 2000.
Source: ILO 2003.

Women are also being drawn into the informal economy where this kind of activity is significant, most notably in southern Europe. The trend of going to work is most noticeable among mothers with young children, the group most likely to drop out of employment in the post-Second World War period. However, workforce participation rates are crude indicators of working women's situations. They reveal nothing about the intensity of men's and women's employment (part-time versus full-time), their relative contribution to paid and unpaid work,

or about different patterns of lifetime participation. These factors complicate the picture.

First, women are under pressure to limit their paid economic activity. In all these countries caring and household work remains predominantly with women, many of whom subordinate employment to family responsibilities. In many countries, some of the care burden of children, the sick and the elderly is shifting to institutions other than the family, but women still have to shoulder a time-consuming household load. Thus many work part-time or drop out of the labour force altogether at far higher rates than men. Even in the Nordic countries where levels of formal participation are highest, many mothers of young children technically in the labour force are actually on parental leave; few men take up their parental leave entitlements. Moreover, where care work is bought in—nannies, nurses, cleaners, minders—it is usually done by women, often from racial or ethnic minorities (see chapter 7). It is invariably underpaid relative to "male" occupations involving similar levels of competence.

Thus the gender division of labour is not disappearing, but modernizing, as women enter the labour force and stay in employment for greater portions of their lives. It is now sometimes argued that gender difference is increasingly based on time, with men working full-time and women working part-time (see figure 5.2). This has replaced the older gender distinction between men's participation in paid work and women's full-time domesticity and absence from the labour market. There is variation in the quality of the work women engage in between countries, as well as in the mix of paid and unpaid work, but the basic pattern is the same: men "specialize" in paid work while doing little at home; women do the bulk of unpaid work, increasingly in combination with employment. There are different views over whether women work more hours overall. The evidence suggests that certain groups of women are hard-pressed, for example employed mothers who work a "second shift" at home.[15]

According to recent ILO estimates, three categories of non-standard or atypical work comprise 30 per cent of overall employment in 15 European countries, and 25 per cent of total employment in the United States: self-employment, part-time work (in which women predominate), and temporary work.[16] This cannot be equated with informal work in developing countries; some of it takes place under contract and falls under the scope of labour legislation. Work of this kind may be a deliberate choice by male and female workers with resources, skills and other options. Part-time and temporary workers are often employed by regular firms and institutions. Nevertheless, atypical workers have fewer protections and benefits than full-time employees, although there are differences between countries. Part-time workers are more likely to be eligible for benefits in Europe than in North America or Japan.[17]

There is also a rising trend of irregular, informal and hidden employment in many industrialized countries. This kind of work is usually undertaken by immigrant women and men, many of whom are undocumented (see chapter 7). It is therefore extremely difficult to obtain reliable figures concerning its extent or the situation of women as opposed to men employees.

Finally, it is important to underline the fact that there is still a substantial earnings gap between men and women in OECD countries, despite an EU policy mindset which assumes that women, like men, work full-time and are financially independent.[18] This is partly because so many women work part-time; but there are also earnings gaps among full-time workers, as table 5.1 clearly shows. These reflect occupational segregation and the fact that "women's jobs" earn lower wages. Interestingly, younger women seem to have much higher relative earnings, which may indicate progress over time toward gender parity. But it may also reflect the fact that the youngest cohorts have not yet entered the prime childrearing years, when women are under greater pressure to scale back on employment in ways that often result in lower pay.

WOMEN'S EMPLOYMENT IN EASTERN AND CENTRAL EUROPE: CRISIS AND DECLINE

The situation with regard to female employment in the formerly centralized command economies of Eastern and Central Europe has undergone more radical shifts, and some reversals. Prior to 1989, these countries had achieved remarkably high rates of female labour-force participation, despite gender segregation of jobs, modest gender wage gaps, and an unchanged distribution of household responsibilities. After the socialist regimes collapsed and economies were liberalized, there was a radical and alarming decline in employment and activity rates for both men and women. During the course of economic transformation, around one-third of all jobs were lost, leading to widespread unemployment. At the same time, state welfare systems

Table 5.1	Women's average annual income/earnings as a percentage of men's, by age groups for full-time, full-year workers in the mid to late 1990s						
	Total 15+	**15–24**	**25–34**	**35–44**	**45–54**	**55–64**	**65+**
Austria	74.9	88.1	80.6	73.4	73.4	65.7	53.0
Canada	73.1	82.5	78.2	74.8	69.9	62.4	–
Denmark	82.8	–	–	–	–	–	–
Finland	77.6	79.5	81.7	74.5	74.7	75.4	–
Ireland	65.0	–	–	–	–	–	–
Italy	81.2	93.9	88.9	79.7	80.2	80.2	67.8
Netherlands	71.2	88.6	86.6	84.1	75.5	77.6	–
Norway [1]	71.2	85.1	71.6	73.4	67.7	79.2	–
Spain	77.9	77.9	85.9	82.1	73.8	63.9	34.4
Sweden	78.7	84.2	80.2	77.4	76.4	76.6	–
Switzerland [2]	76.4	95.1	87.2	80.9	69.6	72.3	–
United Kingdom [3]	73.8	–	–	–	–	–	–
United States [2]	68.0	87.2	81.1	69.6	63.5	53.5	54.8

Notes   (1) Youngest age group is 16–24.
            (2) Median annual income.
            (3) Average weekly earnings; figure refers to Great Britain.
Source: Orloff 2002.

were dismantled. As the real value of wages declined, social benefits were being reduced, pensions lost their value, inequalities increased, and poverty became visible and deepened. Complicating the economic and social crisis, an ideological backlash ensued against the kind of "emancipation" fostered by regimes of the communist era, with worrying implications for gender equality prospects.

In this turbulent and traditionalist-resurgent context, questions were raised about women's ability to maintain their presence in the public sphere. By the early 1990s there had already been reversals in women's labour-force participation. Women were facing new—or perhaps old but previously disguised—forms of discrimination and higher rates of unemployment than men, while benefits for employed mothers were being cut.[19] Were these apprehensions of women's loss of hold in the labour market borne out by subsequent developments?

Apart from Slovenia, the three countries in the region exhibiting the highest level of economic prosperity, the most streamlined progress towards liberal democracy, and the quickest transition into the EU are the Czech Republic, Hungary and Poland. However, concern has been expressed about the "male democracies" taking shape in the region, maybe precisely because of their rapid integration into the globalizing world.[20]

Employment and activity rates for both men and women declined sharply after 1990 and are very low in two of the three countries (Poland and Hungary) (see table 5.2). Czech women have had most success in staying economically active, probably because employment retrenchment in the Czech Republic was generally milder than in the other two countries.[21] Polish women, with a higher rate of inactivity in 1989 than women in the other countries, were less likely to be employed or active in 2001. The low levels of economic activity in Hungary are particularly worrying, especially as far as women with lower qualifications are concerned (see box 5.1). In addition to the mass disappearance of jobs in the early 1990s, high rates of inactivity have been attributed to the legacy of an early retirement age, and generous maternity/parental leave policies which encouraged mothers (but not fathers) to leave work. Women's activity rates are well below the EU average (60 per cent), or even the

Table 5.2   Activity rates and female/male mean wage ratio, Czech Republic, Hungary and Poland

| | Activity rates (percentage of population aged 15 to 64) | | | | Female/male mean wage ratio | | |
| | Male | | Female | | | | |
	1990	2001	1990	2001	1988–1989	1995–1996	1999–2000
Czech Republic	—	71.9	—	67.9	70.6	78.3	73.8
Hungary	83.8	67.8	75.9	52.4	72.1	80.2	80.1
Poland [1]	74.3 [2]	64.3	57.0 [2]	49.7	70.8 [3]	64.9	65.2 [4]

Notes: (1) Wages for white-collars only; (2) Data for 1988; (3) Data for 1985; (4) Data for 1985.
Sources: Pollert 2003; Fultz et al. 2003, cited in Fodor 2004b.

average of the EU accession countries. This is a new phenomenon in Hungary where the drop was the sharpest; in Poland it represents a continuation of earlier trends. Only the Czech Republic maintains a relatively high, if reduced, female activity rate at 68 per cent.

Low economic activity rates cause obvious problems. Few families relying on only one wage enjoy a decent standard of living; thus women's lack of gainful employment may expose a family to poverty. In Poland and Hungary, studies show a significantly higher risk of poverty in households with inactive members; the typical poor family consists of a working husband and an "inactive" wife raising young children. In addition, high divorce rates and inadequate social provisions for mothers on their own, place women outside the labour force in a particularly vulnerable position.

Despite some common patterns across the three countries, there are also some notable diversities in gender hierarchies. In Poland, emphasis on women's domestic roles and a long history of women's labour market disadvantage assigns most women to the household. Women do work, but unemployment is rampant, the gender wage gap is significant, and women seem to have difficulty gaining positions of workplace authority. Since 1989, the Church has strongly influenced social policy, in particular decisions about abortion and contraception, and loudly favours traditional family values and gender roles.[22]

In the Czech Republic, the economic transformation process was slower and less radical than in the other two countries.

Here, women are more likely to be economically active, but they occupy low-level positions at a distinct disadvantage to men. The position of Hungarian women is sharply divided along class and ethnic lines. This differentiation also exists in the other two countries, but the presence of the Roma in Hungary makes social exclusion along the lines of gender, as well as race and class, more visible. Middle class women, especially those who are young, childless and well-educated, have managed to gain or retain their positions in the labour market and win social rights which help them combine paid and household work. Those in low-income groups are left behind, economically inactive, forced into early retirement or welfare subsistence.

In countries in the region where the transition has been more traumatic, many people previously employed in public enterprises or the bureaucracy are now engaged in the informal economy, often in home-based work.[23] Some have been retrenched from the public sector but are entitled to a minimum pension; others may retain a public-sector post but on wages that are too low to cover the rising cost of survival. Members of minority and migrant populations tend to fall into the poorest categories: for example Kosovar and Roma women in Serbia, and Polish women in Lithuania. These women are often excluded from the more lucrative niches in the informal economy, and are forced to manage on very few financial and social resources.

Box 5.1 Women outside the labour market in Hungary

The rate of economic inactivity in Hungary is high and on the rise. From 1.5 million women aged 15–64 in 1999, the number had gone up to 1.7 million in 2001, from 41 to 48 per cent of the age group. (The corresponding rates for men were 23 per cent in 1999 and 34 per cent in 2001.) All age groups are represented, and the majority have very low qualifications. The declared reasons for women not to be working include seeking education (27 per cent), undertaking childcare (21 per cent), and taking early retirement (27 per cent); a quarter give no reason. In 2002, other than those in education or near retirement, the great majority said that they would like to work—far more than the number of active job-seekers. Re-entry into the formal labour market is not easy however, as many companies have been liquidated and former employers are not able to take their ex-employees back. Return is particularly difficult for those who have spent a long spell outside the labour market. Few people can afford to pay for childcare, care for the sick or elderly, or domestic help. Meanwhile most households need a second earner. So those women who are able, undertake a variety of casual work—gardening, taking care of children or older people, cleaning—in their vicinity for a few hours a day or week, bypassing the formal economy. Those engaging in such work are poor, live on a pension or childcare assistance, and so grasp any opportunity they can. The rate of pay has little to do with the official minimum wage. The segmentation of the labour market in Hungary is deep, with few passageways between the unrecognized informal economy and the formal workplace.

Source: Laky 2004.

MIDDLE EAST AND NORTH AFRICA: STALLED INDUSTRIALIZATION AND DIVERSIFICATION

Although the MENA region is often studied as an integrated whole (due to certain shared cultural, religious and historical characteristics, and the prevalence of oil economies), it includes three distinct types of economy: the oil economies (such as Kuwait and Saudi Arabia); the mixed oil economies (such as Algeria, Islamic Republic of Iran, Iraq and Tunisia); and the non-oil economies (such as Jordan, Morocco and Turkey). Women's labour-force participation and access to paid employment in the region are lower than those reported for other developing regions, although they have been rising in recent years (see figure 5.1).

As part of state-directed industrialization during the 1970s and 1980s, the formal sector in most countries in MENA was largely made up of government agencies and state-owned enterprises. High wages and generous social policies for employees were made possible by state oil revenues, and by the capital and labour flows between countries (for example, remittances of workers from non-oil countries working in the oil or mixed-oil economy countries). At the same time, income taxes were among the lowest in the world. A detailed comparative study of wage trends has established that the wages of manufacturing workers were higher in most of these countries than in Asian countries such as the Republic of Korea, Malaysia and the Philippines.[24]

The political economy of oil, however, was a mixed blessing. It weakened accountability mechanisms between the citizens and the state, allowing authoritarian states to dominate the economy and society. There were also important implications as far as employment opportunities and lack of economic diversification were concerned. High wages for male workers, large-scale male migration from the non-oil countries to the oil-rich countries, remittances sent back by (male) migrant workers, and the cultural and legal sanction given to the "male breadwinner" ideal, all served to suppress women's employment. In some labour-sending countries, labour shortages led to a new dependence of the agricultural sector on women workers. But overall, the region did not exhibit the levels of female labour-force participation developing in Southeast Asia or parts of Latin America.

Employed women in the region were professionals, mostly in the social sector. Compared with other parts of the world, women were under-represented in production jobs, clerical and sales work, and administrative and managerial positions.

The ramifications of the near-collapse of oil prices in 1986 (from US$28 per barrel to US$7 per barrel) were widespread. Governments put in place austerity measures, and tried to shift from a state-directed development strategy with large public sectors to a growth strategy favouring the expansion of the private sector. Export industrialization was also encouraged. In Morocco and Tunisia, as well as in Turkey, there has been a significant absorption of women into manufacturing for export. Outside North Africa and Turkey, modern manufacturing industries for export have failed to take hold. In Islamic Republic of Iran, significant numbers of women are recorded in census figures as working in manufacturing, but this is predominantly informal activity, rural and family-based, such as rug-weaving and handicrafts.

The impacts of the changing political economy on female employment and gender hierarchies in labour markets have been mixed. Some trends stand out and need to be studied more closely. First, there has been an increase in the supply of job-seeking women, and an emergence of very high rates of unemployment among women (see table 5.3).

Another is the expansion of women's non-governmental organizations (NGOs), which appear to be playing important roles culturally, politically and socially, while also providing employment opportunities for women who might otherwise not find them in the government or private sectors.

The contraction of public-sector employment has contributed heavily to job losses, especially in the former state-owned enterprises, but women have been surprisingly little affected. In the Islamic Republic of Iran, for example, women's share of civil service employment grew from 30 per cent in 1986 to 38 per cent in 1996. Throughout the region, there is an increasing presence of women in government employment. The feminization of the civil service seems to be linked to two factors: the rising educational attainment of women, and the downgrading of the public sector and gravitation of men into

Table 5.3 Unemployment rates, selected MENA countries, 1990s

Country	Year	Male (per cent)	Female (per cent)	Total (per cent)
Algeria	1992	24.2	20.3	23.8
	1997	26.9	24.0	26.4
	2001	-	-	27.3
Bahrain	1991	5.5	13.4	6.8
Egypt	1995	7.0	22.1	10.4
Iran, Islamic Republic of (urban)	1991	8.9	21.5	14.5
	1996	8.3	12.5	10.2
Jordan	1991	14.4	34.1	17.1
	1994	12.9	28.3	15.0
	1997	11.7	28.5	14.4
	2000 (Nov.)	12.6	19.8	13.7
Lebanon	1996	8.6	7.2	7.0
Morocco (urban)	1992	13.0	25.3	16.0
	1998	17.4	22.9	18.7
Oman	1993	4.7	8.7	5.1
Syrian Arab Republic	1981	3.2	2.0	3.0
	1991	5.2	14.0	6.8
	1995	5.1	11.6	6.5
Tunisia	1993	14.7	21.9	16.1
Yemen	1991	14.0	6.0	12.3
	1994	10.1	5.4	9.1

Sources: World Bank 1995a:5; ERF 1996:103; ERF 1998:128; ESCWA 2000:37; ILO 1999; Moghadam 1998; Yemen Ministry of Planning & Development 1998; Jordan Department of Statistics various dates; IRI 1993:table 8, p.64; IRI 1997:table 3-1, p.70; Republique Algerienne 2000; World Bank 2004a, cited in Moghadam 2004.

the expanding and more lucrative private sector. The jobs obtained by women are not necessarily at high levels: they have minimal presence in administrative and managerial positions. In the late 1990s, the percentages ranged from a low of under 6 per cent in Algeria, Islamic Republic of Iran, Jordan, Kuwait and Syrian Arab Republic, to 10–13 per cent in Egypt, Tunisia and Turkey.[25]

One distinctive feature, long noted by researchers, is women's disinclination to enter sales work and service occupations in the private sector, confirmed by wage employment data showing their under-representation in retailing, services, hotels and restaurants. Women's "avoidance" of these occupations has been explained in terms of cultural norms, as these are occupations with the highest likelihood of indiscriminate contact with male outsiders. But the traditional urban markets—bazaars or souks—are the province of a male merchant class and imbued by a masculinist and elitist culture. Thus exclusionary forces operating through male networks are even more likely than women's own "disinclination" to have kept them out of this domain. Some change is under way, however. In Tunisia, for example, women are finding their way into the more open niches, and gender divisions are slowly melting away.

Challenges facing women in the labour market besides high rates of unemployment are structural weaknesses in the economies; widening within-country inequalities; continued high rates of illiteracy in some countries (such as Egypt, Iraq, Morocco, Syrian Arab Republic and Yemen); and the gap between anachronistic laws and norms and the realities of women's lives. In Tunisia, furthermore, women's employment and access to social programmes could be undermined when the Free Trade Agreement with the EU comes into effect in 2007. The elimination of tariff barriers may increase imports and trade deficits, diminish state revenue from tariffs, and adversely affect the social welfare programmes administered by the state, as well as retrench thousands of women workers.

Anecdotal accounts and ethnographic studies suggest that self-employment and other forms of informal work—both high-end and low-end—have been expanding, as different groups of women search for a toe-hold in a differentiated informal economy. However, more qualitative and quantitative studies are needed to determine the extent and types of informal activities that women (and men) are undertaking, the constraints they face, and how gender hierarchies interact with other types of segmentation within the informal economy.

THE INFORMAL ECONOMY

The informal economy is sometimes defined in terms of what it is not: economic activity and enterprises that are not registered, not regulated, and do not pay taxes. But it is being increasingly recognized that registered companies which belong to the formal economy may also engage workers on their own premises on an informal basis, without secure contracts, worker benefits or legal protection. They also have complex subcontracting arrangements whereby individual homeworkers are informally employed. Finally, some of those who are "self-employed" are highly vulnerable; "self-employment" is a category covering a great range of contractual conditions, including thinly disguised forms of wage labour.[26]

At the 2002 International Labour Conference, therefore, a new and broader definition of the informal economy was endorsed, which accommodates this diversity. The new concept of "informal employment" defines it as employment without secure contracts, worker benefits or social protection, and encompasses the following situations:

- self-employment in *informal enterprises* (that is, small and/or unregistered enterprises)
  - employers
  - own-account workers
  - unpaid contributing family members
- wage employment in *informal jobs* (that is, without secure contracts, worker benefits or legal protection)
  - employees of informal enterprises
  - informal wage workers for formal firms or households: casual day labourers, domestic workers, contract workers, temporary and part-time workers (without protection).[27]

The ILO has recently provided a statistical picture of the informal economy, which helps shed light on the male–female share of informal employment, job status and incomes earned.[28] Some of the findings are summarized below.

In developing countries

- Informal employment comprises one half to three-quarters of non-agricultural employment: 48 per cent in North Africa, 51 per cent in Latin America, 65 per cent in Asia, 72 per cent in sub-Saharan Africa (table 5.4).
- Informal employment tends to be a larger source of employment for women than for men in all developing regions except North Africa (table 5.4).
- Self-employment comprises a greater share of informal employment (outside agriculture) than wage employment in all developing regions. In most countries this share is greater for women than for men (table 5.5).

- Although women's labour force participation rates are lower than men's, the limited data available point to the importance of women in home-based work and street vending.
- Those who work in the informal economy are generally not covered by labour legislation for social protection and earn less, on average, than workers in the formal economy.

Women in all parts of the world speak of the advantages—notably the flexibility—of part-time and home-based work. But this type of labour market adaptation is generally one-sided, derived from the needs of employers to access workers whose domestic responsibilities would otherwise exclude them.[29] Much of this work is low-paid and insecure. Typically there are no contractual rights to paid leave, for sickness, maternity or vacation. Nor are pension rights included. There is an assumption that a husband or son will provide support for the retired worker in her old age.[30] Even the presumed advantages of "flexible" work—accommodation of women's caring responsibilities—may be less relevant in settings where the potential domestic pool is

Table 5.4 Informal employment in non-agricultural employment, by sex, different regions and selected countries (1994–2000)

Region /country	Informal employment as percentage of non-agricultural employment	Women's informal employment as percentage of women's non-agricultural employment	Men's informal employment as percentage of men's non-agricultural employment
North Africa	**48**	**43**	**49**
Algeria	43	41	43
Egypt	55	46	57
Sub-Saharan Africa	**72**	**84**	**63**
Chad	74	95	60
Kenya	72	83	59
South Africa	51	58	44
Latin America	**51**	**58**	**48**
Bolivia	63	74	55
Brazil	60	67	55
Chile	36	44	31
El Salvador	57	69	46
Mexico	55	55	54
Asia	**65**	**65**	**65**
India	83	86	83
Indonesia	78	77	78
Thailand	51	54	49
Syrian Arab Republic	42	35	43

Source: ILO 2002b.

Table 5.5 Wage and self-employment in the non-agricultural informal sector by sex, different regions and selected countries (1994–2000)

Country/region	Self-employment as percentage of non-agricultural informal employment			Wage employment as a percentage of non-agricultural informal employment		
	Total	Women	Men	Total	Women	Men
North Africa	**62**	**72**	**60**	**38**	**28**	**40**
Algeria	67	81	64	33	19	36
Egypt	50	67	47	50	33	53
Sub-Saharan Africa	**70**	**71**	**70**	**30**	**29**	**30**
Chad	93	99	86	7	1	14
Kenya	42	33	56	58	67	44
South Africa	25	27	23	75	73	77
Latin America	**60**	**58**	**61**	**40**	**42**	**39**
Bolivia	81	91	71	19	9	29
Brazil	41	32	50	59	68	50
Chile	52	39	64	48	61	36
El Salvador	65	71	57	35	29	43
Mexico	54	53	54	46	47	46
Asia	**59**	**63**	**55**	**41**	**37**	**45**
India	52	57	51	48	43	49
Indonesia	63	70	59	37	30	41
Thailand	66	68	64	34	32	36
Syrian Arab Republic	65	57	67	35	43	33

Source: ILO 2002b.

wide, paid domestic labour is cheap, and where many women are the sole income earners within their households.[31]

Rural migrants entering the urban informal economy

A more in-depth gendered analysis of the informal economy can be gained by drawing on a range of relevant case studies. Rural impoverishment has historically contributed to migration into urban areas and continues to do so. Migrants come from all strata of society, and those who have capital, skills and contacts tend to go furthest and do best.[32] Women who migrate are often seen as "associational", simply accompanying their husbands: in India, for example, even though female migrants predominate, only 1 per cent are recorded as migrating for employment. However

wives do look for work, returning home if they fail, and the many who stay are migrants in their own right.[33] Women's patterns of migration can also change rapidly depending on workplace opportunity, as has recently happened in Bangladesh.[34]

The employment of young, rural, migrant women in export-oriented manufacturing industries has been studied extensively over the past decade, with conflicting interpretations of what such employment means to the women involved. However, a much larger contingent of women can be found on the lowest, least visible rung of the informal employment ladder. Many lack the skills and connections needed to secure more stable jobs with decent pay. They usually live in slum housing without even the most basic amenities, and are often at the mercy of local "strongmen".[35]

Particularly pertinent in the context of an overall concern with liberalization is a study in Dhaka (Bangladesh) comparing pay and working conditions of women workers in export garment industries with those of women working for domestic markets.[36] Compared with those working for the export industry, the working conditions of those employed in non-export firms were much less formalized. They rarely received a contract letter of any sort (4 per cent), maternity leave (18 per cent), overtime pay (8 per cent) or medical care at work (13 per cent). Women in export garment-industry jobs, especially those employed in the Export Processing Zones, tend to be younger, from distinctly better-off backgrounds, and better educated; primary-school qualification is needed for entry.

The majority of women working in the domestic informal economy, whether self-employed or waged, were clustered in a limited range of occupations. Those in waged work were concentrated in domestic service, casual manual work (often on construction sites), and small-scale manufacturing; the self-employed had small shops or tailoring businesses, or were vendors in petty trade. Over half (52 per cent) had been without work for some period of the past year, a serious problem for informal workers. Their shorter working hours, compared to the long hours put in by export garment workers, were not indicative of an active choice on their part. Casual work, while more flexible than factory work, often entails high levels of underemployment, which means fluctuating and low earnings.

In Bangladesh the export garment industry has been nurtured by national capital under the protection of the Multi-Fibre Arrangement (MFA), providing jobs to 1.5 million women (1.8 million workers altogether).[37] Although working conditions in many of these factories are below international standards, the expansion of employment for women in a highly patriarchal society has been judged positively by many observers and by women workers interviewed by researchers.[38] In other countries, however, global integration has not produced dynamic export industries, nor has it lured global firms to tap into a potentially vast labour force. Many countries in Africa have experienced de-industrialization, while extractive sectors (mining and logging) and trading activities have grown. Even in the early 1990s, while trading constituted 50 per cent of enterprise in Swaziland, more than 60 per cent in Botswana and close to 70 per cent in Kenya and South Africa, manufacturing only

constituted 17 per cent in South Africa and Botswana, and 35 per cent in Lesotho. Zimbabwe was exceptional with a high manufacturing component of 65 per cent, but liberalization has since pushed Zimbabwe increasingly into trade.[39] Export-oriented industries have failed to take hold, and much of women's work is in trading and services rather than in manufacturing.[40]

Many women in the urban informal economy in sub-Saharan Africa are working for others, or have done so at some stage. These employer/employee relations within the urban informal economy have been described as "ubiquitous and vicious networks of micro-exploitation of the poor exploiting the very poor".[41] An example is the female head porters or *kayaye* in urban markets in southern Ghana. Most are young women migrants from rural areas in northern Ghana, eking out a living portering goods on their heads at the service of sellers or purchasers (see box 5.2). Low growth in the "lost decade" of 1980s in Latin America led to the expansion of open unemployment, as well as the accelerated expansion of low quality employment, mostly in informal activities. During the 1980s and 1990s, eight out of every ten new jobs created were in the informal sector, while the 1999 manufacturing wage was only 3 percent higher than its 1980 counterpart.[42]

Both Ecuador and Bolivia, for example, have seen a rapid expansion in their non-farm informal economies in the last decade, as an outcome of severe macroeconomic and financial crises and restructuring. Global integration has taken place, but without an expanding export-oriented manufacturing sector or foreign capital inflows. A recent survey highlights the extensive nature of informal work, its variability in incomes, and the high vulnerability for the workers concerned, especially women.[43] In the low-income urban communities surveyed, only 18–20 per cent of workers were formally employed, and they were predominantly men. Women were typically engaged in small-scale domestic production in traditional crafts, furniture, shoes, leather and garments; these informal markets have recently suffered from the invasion of large amounts of second-hand products, mostly from the United States. El Alto, a de facto annex to the city of La Paz (Bolivia's capital), has become the quintessential indigenous "informal city", with the great majority of its inhabitants surviving from microenterprises,

---

Box 5.2   *Kayaye* in Ghana: The poor exploiting the very poor

Commercial head-loading by girls and women known as *kayaye* is commonplace in large towns and city areas in Ghana, where women traders and buyers employ these women to move their goods between purchasing points and transport facilities. Head-load portering is women's work in Ghana as elsewhere in Africa, while portering by men involves the use of wheeled equipment such as a hand-pulled cart or wheelbarrow.

The female portering trade depends on a network of ethnic ties. These facilitate the migration of girls from rural areas and their incorporation into city life, supplying them with accommodation, working tools and access to savings schemes. Most are from northern Ghana, the most economically deprived region in the country; the majority of the *kayaye* in Accra, for example, come from northern Ghana and spend six months to a year in the city. They maintain close ties with their families and send them part of their income. They share accommodation and form savings clubs as part of their strategy to survive.

Kayaye typically live in wooden sheds around the markets. These are used for trading by day, and as shelter when the trading day is over. They pay a fee and sleep on cardboard, sacks or on a piece of cloth. Only at night can they use the sheds for sleeping, so they have difficulty storing their belongings and caring for their children. Mothers leave their children in the care of girls aged as young as six, who operate as child minders before graduating into porterage themselves. The *kayayes'* housing situation makes them vulnerable to sexual abuse.

Kayaye are members of a growing urban homeless contingent. After porterage and petty trading, commercial sex is the next most popular activity among females in this category. *Kayaye* may also engage in commercial sex work at night to augment their meagre earnings. Children as young as ten are involved in commercial sex, for which there is a high demand. Just as these girls are not able to demand fair wages for their services as porters, they are not able to negotiate safe sex or reasonable wages for sex. They rarely have access to reproductive health services, including safe abortions.

Source: UNICEF 2002.

---

street vending and similar activities. In both countries, the informal economy is dominated by low-return and low-productivity activities pursued as a means of survival.

Perpetuation of informality to disguise real employment

In many parts of the world, types of employment relationship are emerging that are purposely disguised as something else, or not clearly defined. Recruitment into more secure positions tends to be selective, drawing on male candidates with their higher educational qualifications and other advantages; successful applicants for jobs are also often from socially privileged or ethnically favoured groups. Women cannot transcend the many biases against them and remain locked into the casual workforce.

Box 5.3 describes the process of labour segmentation in agro-processing in south India. In many such situations, although there is clearly an employment relationship, the worker is not covered by labour legislation, and receives no social benefits. In other cases there may be a contract, but the relationship is deliberately disguised as commercial transaction. This is done so that the employer can sidestep labour legislation and avoid even basic occupational health and safety responsibilities, not to mention social benefits. A variation is to acknowledge the employment, but to hire the same worker on repeated short-term contracts—"permanent temporary work"—so that social benefits and customary entitlements can be denied.

There are also cases where the employment relationship is ambiguous: for example, where dependent workers operate at home on a piece-rate basis rather than attend an organized work-

Box 5.3	Stratified markets in south India entrench insecurity

In small south Indian towns dominated by agro-processing activity there are several fault lines in the security of labour. The typical informal unit is tightly controlled by patriarchal male family members who confer or withdraw security at their whim. Workers are selected by origin (local), caste (usually avoiding Scheduled Castes) and gender (male). There are a number of permanent jobs, highly sought after, in livelihoods ranging from the night watch to accountancy. Contracts are individualized and verbal. Payment periods vary, and may be confined to yearly disbursement, while dismissal is instant. Some permanent jobs can be part-time, others seasonal. A form of occupational welfare is usually extended to this workforce in the form of loans and gifts of cash for medical costs, education and marriages. These can be seen as primitive imitations of regular state protections, but their other purpose is to tie down employees valued by the employer.

Meanwhile the casual workforce is entirely at the mercy of the employer and receives no benefits of any kind. Pay is low and fluctuating, the job turnover is high and security is nonexistent. Labour recruiters belong in the upper category and enjoy annual bonuses and small loans; but they are encouraged to turn labour over fast so as to reduce customary entitlement to annual "gifts" and avoid protective obligations. Male casual labour is occasionally unionized, but the multiplicity of unions leads to the political mediation of disputes; the state effectively enforces the labour laws, rarely in the workers' favour. Factory inspectors with huge territories to cover and few resources for enforcing the law are often corruptly implicated with bosses in the evasion of laws and the erosion of labour rights.

Female casual labour is subjected to extremes of casualization, negligence and harassment and to unsafe and unsanitary working conditions, their wages often being reported by bosses as "pocket money". In such firms, work has for decades been subcontracted, often exported to rural sites to avoid inspection and to profit from cheap or unwaged family labour, from low rents, and from the ease of evasion of any welfare obligations and taxes. Thus capital uses informal practices and a selective idiom of social protection to render the majority of the workforce extremely insecure, and a small valued minority less insecure.

Source: Harriss-White 2000.

place. Increasing numbers of people work in situations where brokers or subcontractors intermediate between the person doing the work, and the firm for which it is being done. The worker only has contact with the supplier of materials and collector of the finished goods. The broker himself or herself may be operating on slim profit margins, and also be vulnerable and insecure.

After the Asian crisis, the garment industry in the Philippines was restructured; many women lost their formal jobs, yet remained in the industry. One woman became a labour supplier for the same firm she had previously worked for, organizing women she had formerly worked with, to produce the embroidered smocking on children's clothes. She is Gloria Bularin, in box 5.4 below. This illustrates the many-layered nature of subcontracted work. It also shows the exceptionally low wages at the lower end of the chain. Information about the earnings of middle-level subcontractors is invariably difficult to obtain.

The informalization process: Outsourcing

Since informalization of employment is growing, it is important to understand the process which leads to the deconstruction of jobs and their removal from the protected workplace. The increased organization of the workplace cannot be guaranteed; on the contrary. Previous assumptions that certain occupations and enterprises were fixed in the formal or informal economy have turned out to be misleading; some that were formal have become informal, often with the same worker in place. Textile, clothing, leather and footwear industries in South Africa, protected and subsidized under the old apartheid regime, show these characteristics, according to a study documenting the impacts of labour retrenchment and the introduction of subcontracting and other "flexible" labour practices in

Box 5.4	Subcontracting and pricing in clothing, the Philippines

Angono in the Philippines is a town well known for its embroidery work. Demand comes from Carol's, a major local retailer of children's wear. In this domestic chain of production, baby dresses with hand embroidery sell for between US$6.86 and US$9.80. Diana Juan is a supplier to Carol's. She has live-in workers doing the straight sewing, and subcontracts the hand embroidery through Marisol Ugarte, who gets US$0.03 a line. Marisol Ugarte subcontracts to Gloria Bularin at US$0.02 per line. Gloria Bularin in turn organizes homeworkers, who she pays US$0.01 to US$0.015 per line.

Source: Doane et al. 2003, cited in Lund 2004.

the context of liberalization.[44] With the lowering of trade barriers, imports began to flood the economy. By the late 1990s, both employment and production in the footwear industry began to decline, with the clothing, leather and textile sectors later following suit. Restructuring and "rationalization" in these labour-intensive industries resulted in massive job losses.

As far as women are concerned, the negative employment effects stem from the increasing informalization of the workplace. "Rationalization" is achieved through job rotation, outsourcing and subcontracting. Some retrenched workers have been encouraged to buy their equipment and set up in home-based production. At the same time, growing numbers of women evicted from these clothing and textile industries are ending up in street trading and other survival activities in the informal economy. Despite official commitment to aid small and medium-sized enterprises, there is no access to state support, at least from the central government.[45]

In many countries, the phenomenon of homeworkers is growing; most of them are women. Millions of these subcontracted employees, working on a piece-rate basis, feed productive profit-making output from their homes into the more formal manufacturing companies or their intermediaries. The payment they receive is extremely low, and they may have to work extremely long hours or at night to make enough money to survive; many also use their children as subsidiary workers. These areas are untouched by labour laws and social welfare. The fact that homeworkers are dispersed raises special challenges for collective action, but to change the conditions under

which they work they need to bargain for more regular work orders, higher piece rates and more prompt payment (see box 5.5).

Many female homeworkers process products in the global value chain, while others work on articles destined for the domestic market. In the garments industry workforce alone, the percentage of homeworkers in the mid-1990s was estimated at 38 per cent in Thailand, between 25–39 per cent in the Philippines, 30 per cent in one region of Mexico, between 30–60 per cent in Chile and 45 per cent in Venezuela.[46] Very recent research indicates that some of this "soft" employment is facing a crisis as textile and garment exports face growing competition in world markets, and companies try to cut costs still further.

Informalization and public-sector retrenchment

In many low-income countries, public-sector workers have also been crowding into the informal economy, even when they have managed to maintain their jobs despite public-sector retrenchment. The civil service reforms of the early 1990s often entailed radical downsizing; today more emphasis is placed on "new public management" reforms which seek to change the incentive structures and outsource some of the functions of the public administration (see chapter 11).[47]

Cameroon is a case in point. Like many other African countries, Cameroon underwent an economic recession in the

Box 5.5   Homeworkers and the self-employed

The problems and constraints faced by self-employed home-based workers and homeworkers are quite different, although both typically lack bargaining power and have to provide their own social protection. Homeworkers are often forced by circumstances to work for low wages without secure contracts or fringe benefits and to cover some production costs ... Most self-employed home-based workers, except high-end professionals, face limited access to and/or competition in relevant markets. To improve their situation homeworkers need to strengthen their capacity to bargain for regular work orders, higher piece rates, and overdue back pay (a common problem faced by homeworkers worldwide); while home-based self-employed need better access to financial markets and enhanced capacity to compete in product markets. In effect, homeworkers often face problems of *exploitation* while the self-employed often face problems of *exclusion*. The strategies to address problems of exploitation in labour markets-such as collective bargaining for higher wages-are different than the strategies to address problems of exclusion in capital and product markets—such as providing access to financial, marketing, and business services.

Source: ILO 2002b.

mid-1980s, and subsequently embarked on a structural adjustment programme. One target of the reforms was the civil service. In addition to downsizing of the public sector through retrenchments and retirements (in 1995/96 alone, seven ministries fired significant numbers of workers), the terms and conditions of service for public employees were drastically trimmed. Within three years, civil servants experienced salary cuts of up to 60 per cent, and payments fell heavily into arrears. As in many other African countries, civil servants forced to compensate for loss of earnings and falling living standards began to make forays into the informal economy, along diverse lines (see box 5.6).[48]

Women and men are not evenly placed within the public service. Women generally tend to have a minimal presence in administrative and managerial positions; they also tend to cluster within services such as health and education. Reliable statistics showing how women and men have fared comparatively in terms of retrenchment from the public sector are difficult to find; much depends on where the staff cuts have been made. But public-sector reforms also generate downward pressures on wages and working conditions, and these are likely to have fallen particularly on lower-level staff. These pressures are affecting women health workers and their interactions with women health users, as explored in chapter 8.

The case of China

In China where women have been intensively employed in state-owned enterprises, the process of industrial restructuring has dealt a heavy blow to their employment prospects and security. China is often cited as threatening jobs prospects in other parts of the world, with its dynamic export-oriented industries attracting millions of young rural migrants each year: 48 per cent of all migrant workers in China are women (figures for 2000).

The view of China as the "workshop of the world" is one-sided. Often overlooked are the huge inequalities—class, regional, rural/urban, age, gender—stemming from a quarter-century of market reform which has drastically restructured the economy and workforce. The privatization of industry has dealt a severe blow to permanent state workers' entitlements, shattering their prized employment and livelihood security. Workers in collective enterprises, which previously functioned as state subsidiaries, also suffered huge layoffs. In 1993 the official union found that women workers accounted for 37 per cent of all state workers but 60 per cent of those laid off and unemployed. By 1999 women accounted for 45 per cent of all laid-off workers.[49]

Informal work, termed "flexible employment" by some Chinese researchers, has become a major source of income for the unemployed. The availability of such employment varies

Box 5.6   Straddling strategies by teachers and health workers in the South West Province of Cameroon

Before the economic crisis, teachers were among the best-paid civil servants in Cameroon. Once the reforms began to bite, teachers began to supplement their falling wages with informal activities. They now comprise the largest number of formal employees working as newcomer entrants into the informal economy: 67 out of 75 of the teachers interviewed in a study undertook such activities. Health workers are now joining them, as are clerical staff.

These public-sector workers use their position, equipment and time in the regular workplace to undertake other profit-making work on an informal basis. The different ways they do this depend on the existing job and to a considerable extent on gender. In the case of teachers, while men, and a few women, provided supplementary private tuition for individual students or classes, and sold reproductions of lecture notes to secondary and high-school students, women teachers mostly undertook petty trading in food. They sold meals at lunch time and a variety of snacks, as well as non-food items. The capital base of such trade is very small.

Nurses, like teachers, were involved in informal activities related to their formal work. From being a secretive sporadic activity, private practice or "PP" became widespread and open after general and hospital strikes of the early 1990s failed to obtain improved working conditions and salaries. PP commonly involves minor consultations and drug sales to patients outside the hospital, sales of drugs within hospital premises during working hours, home-care nursing, or a combination of informal health care and petty trading.

Source: Agbaw 2000, cited in Tsikata 2004.

across cities and regions, but the Ministry of Labour has estimated that of 25 million unemployed and laid-off workers nationwide, 15 million have found jobs in the informal economy.[50] Those with financial means have opened up private or family businesses such as restaurants, salons or neighbourhood stores. At the other end of the spectrum, especially in the northeast "rust belt" where economic growth has been sluggish, casual work only is available. Men work as day labourers in construction, help out in private enterprises or trade on the street. Unemployed women workers sometimes turn to prostitution. In one study in three northeastern cities, of more than 100 sex workers, 74 per cent were former state-owned-enterprise workers, and most (92 per cent) had become sex workers after seeking alternative employment for over four years.[51]

There are no clear patterns of gender disparity in the re-employment of laid-off workers. Qualitative studies have offered divergent interpretations. One study in Wuhan finds that female laid-off workers have a better chance starting a service-oriented business than male counterparts; these are more averse to service roles but have more success in finding positions in established companies.[52] Another study in three cities finds that age discrimination is at least as serious as sex discrimination. Almost every interviewee aged over 30 cited this rather than gender as a major obstacle to finding re-employment. This situation is compounded by the cohort experience of the over-30s as the unlucky generation sent out to the countryside during the Cultural Revolution and deprived of a sound education.[53]

Another issue often overlooked in discussions about China is the sharp increase in labour conflicts. There has been a proliferation of conventional and irregular labour activism, from petitions, labour arbitration and litigation, through protests, marches and road blockages. The state has responded with measured mixes of concession and repression. Economic and livelihood demands are recognized and often partially answered by swift financial compensation doled out by the central or provincial government. However political demands such as for the removal of officials and cross-factory actions are relentlessly suppressed and harshly punished. There is only one legal union in China, the All China Federation of Trade Unions (ACFTU). Independent unions are illegal, and attempts at forming autonomous unions have been designated as treason or subversion. However, even where trade unions and NGOs are legal and tolerated, the organization of women workers in the informal economy presents formidable challenges.

ORGANIZATIONS OF INFORMAL WORKERS

One of the promising developments of the 1990s was the emergence of new forms of organizing among women workers in the informal economy, both domestically and internationally. The Self Employed Women's Association (SEWA), in Gujarat, India, with 700,000 members, is one of the oldest and best-known; many others have emerged over the past decade, some taking SEWA as their model, as did the South African Self-Employed Women's Union (SEWU), formed in 1993. These organizations include street vendors, home-based workers and small agricultural producers. Other women's associations—some independently and some as part of national trade union federations—have focused on organizing domestic workers; these remain a highly vulnerable section of the female workforce in many countries, both developed and developing.

Historically, women workers have found it very difficult to voice their concerns from within male-dominated trade unions. In the 19th and early 20th century industrial revolution, trade unions were hostile to women workers' presence in the industrial workforce; they used protective legislation and the construct of the "family wage" to relegate women to the sphere of unpaid work in the home.[54] The picture has changed dramatically down the years, largely through women's efforts to reform workplace procedures, goals and cultures, both from within mainstream trade unions and by building independent trade unions. However, women's attempts to secure gender justice and parity within labour organizations are often resisted or sidelined.

Responsiveness to women workers has been equally problematic in the developing world. Even where an explicit commitment to women workers' rights has been made, it is rarely recognized that women workers may have different priorities from male workers: childcare support, for example, may be more important to them than a minimum wage.[55] An illustration of "gender blindness" comes from an electronics factory in India. Women workers organized to make certain demands: a company bus so as to avoid sexual harassment on public transport, especially late in the evening and uniforms, to reduce the hierarchies and problems arising from the fact that women in this factory came from different socioeconomic backgrounds. These demands were agreed by management, but the male workers were dismissive: "Girls do not know how to raise demands. They fall into the trap laid by management. They ask for general facilities while the real issue is wages … now the girls have a bus, uniforms so they are just happy with that. They don't ask for wages."[56]

The attitude of Indian trade unions to informal workers in general has been described as "indifference, rising almost to enmity", underpinned by "fear that pressure from below would lead to the gradual erosion of the rights gained during a long struggle by protected labour".[57] Homeworkers have been seen by unions as "outlaws" or "scab labour", undercutting the organized workplace. These fears are understandable, especially in economies where the formal regulated workforce is no more than 10 per cent of the total workforce. However, this demonstrates that the culture and procedures of the trade union movement, primarily a champion of male workers in the formal sector, are biased towards male preoccupations and are out of tune with the lives of predominantly informally working women.[58] Not surprisingly, women have tended to create a "separate space", either within mainstream trade unions or independently, where their concerns can receive a better hearing.

Today, there are many women workers' organizations of different origins and types. Some are independent organizations that have arisen outside the framework of the traditional trade union movement; others are independent within established trade union structures; yet others are part of unions originating in the formal economy but organizing informal workers. They cover a great variety of industrial sectors and services, as well as agriculture and rural occupations. In some developing countries, however, NGOs have taken up the needs and rights of women workers. Some offer affordable services, such as child-care facilities, low-cost residences and legal support. New kinds of labour organizations are also emerging that base themselves within the community, and offer a much wider range of support services than do traditional trade unions.[59]

Many of these new trade unions, as well as NGOs and community-based organizations (CBOs) responding to women workers' rights, face major difficulties in expanding their reach and becoming sustainable. SEWU's main challenge, for example, remains its persistent inability to become financially self-sufficient: after 10 years, its paid-up membership remains less than 5,000, while more than 10,000 members have allowed their membership to lapse by non-payment of dues. This is a problem shared by other unions of vulnerable workers in South Africa and elsewhere.

NGOs have greater flexibility because they are not membership-based organizations and seldom have a single constituency; but this also raises questions about their accountability, which is not usually democratic and is rarely transparent to their beneficiaries. Both trade unions and NGOs face challenges in alliance-building to broaden the scope and reach of their efforts. While there is wide scope for trade unions and NGOs to support each others' aims—and there are some exemplary cases of collaboration—relations between them have often suffered from tensions and rivalries rooted in ideological and organizational differences.[60]

Despite such caveats these developments are promising. Only through collective action have workers historically regulated their wages and working conditions, and eliminated the worst forms of exploitation; they were responsible, in effect, for the formalization of the workplace. But the stresses of the last couple of decades have other ramifications. Not only have new union and NGO workers' champions emerged, but the trade union movement has itself suffered a major shake-up. Older organizations have seen their membership and influence decline and been forced to adjust to new realities in the world of work.

The General Agricultural Workers' Union (GAWU) of Ghana is a case in point. It expanded its membership to non-waged workers and subsistence farmers after structural adjustment caused its membership to drop from 130,000 to 30,000. Another example is the Uganda Public Employees Union (UPEU). In the 1990s, membership dropped from 108,000 to 700 as a result of public sector reforms. The union then transformed its outlook and scope: it revised the concept of "public employee" from the narrow meaning of "civil servant" to a much broader concept of engagement in serving the public, including such groups as street vendors. As a result of this change and an organizational drive, its membership grew to 17,000 by 1999.[61]

International campaigns and alliances

In recent years the issue of labour standards has become divisive in view of proposals being made for its enforcement through international trade agreements and trade sanctions. There are, understandably, concerns among Southern governments and civil-society groups about protectionist motives lurking behind such proposals. More to the point, it is not just the traded sectors that require labour-market regulation.

While transnational alliances between trade unions and NGOs have been effective in campaigning for workers' rights, these campaigns have been limited to workers in traded goods visible to Northern consumers. The direct benefits are often limited to workers with jobs dependent on multinational companies and their subcontractors, who are often among the more privileged and best-paid members of the workforce.[62] Where a much larger proportion of the workforce operates in the informal economy in far worse conditions, they are beyond the reach of such campaigns. However, the different segments of the workforce do not necessarily live in isolation from each other. Successful campaigns and organizations affecting one segment are likely to have ripple effects on power relations elsewhere. The female working class is less segmented than sometimes appears, and changes in one part are likely to have implications in others.

For women with virtually no assets and who work in the informal economy, collective action through democratic organizational routes presents the only practicable avenue for regulating or improving their working conditions. The idea that the formalization of property rights constitutes the solution to the problems of the informal economy is a complete misconception as far as working women are concerned (see box 5.7).

Box 5.7   "Property rights" are no panacea for the informal economy

The influential work of Hernando de Soto has paved the way for a particular policy perspective on the informal economy.[63] According to de Soto the transition of informal into formal work is constrained by a deficient framework of property rights. Allegedly, lack of legal recognition for some forms of property constrains access to institutional sources of credit. A similar perspective informed the World Commission on the Social Dimensions of Globalization. Its report sees the legalization of de facto property rights as:

> a vital step in the transformation of the informal economy. To achieve this, governments need to: identify the people and assets concerned; identify the practices and customs which govern the ownership, use and transfer of these assets, so as to root property law in the prevailing social context; and identify administrative, bureaucratic and legal bottlenecks and obstacles to market access.[64]

The axiomatic understanding of such a position is that the informal economy is inherently vibrant, flexible and dynamic, and that it can effectively compete with larger units in the formal sector once constraints—such as lack of access to credit— are removed. This ignores a number of the informal economy's key features, and the problems faced by its many and varied practitioners.

The size of its units—typically individuals and households—is critical in many ways. For example, market access is fundamentally dependent not on legal status, but on output. Larger size allows organizational economies of scale. Increased access to markets by small units usually requires some degree of co-operation between them; alternatively, they might make arrangements with a larger unit or obtain public intervention through marketing bodies. As for credit, access is typically more difficult for all small units, even in the formal sector, not only because of the lack of collateral and high administrative costs, but because they are perceived to be inherently more risk-prone.

Looking at the issue of property rights itself, there are problems and risks associated with the establishment of rights, such as regulated tenure and ownership of land. The evidence from sub-Saharan Africa shows that the customary rights of women, and of other marginal groups, are often lost in the process of titling and registration. A large number of workers in the informal economy anyway have no "property" to be registered; they are engaged in informal activities only because they cannot find work in the formal sector. Most women workers are in this category.

Finally, and perhaps most crucially, it is a mistake to assume that all informal activity is effectively self-employment and that employer–worker relationships do not exist. As already demonstrated, a main attraction of the informal economy for employers is precisely the absence of labour regulation, allowing lower labour costs and greater exploitation of workers. Increasingly, formal sector organizations depend on units of the informal sector to undertake production by means of sub-contracting; the line between the two sectors has thus become much harder to draw. This means that the most basic difference between formal and informal parts of the economy is not the access to credit or markets, but the absence of regulation and lack of protection for workers in the informal economy, as well as the latter's lack of voice and political influence.

Source: Ghosh 2004b.

Notes

1 Figure 5.1 includes countries in the MENA region for which data were available. Because of certain shared characteristics, including culture, religion, history, and the prevalence of oil economies, the MENA region is considered an appropriate site for regional analysis, not only by international organizations such as the World Bank but also by scholarly organizations such as the Middle East Studies Association.

2 Elson 1999.

3 Anker et al. 2003; Anker 1998.

4 Kabeer 1995.

5 Elson 1999; Folbre 1994.

6 ILO 2002b.

7 Standing 1999.

8 Pearson 2004.

9 Ghosh 2003a.

10 Ghosh 2003a.

11 UN 1999.

12 Ghosh 2003a.

13 This section draws heavily on Orloff 2002.

14 Orloff 2002.

15 Hochschild 1989.

16 ILO 2002b.

17 ILO 2002b:27.

18 Lewis and Giullari 2004.

19 Einhorn 1993.

20 Eisenstein 1993.

21 Fodor 2004b.

22 Heinen and Portet 2002.

23 Pearson 2004.

24 Karshenas 2001 cited in Moghadam 2004.

25 Moghadam 2004.

26 Harriss-White 2000.

27 ILO 2002b.

28 ILO 2002b.

29 Elson 1999.

30 Elson 1999.

31 Pape 2000 cited in Tsikata 2004.

32 Breman 1996.

33 Jackson and Rao 2004.

34 Kabeer and Mahmud 2004.

35 Roy 2003.

36 Kabeer and Mahmud 2004:tables 7 and 8.

37 Kabeer and Mahmud 2004.

38 Kabeer 2004.

39 Rogerson 1997 cited in Tsikata 2004.

40 Tsikata 2004; Hart 2004.

41 Davis 2004:22 cited in Tsikata 2004.

42 Tokam 2002.

43 Beneria and Floro 2004.

44 Deedat 2003; see also Hart 2004.

45 Lund et al. 2000.

46 Chen et al. 1999.

47 Bangura 1994, 2000.

48 Agbaw 2000, cited in Tsikata 2004.

49 Chang 1995; China Employment Report 2002 cited in Lee 2004.

50 Institute for Labour Studies of the Ministry of Labour and Social Security of China 2002, cited in Lee 2004.

51 Huang and Wuanming 2003, cited in Lee 2004.

52 Tsui 2002, cited in Lee 2004.

53 Cook and Jolly 2001.

54 Hartman 1979; Gallin and Horn 2004.

55 Chhachhi and Pittin 1996; Rowbotham and Mitter 1994.

56 Chhachhi and Pittin 1996:115–16.

57 Breman 1996:247.

58 Mitter 1994.

59 Kabeer 2004.

60 Eade 2004.

61 Gallin 2004.

62 Anner and Evans 2004; UNRISD 2004.

63 De Soto 2000.

64 ILO 2004e: 61.

Chapter 6
The changing terms of rural living

Famines and food crises expose the precariousness of the livelihoods of those affected. In 2002 several countries in southern Africa experienced serious food shortage. The effects were widespread: 14 million people suffered hunger and hardship. The immediate causes were drought and severe local flooding, but the impacts were made greater by the lack of food security to which many households were already acutely vulnerable. The ravages of HIV/AIDS had helped erode assets and social support networks. As critically, the onslaught of economic liberalization over two decades, undermining smallholders' ability to construct viable livelihoods, had helped to deepen rural poverty.[1]

At around the same time, India experienced a spate of suicides by hopelessly indebted cotton farmers. In response to rising world prices for cotton during the early 1990s and official encouragement as trade was liberalized, farmers had converted to cotton land that had been under food grain cultivation, particularly in Andhra Pradesh but also in northern Karnataka and Punjab. After a peak in the mid-1990s, world cotton prices suddenly declined. In the early 2000s, swamped by debt, thousands of farmers committed suicide, often by swallowing pesticides.[2]

These examples of severe distress are connected. Both, whatever their incidental causes, are unanticipated outcomes of systemic policy choices by powerful governments and international financial institutions (IFIs). The food crisis in southern Africa threw a spotlight onto what had been happening to the lives of farming people in poverty-stricken and indebted countries forced onto a diet of liberalization. The story of cotton encapsulates the risks associated with reliance on the export of volatile primary commodities—cotton is by no means the only

case—whose prices in global markets are unstable and which experience sharp, sometimes prolonged, falls. At the end of 2001, real non-fuel commodity prices had plunged to about one-half of their annual average for the period 1979–81, leading to the build-up of unsustainable external debt in the non-oil commodity exporters.[3] Such crises, of which many other examples could be cited, raise serious questions about liberalization as a universal policy model for developing countries with high proportions of rural populations dependent on agriculture.

The distortions within the current agricultural trading system, whereby European and US farmers enjoy protection and subsidies and Southerners find their produce excluded from Northern markets, have been strongly protested by governments from the South; despite protracted negotiations within the World Trade Organization (WTO), these tensions remain unresolved and the future directions of agricultural trading policy remain unclear.[4] Such grand-scale North–South discrimination within the global trading system attracts widespread attention. But other ways in which the outcome of economic liberalization in the agricultural sphere discriminates between social groups are frequently overlooked. The gender perspective—differentiated impacts on women and men, girls and boys—has been neglected.

This chapter scrutinizes agricultural liberalization from a gender perspective, highlighting the changes in rural women's, as compared to rural men's, earning opportunities, farming and family responsibilities, and access to resources. Liberalization has contributed to the vulnerability of smallholders, and to women's workloads, but without producing the anticipated growth rates and the sought stimulus to production, to techno-logical change and to a restructured composition of the rural economy. It has also shaken up social relations and triggered changes in gender relations.

THE IMPLICATIONS OF LIBERALIZATION FOR RURAL POVERTY

In both sub-Saharan Africa and South Asia, a high proportion of the population continues to live in rural areas, and agricul-ture is vital to GDP and to people's livelihoods (table 6.1). Rural poverty, including female poverty, is behind the selection of these regions for examination. By contrast, Latin America is much more urbanized and farming contributes a relatively small share of GDP. However, agricultural products remain an important source of foreign exchange, and the IFIs have praised Latin American success in shifting into high-value agricultural export (HVAE) production. This strategy relies heavily on female agricultural workers, and its implications are therefore worth exploring.

During the 1980s, many African and Latin American coun-tries suffered economic crises, and this was diagnosed by the IFIs as stemming directly from heavy state involvement in the econ-omy. The agricultural sector was seen as a prime victim of state-directed regimes; cheap food policies, for example, distorted prices and depressed farming incomes. If instead the market were to determine prices, they would rise naturally and benefit producers; meanwhile currency devaluations and lowered export taxes would help promote agricultural exports. That, at least, was the accepted international policy view.[5]

In truth most developing country states were heavily involved in the economy. In the newly independent states in Africa in the 1960s, for example, there was a widespread view that markets were not adequate to build a strong economy. State marketing boards were set up to govern production and trade in major agricultural products; these provided subsidies, and usually paid the same prices to farmers in remote areas as to those close to urban markets. In Latin America, agricultural

prices were artificially depressed by an overvalued exchange rate and export taxes; but this was to some extent redressed through positive resource transfer into the sector via public investment, subsidized credit and agricultural services.[6]

In both regions, there were wide fluctuations in marketed agricultural output over the period (see figure 6.1). In Latin America, growth was respectable in the 1970s at an average annual rate of 3.3 per cent. During the 1980s—the first reform decade—the rate veered widely; this crisis-ridden period also saw an overall increase in poverty, from 41 to 48 per cent of all households. During the 1990s agricultural growth averaged only 2.2 per cent. Poverty indices improved, but only at a lag-gardly pace, so that Latin America entered the new millennium with a higher proportion of poor and indigent rural people than in 1980 (see table 6.2). At the same time, the economic reforms tended to reinforce existing divides between regions and pro-ducers.[7] The most dynamic products of the 1990s were those grown by modern, capitalized farmers with links to international agro-industry and export markets. Those in decline were largely pro-duced by small farmers. One of the downsides of liberalization in Latin America has been the rise in agricultural imports.[8]

Nowhere have the rural effects of liberalization policies been more profound than among the agriculturally dependent populations of sub-Saharan Africa. Compared with other devel-oping regions, agriculture had been a sluggish earner before liberalization, although not uniformly. State bodies were per-ceived as significantly to blame: a costly drain on government revenue, they were also inefficient in delivering inputs and paying farmers. Adjustment policies, notably the reduction of state involvement, were supposed to reverse African agricul-tural fortunes.

Over the past 30 years, agricultural growth rates in sub-Saharan Africa have fluctuated wildly (see figure 6.1). Both high and low—some years have been negative—growth rates have been the product of special circumstances, mitigating the impact of liberal reforms. Uganda, often glowingly cited as a reform success story, is a case in point. High growth rates have been achieved, but the turmoil of the years preceding reform had hit the economy to such an extent that the baseline for measuring performance was extremely low.

Table 6.1 Economically active population in agriculture, agricultural value added and agricultural exports, regional averages and some country examples (1980–2000)

	Proportion of economically active population in agriculture [1]			Agriculture, value added (% of GDP) [2]			Agricultural exports (% of merchandise exports) [2]		
	1980	1990	2000	1980	1990	2000	1980	1990	2000
Africa	**69**	**64**	**59**	**29**	**29**	**27**	**51**	**45**	**43**
North Africa	*44*	*32*	*27*	*15*	*16*	*13*	*16*	*15*	*11*
Egypt	57	41	34	18	19	17	22	19	-
Tunisia	39	28	25	14	16	12	8	12	9
Sub-Saharan Africa	*72*	*68*	*63*	*31*	*30*	*28*	*59*	*55*	*52*
Cameroon	73	70	59	31	25	43	64	35	36
South Africa	17	14	10	6	5	3	11	12	12
Tanzania	86	84	80	-	46	45	76	-	-
Zimbabwe	72	68	63	16	16	18	43	51	60
Latin America and the Caribbean	**31**	**25**	**21**	**16**	**14**	**10**	**47**	**47**	**44**
Caribbean	*26*	*22*	*17*	*14*	*11*	*7*	*38*	*36*	*43*
Dominican Rep.	32	25	17	20	13	11	73	-	-
Jamaica	31	25	21	8	7	6	14	20	23
Central America	*42*	*34*	*27*	*22*	*19*	*13*	*65*	*68*	*57*
Guatemala	54	52	46	25	26	23	70	73	60
Mexico	36	28	21	9	8	4	15	13	5
Nicaragua	42	34	27	23	31	-	83	91	90
South America	*31*	*25*	*21*	*13*	*14*	*12*	*42*	*39*	*36*
Argentina	13	12	10	6	8	5	71	61	45
Brazil	37	23	17	11	8	7	50	31	28
Paraguay	45	39	34	29	28	20	88	90	80
Asia	**46**	**41**	**36**	**21**	**23**	**23**	**28**	**15**	**11**
East Asia	*49*	*40*	*33*	*15*	*13*	*13*	*5*	*6*	*3*
China	74	72	67	30	27	16	-	16	7
Republic of Korea	37	18	10	15	9	5	9	5	3
Southeast Asia	*56*	*52*	*48*	*21*	*29*	*25*	*31*	*17*	*9*
Indonesia	58	55	48	24	20	17	22	16	13
Thailand	71	64	56	23	13	10	58	34	18
South Asia	*67*	*61*	*57*	*40*	*33*	*27*	*48*	*23*	*19*
India	70	64	60	39	31	25	33	20	14
Pakistan	63	52	47	30	26	27	44	20	13
Central Asia	*-*	*-*	*-*	*-*	*33*	*32*	*-*	*-*	*-*
Kazakhstan	-	-	18	-	-	9	-	-	8
Uzbekistan	-	-	28	-	33	34	-	-	-
West Asia	*26*	*20*	*15*	*9*	*14*	*17*	*19*	*12*	*12*
Jordan	18	15	11	8	8	2	25	11	16
Syrian Arab Rep.	39	33	28	20	28	23	13	18	13
Oceania	**48**	**43**	**37**	**27**	**21**	**19**	**70**	**71**	**43**
Developed regions	**15**	**11**	**8**	**8**	**10**	**7**	**23**	**19**	**14**
Eastern Europe	*28*	*23*	*17*	*20*	*18*	*12*	*17*	*15*	*9*
Western Europe	*12*	*8*	*5*	*7*	*5*	*3*	*21*	*17*	*13*
Other developed	*7*	*5*	*4*	*6*	*4*	*2*	*34*	*27*	*22*
World	**43**	**38**	**34**	**20**	**20**	**18**	**39**	**32**	**29**

Note: Regional averages for each variable have been calculated from countries with available data for at least two of the periods considered. Agricultural exports comprise exports of food and of agricultural raw materials.
Sources: (1) Calculated from FAO 2004; (2) World Bank 2004b.

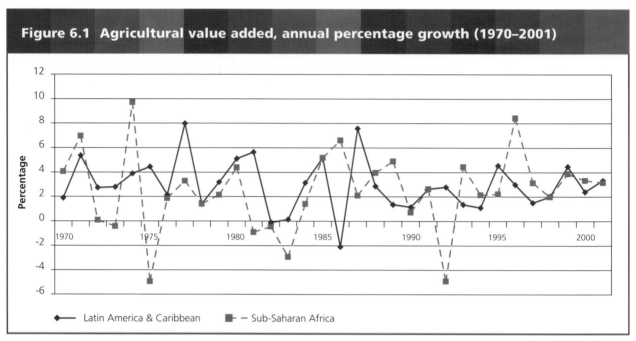

Figure 6.1 Agricultural value added, annual percentage growth (1970–2001)

Source: Calculated from World Bank 2004b.

Table 6.2 Poverty and indigence rates in Latin America, percentage of population (1980–2002)

Year	Poor			Indigent		
	Total	Urban	Rural	Total	Urban	Rural
1980	41	30	60	19	11	33
1990	48	41	65	23	15	40
2000	43	36	63	18	12	38
2002	44	38	62	19	14	38

Source: ECLAC 2004.

Over the years, proponents of reform have increasingly accepted that African agriculture's response to liberalization has been disappointing.[9] Larger-scale commercial farmers and estate proprietors have been in a better position to take advantage of improved prices and new markets than have smallholders, who are everywhere in the vast majority. In several countries and for particular commodities, liberalization did produce spurts in smallholder production of export crops, but these gains have not been maintained. As figure 6.2 indicates, throughout the 1980s and 1990s as liberalization progressed, sub-Saharan Africa witnessed the steady decline of its agricultural exports as a share of world agricultural trade.[10]

Meanwhile the problems surrounding food production and security are far from resolved. The 2002 shortages in southern Africa, as already noted, showed up the increasingly parlous state of rural livelihoods. Deteriorating household food security in Malawi, Zambia and Zimbabwe has been attributed to the loss of subsidies for fertilizers and seeds and of rural credit, and the

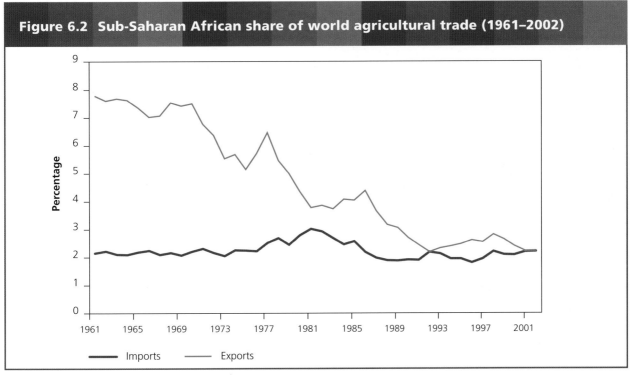

Figure 6.2 Sub-Saharan African share of world agricultural trade (1961–2002)

Source: Calculated from FAO 2004.

erosion of agricultural marketing services, especially in remote areas.[11] Although much derided, marketing boards serviced small-holders' needs for inputs, provided marketing channels to remote and widely dispersed farms, and enforced commodity standards. Their dismantling has led to expressions of serious concern.[12] The private traders who have taken their place provide patchy ser-vices, bypass farmers in areas where transport costs are high, and do not carry out adequate checks or enforce quality control.[13]

THE GENDERED IMPACTS OF ECONOMIC REFORM

Gender-differentiated examination of the implications of eco-nomic reform on rural livelihoods is hard. The evidence base for a generalized gender analysis of agrarian change is poor; information from selected countries is the only usable guide to regional trends, which are hard to extrapolate from sparse and unindicative data.[14]

National agricultural statistics are inadequate in a number of key respects, some of which stem from using either the indi-vidual holder, or the holding, as the unit of analysis, which means that the relationships between the farming of household members cannot be assessed. It also remains the case that accu-rate information about women's own-account farming, which is ostensibly collected in national agricultural statistics, is rare, largely because of the techniques and methodologies of data collection. While labour-force surveys provide gender-disag-gregated data, their information is frequently unreliable or misleading. Much of the suggested increase in rural women's economic activity in Latin America between 1980 and 2000 is simply a reflection of their previous under-enumeration (see figure 6.3). This makes it difficult to draw accurate conclusions about rural women's employment trends, especially as the data implies against all probability that women workers are concen-trated in non-agricultural activities.[15]

Case studies of changing gender relations under the unfold-ing impact of liberalization are few and far between, especially

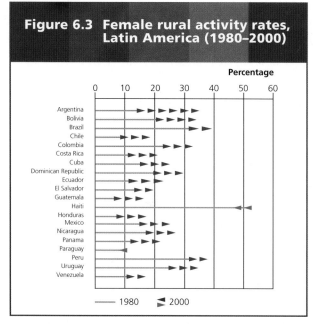

Figure 6.3 Female rural activity rates, Latin America (1980–2000)

Note: Data refer to population aged 10 years and over.
Source: ECLAC 2002.

from sub-Saharan Africa. From Latin America, there are case studies on HVAE where women workers are highly visible; but there is much less information on the gender impacts of liberalization on smallholder production of traditional commodities.

This chapter first considers smallholder farming, agricultural production that is organized on a household basis with the unit of production and consumption overlapping, and where typically a proportion of what is produced does not enter the market system but is consumed by the household. This remains a key institution within the agricultural economy in many developing regions, especially in sub-Saharan Africa. Smallholder farming has come under severe stress over the past two decades. The chapter then goes on to explore rural wage employment in large-scale corporate export farming. This has emerged as a significant new source of employment for rural women, especially in Latin America where levels of socioeconomic differentiation are very high and a sizeable stratum of households is landless or near landless and dependent on wages. The third section looks at the more general diversification of smallholder livelihoods, in which men, women and child household members are increasingly involved. The

unpaid domestic and care economy is central to rural livelihoods in all their diversities.

The invisible economy: Unpaid household-based work

The unpaid domestic economy, whereby households are managed and their members' needs met, is central to rural livelihoods. Women undertake multiple roles in this context. They often help in domestic food cultivation and small livestock management, as well as food processing and preparation; they are exclusively responsible for fuel and water collection, childraising and care of the sick and elderly; they also often earn small amounts of cash from informal entrepreneurship including sale of surplus horticultural produce and brewing. All these activities consume time and energy and carry economic significance for the household. Livelihood research pays lip service to them, but few studies collect systematic data concerning women's unpaid work. As a result, it is difficult to trace the implications of liberalization on unpaid work burdens and on health and nutrition indicators. The latter may only become manifest over the long term.

In sub-Saharan Africa, rural women typically spend 3.5 to 5 hours a day fetching water and fuel, preparing food and looking after children; they also work in the fields alongside men. HIV/AIDS has intensified the burden carried by many African women and girls, since they have to nurse patients through their long decline. Girls may be withdrawn from school to support the family; older women are left to provide for many dependent orphans of their own deceased sons and daughters. The responsibilities and family costs associated with caring for the sick are heaviest in countries where the health and social infrastructure is minimal.[16] Accordingly, reductions in services and the introduction of user fees associated with economic reform agendas discriminate against women by throwing extra work onto their shoulders (see also chapter 8).

In addition to the implications of reduced public subsidies for health services and utilities provision—water, sanitation, electricity—pressure on women's resources of time and energy have also been increased by environmental degradation and the marketization of natural resources.[17] The collection of fuel and water is more time-consuming and costly. In a study of women's adoption of bicycles in a drought-prone area of Tamil Nadu (India), a major use was to collect drinking water from distant sources.[18] Public investment in technologically appropriate, low-cost infrastructure and delivery of basic services would offset growing disadvantage; but that is not the thrust of policy agendas emphasizing service and utility privatization.

Domestic burdens can be said to inflict upon many African women a "time famine", limiting their possibilities of engaging in productive work.[19] Others already spend a great deal of time on very poorly rewarded work, where such work is available.[20] Even if they do not suffer the acute gender discrimination over access to food that occurs in South Asia, their general level of physical well-being is affected by the long hours they spend on energy-intensive work, and by repeated childbearing.[21] Maternal mortality rates are high compared with other regions, and have been rising in recent years.[22] Even where there is no demonstrable direct effect of women's unpaid care burdens on measurable economic productivity, the women's health and nutritional status, and their children's, suffer. There are therefore good reasons for reducing women's unpaid work burdens, even if these burdens do not operate as an inevitable binding constraint on the daily allocation of their time to so-called "productive" pursuits.

Smallholder farming in the context of liberalization

Liberalization and smallholders in sub-Saharan Africa

Tanzania is a rare case where there is excellent research into the effects of liberalization in rural areas, including its gender differences. One of the features of Tanzania's post-independence rural development policy was to boost smallholder incomes and favour food rather than export crops. However, state support for agriculture proved costly and became increasingly inefficient. Production declined, contributing to severe economic crisis by the early 1980s. IMF loans for economic recovery were conditional on structural adjustment programmes, in which reform of the agricultural sector was a high priority.

The effects of liberalization on particular crops—coffee, cotton, cashew nuts—have since been studied extensively.[23] Problems identified include the collapse of credit systems; a sharp decline in inputs especially among smallholders; the imposition of complex and onerous local taxes; and the volatility of world agricultural commodity prices. Similar constraints affect smallholders throughout the region, contributing to the low or even stagnant growth rates in agriculture over the period from the start of liberalization in the early 1980s until today. Food crop production has not increased, while the performance of export crops is very uneven.

Changes in the Tanzanian market include a large increase in cashew exports. Where they can, smallholders have moved out of traditional cash crops into cashew production. The results of this move have been mixed. Farmers and district officials questioned in a study conducted by Action Aid distinguished sharply between a "honeymoon" period, starting soon after the market reforms of the mid-1990s when the world price was high and continuing until 2000, and a crisis period, starting in 2000 and still ongoing.[24] During the honeymoon, small producers benefited a great deal from the liberalization of the cashew nut trade. Competition between buyers in the newly privatized sector was stiff, and farmers received good and rising prices. The area under cashew nuts expanded, as did the yields per hectare, the export price and the producer price. But by 2001 crisis had set in, led by drastic cuts in world market prices. Apart from the falling prices, the buyers had established cartels through which they were able to squeeze the small producers.

How have these changing fortunes affected male and female household producers? Men traditionally own cashew nut trees, and women provide most of the labour. In the honeymoon period, women were remunerated better for their work and extra labour was hired to assist them. Nevertheless, the study found that women gained less than men. This is partly because men control the sale of the cashew crop, negotiating the prices with the buyers; therefore women have little idea about the quantity sold or at what price. There is also indication of an increase in gender tensions during the time of lucrative income.

As producer prices rose, so did the divorce rate according to the women. Husbands, they complained, used their wives' labour during the cashew nut season, only to abandon them for new wives when the season was over.

Despite these protestations after the event, women did gain temporarily from the boom. They did not object to having to work much harder in the honeymoon era, did share in the rising household incomes, and were better off in the initial post-liberalization period than after 2001. Their families had then been able to hire labour to assist on the farms, but this was no longer possible. Some women could no longer afford to buy even a small quantity of paraffin for a lamp, and spent their evenings in the dark.

More detailed gender impacts of liberalization within cashew nut production and processing are reported in an extensive study from Mozambique.[25] This confirms that impacts depend on differences between male and female control over key resources, crop income and labour inputs. The extra work burden carried by women does not appear to create gender conflict. The more important effects are on the household economy, with their special implications for family well-being. Liberalization has brought a loss of real income, and increased exposure to powerful traders and volatile global markets. The lessons from these case studies, borne out by other country examples, are that the private sector provides inadequate markets for smallholders, and that exposure to world markets brings increased vulnerability.

Changes in work burdens, as these cases demonstrate, have a potential for male–female tensions. A view which gained currency in the 1990s, especially within the World Bank, was that the weak "supply response" of African agriculture to liberalization could be ascribed to the inflexibility of gender roles within households, and women's unwillingness to contribute unpaid labour to cash crops controlled by their husbands.[26] An alternative proposition is that these intrahousehold gender constraints and conflicts of interest, while they do occur between husbands and wives, have been overemphasized. There are significant areas of common interest between husbands and wives in smallholder households, and there is considerable evidence of flexibility in gender roles in agriculture more generally. If liberalization has

failed to enhance agricultural production, it has much more to do with the broader constraints on smallholders that liberalization itself has exacerbated, rather than the economic consequences of intrahousehold gender roles and conflicts. Gender conflict itself is often one form in which the deleterious outcomes of liberalization for households and communities are experienced. In this sense, it is a symptom of economic malaise and not a cause.

Liberalization and farming households in Latin America

Several overlapping processes over the past 30 years have contributed to changes in the gender division of labour among Latin American smallholders, sometimes described as a tendency towards the "feminization of agriculture".[27] The leading cause has been the emergence of a class of impoverished and dispossessed smallholders, a process which gained momentum in the 1960s and 1970s, and is generally associated with men becoming landless or land-poor labourers. Male participation in temporary wage labour, particularly when it involves seasonal migration, has everywhere been associated with higher female participation in agriculture. This has as its basis the general flexibility of the gender division of labour in smallholder agriculture.

During the liberalization era, women's participation in agriculture appears to have changed: they are no longer merely "secondary" workers. Women are emerging as farm managers, providing the bulk of family farm labour and taking on extra tasks as men migrate in search of alternative sources of income. By withdrawing direct state support to domestic food production, agricultural reform has galvanized this process. In addition, exports of traditional agricultural products such as coffee have declined as a result of global trade liberalization and depressed commodity markets. The "feminization of agriculture" is therefore a phenomenon associated with the lack of viability of smallholder agricultural production in the current era.

The degree of distress to smallholder farming inflicted by liberalization largely depends on the degree of state support smallholders previously received, and the extent to which they previously supplied basic foodstuffs to the market. Subsistence producers in countries such as Peru and Bolivia have been less directly affected by such policies than by changes in urban and rural labour markets. Those most negatively affected have been the small and medium producers, the beneficiaries of previous rural development initiatives. The withdrawal of previous state support and the pace of external liberalization are critical.

These factors distinguish the case of Mexico. From 1970 through 1982, successive Mexican governments pursued a policy of "food sovereignty", investing in rural social and physical infrastructure and providing credit and technical back-up to smallholders. The stabilization and adjustment policies associated with the debt crisis of 1982, combined with the general opening of the economy and the dismantling of state institutions supporting agriculture, had severe implications for smallholder profitability. The pressures were compounded after the implementation of the North Atlantic Free Trade Agreement (NAFTA) in 1994; corn imports from the United States suddenly increased. This drove down prices to such an extent that the government's compensatory measures to maintain farm incomes became wholly inadequate.

The "feminization of agriculture" in Mexico is directly associated with the increase in long-distance male migration in the 1980s and 1990s, and particularly with migration from rural areas to the United States. Women, particularly married women, become farm managers when both sons and husbands are absent for considerable periods of time. Similar processes appear to be at work in Central America, where the state has gradually cut back support to basic grain production.[28] Since it is more common for men to seek wage work through long-distance migration, it is usually women who maintain agricultural production and guarantee the household's food security. This also explains the high share of female-headed households in the region.

The Indian experience

The feminization of agriculture in India has taken a different form. Between 1972/3 and 1999/2000, the proportion of rural workers in agriculture declined from 84 to 76 per cent. This was largely due to male workers moving out of agriculture entirely, while women substantially remained. Since 1987/8, whatever absorption there was of women into the non-agricultural sector has slowed down, and since the economic reform programme

began in 1991, this deceleration has been dramatic.[29] Indeed, rural women's employment at the all-India level has shown remarkable stability over the years. In 1961, nearly 90 per cent of rural women workers were in agriculture; in 1994 the figure was 86 per cent, a marginal drop. Women comprise an increasingly important proportion of the casual labour force in rural areas, as men withdraw from agriculture into other occupations. Some analysts therefore claim that rural India has also been witnessing a feminization of agriculture.[30] But feminization of agricultural wage labour—often fieldwork of the most laborious, worst paid and lowest-status kind—is not the same as the feminization of farm management.[31] As far as India is concerned there is little evidence that farm management is being assumed by women.

The diversification of rural livelihoods

Two important trends have emerged as companions to liberalization. The first and most directly attributable is the growth of large-scale corporate export farming, particularly of high-value horticultural products such as flowers, fruits and vegetables. This is a significant new source of employment for rural women in many parts of the world. The second is the more general diversification of smallholder livelihoods, into which men, women and child household members are increasingly propelled. Two key gender-related questions in connection to both trends are as follows. What kind of diversification strategies are women pursuing, and what are their effects? And what kinds of changes are taking place in gender relations within rural households as a result of these new agricultural lifestyle developments?

New forms of agricultural employment

Corporate farming is a relatively new and growing source of employment for rural women in India. In Andhra Pradesh and Punjab respectively, hybrid cottonseed and tomatoes have become the mainstay of new-style corporate farming. These consolidated farming units have led to the alienation of land from smallholders, and have drawn on an extremely casual and vulnerable labour force composed mainly of women and children.[32]

Table 6.3 Women's employment in high-value agricultural export production

	Numbers employed	Gender composition (% females)	Age (range or median)	Employment status
Cut flowers				
Kenya	40,000 (+ 4,000 to 5,000 small holders)	75	20–34	Seasonal
Uganda	3,000	75–85	–	Permanent
Zimbabwe	27,000	79–87	–	Seasonal & permanent
Colombia	70,000 (+50,000 in female packing industry)	60–80	15–28	Permanent & contract
Ecuador	30,000 – 50,000	50–70	16–29	Permanent & contract
Fruit				
South Africa	280,000	53	31	Seasonal, temporary & contract
Brazil	–	65	–	Permanent
Chile	336,739	45	30	Temporary
Vegetables				
Kenya	20,000–32,000	66	18–29	Temporary
Guatemala	18,000 smallholders	33 in field work 100 in processing	–	–
Mexico	1.2 million	50–90	–	Temporary, seasonal

Source: Adapted from Dolan and Sorby 2003.

A study in Punjab showed women labourers accounting for 60 per cent of tomato production while receiving 60–75 per cent of male wages.

HVAE crops are also grown in several countries in sub-Saharan Africa, mainly supplying European markets during their off-season. Exports of cut flowers and vegetables are expending in Kenya, Uganda, South Africa and Zimbabwe, although as table 6.3 indicates, the numbers of workers involved mostly remain small. Women form a high proportion of this new workforce.

The trend towards corporate agriculture and its exploitation of a supremely casual, mainly female labour force has been most marked in Latin America, and of much longer duration there than elsewhere. Historically, land distribution has been very skewed in this region, with a substantial number of households being landless or near-landless, and relying on wage work. The economic reform policies of the 1980s and 1990s prompted an increase in the wage-labour force necessary for the take-off of corporate export farming. Women constitute between 40 to 60 per cent of the labour engaged in fieldwork for these crops, as well as the overwhelming majority of those employed in packing houses.[33]

Several factors undermine the positive livelihood effects of this new form of employment for women. Significantly, corporate farms use a gender-segregated workforce, and women are overwhelmingly employed in more insecure, less well-paid, and lower-skilled activities, without opportunities for advancement. The work is often seasonal, with long hours of work, poor health and safety conditions and no social protection.[34] The use of toxic inputs without adequate training and protective clothing is identified as a major health risk. There are also possible longer-term health effects which are not being sufficiently researched.[35] In some countries producing HVAE (including South Africa, Chile and Argentina) there has been a notable rise in the use of contract labour, both male and female, hired by third-party contractors. This reduces labour costs and facilitates the flexibility of export production as contractors move their teams from site to site. But contract labourers rarely enjoy any employment benefits or social protection, and constitute a highly vulnerable worker group.

However, women's new opportunities have also triggered some positive social changes. Young women now have an alternative to rural–urban migration and domestic employment, and a degree of economic autonomy, physical mobility, and possible choice over who they marry. Young single women tend to be preferred as job candidates over married women with children, particularly in the packing houses, but these jobs have also become crucial to the growing number of female household heads. Greater bargaining power, derived from their higher contribution to household income, has given married women greater leverage over household decision making. It has also, however, increased tensions within households as women attempt to exert more influence over family decision making.

Addressing the high level of insecurity and low levels of income and social protection suffered by women workers would require some form of collective action on their part. Nurturing labour and community organizations amongst seasonal, physically dispersed and often isolated workers is a major challenge, although some efforts are being made, notably among the *temporeras* (temporary women workers) in the fruit sector in Chile (see box 6.1).

Gender impacts of livelihood diversification

"Income diversification"—the term used when farming households take on activities other than agricultural production to expand their sources of living—has become widespread in many rural settings over the past 20 years. This includes seasonal migration in search of work, a longstanding feature of rural livelihoods in many parts of Africa, Asia and Latin America.

Box 6.1   Fruit *temporeras* in Chile

In Chile's expanding fruit export sector, a high proportion of seasonal workers are women, many employed in packing. Working collectively in the packing houses should provide an opportunity to organize; however, temporary workers in Chile are still dispersed and have difficulties in organizing long-term collective activities. In 1998, only 1 per cent of temporary fruit workers belonged to a trade union.

Low union membership is in part a reflection of the repressive policies of the military regime at the time that the sector was expanding. However, even in the new democratic era, unions do not have collective negotiating power on behalf of temporary workers. In the specific case of women *temporeras,* many of their needs—childcare facilities since the working season coincides with school closure; out-of-season employment, education and training—are not addressed by trade unions, and this acts as a disincentive to membership.

The women tend to look elsewhere. One avenue for advancing their needs has been through participation in community-based organizations outside the workplace supported by churches and non-governmental organizations. These organizations have an advantage over trade unions: they can adapt to the specific needs of female seasonal workers, acting as focal points during periods of unemployment, dovetailing work-related demands with social, self-help and out-of-season projects. But community-based initiatives also have their limitations: they lack co-ordination and depend on external sources of funding, which have been in decline following the return to democracy. They may also not be able or willing to assist migrant workers.

Within the workplace, women *temporeras* use their own strategies to improve working conditions. For instance, they resort to wildcat strikes to raise their rates. Women refer to this type of stoppage as *cruzando los brazos* (crossing the arms): by taking advantage of the perishable nature of the products they handle, *temporeras* only have to cross their arms and let the fruit rot in order to gain some bargaining power. Key to success is the number of workers participating, which in turn is heavily dependent on social networks of families and friends. The heterogeneity of *temporeras* as a social group, and the fact that the basis for their unity dissolves at the end of each season, make sustained unified response difficult.

Sources: Barrientos et al. 1999; Barrientos and Barrientos 2002.

Diversification is therefore hardly new, but appears to be intensifying. There are different schools of thought about whether this trend is positive or negative for those involved, and for the rural economy more generally.

Diversification of income sources is welcomed by policy makers, who stress that it indicates a "thickening" of the rural economy and rural markets to include a wider range of activities, including rural industries. Enhanced linkages backwards and forwards to agriculture are said to be important for rural poverty reduction. However, increasing concern has been expressed at some of the forms income diversification is taking. Some analysts claim that the increasing move into off-farm income generation represents a search for survival under conditions of increasing economic stress. This has led authors to underline that there are in effect two different kinds of link with poverty. Some off-farm incomes provide routes out of poverty, either because diversification itself gives higher and more secure incomes, or because such incomes can be reinvested in farming. In other cases, incomes earned are so poor that diversification in fact contributes to a cycle of impoverishment.[36]

Relatively few studies examine the process of diversification from a gender perspective. One detailed research project that does so covers four village-level studies in southern Tanzania.[37] This showed the following four trends. First, there is a major diversification in rural incomes away from farming, and this diversification is into mainly non-agrarian rather than agrarian sectors. Second, new forms of migration are important in contemporary diversification strategies; and third, diversification does not provide the kind of savings needed to invest in farming. Instead it is dominated by petty trading, often of cheap imported consumer goods from South and East Asia, second-hand clothes and imported foodstuffs. Finally, most of the opportunities taken up by young men and young women are of the low-entry and low-return type, producing poor incomes; a few young men achieve better-remunerated activities.

There are parallel findings from elsewhere. Studies into off-farm employment and incomes in Ecuador, El Salvador and northeast Brazil suggest that women tend to be more likely than men to engage in low-productivity, poorly paid, non-agricultural activities.[38] A detailed qualitative study of livelihood strategies in rural Uzbekistan also shows women largely confined to the survivalist, low-return strategies in over-crowded segments of the informal economy.[39]

A survival strategy adopted by impoverished women is to undertake casual work in smallholder or commercial farming, remunerated in cash or in kind. The available research evidence suggests that this is a growing area of diversification in sub-Saharan Africa. Little is known about the wage rates for this kind of work, or about its effects on women's own farming; there is, however, evidence from Malawi that this suffers when women are forced into *ganyu* labour (casual agricultural piece-rate work).[40] Estimates suggest that women are paid from one-third to one-half of the rate paid to men for a day's work, and that engaging in casual farm work of this kind is a sign of extreme poverty. Studies carried out in Uganda, Mozambique and South Africa, however, find that wage work brings in more income than self-employment. In South Africa, employment on large-scale state or agribusiness farms can provide women with far more reliable and secure earnings than those available on small-scale farms or through other forms of self-employment.[41]

Diversification's darker side

The picture is sometimes grim. A study of the female labour market in Zimbabwe examined a sugar cane factory employing 3,400 permanent employees and a smaller cohort of casual workers, many of whom were women. Although the casual wage rate was relatively good, employment was seasonal. The critical factor affecting overall earnings was the length of the working period, which varied from year to year. Many women were in dire circumstances, especially when their contracts expired. Mostly single, they had migrated for work, left children behind in their home villages, and lived near the factory all year round. When they were not needed, their only option was selling sex. They lacked the protection of family and kin, and some entered partnerships with men just to get a place to live.[42]

The Zimbabwe study shows how livelihood predicaments have reduced some women who are not regular sex workers to trading sex for money or goods on an occasional basis. A similar finding is shown by a study on women sex workers in the Indian state of Orissa. This documents the phenomenon of "flying sex workers": married women with children who come to town in the evening to earn extra money, especially before festivals.[43] In these instances, sex work is part of a portfolio of activities that women—and some men—engage in sporadically, not a specialized occupation.

As already noted, diversification out of agriculture among rural workers in India has mostly been confined to men; but it has a variety of gender impacts, and the mobility involved has also made a contribution to changing family structures (see box 6.2). In non-farm activity, the main sectors of growth appear to be construction, transport, storage, retailing, hotels and restaurants, all of which prefer male workers. Female employment has remained more or less confined to the agricultural sector, sometimes involving rural–rural seasonal migration.[44] In some areas and among some social groups, joint family migration is the norm. Many such families are landless, low-caste and illiterate, and work in unskilled jobs in brick kilns and construction, fish processing, and seasonal agriculture; women only occupy the most menial and low-paid activities. In such cases, gender relations remain undisturbed.[45] After a whole day's labour, women still have to cook for the family group and fetch water and fuel, while men relax. Also, the control of the women's wages remains with the men as heads of households.

One of the most significant aspects of labour-force segmentation is the divergence of low-entry, low-return activities and higher-entry, higher-return occupations. Not surprisingly, women are overwhelmingly clustered in low-entry, low-return activities to which they are driven by survival needs, as are men, but some men also occupy high-entry, high-return positions. The pittance that women receive from their new sources of income contributes to a vicious circle of under-capitalization. Men's savings from migrant labour or formal wage employment have often been used for investment in higher-value agriculture or family enterprise, enabling them to market an increasing output commercially. Women are much less likely to earn sufficient off-farm income to provide savings for agricultural investment.[46]

There are exceptions, notably in West Africa where women dominate the marketing of agricultural products. In southern Ghana where women traders are prominent, they are more likely than men to be found in low-entry, low-return type of activities, but there are a minority who operate on a very large scale, including at international level. One of the impacts of

---

Box 6.2 Diversification and changing household structures in India

Changes in marriage practices have been observed across India, some of which interact with rural income diversification. These changes include rising age at marriage, intensification and spread of dowry, and the trend towards household nucleation. Households may split into nuclear components when members move from agriculture to other occupations, or migrate separately for work; and when members seek to control earnings rather than share with the wider group. This may be a survival strategy for some people within an impoverished family unit, or it may derive from upward social mobility.

Part of the logic underpinning large birth orders and an extended family structure is to provide labour and mutual support for a farming family; thus the trend towards nuclear households is connected to declining land ownership and diversification from agriculture into non-farm occupations. Among better-off and more educated groups, it may also reflect the desire of daughters-in-law to escape the iron rod of mothers-in-law and their domestic labour demands, as well as their competition for their husbands' allegiance, and to have more control over household finance.

Since women are themselves influential in this trend, it must be perceived by them as in their interests, although there are losses too: assistance with domestic work and provision of childcare is less easy for women to procure within the nuclear family. Since liberalization tends to accelerate the diversification of livelihoods away from agriculture and reinforce landlessness, it can also be seen as supporting the process of family nucleation—which is likely to continue.

Source: Jackson and Rao 2004.

trade liberalization on market women in Ghana has been tougher competition; more resources and skills are needed to compete, and women who are poor and disadvantaged lose out to larger operators.

Where young migrant women seek employment in cities, opportunities arise for economic mobility, and social norms and practices can change dramatically. In countries such as China and Bangladesh where manufacturing industries employing women have expanded in recent years (see chapter 5), significant numbers of young rural women have gained access to salaried employment for the first time.[47] Many maintain their family links and invest their savings in land, agricultural inputs, housing, and tuition in vocational skills. Married migrant workers spend heavily on children's school fees, a potential route for upward mobility.[48] Unfortunately in some countries, especially in sub-Saharan Africa, rapid liberalization has been accompanied by the collapse of national industries, and there is thus a dearth of jobs to absorb rural migrants in search of new life chances.

Constraints on women's diversification

There are a number of reasons that rural labour markets in different settings remain so strongly gender-segmented. Some are straightforward and strictly economic, relating to entry costs (capital requirements), and the value that job-seekers place on their own labour. Many typical off-farm employment opportunities for women are in small-scale enterprises based on very low start-up costs.

The reasons that women are willing to work for very low wages compared with men are complex. Important considerations include the low income potential of their own production, and pressing family needs—to feed their children, for example. There are often few local earning opportunities for the large numbers of women seeking work to meet basic survival requirements, which male heads of household cannot or do not provide. Men's higher standing as farmers and their greater access to land and credit give them a stronger fall-back position and offer them opportunities with better returns. Social and cultural constraints on women can play an even more critical role than economic factors. In many parts of Asia only women in the lowest social groups work for pay on other people's farms,

while at the same time trust, reputation and social contacts preserve certain lucrative niches of the labour market for men.

Access to resources: Land and credit

Gender and land

One of the major lessons of the experience of economic reform and liberalization is that the resource poverty of farmers prevents them from taking up new opportunities. A critical asset in the rural economy remains land.[49] During the 1990s, land-tenure institutions were subject to reform in a number of countries. International donors have been heavily involved in the design of these reforms in many cases, underpinned by the view that having the "right institutions" (that is, private property rights through registration and titling) would strengthen markets, facilitate the entry of foreign capital into the agricultural sector, and enhance overall development.

In many countries women's rights activists have been closely involved in policy debates on land, often alongside other civil society groups such as rural trade unions, NGOs and social movements. Women's claims to be entitled to hold or own land have provoked contention, showing up deep divisions within civil society and generating accusations that some individual women or groups are willing to be co-opted by the state or by external donors. This occurred during debates on the recent land tenure reforms in Tanzania, which culminated in the passage of two pieces of detailed legislation in 1999.[50] Where rural social movements and trade unions have embraced women's landholding interests—as in the case of the *Movimento dos Trabalhadores Rurais Sem Terra* (movement of landless rural workers) and the *Confederação Nacional dos Trabalhadores na Agricultura* (national confederation of agricultural workers) in Brazil—this has only happened after many years of feminist activism within and outside the movements in question.[51]

Such efforts led to significant progress in the passage of more gender-equitable land-tenure laws during the 1990s. The reform of civil codes in Latin America has gradually expanded the property rights of married women and those in consensual unions. Women have also gained access to land via state programmes of land distribution and registration over the past decade, largely as a result of the rise and consolidation of national rural women's organizations and their success in pursuing their demands.[52] In India, the Ninth Five-Year Plan (1997–2002) paid particular attention to the land rights of women and of tribal populations, both groups heavily represented within smallholder agriculture.[53]

In sub-Saharan Africa, women's access to land has historically been sanctioned within indigenous or "customary" systems of land tenure. However, since the early 1950s, women's position has receded in the face of land registration and the introduction of land title and individual proprietorship. The assignment of formal landowning rights has tended to promote inequality and enhanced insecurity: the customary access rights of women, and of pastoralists and minority tribes, have often been denied recognition during registration processes.[54] The experience in Kenya is often cited as emblematic of how processes of land titling and registration fail women. In the recent wave of land tenure legislation and titling programmes in Tanzania, Uganda, Malawi, Côte d'Ivoire, Niger, Ghana, Zimbabwe and South Africa, women's interests in land have been given greater, although uneven, recognition.

Even where women's rights are formally recognized, there continues to be a substantial gap between the legal recognition of their right to own or hold land, and women's effective access to land as an income source. The reasons for this gap are complex, and vary from place to place. But two significant policy trends require attention if poorer women especially are to access land on a secure basis: the emphasis on developing markets in land, and the resurgence of policy interest in local and informal mechanisms for land management.

Creating land markets

If poorer women in particular are to access land on a secure basis, attention will have to be paid to the over-emphasis within current policies on the creation of markets in land by registration and the conferring of title. These are far from being a complete solution to under-capitalization, lack of farm improvement and depressed smallholder incomes. Evidence from different countries suggests that land markets rarely favour the rural poor, nor are they gender-neutral; see table 6.4 for information from Latin America.

Table 6.4 Form of acquisition of land ownership by gender (in percentages)

	Inheritance	Community	State	Market	Other	Total	
Brazil							
Women	54.2	—	0.6	37.4	7.8	100	n = 4,345
Men	22.0	—	1.0	73.1	3.9	100	n = 34,593
Chile							
Women	84.1	—	1.9	8.1	5.9	100	n = 271
Men	65.4	—	2.7	25.1	6.8	100	n = 411
Ecuador							
Women	42.5	—	5.0	44.9	7.6	100	n = 497
Men	34.5	—	6.5	43.3	15.6	100	n = 1,593
Mexico							
Women	81.1	1.8	5.3	8.1	3.7	100	n = 512
Men	44.7	14.8	19.6	12.0	8.9	100	n = 2,547
Nicaragua							
Women	57.0	—	10.0	33.0	—	100	n = 125
Men	32.0	—	16.0	52.0	—	100	n = 656
Peru							
Women	75.2	1.9	5.2	16.4	1.3	100	n = 310
Men	48.7	6.3	12.4	26.6	6.0	100	n = 1,512
Couples	37.3	1.6	7.7	52.6	0.8	100	n = 247

Source: Deere and León 2003: table 3.

A comprehensive study of continent-wide evidence on the effects of land privatization in sub-Saharan Africa also finds that recent processes of privatization and land concentration (rather than national land registration schemes per se) have reduced women's rights over land.[55] In the context of the reforms in Tanzania noted above, in which a Gender Land Task Force (GLTF) was created, some feminists argue that whereas women's rights to land as wives are protected under the new Village Land Law, their rights as community members are at risk given the liberalization principles and the administrative structures that have now been established.[56]

Not all women's advocates, however, share this dim view of liberalization. Some of the most influential groups in the Tanzanian GLTF supported land titling, registration and the creation of land markets, since it would allow women to purchase land and have it registered in their own name to be inherited by their descendants. However, such optimism may prove misplaced, especially as far as low-income women are concerned; in the context of commercialization and marketization, the tendency is for weaker groups, including poorer women, to lose customary rights they once had, while powerful contestants for control over such a vital resource consolidate their hold.

In South Africa land reform is a somewhat different process, operating against the historical background of apartheid. Here, reform has followed a "willing buyer–willing seller" model of exchange; commitment to gender equity has operated mainly at the level of lofty principle due to the absence of political accountability around women's land rights, as well as institutional and operational weaknesses. Concern with the process has centred on the state's inability, within the market-friendly straightjacket, to acquire and redistribute productive land proactively and on a large scale. By June 2000, the national average of transfer of farmland to new owners was 1 per cent—a paltry achievement relative to the need and the demand. A strictly demand-driven programme conflicts with the policy aim of reaching women as a constituency, because it overlooks the way in which power relations and divisions within communities influence the way in which "demand" is articulated.[57] The major achievement to date has been to ensure that women are chosen to serve on project committees along with men; however, given the difficulties

that women often experience in voicing their views in such circumstances, this cannot guarantee representation for women's interests in project planning. Nor is the representation of women in the future assured.[58]

The lack of an overall agrarian policy—in South Africa as in many other countries—further limits the effectiveness of land reform and proprietorship as agents of development. Given this policy vacuum, it is not at all clear that having secure access to a parcel of land is enough to provide the basis for a decent livelihood. In the case of India for example, the slow growth in the agricultural sector, the decline in public investment and other signs of rural stagnation are serious causes for alarm. Whether a change such as recognition of women's right to hold *patta* (title) to land, or the provision of training and extension services for rural women, would really make a difference is at least questionable.

The (re)turn to local and informal institutions

Recently there has been a resurgence of policy interest in informal, local-level "customary" mechanisms for land management, as part of the wider interest in decentralization and the strengthening of local government.[59] But so far there has been little discussion as to how these local-level systems work in practice, including their capacity to deliver more gender-equitable resource allocations. In most Asian and African settings, women have little power at any decision-making level involved in land tenure, not only within formal institutions of government and the law, but also, and especially, in informal local decision making. In several countries including South Africa and Ghana, there are serious concerns about the place to be assigned to "traditional" authorities in rural local government, since the basis of their power is not always democratically anchored and the "traditionalism" they espouse can be inimical to women's interests.[60]

Where decision making regarding land has been devolved to informal community-based institutions, as in Uganda which has gone furthest along this road, women are finding the "justice" delivered by local councils highly discriminatory. An observer explains: "Women ponder openly whether they, as quintessential outsiders in patrilineal and patrilocal society, can obtain an impartial judgement before a local council constituted by their husbands' family and friends".[61] Similar concerns have been raised about the decentralization of land administration in China. Here the shift of power to local authorities, unaccompanied by clear instructions from the central government, has led to the development of local practices that violate national laws intended to safeguard women's rights to land.[62]

Access to credit

Capital constraints are extremely important to both men and women farmers. All smallholder farming requires some capital, even subsistence farming for which there must be seeds and tools, but cash crop farming, whether of food or export crops, requires much more outlay. The sums involved are often beyond the reach of many women, through whose hands pitifully little cash may pass during the normal year.

Over the past decade, considerable policy attention has been given to micro-credit interventions for poverty reduction. Women have frequently been the specific targets of micro-credit facilities, as was mandated by the Beijing Declaration and Platform for Action. Given rural women's lack of independent access to all kinds of resources including capital, this policy attention to credit has been a boon.

South Asia has been home to some of the most active campaigns for extending micro-credit to women. In India the provision of adequate and timely credit, at reasonable rates of interest, has been a stated objective of public policy since Independence. Formal-sector lending institutions have been expanded accordingly, and concessional or subsidized credit has been made available to socially disadvantaged groups through the Integrated Rural Development Programme (IRDP) and other bank lending routes. However, there were many bureaucratic problems as well as a lack of sensitivity to the social and economic context in which these programmes operated.

A period of banking reform began in 1991, alongside other reforms directed at liberalization. Recent research on credit provision shows that the share of agriculture in total credit disbursement declined between 1985 and 2001. More significantly, the share of agricultural credit to marginal farmers, who in

1990 accounted for 30 per cent of agricultural credit from commercial banks, declined to 24 per cent in 1999–2000. During the same period, the number of beneficiaries receiving credit through the IRDP also declined from 2.9 million to 1.3 million.[63] While gender-disaggregated data is not available, it is likely that an insignificant proportion of this went to women due to the need for land as collateral for agricultural credit and the lack of land titles with most women.[64]

The government has sought to fill this gap through a rapid expansion in micro-credit provision through the formation of self-help groups (SHGs), mainly among women. These aim to overcome the problems of inaccessibility, high transaction costs and poor repayments encountered by the formal institutions. From support to 500 groups in 1992 the programme extended to 500,000 groups in 2002, altogether covering over 40 million people of whom 90 per cent are women—a significant achievement.[65]

There are however some shortcomings in the outreach of credit to women in the poorest sections of society. NGOs are responsible for linking women members to credit sources in 70 per cent of cases; thus the presence of NGOs active in microfinance dictates the spread of credit to potential customers. Such NGOs are unevenly spread across the country, tending to be concentrated in certain states and areas. It is also disappointing that, despite women's involvement in livestock-raising throughout rural India, the share of animal husbandry and dairying was only 6 per cent of the total small-scale credit offered for agriculture and allied activities during 1999–2000. Another problem is the relatively small size of average loans: R1,000 is the amount typically given to members of SHGs. This low loan level has often in the past led women into a trap of under-capitalization in income-generation projects and failure to create economic lift-off.

A study of women's SHGs in Andhra Pradesh points out that while the organization of women into groups is indeed a strategy in the right direction, it does not automatically contribute to changing social norms and gender equality.[66] From Bangladesh—another South Asian country where micro-credit schemes have mushroomed in recent decades—the evidence is mixed. Some studies show that women's bargaining position within households is strengthened by access to credit and the control over income and assets it brings, while other researchers argue that the loans and the pressure to repay lead to stress, and to higher levels of domestic violence.[67]

DETECTING CHANGE IN GENDER RELATIONS

During the 1990s, eroding state support for domestic agriculture and exposure to highly volatile and generally depressed global commodity markets have dealt heavy blows to many smallholder households in developing countries. Although few researchers have singled out for study the changes in gender relations within these communities and households, there is no doubt that severe economic pressures have provided a context for family disruption, interchange of gender roles, and shifts in resource control and male–female relations. In many countries where permanent or seasonal male out-migration has been heavy, women have assumed sole responsibility for the farming household. In contexts where liberalization has failed to produce a sustained rise in agricultural incomes, gender tensions and conflicts are a potential outcome of the livelihood adaptations households have been forced to undertake.

A few studies do give specific insights into the effects on gender relations in rural societies of the processes set in train by liberalization, including the Tanzania study previously referred to.[68] Here, the "scramble for cash" caused an upheaval in age-old gender and generation divisions of labour. The previous distribution of work between men and women has broken down, and men have generally accepted that their wives and daughters now work outside the home. Women often talk of their new income-earning roles as having been thrust upon them by worsening economic circumstances. While the range of cash-earning activities that women pursue constantly widens, some men have also taken on tasks traditionally assigned to women, such as beer brewing. As age and gender barriers to market entry melt away, a growing divide has appeared between those with and those without sufficient capital to enter non-agricultural opportunities yielding high returns.

The Tanzanian study also points to profound effects on gender and generational relations. While men seemed willing to acquiesce in women's new cash-earning opportunities, they were much less willing to accept a restructuring of household relations. Women complained of an intensified working day, and in communities where women have gained cash relative to men, they may face complaints from demoralized husbands who resent their wives' efforts to realize extra cash from trade and beer-brewing. Wife beating was also cited as an increasing problem.

The difficulties in renegotiating conjugal relations and responsibilities are echoed in another study into the effects of liberalization on gender relations and food security in two villages in rural Kenya.[69] Here men's income and employment opportunities have been undermined by liberalization, but women have sought out new opportunities both on and off their farms. Gender conflicts have subsequently ensued over control of income, decision making and questions of family respect. Pressures on the household and men's loss of their breadwinning role have exacerbated problems, and domestic violence has increased. Women's cash-earning work leaves less time for household and childcare tasks, and their expenditure choices have provoked men's suspicion and distrust.

This is part of a classic picture stemming from declining returns to smallholder farming and the intensification by rural households of long-standing income diversification, in the process of which gender and generational divisions of labour and authority are shaken up. As well as leading to strained gender relations, this has also produced new spaces of personal autonomy which women have seized. The process of diversification has taken varied forms. The negotiation of gendered responsibilities at lower levels of overall income is likely to lead to gender conflicts, and is also likely to be the most widespread effect of liberalization. As this chapter has shown, although there are some women who are diversifying into better incomes, for the vast majority of rural women diversification is more of a survival strategy than a route out of poverty. In some circumstances, where both men and women household members need to earn non-farm incomes to survive, there may be more opportunities for women to do so, but then there may be gender tensions over women's new earning opportunities, especially if men cannot find employment or men's farming income is going down.

Notes

1 House of Commons, International Development Committee 2003:15; Devereux 2002.

2 Patnaik 2003.

3 UNCTAD 2002; Gore 2003.

4 TWN 2003; Raghavan 2004.

5 World Bank 1981.

6 For Latin America, see Spoor 2002.

7 David et al. 2001.

8 Deere 2004:table 2, based on FAOSTAT for 43 countries and territories.

9 World Bank 1994:171.

10 Moyo 2002.

11 Abalu and Hassin 1999.

12 Bryceson 1999a, 1999b; Deininger and Olinto 2000; MAFF 1999; Oxfam/IDS 1999; Wold 1997.

13 Bryceson 2002.

14 For an extensive discussion of the statistical and methodological problems see Deere 2004 for Latin America, Whitehead 2004 for sub-Saharan Africa, Jackson and Rao 2004 for India.

15 See Deere 2004.

16 Msimang and Ambert 2004; Mackintosh and Tibandebage 2004; on elderly women in Thailand, see Knodel et al. 2001.

17 Heyzer 1996.

18 Rao 1999.

19 See Blackden 1997 for Zambia, and Dolan 1997 for Kenya.

20 Whitehead 2001.

21 Kabeer 2003:155.

22 Galli and Funk 1995; Bijlmakers et al. 1996.

23 Rweyemamu 2003; Mung'ong'o 2000; Sen 2002; Bigsten et al. 2001; Ellis and Mdoe 2002; Baffes 2002a, 2002b.

24 ActionAid 2004.

25 Kanji and Vijfhuizen 2003.

26 Blackden and Bhanu 1999; see Whitehead 2001 for a critical review of the empirical literature.

27 Arizpe et al. 1989.

28 Chiriboga et al. 1996.

29 Agarwal 2003.

30 Agarwal 2003; da Corta and Venkateshwarlu 1999.

31 Jackson 2003.

32 Gill 2001; da Corta and Venkateshwarlu 1999.

33 The extensive case study material for Latin America is reviewed by Deere 2004.

34 Dolan 1997; Oxfam/IDS 1999; Dolan and Sorby 2003.

35 Barrientos and Barrientos 2002.

36 Ellis 2000; Reardon 1997.

37 Bryceson 1999a, 1999b.

38 Lanjouw 2001; Ferreira and Lanjouw 2001; Elbers and Lanjouw 2001.

39 Kandiyoti 2003.

40 Whiteside 2000.

41 Sender 2002; Sender et al. 2004.

42 Adams 1991 cited in Whitehead 2004.

43 Gangoli 2003.

44 Breman 1985; Teerink 1995.

45 Mitra 1989/90.

46 Moore and Vaughan 1994.

47 Kabeer 2000; Gulati 1993.

48 Lee 2004.

49 Agarwal 1994.

50 Tsikata 2003b.

51 Deere 2003.

52 Deere 2003.

53 Jackson and Rao 2004.

54 Platteau 1995.

55 Lastarria-Cornhiel 1997.

56 Mbilinyi 1999:5 cited in Tsikata 2003b.

57 Walker 2003.

58 Walker 2003.

59 Whitehead and Tsikata 2003.

60 Tsikata 2003a.

61 Khadiagala 2001:67.

62 Zongmin 2004.

63 Ramachandran and Swaminathan 2004.

64 Jackson and Rao 2004,

65 NABARD 2004.

66 Deshmukh-Ranadive 2003.

67 Schuler et al. 1996; Goetz and Sengupta 1996.

68 Bryceson 1999a, 1999b.

69 RODI-Kenya 2004.

Chapter 7
Cross-border migration of workers

The discussion of rural and urban livelihoods in the previous two chapters indicates that movement—whether seasonal, circular, temporary or permanent—is integral to people's livelihoods in many parts of the developing world. For many of those with deteriorating incomes, migration offers the promise of survival or of a better life for themselves and their families. This can involve seasonal migration; it can also involve longer-term or even permanent stays in towns or cities in the hope of finding better-paid work than is available in rural areas. Yet another scenario involves crossing international borders in the search for earning opportunities.

It is often assumed that international migration almost invariably involves the movement of people from poor to more affluent countries. However, the reality is more complex; today's migrant workforce comprises workers with a variety of skills moving to an increasing variety of destinations. Considerable migration takes place between industrialized countries.[1] This diversity of worker migration has led to the emergence around the world of complex systems of workforce stratification according to ethnic origin, migration status and gender.[2] Given the increasing income gaps between countries in different regions over the past couple of decades,[3] it is reasonable to assume that there has been a surge in both short-range and long-range movements.

The international migration of workers has attracted a great deal of policy attention in recent years. The reasons stem in part from xenophobic political considerations in destination countries, and also from the process of ageing under way in most industrialized countries, with greater longevity imposing new demands on the care economy. There are also concerns about brain and skills drains from developing countries which they can ill afford. Countries of origin have also begun to show increasing interest in their diasporas and the benefits of their remittances; this has been assisted in some cases by programmes such as the Migration for Development in Africa initiative by the International Organization for Migration (IOM).[4] Total diaspora remittances worldwide are estimated at around US$100 million annually; they thus keep entire economies afloat.[5]

Within and beyond these considerations, there are gendered ramifications of migratory processes. Gender-differentiated population movement often reflects the way in which gender divisions of labour are incorporated into uneven economic development processes.[6] Prejudices attached to immigration, combined with racial and gender inequalities, make migrant women "triply disadvantaged" and likely to be over-represented in marginal, unregulated and poorly paid jobs. At the same time, the upheaval of migration—whether by women on their own or jointly with men—has the potential to reconfigure gender relations and power inequalities. Opportunities emerge to improve lives and escape previously oppressive situations.

These, however, are accompanied by new vulnerabilities. In unfamiliar environments, migrants can be exposed to exploitation and abuse in the living environment and workplace, and to breakdowns of norms within their own social networks. Families are often split apart. The departure of one or both spouses to other countries, sometimes together, sometimes apart, has negative implications for children left behind and can lead

Box 7.1   "Illegal", "undocumented", "irregular": A note on terminology

Migrants without documentation or work permits are typically referred to as "illegal", which is misleading as it conveys the idea of criminality. Many studies have shown that migrants shift between the status of legality and illegality for various reasons, often beyond their control or knowledge. The term "undocumented" is preferable, but does not cover migrants who enter the destination country legally but later violate their original entry visa. At the 1999 International Symposium on Migration in Bangkok in 1999, 21 participating countries agreed to use the term "irregular migrants", which has since become common practice.

to permanent family break-up.[7] The risk of sexually transmitted disease also rises. Migrant workers tend to have higher HIV infection rates than non-migrants, no matter what the HIV prevalence is at sites of departure or destination; this has been documented in Mexico, Senegal, Ecuador and southeast Ghana.[8]

INTERNATIONAL MIGRATORY FLOWS

All regions are implicated in the rising mobility of people in search of work and earning opportunities, and the associated policy issues have correspondingly risen on political agendas. Although transnational workers still represent a small percentage of industrialized countries' total workforce (4 per cent), migratory flows of workers from the developing to the industrialized countries have been rising in recent decades. The United States received the largest proportion (81 per cent), followed by Canada and Australia (11 per cent) and the European Union.[9] Women account for an increasing proportion of international migrants (49 per cent in 2000), reflecting their increasing role as primary income earners. The out-migration of women workers is most evident from Asia, with the majority migrating as domestics, workers in the entertainment industry, and to a lesser extent as nurses and teachers.[10]

Despite women's increasing presence in migratory flows, there are few statistics on international migration by gender; the data is also uneven across countries.[11] Surveys inevitably underestimate those entering in an undocumented manner or working irregularly, as well as the extent of transient circulation.

The lowly position of women in the labour market, the poor value accorded to domestic work, the lack of protection in informal and irregular occupations, especially those dominating the entertainment and hospitality industries, and involvement in (illegal) commercial sex, mean that many women are vulnerable to exploitation. Gender considerations cannot, therefore, be confined to male/female breakdowns of formal labour migration statistics, but should embrace the factors influencing standard male/female roles and access to jobs and resources.

CHANGING "MIGRATION REGIMES": WHO GETS IN?

Regulations and practices—"migration regimes"—govern the entry and continued residence of migrants. Despite a history of excluding certain groups of migrants, the so-called "settlement countries" (Canada, the United States, Australia, New Zealand) grant most migrants the right to settle permanently. Today, migrants from Asia (in Canada, the United States, Australia and New Zealand), and from Latin America (in the United States), have displaced earlier patterns of migration from Europe to the "New World". The pattern in Europe has been different. The postcolonial policy of bringing in temporary workers and limiting long-term immigration has led to distinctions between "settlers", "guest workers" and "colonial" migration. All four settlement countries still welcome large-scale immigration, and access to both labour markets and citizenship is straightforward in comparison with much of Europe.

In North America

However, there has recently been a change in attitudes towards immigration in North America. Both Canada and the United States admit permanent residents on the basis of three long-established principles: family reunification, economic contribution and humanitarian concerns. There are now moves towards a dilution of these "settlement" principles in ways that favour the needs of the labour market. Policy makers are increasingly urged to tailor immigrant selection to meet long-term demographic needs based on those human-capital characteristics most likely to ensure net national advantage. They thus appear to be moving closer to a "guest worker" regime.

The number of temporary residents in both the United States and Canada has grown rapidly in the recent past. They include both skilled workers, such as managerial, professional, and information technology (IT) workers, and low-skill workers such as live-in caregivers and seasonal agricultural workers. Most active recruitment has been in the skilled categories. There is a belief that skilled and educated workers will integrate more easily, whereas immigrants with low educational attainments are regarded as hard on the public purse. In both countries it has recently been proposed to legalize irregular immigrants by granting them temporary-worker status.

The targeting of young, highly skilled entrants for permanent residence is most evident in Canada, where a series of regulatory changes in the 1980s and 1990s restricted immigration based on family reunification, and emphasized the intake of those who would make economic contributions. By the end of the 1990s, the majority of new immigrants to Canada consisted of "economic immigrants" and their immediate families (see figure 7.1). In the United States meanwhile, despite frequent calls from economists and policy makers to change immigration policy so as to improve immigrant "quality", most still come in as relatives of legal residents (see figure 7.2). A variety of political and administrative factors militate against the adoption of more selective entrance requirements in the United States, not least the politicized nature of the debate at a time when the electoral importance of the huge Hispanic population is taken very seriously by both political parties.

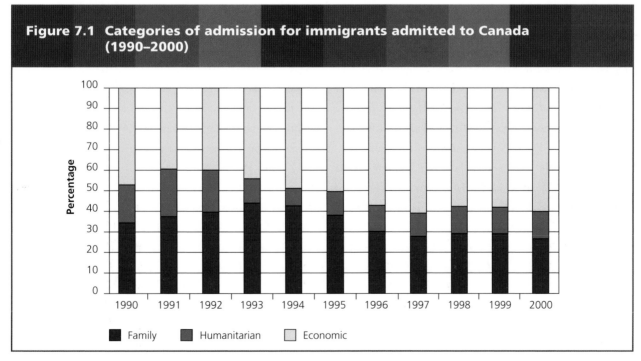

Figure 7.1 Categories of admission for immigrants admitted to Canada (1990–2000)

Note: Years ranging from January 1 to December 31.
Sources: Minister of Supply and Services Canada 1991, 1992, 1996; Minister of Public Works and Government Services Canada 1994, 1997, 1998, 1999a, 1999b, 2000, 2001, cited in Boyd and Pikkov 2004.

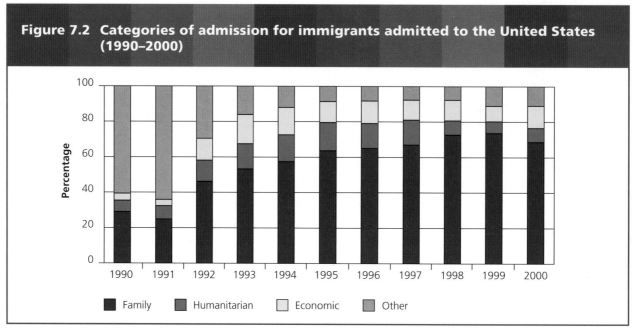

Figure 7.2 Categories of admission for immigrants admitted to the United States (1990–2000)

Note: Years ranging from April 1 to March 31.
Source: Department of Homeland Security, United States 2003, cited in Boyd and Pikkov 2004.

In Europe

In Europe, the debates surrounding immigration are also politicized; populist protests fed by far-right elements vociferously demand restrictions on migrants, whether for work, family reunification or asylum. In countries where right-wing parties have gained power in recent elections, as in Denmark, France, Italy and the Netherlands, one of the first policy areas to be addressed has been that of immigration control. Several countries have recently introduced legislation to tighten rules concerning family reunification and other areas of the migration regime. In the wake of 9/11, Denmark, France and Germany have also introduced or reinforced compulsory integration programmes. The increasing pressure for "integration" and "assimilation" has served to reinforce suspicion towards Muslim populations in particular, who are wrongly and simplistically depicted as inimical to Western values, especially in their views of gender relations.

Within more restrictive and punitive regimes, however, a distinction has been drawn between the skilled who are welcome, and the less skilled whose numbers are to be controlled. Some countries offer easier entry to the skilled: the right to be accompanied by one's family, family members' right to work, a permanent residence permit and citizenship. Some new systems—those under Germany's new immigration law, and in the United Kingdom—operate a points system; in the United Kingdom this prioritizes income, job status and educational level. The less skilled generally enter as contract labour or under a guest worker system, without the possibility of transition to settlement or the right to bring in family members. Where quotas are insufficient to meet employers' demands, migrant workers enter in a forced state of irregularity.

In Asian countries

In East and Southeast Asian countries, hosts to millions of migrant workers from poorer regional neighbours, contract labour is also prevalent. Since the mid-1970s when significant worker migration began, measures to control flows and at the same time provide employers with a pool of flexible labour have gradually been introduced. Workers are categorized according to skills: registered professionals and highly skilled workers;

authorized unskilled workers on contract; and unskilled workers with neither contract nor permission of entry, who are therefore unauthorized. Notably absent from this is any right of admission based on humanitarian concerns. In contrast with Europe and the traditional "settler" countries, Asian countries officially prevent unskilled migrants from settling and reuniting with their families.

Although multi-ethnic and multi-religious societies such as Malaysia, Singapore and Hong Kong (SAR China) were historically formed by migration, maintaining ethnic balances is a contributing reason for rigid migration policies today. In some countries—Thailand, for example—some national minority groups do not even have full citizenship rights. Acquisition of permanent residence status, let alone citizenship, is therefore out of reach for most inter-country Asian migrants. In the multi-ethnic societies, migrants usually enter to work on contract at well-defined jobs for a specified number of years. In the more mono-ethnic countries of East Asia, such as the Republic of Korea and Japan, there is no admission of unskilled migrants—except for those with ethnic ties (the so-called *nikkeijin* in Japan and Korean-Chinese in Korea). Skilled foreigners are admitted for selected occupations. Despite the official policy of prohibiting unskilled foreigners from employment, both countries have been home for many years to 200,000–300,000 unskilled migrants, either legally under the cover of "traineeship programmes" or irregularly in an undocumented manner.

WOMEN WORKERS' MODES OF ENTRY

Family reunification

In both North America (table 7.1) and Europe, women predominate among migrants entering on the basis of family reunification, while they are less than half of those entering on the basis of economic criteria. This statement is based on data concerning both sexes, regardless of whether they enter as principal applicants or as family members. Earlier research for North America confirms that when women enter on the basis of humanitarian or economic criteria of admissibility, they are most likely to be the spouses or dependents of male principal applicants.[12] Only where labour flows are destined for female-typed jobs, such as nurses and domestics (see below), do women predominate as economic migrants. The mode of entry for women thus tends to reflect their stereotypical roles as wives, daughters and caregivers.

Table 7.1 Percentage of total admissions of immigrants in the family, humanitarian and economic categories who are females [1] (1990–2000)

	Canada [2]			United States [3]		
	Family	Humanitarian	Economic	Family	Humanitarian	Economic
1990	54.9	40.3	49.2	54.2	46.7	50.9
1991	56.0	38.5	50.2	54.8	48.1	50.3
1992	57.1	38.7	50.1	56.5	48.2	48.6
1993	58.0	42.6	51.6	56.4	49.0	47.7
1994	57.5	43.7	50.7	56.6	49.1	49.0
1995	58.3	43.1	49.5	56.9	48.5	49.5
1996	58.8	45.7	48.3	57.1	47.6	49.9
1997	59.8	44.6	47.8	57.6	46.8	49.2
1998	60.9	46.0	47.5	56.8	46.6	48.1
1999	61.2	45.9	47.1	57.4	48.7	49.5
2000	61.6	46.4	46.7	58.5	48.0	49.4

Notes   (1) For example of all persons admitted to Canada in 1990 as immigrants (permanent residents) on the basis of family ties, 54.9% were female.
          (2) Calendar years, ranging from January 1–December 31.
          (3) Fiscal years, ranging from April 1–March 31.
Sources: Minister of Supply and Services Canada 1991, 1992, 1996; Minister of Public Works and Government Services Canada 1994, 1997, 1998, 1999a, 1999b, 2000, 2001; Department of Homeland Security, United States, 2003, cited in Boyd and Pikkov 2004.

Despite the significance of migration for family reasons, it receives virtually no attention in migration research. This is mainly due to its association with female "dependency". The assumption is that most women migrants do not enter the labour force and are not concerned about work. Virtually nothing is known of their employment aspirations. With the expansion in skilled male migration and the likelihood that the wives of skilled males may also be skilled, an increasing number of educated women are likely to be blocked from careers. There has recently been some relaxation in regulations for spouses of skilled migrants; but difficulties of recognition for professional qualifications obtained elsewhere typically remain.

In the European Union (EU) and North America, another regulatory inhibition is that the "family" for immigration purposes is defined by the state, and although it includes spouses and dependent children under the age of 18 years, it does not normally include parents unless they are dependent or in serious difficulties. Thus the more limited concept of family leaves little consideration for caring at a distance, cultural differences

in familial relationships, and the role of grandparents or other relations in providing nurturing and support for different members of the family (see table 7.2).

Asylum and refugee migration

The other significant category is humanitarian-based admissions: asylum seekers and refugees. Although laws and procedures for such admissions are couched in gender-neutral language, this does not guarantee gender parity in outcomes. Statistics for camp populations assisted by the United Nations High Commissioner for Refugees (UNHCR) show that women aged 18–59 equal or outnumber their male counterparts; but throughout the 1990s, women of all ages represented less than half of refugee and asylum seekers in the United States, and of Canadian refugee admissions (table 7.1). The gender gap in admissions is larger when using data on principal applicants, since this excludes spouses and dependants: 33 per cent of

Table 7.2 Beneficiaries of family reunification in the European Union

Country	Spouse	Children	Parents	Others
Belgium	Yes	Less than 18 dependent		
Denmark	Yes (also de facto partner)	Less than 18 living with person with parental responsibility	Over 60 dependent	For special reasons
France	Yes	Less than 18; less than 21 for member states to the European charter	Not considered	
Germany	Yes	Less than 16 unmarried; less than 18 for specific cases	For humanitarian reasons	
Greece	Yes	Less than 18	Dependent	
Ireland	Yes	Depending on individual circumstances	Depending on the individual circumstances	Depending on the individual circumstances
Italy	Yes	Less than 18 dependent	Dependent	Non-minor children
Luxembourg	Yes	Less than 18	Yes	Non-minor children
Netherlands	Yes (also de facto partner)	Less than 18 dependent	If non-reunification causes difficulties	In exceptional circumstances
Portugal	Yes	Dependent	Dependent	May be considered
Spain	Yes	Less than 18	Dependent	Non-minor children
United Kingdom	Yes	Less than 18 dependent, unmarried	Dependent widow mother; widower father	For extraordinary reasons

Source: European Commission 2003.

principal applicants as refugees to Canada were women in 2000. In the UK the majority of asylum applicants in 2002 were men (78 per cent), but the rates of recognition of the right to claim refugee status did not vary markedly between women and men.

Within the asylum processing or refugee recognition process, factors relating to gender—such as vulnerability to sexual violence, discrimination based on behaviour or dress—may not be given consideration. The definition of a refugee should be gender-neutral, but the exclusion of gendered forms of discrimination or vulnerability amounts to male bias. Women's political activities, often located in the private sphere or comprising domestic support for dissidents, may not qualify as likely to provoke persecution. In Australia, Canada and New Zealand, guidelines for gender persecution in the asylum process are already in place, and European states (Denmark, Germany, Ireland, Norway, Sweden and the United Kingdom), are increasingly following suit. Norway and Sweden operate affirmative policies, providing women to be resettled with travel grants and applying selection criteria which include vulnerability as well as political persecution; similar proposals are being considered in the United Kingdom.

Countries which resettle refugees often add admissibility criteria to the basic eligibility criteria. These reflect concerns that the refugees should not pose health or security threats, and that they should not require extensive and long-term social assistance. For the most part, eligibility is a necessary, but not sufficient, criterion of admissibility, which also depends on education, job skills and the potential for economic self-sufficiency. The gender stratification typical of most societies means that women usually have less education than men, and have lower skills and fewer working experiences; they are therefore likely to encounter greater difficulties in meeting "self-sufficiency" criteria. Canada's pioneering Woman at Risk programme, which began in 1988 in response to a request from UNHCR for special assistance in the protection and resettlement of vulnerable women refugees, still only receives modest numbers. Only 2,250 women and their dependents have been resettled since admissions began. This stems from the real difficulties of economic integration and the long time-frame required, and the high cost of caring for these individuals from private and state funds.[13]

Trends in East and Southeast Asia

Contrary to the North American and European stereotype of women migrants as dependants, East and Southeast Asian women overwhelmingly migrate as independent workers, either as single women or as married women without their husbands or children. A channel of migration increasingly used by Asian women is "marriage migration". Either marriage is the result of labour migration, when for example a hospitality or entertainment worker marries a host-country customer; or marriage is the purpose, as is the case with "mail-order brides".[14] There has been such a significant increase in inter-country marriages in East Asia, with the majority of couples involving local men (in Japan, Republic of Korea and Taiwan Province of China) and women from Southeast Asia, that East Asian governments are revisiting their residence and citizenship regulations. In Singapore, marriages between unskilled foreign domestic workers and local men are prohibited by law.

As already noted, migration destination countries in Asia do not recognize family reunification as a criterion of immigration. The number of immigrants formally admitted on humanitarian grounds (refugees and asylum seekers) is also insignificant. Table 7.3 shows outflows of female migrant workers, mostly live-in domestics, from the four major sending countries in Asia from 1979 to 1996. The data shows that the feminization of migration from these countries began in the late 1970s, when Sri Lanka despatched significant numbers of women domestic workers, mostly to the Middle East. By the mid-1990s other countries were contributing to this flow, with women constituting up to 70 per cent of their migrant worker outflows. These women were employed in the Middle East, Europe, North America and Oceania.

Turning to the presence of migrant women in Asia's labour-importing countries, table 7.4 lists by country the number and proportion of females to the total migrant population in various occupations. By 2002 there were at least 1.3 million foreign women working in the seven major labour-importing countries: Singapore, Malaysia, Thailand, Taiwan Province of China, Hong Kong (SAR China), Republic of Korea and Japan. In some, these women constituted a high proportion of the total immigrant labour force.

Table 7.3	Number of female migrant workers by sending country and proportion of females in total outflows (1979–1996)							
	Sri Lanka		Indonesia		Philippines		Thailand	
	Total number	% of females	Total number	% of females	Total number	% of females	Total number	% of females
1979	12,251	47.3	—	—	—	—	—	—
1980	14,529	50.8	—	—	3,862	18.0	—	—
1981	30,135	52.5	—	—	—	—	—	—
1982	5,400	24.0	—	—	—	—	—	—
1983	7,819	43.2	12,018	48.4	—	—	—	—
1984	5,762	36.7	20,425	48.0	—	—	—	—
1985	11,792	95.1	39,960	49.4	—	—	—	—
1986	5,150	31.4	39,078	47.7	—	—	7,194	6.4
1987	5,474	34.0	44,291	49.0	180,441	47.2	9,752	9.2
1988	10,119	54.9	49,586	48.6	—	—	15,062	12.7
1989	16,044	58.4	—	—	—	—	—	—
1990	27,248	63.9	—	—	—	—	—	—
1991	43,612	67.0	—	—	—	—	—	—
1992	29,159	65.3	—	—	—	—	—	—
1993	31,600	64.8	85,696	66.0	138,242*	54.0	41,830	19.4
1994	43,796	72.8	—	—	153,504*	59.2	—	—
1995	125,988	73.3	—	—	124,822*	58.3	31,586	15.6
1996	119,456	73.5	—	—	111,487*	54.2	28,642	13.3

Note: * Numbers of newly hired only.
Source: UNDESA Population Division 2003, cited in Yamanaka and Piper 2004.

Irregular migration

As table 7.4 suggests, irregular or unauthorized migrants are an important contingent in the Asian countries. This is a product of uneven economic development and the fact that neighbouring countries contain populations with a shared history, language and religion. Borders between Malaysia, Indonesia and the Philippines have been porous, as have those between Thailand and Myanmar, Laos, Viet Nam and Cambodia. Reliable information is not available, but the total number of unauthorized workers in these areas is estimated at 1.5 to 2 million. Studies of undocumented migration in Southeast Asia report considerable numbers of migrant women from the Philippines, Indonesia, Myanmar and Laos working under strenuous conditions with little legal protection in a wide range of occupations, as domestic workers, vendors, plantation workers, factory workers, construction labourers and fish-farm hands. The border areas between Thailand and Myanmar host large numbers of women, often belonging to ethnic minorities, who engage in sex work.[15] The many legal and human rights contradictions inherent in the status of many of these women migrants have triggered mushrooming activism by non-governmental organizations (NGOs).[16]

At the US–Mexican border, where unauthorized labour enters North America, migrants face similar or worse discriminations and difficulties. The irregular population in the United States is estimated at about 9.3 million, representing a little over one-quarter of all foreign-born in the country; 41 per cent are women. Backlogs are thought to be responsible for a considerable proportion, as family members can wait 10 years for a visa. Ninety-six per cent of the men are in the workforce, as are an estimated 62 per cent of the women. The 6 million altogether

Table 7.4 Occupation, immigration status, country of origin, and number of unskilled female migrant workers by receiving country and percentage of total number in the early 2000s

Country/ economy	Major occupation	Immigration status	Country of origin	Number of women	% of women to total number
Singapore	Domestic worker	Contract worker	Philippines, Indonesia, Sri Lanka	140,000	43.8
Malaysia	Domestic worker	Contract worker	Indonesia, Philippines	162,000	20.5
		Unauthorized migrant		-	-
Thailand	Domestic worker	Registered migrant	Myanmar, Lao PDR	244,000	43.0
		Unauthorized migrant	Cambodia	-	-
Hong Kong (SAR China)	Domestic worker	Contract worker	Philippines, Indonesia, Thailand, Sri Lanka, Nepal, India, Other	201,000	70.0
Taiwan Prov. of China	Domestic worker, Caregiver	Contract worker	Indonesia, Philippines, Viet Nam	170,000	56.0
Republic of Korea	Factory worker	Industrial trainee	China, Philippines, Viet Nam	35,000	35.1
		Unauthorized migrant	Mongolia, Thailand, Other		-
	Service worker	Unauthorized migrant	Korean-Chinese, Chinese	43,000	-
	Entertainer	Entertainer	Philippines, Russia	5,000	-
	Unknown	Unauthorized migrant	Thailand, Mongolia, Other	19,000	-
	Foreign Wives	Spouse of Citizen	China, Philippines, Thailand	57,000*	-
Japan	Factory worker	Long-term resident	Brazil, Peru	120,000	45.1
	Entertainer	Entertainer	Philippines, Russia, Rep. of Korea	40,000	84.1
	Unknown	Unauthorized migrant	Rep. of Korea, Philippines, Thailand, China	106,000	47.3
	Foreign wives	Spouse of citizen	China, Philippines, Rep. of Korea, Thailand	89,000**	-

Notes   *Total for 2000 and 2001.
              ** Total for 1989 to 1999.
Sources: Huang and Yeoh 2003; Chin 2003; Tantiwiramanond 2002; Hong Kong Census and Statistics Department 2002; Lan 2003; Lee 2003; Yamanaka 2003, cited in Yamanaka and Piper 2004.

who are thought to work account for 5 per cent of the work force, and contribute 10 per cent of the US economy.[17] These workers earn less than others; two-thirds make less than twice the minimum wage.

In the face of this tidal flow of migrant workers playing a significant role in the US economy, a shaky political consensus has formed in favour of conferring some kind of legal status to at least some part of the undocumented population. President George W. Bush's 2004 immigration policy reform proposal and its programme for legalization bear a striking resemblance to European guest-worker policies, and may well lead to the institutionalization of a class of legal residents with second-class status.

Trafficking

People trafficking is the most notorious feature of irregular migration, and trafficking for the purpose of sexual exploitation frequently constitutes the gravest violation of human rights. Trafficking in human beings is far from being a new phenomenon, but like other migratory flows, it appears to be growing in scope and magnitude. Migration and trafficking are often distinguished from one another by the notion that migration is characterized by choice, and trafficking by coercion, deception or force. However, in today's globalized economic context and in the face of heavy restrictions on freedom of movement, cross-border trafficking and migration exist along a continuum. In addition, war and conflict situations tend to result in higher incidences of trafficking (see chapter 13).

A problematic issue is the definition of trafficking, which is differently interpreted according to differing interests, viewpoints and policy objectives. Views vary as to whether non-coerced, adult migrant prostitution should be included. Too narrow a definition of trafficking may obscure the different pressures pushing women to migrate in search of work in the sex industry. There is increasing evidence that migrant women rarely fit the perfect victim image. Many fully understand prior to migration what their working destination consists of, and even if their choice is constrained by economic and social circumstances, they actively co-operate in it. What such women need is a legal status and employment rights, which would allow them to leave commercial sex for other types of work. Another problem with the common definition of trafficking is its focus on sexual exploitation only, omitting those who are the objects of other types of work-related trafficking.

In the context of cross-border movements, destination countries have commonly treated human trafficking first and foremost as an issue of illegal immigration. The danger with this approach is that it involves a shift of focus away from the problem of human rights violations to that of illegal entry and stay, so that ultimately the receiving state, rather than the trafficked person, is perceived as the "victim".

This also explains the reasoning behind victim support systems recently put in place by some destination countries, which require women to testify in court against their traffickers in order to receive residence permits. Temporary residence, however, does not result in long-term security for the women involved. The practice of entwining the selling of sex by migrant women with debates over illegal immigration usually results in the latter taking precedence, with many women being deported upon

detection. This also explains governments' reluctance to regularize the presence of foreign sex workers, as such a move is seen as encouraging illegal immigration.[18]

One of the harshest realities for undocumented migrants is that they are vulnerable to deportation at any time for any infraction of the law. While this has implications for trafficked women, undocumented immigrant women who suffer physical abuse at the hands of employers or spouses are also vulnerable. In the United States, battered women's advocates pressured the US Congress to create a provision in the 1994 Violence Against Women Act to reserve green cards for undocumented immigrant women who have been physically abused by a (legally resident) spouse, and allow them to petition for permanent residency without the knowledge of their husbands. By 2001, 17,907 women had applied under the provision. Destination countries of women trafficked for sexual exploitation have also begun to put in place victim support programmes and provide visa categories that allow identified victims to postpone, or even avoid, deportation; Italy is a case in point.

STRATIFIED LABOUR MARKETS

Immigrant women have low participation in the labour force, and occupy low-status jobs with poor working conditions and low earnings (see figure 7.3 and table 7.5). In North America, foreign-born women were the least likely of all groups, defined by birth-place and gender, to be in the formal labour force in the 1990s.[19] Although some foreign women, including some of those from the developing world, are present among skilled workers, they are disproportionately visible at the bottom rungs of stratified services, retail and manufacturing sectors. African, Latin American and Hispanic women are most likely to be in low-skilled jobs.[20]

In Northern Europe, the rate of participation in the labour force of migrant women is lower than for national women, although it has recently been increasing. Within each country there are also considerable variations between nationalities. Refugee women find it particularly difficult to enter the labour market, according to Norwegian data, and fewer women participate in

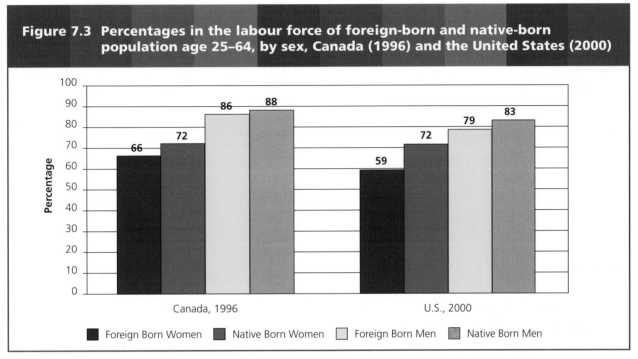

Figure 7.3 Percentages in the labour force of foreign-born and native-born population age 25–64, by sex, Canada (1996) and the United States (2000)

Sources: Calculated from Statistics Canada 1996 and United States Census Bureau 2000, cited in Boyd and Pikkov 2004.

labour market schemes than men.[21] In many countries asylum seekers are barred from employment, at least initially. Being the non-principal applicant for asylum can also make it more difficult to obtain the right to work. Refugees generally confront cultural and language barriers, racism, prejudice and lack of recognition of qualifications; but women refugees have additional burdens of childcare and may also face opposition from male family members to employment outside the home.

While some of the disparity between groups may be explained by such factors as greater numbers of children in immigrant families and culturally conditioned choices of suitable female employment, these low rates also reflect difficulties in finding jobs, and the quality of employment on offer.

The rise in women's employment in many Organization for Economic Co-operation and Development (OECD) countries, especially where many mothers of young children work full-time as in Sweden and France, has created extra demands for childcare and other social services. Although family members, especially grandmothers, may provide significant informal support, there is also increasing resort to formal service provision,

either in the public sector, or via the market, or by less formal community networks.

The service sectors in which jobs are created are prime generators of insecure and low-waged jobs, especially where government is off-loading social services to the private, community and voluntary sectors. In the new global economy, men and women circulate differently. Men tend to occupy an elite space in a high-tech world of global finance, production and technology: the commanding heights of the "knowledge economy". They move more easily within transnational corporations and in the IT and scientific sectors, while women provide the services associated with a wife's traditional role: care of children and the elderly, home-making and sex. Although women are not absent from the ranks of the skilled, demands in such industries as IT for constant physical mobility and flexibility between workplaces are difficult for migrant women workers to meet.

Migrant women thus fill expanded needs for care in advanced economies, enabling their growth to take place under neoliberal conditions of welfare restriction and flexible labour forces.[22] The role of migrant women in providing care for the

Table 7.5 Participation rate and unemployment rate of nationals and foreigners by sex in selected OECD countries, 2001-2002 average

	Participation rate				Unemployment rate			
	Men		Women		Men		Women	
	Nationals	Foreigners	Nationals	Foreigners	Nationals	Foreigners	Nationals	Foreigners
Austria	78.7	84.6	63.2	63.1	4.0	9.3	4.0	8.2
Belgium	72.8	71.2	56.2	42.7	5.1	14.3	6.6	17.8
Czech Republic	78.5	84.1	62.8	61.6	6.3	9.1	9.1	13.2
France	75.2	76.1	63.4	48.4	6.7	16.6	9.6	21.0
Germany	78.9	77.6	65.2	51.5	7.7	13.7	7.7	12.1
Greece	75.8	89.4	49.1	57.8	6.6	6.9	15.2	16.1
Hungary (2001)	67.5	77.3	52.4	53.1	6.3	2.2	5.0	7.7
Ireland	78.8	77.3	56.7	56.4	4.3	4.9	3.6	5.5
Luxembourg	73.0	81.8	48.4	59.1	1.3	2.4	1.9	4.2
Netherlands	85.3	68.9	68.1	52.1	2.0	4.4	2.6	5.0
Spain	78.3	88.3	51.2	63.8	7.4	11.4	15.7	17.0
Sweden	80.5	71.0	76.9	60.4	4.9	12.1	4.3	9.3
Switzerland	88.8	89.6	74.1	71.2	1.7	4.6	2.6	6.2
United Kingdom	82.7	76.4	68.7	56.3	5.3	8.4	4.1	7.5
Australia (2001)[1]	81.7	77.8	67.6	59.3	7.8	8.6	6.2	8.1
Canada (2001)[1]	73.9	68.7	62.3	54.6	7.8	6.8	7.0	8.1
United States[1]	82.0	86.5	72.2	62.6	6.0	5.6	4.7	6.3

Notes: Calculations are made on labour force aged 15 to 64 with the exception of Canada (15 and over) and the United States (16 to 64 years old).
(1) The data refer to the native and foreign-born populations.
Source: OECD 2004b.

elderly, children, the disabled, in paid, unpaid, formal and informal capacities is a factor too little addressed in the context of changes in the care economy and the welfare state.[23] In some countries migrant labour contributes substantially to employment in schools, hospitals, residential homes for the elderly and childcare centres. The Scandinavian countries and the United Kingdom have the highest percentages of migrant women employed in education and health. In Sweden these accounted for 27 per cent of migrant female employment in 2001–2, in Finland and the United Kingdom for 22 per cent. In other European countries the proportions are much lower: 8 per cent in France, 10 per cent in Germany and 5 per cent in Spain.

As far as domestic work and household care is concerned, the most widespread problems are the low pay and long working hours, the inferior positions of domestic workers, and the personalized relationships with employers which make it difficult to negotiate reasonable and timely pay or time off. The prospects of exploitation are greater if the worker is young, especially if she is below official working age. The health and safety situation in the home may not be satisfactory, education and personal growth opportunities may be lost, and if the worker is ill she may not be paid and may even lose her job. There are also risks of psychological, physical and sexual abuse. Chances of redress are low since domestic work is not usually covered by

Box 7.2   How commuters from the margins help the elite live in clover

Ewa, a single mother in the small Polish town of Siemiatycze near the border with Belarus, has been shuttling back and forth to Brussels for four-month stints for the past seven years. The mother of a 12-year-old boy, Ewa operates a job-share with her mother. They take it in turns to manage their Brussels employers' domestic load—cooking, cleaning, minding the children, and running the errands—to free them for leisure or professional employment.

Thousands of people in Siemiatycze regularly commute to Brussels to provide an underclass of cheap and irregular labour to the upper crust of Western Europe. Lack of jobs at home and the huge wealth gap between east and west foment this flow of people in search of work. There are no official figures, but around 5,000 people from a town of only 16,000 are thought to be working in or near Brussels at any given time.

Ewa and her mother are typical of many families sharing jobs which take them far away and break up their own opportunities for an integrated family life. The rewards are too important to pass up. The bus journey takes around 22 hours, and in four months the worker can earn £3,000, the amount it would take two years to earn in a local job, if one was to be found. Ewa's sisters and their husbands, her two brothers and their wives are all commuting 1,000 miles once or twice a year to do similar jobs. Ewa speaks approvingly of her employers. "They treat me really nicely. I wouldn't dream of changing them," she says.

There have been some alarmist projections, many ill-founded, about the volume of migration to be expected from new EU accession states into the better-off countries. However, Brussels projects that because of demographic decline, the new Europe's working-age population will fall by 20 million within a generation, necessitating an influx of immigrant labour. Meanwhile the phenomenon of the Polish underclass servicing the west European elite has been going on for a long time and is unlikely to change very much soon.

Source: Traynor 2004.

labour legislation. In East and Southeast Asia, various countries and territories—Hong Kong (SAR China), Singapore, Malaysia and Taiwan Province of China—recognize domestic work for visa purposes, but except in Hong Kong (SAR China) they explicitly exclude it from labour standards.

Many migrant women with full high-school experience and even university degrees experience deskilling and lack of recognition for qualifications. This applies particularly to women from the Philippines, Eastern Europe and Latin America. Many enter a host country as a student or a tourist and then overstay. The boundaries between the legal and the irregular become blurred; this is particularly true for Latin American and Southeast Asian women workers, since Eastern European women do have rights of residence for up to three months and often rotate a job between several people (see box 7.2).[24]

In Germany, it has become possible since February 2002 for citizens of countries joining the EU to work legally for up to three years in households that are taking care of a relative and are receiving benefits from the state care insurance system. Though legally employed and paid at German rates, the state stipulates that these carers cannot compete against German-trained home-care employees and their permit must be for "household assistant"; by suggesting that "untrained foreign workers" may put those they care for at risk, they have in effect sanctioned deskilling. This resolution of a labour shortage contrasts with that of IT workers; these are employed at the same grades as Germans.

Although migrant women's qualifications may not be recognized, and they may suffer in jobs for which they are overequipped, their and their family's position in their home community often rises. Several studies have explored the contradictory class position in which some labour migrants find themselves, especially the well educated from such sources as the Philippines or Eastern Europe. Migration can mean a simultaneous experience of upward and downward mobility. Discrimination and the erosion of skills at destination sites may be offset by upward mobility at home, as remittances are invested in small businesses, housing and children's education.

MIGRANT HEALTH WORKERS

Historically, women have tended to enter the welfare and social professions (education, health and social work). An analysis of UK work permit data for 2000 showed that sectors with high proportions of female staff constituted some of the fastest-growing sectors of migrant employment. A crisis in nursing in the United Kingdom and Ireland, as well as in Canada and the United States, has created a truly global labour market. Globally, the Philippines has supplied the overwhelming number of nurses for work overseas, followed by countries in Africa such as Ghana and Nigeria. Not only do the prospects of better pay attract them to the North, but the state of the health sector at home constitutes an important push factor (see chapter 8). Ireland too has become heavily dependent on overseas nurses, with Filipinas supplying the largest contingent. In order to address skills and brain drain concerns, the United Kingdom is introducing a code of conduct to cover foreign health worker recruitment, but doubts remain whether it will be enforced in the private sector.

In a study of international nursing recruits in the United Kingdom, mainly from Europe, Australia, Africa and the Philippines, many felt that their skills were not appreciated or respected; that they were downgraded; and that they confronted racism and xenophobia. Experiences varied considerably between the National Health Service, judged in more positive terms, and the private independent sector where they were frequently used as care assistants.[25]

These findings are echoed in similar studies carried out into the situation of foreign-born nurses in North America. These may receive higher salaries than in their countries of origin, but there is much potential for exploitation. Nurses are frequently employed as nursing aides rather than as registered nurses, and face discrimination in the form of lower pay, fewer promotions,

higher risk of being fired, and more common assignment to high-stress units.[26] The connection of the recent demand for foreign nurses with the restructuring of health care systems raises the possibility of deteriorating work conditions, lower pay and a negative climate for patient care. Hospitals in the United States with shortages of nursing personnel are often municipally run and located in inner-city areas.

In Canada, all highly trained immigrant workers, including nurses, are affected by licensing and recertification requirements for professionals. Regulated occupations, such as those in certain trades, law, engineering and health areas, require statutory certification or licensing, primarily through professional associations. While the purpose is to maintain standards and assure public health and safety, these practices also are the defining characteristics of segmented labour markets which create monopolies by controlling labour supply. In Canada, certification requirements can be seen as a form of systemic discrimination; criteria may be applied to the Canadian-born and foreign-born alike, but they disproportionately restrict the access of the foreign-born to trades or professions. Devaluation of education credentials becomes part of this systemic discrimination when professional associations do not recognize foreign degrees as equivalent to those obtained within the country.

While the most publicized, nursing is not the only area of professional health personnel shortage. In the United Kingdom, overseas doctors (non-European Economic Area (EEA) qualified) form a large percentage of the hospital medical workforce; in 2000 they constituted 26 per cent. In an increasingly feminized occupation, women form a significant proportion of migrant doctors—over half of those registering with the General Medical Council in 1998. Most are appointed in the lower and middle grades, and are seeking further qualifications and training.

Even if many of the skilled women migrants do not intend to settle, they have the possibility of renewing their contracts, of eventually acquiring citizenship and bringing their families—entitlements that are not available to the less skilled. So although fewer in numbers, the expansion of skilled opportunities for female migrants highlights the diversity of migratory circuits and potential entitlements.

Notes

1   See for example Hugo et al. 2003.

2   Castles 2003; Kofman 2004.

3   Milanovic 2003; see also IDEAS 2002.

4   IOM 2004.

5   Newland 2003.

6   Chant and Radcliffe 1992.

7   Asis, Huang and Yeoh 2004.

8   Collins and Rau 2000.

9   ILO 2004f:5.

10 ILO 2004f:10–11; Yamanaka and Piper 2004.

11 Zlotnik 2003.

12 Boyd 1992; Freedman 2003a.

13 Boyd and Pikkov 2004.

14 Piper and Roces 2003.

15 Battistella and Asis 2003; Asia Watch and Women's Rights Project 1993.

16 Piper 2003, 2004.

17 Jimenez 2003.

18 Gallagher 2001; Freedman 2003b; Piper 2004.

19 Bean and Stevens 2003; Schoeni 1998.

20 Boyd 2001; Shumway and Cooke 1998; Wright and Ellis 2000.

21 Hauge Byberg 2002.

22 Ehrenreich and Hochschild 2003; Hochschild 2000; Sassen 2000.

23 Williams 2003.

24 Morokvasic 1996.

25 Allan and Aggergaard Larsen 2003.

26 Stasiulis and Bakan 2003.

Chapter 8
The search for a new
social policy agenda

Livelihoods in today's world are subject to a range of insecurities. These are acute in contexts where few people work with an employment contract and the associated rights to work-related benefits, and where domestic production processes are increasingly exposed to fluctuations and recessions in global markets. When earnings and incomes have plummeted and jobs have disappeared, people have little to fall back on. Not only are formal social protection mechanisms missing in many developing countries for the millions of women and men who work in the informal economy, but contingencies such as ill-health, childbirth and old age are themselves powerful drivers of impoverishment, as earnings fall and assets are depleted to purchase health care in increasingly commercialized contexts.

There has recently been more recognition of these realities. The 1990s saw a dramatic shift in global policy pronouncements acknowledging the vital role of social policy to the development process. That this was not just a rhetorical shift is apparent from figure 8.1, which shows that the social sectors now account for nearly one-third of all donor funding to developing countries.[1] This was a far cry from the "market fundamentalism" of the early 1980s, which focused narrowly on "getting prices right", and never mind the social consequences.

The period of austerity in the social sectors was a direct outcome of the virtually universal and standardized pattern of reform imposed as a condition of loan and adjustment packages. Social spending was drastically curtailed, and "user fees" were imposed for health, education and other social services. By the late 1980s it became increasingly evident that the poverty and social disruptions caused by stabilization and adjustment

were not the "transitional phenomenon" or "frictional difficulties" the international financial institutions (IFIs) had initially assumed; they were pervasive, long-term and systemic. Studies into the impacts of adjustment and popular opposition to key adjustment-related measures combined to bring into question the orthodox policy prescriptions of the day.[2]

By 1990 the World Bank had accepted that adjustment packages paid too little attention to social privations, and that it would be wise to prevent the "depreciation of human capital" during the adjustment process. The dilemma of how to increase social support while remaining within the constraints of stabilization and fiscal propriety was resolved by attempting to "target" social expenditures to those populations most in need. Certain existing expenditures were reallocated, for example from secondary to primary education; and supplementary programmes or "safety nets" for the poor were created. The underlying thesis in social sector restructuring was residualist: social welfare institutions should come into play only when the "normal" structures of supply—the family and the market—broke down.[3] The safety nets put in place often came too late: they waited for people to "fall" rather than tried to prevent them from falling in the first place; they were too narrowly targeted and even mistargeted; and they were not commensurate with the scale and nature of poverty and deprivation in the context of adjustment.[4]

By the late 1990s, the view that the vulnerabilities experienced in many developing countries required institutionalized systems of social protection—a view informed by the history of the European welfare state—began to fall on more receptive ears. A crescendo of criticism and civil society activism helped

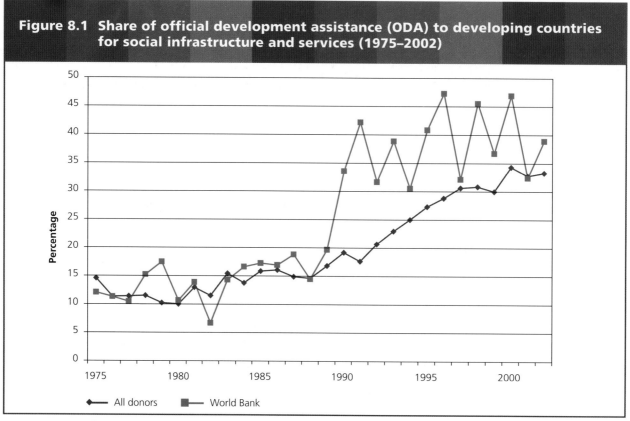

Figure 8.1 Share of official development assistance (ODA) to developing countries for social infrastructure and services (1975–2002)

Note: Social infrastructure and services includes education, health, population programmes, water supply and sanitation, government and
          civil society, and other social infrastructure and services.
Source: Calculated from OECD 2004a.

restore levels of public social spending in several countries, including Chile, Sri Lanka, Tunisia and Mexico (see table 3.3). A concern for "the social" resurfaced in unlikely quarters; even the International Monetary Fund (IMF) was compelled to give explicit recognition to the importance of social policies.[5] The World Bank's mindset change was indicated by the subject of its **World Development Report 2000/2001: Attacking Poverty**; this identified "social risk management" as the most sustainable basis for poverty reduction.[6] Building on critiques of philanthropy and drawing on notions of "participation", this proposed to avoid a "culture of dependency" by helping the poor develop the capacity "to cope with, mitigate or reduce" their risks.

A shared vocabulary of "poverty", "social protection", "participation" and "citizenship" became widely applied; but the consensus it indicated was more apparent than real. Diverse

interpretations of the causes of social disadvantage, and equally diverse views of the necessary social policy responses, continue to vie for attention. The World Bank carries power and prominence in the policy arena, due to its weight as a lender to social sectors in developing regions, especially in South Asia and sub-Saharan Africa (see figure 8.2), and because of its leadership of the "poverty reduction strategy paper" (PRSP) process which it began to promote in 1999. At the policy level, however, its residualist approach to social policy, based on the notion of the state as "gap-filler", is in conflict with a concept of social policy which holds that its purpose is redistributive and that the state has to be a major player. This position is advocated by many organizations, activists and academic networks.[7]

In the "social risk management" framework, the state is only expected to provide "social safety nets for risk coping" and "risk

Figure 8.2 World Bank's share of total ODA for social infrastructure and services, selected regions (1975–2002)

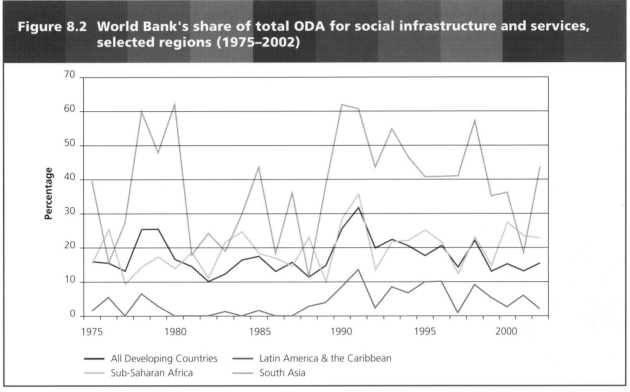

Note: This variable has been calculated for each region as World Bank's ODA for social infrastructure and services divided by the ODA from all donors for social infrastructure and services. These include education, health, population programmes, water supply and sanitation, government and civil society, and other social infrastructure and services.

Source: Calculated from OECD 2004a.

management instruments" to be operated where or when the private sector fails; there are strong continuities here with the earlier generation of minimal safety nets. In the **World Development Report 2004: Making Services Work for the Poor** acknowledgement is given to the need for "governments to invest in purchasing key services to protect poor households"; it is also allowed that: "making services work for poor people means making services work for everybody while ensuring poor people have access to those services".[8] But this report speaks with many different voices, and its impact on the operational guidelines for Bank lending to the social sectors is still far from clear.

In contrast, the redistributive view of social policy underlines the importance of equity and universal social provision. In the context of a developing society, it perceives the state as having a central role to play not only as the regulator of institutions and structures, but also as a significant provider. In situations of widespread poverty, where insurance mechanisms for the poor are ineffective, and there is likely to be serious underprovision by private providers, the case for public intervention by the state is very strong.[9]

The underlying assumption of much recent literature on social policy from the IFIs is that targeted public provision is the way to achieve greater social inclusion. This assumption, however, is open to question. Means testing and targeting are often the last resort of unequal societies; they can trap people in poverty and they can enhance inequality, rather than deal with inequality through redistribution; they are also very demanding in terms of state administrative capacity. At the same time more inclusive systems—where access is a publicly debated issue, where cross-subsidy occurs, and different social classes come across each other in the same institutions—are likely to be associated with more progressive behaviour by the state.[10]

European experience suggests that countries with the lowest poverty rates have income transfer systems that include universalistic basic flat-rate benefits financed from general tax revenue, public earnings-related benefits financed by employer and employee contributions, as well as social assistance supplements for those still in need. Universalistic basic pension benefits and child allowances are particularly effective in keeping vulnerable groups—the elderly, families with many children, and single mothers—out of poverty. The second major pillar of a comprehensive approach to improving the life chances of the majority of the population is the provision of good quality and universally accessible education and health care.

The fundamental principle behind social policy is that vulnerabilities and risks require collective responses. This is because many people, especially people with low incomes, cannot afford the services provided by the modern private sector, whether these are health or education services, or insurance premiums of various kinds. Attempts to create long-term formal and informal savings (by low-income people themselves and by external agencies) often founder because of the pressing needs of the present. Efforts to co-insure among poor people only, without the wider pooling of risk which comes from including the better-off, are bound to fail, as the core social insurance principle (contribution in relation to income, and benefit in relation to need) is absent. This is why social policies that are founded on principles of universalism and solidarity (risk-sharing)—with strong cross-subsidies from the better-off—tend to be more sustainable, both financially and politically.[11]

This debate about key principles forms a backdrop to considerations of gender in the context of social policy. For reasons which seem inexplicable, the gender premises and implications of the social policy reform agenda have largely been ignored.

GENDER: THE "SILENT TERM"

Both the process of social policy reform and its outcomes are inescapably gendered. And both tend to operate to the detriment of women, especially to women in the least well-off sections of society. Yet mainstream debates on social policy have failed to engage with these concerns; gender has indeed been the "silent term".[12] This omission has characterized both sides of the debate, including those aligned with the residualist and targeted policy perspective espoused by the World Bank, and those associated with the redistributive and universalist school of thought.

What, then, would a gender perspective add to current social policy debates? The first point to underline is that, while social sector reforms have on the whole been detrimental to women, it would be a mistake to assume that women were social policy beneficiaries, as citizens with social rights, prior to the neoliberal policy turn. Indeed, seen from a gender perspective, the 1960s and 1970s were not a "Golden Age". The fact that the formal economy remained small in most developing countries meant that job security and work-related benefits were privileges available to only a small stratum of workers in most countries, most of whom were male.

In Latin America, male-dominated trade unions were the principal beneficiaries of corporatist social contracts through which wages, working conditions and social security were negotiated.[13] While women may have benefited as wives or daughters of "male breadwinners", a pension in old age or entitlement to maternity leave remained distant dreams to the majority. The little security that there was came from paid work where it could be found, from marriage, kin and community, from the church and also through the "protection and patronage" of informal employers.[14] In sub-Saharan Africa, women's small informal groups for credit and mutual help were also popular, especially among market women and traders. But the effectiveness of many of these systems in providing social protection is often limited by their low capital base.

However, while the early effort at formal social protection in many developing countries could have been reformed, extended and built upon in order to cover a much wider range of people, there has in fact been a reversal over the past two decades; in many regions there has been a strong thrust towards the commodification of social services and social protection. Hence, the "male breadwinner model" is being eroded not by gender-equitable reform of state-based entitlements, but by their drastic reduction. These have been replaced by market-based, individualized entitlements for those who can afford them: private pensions, private health insurance, private hospitals, private schools, private retirement homes, private paid care for children and old people.[15]

The impacts of commodification are likely to be felt most strongly by women. The factors explaining why the pressures have gender-differentiated impacts include the following:

- Gender bias in intrahousehold resource allocation: Social norms in many parts of the world, especially South and East Asia, favour boys and men over girls and women in allocation of resources within the household. Where low-income families have to pay for access to services such as emergency health care, the needs of boys and men are likely to be given a higher priority than those of women and girls.

- Gender stratification in markets: Women tend to be more cash-constrained than men, given their disadvantages in labour and credit markets; this is likely to restrict their ability to access market-based services and social protection for themselves and their children. Where women have been traditionally responsible for a significant part of their own and their children's health and education expenses, as is the case in many parts of Africa, their problems are more acute. Where women work, they are also likely to accumulate fewer employment-related social benefits than men, given that they typically work for fewer years, earn less, and are more likely to be informally employed.

- Gender ordering of the unpaid care economy: When formal service provision remains out of reach, informal carers—mothers, sisters, grandmothers, daughters—have to provide unpaid care. Social sector reforms often make unjustified assumptions about the availability of women's and girls' "free" time for caring work.

- Gender stratification in the public social care sector: The working pressures generated during reform, including loss of wages in public sector services, are likely to fall most heavily on women workers, given that they are predominantly located at the lowest rungs of skill, authority and remuneration.

These issues are elaborated in the sections that follow.

GENDER ORDERING/ STRATIFICATION AND INSTITUTIONAL CHANGE

Given the limitations of space, the chapter has selectively chosen to focus on health sector reforms (relevant to many low-income developing countries); pension reforms (more relevant to middle-income countries); reforms and innovations in social protection schemes to include informal workers (both low and middle-income countries); and anti-poverty programmes targeted on low-income women. The education sector is omitted, since an extensive literature and ongoing analysis already exists.[16]

The following analysis of the systemic changes in the social sectors demonstrates how institutional reforms are affecting men and women differently. One of the main contributions of the "welfare regime" literature was to move away from a simple measure of public expenditure and to look at the institutional content of welfare states, in terms of such issues as conditions of eligibility, coverage, and the nature of benefits.[17] The importance of institutions in mediating the link between public expenditure and welfare outcomes is now widely acknowledged. As the **World Development Report (WDR) 2004** stresses, there is no simple relationship between public spending on health and education and outcomes; it is the institutions—seen in the WDR mainly in terms of accountability of service providers to poor clients—that matter. Here, some of the institutional changes that current social sector reforms have brought about are assessed through a gender lens—a perspective with which neither **WDR 2004** nor the first generation of "welfare regime" theorists have seriously engaged. The chapter does not provide a gender-disaggregated analysis of public (and donor) expenditure on the social sectors.

Health sector reforms and gender [18]

Health has been a key area of social sector reform. From a gender perspective, health is especially important, not only because men and women need different types of health support to sustain well-being, reproductive care for women being the most obvious example, but because institutionally health systems are gendered structures, reflecting gender inequalities in the wider society. Hierarchies in the health service usually find men in the senior positions as doctors, policy makers and administrators; while women predominate in lower-status professions and jobs, such as nurses, paramedical staff and orderlies.

The services offered to women often fail to recognize social and cultural norms which deny women decision-making capacity over health-related behaviours, for example, over sexual relations and the use of contraception for child spacing. Meanwhile, where services and personnel are sensitive to women's needs, especially those of the seriously disadvantaged, this can help redress some of the discriminations and difficulties they face. This may be reinforced by the fact that most day-to-day working relations between health care staff and clients tend to be relations among women; they usually take place in the context of mother and child health (MCH) concerns. The woman-to-woman confidence that can build up during routine interactions provides opportunities for promoting health-related behavioural change.

Donors have been heavily involved in the design of health sector reforms in many economic-crisis countries. The standard package is essentially based on the liberalization of clinical care and drugs provision, emphasizing commodification and the use of market mechanisms; the reduction of government; decentralization of delivery systems; and greater attention to cost-effectiveness in government spending. The model usually includes some or all of the following features:

- Retreat of government towards a mainly regulatory and priority-setting role, with responsibility for direct provision of services in public health and for ensuring access to primary care for the poorest.
- Liberalization of private clinical provision and pharmaceutical sales, and the promotion of a "mix" of public, private and voluntary providers.
- Increased contracting-out of government-funded services to independent groups and companies.
- An increase in the autonomy of hospital management and finance; some hospital privatization.

- A shift from tax-based financing mechanisms towards insurance, including mutual insurance schemes.
- The decentralization of health delivery systems to local government control.
- User charges for government-run health services, for government-provided drugs and supplies, and for community-based health services.

This section addresses the impacts of health service reforms on women's access to, and utilization of, health services as users of health care services (for themselves and their dependents); on women's work conditions as health sector workers; and on women as providers of unpaid care, especially when formal mechanisms fail to meet the need for care.

Health care charges: The impact on users

In many countries, reforms to the health sector have been implemented in a context of generalized and severe poverty, and often in the wake of an economic crisis marked by worsening diets and increasing workloads.[19] The period of reform has also coincided with the spread of HIV/AIDS and the severe physical, economic and social strains the epidemic has imposed on families, especially in Africa. Thus needs and demands have grown at the same time that free or affordable health care has become more difficult to access. User fees, first introduced into hospitals in the early 1980s, have since been extended to lower-level government health facilities such as health centres and subcentres providing basic care and emergency treatment. A number of studies have confirmed that user fees and ineffective exemption systems lead to the exclusion of those unable to pay. While few studies have looked specifically at gender-differentiated impacts, studies of reproductive health trends in Zimbabwe, Tanzania and Nigeria show that the introduction of user fees in MCH facilities has been associated with a decline in admissions of pregnant women, and increased morbidity rates during or after birth in both mothers and the newborn.[20]

In India, the 1990s saw a substantial increase in private health provision at the cost of public health care.[21] Growing privatization of services seems to have excluded or marginalized rural people, particularly women in the 15–29 age group as well as tribal populations. This reflects the relative lack of value attached to girls and women compared with boys and men: while both are affected by the lack of affordable services, scarce family resources may be stretched to take boys for treatment while the illness of girls is regarded as less significant and correspondingly neglected. Cases of untreated illnesses were common among the poor, and more common among women and girls.[22] Meanwhile, it is also true that widespread improvement in reproductive health facilities over time has had an important positive effect on maternal and child mortality and morbidity rates.

Where fees are charged for any kind of professional health care, women suffer disproportionately given their and their small children's MCH needs, and their reduced access to cash and income-earning opportunities. Where it is customary for women to be held responsible for the bulk of expenditures on their children such as food, medical treatment, clothing and school expenditures, which is the case in much of sub-Saharan Africa, the burden on women of fees and charges is particularly onerous. Many forms of mutual support for health care exist in poor communities: for example, payment of birth attendants in kind, free care for indigent mothers, sharing domestic work to allow others to work for cash, and mutual loans and gifts. African societies in particular abound in mutual savings schemes run for and by women. However, there is also evidence that falling incomes and economic crisis undermine women's participation in these networks of mutual financial support.[23]

The growth of health insurance

In the face of strong popular opposition to user fees, health financing reforms have recently begun to focus on schemes of health insurance. In the context of social health insurance for those in formal employment, the key gender question is that of equity. Since a small proportion of the population enjoy formal employment, and since these employees are among the most skilled and educated in the society, such schemes mainly cover more advantaged, male-breadwinner members of the workforce. Although these schemes usually cover dependants, still the number of women that can be reached is small.

Given their limited reach, an alternative mechanism of health care financing which aims to promote the inclusion of

poor and vulnerable groups is mutual health insurance (MHI). These schemes have mushroomed in recent years, and in sub-Saharan Africa have taken the form of community-based schemes of voluntary prepayment. Premiums can be paid in instalments; local committees can decide to exempt members unable to pay; and accommodation can be made for those with unsteady or seasonal incomes, by postponement to harvest-time or some agreed date.

Although this is a promising development, these schemes show the same drawbacks as other types of community saving and loan programmes. Rapid start-up may be followed by dwindling membership, unaffordable contributions and payment collection problems.[24] It appears that building on existing co-operative savings and loan schemes has better success, since existing patterns of solidarity exist and can absorb some of the administrative costs. This is the case with the Integrated Insurance Scheme run by SEWA in Gujarat, India (discussed below). However, donors are more inclined to support new stand-alone schemes.

Health sector reforms and women health workers

Research on the privatization of health services and the impacts on the medical workforce appears to ignore gender, at least explicitly. However, since in most countries this workforce is predominantly female and women predominate in lower-status occupations, the downward pressure on wages is likely to have hit women workers particularly hard. While at the upper end, the private clinics frequently appear to provide nurses with better working conditions than the public sector, the same does not apply at the lower echelons, where private employers try to keep down costs by reducing wages and abandoning training. Those who employ trained staff on decent wages find themselves undercut by those who do not.[25] As a result, the poorest women users pay fees they cannot afford to low-paid and low-skilled women medical personnel: a vicious circle of gender disadvantage.

Liberalization, privatization and commodification have contributed to the crisis in health care, and to the strains and demoralization experienced by nurses working in public facilities. There are accusations of abusive behaviour, especially towards

---

Box 8.1   Women health workers on the ward: A snapshot from Tanzania

This kind of thing [bad behaviour] happens, and it is because of poor morale, low commitment, severe overwork and low salaries. Imagine, you are a nurse on duty for 12 hours. You start at 6 am, you may get away at 7.30 pm. You may have a ward of 40 or 60 seriously ill patients. In gynaecology, you are likely to have several emergencies, some operations, postoperative patients, very sick patients. You are two trained people at best. How will you divide yourself? You are constantly overworking and under pressure. You are worried about family problems and commitments. For 12 hours you do not know what is happening to your children. And you may not have as much as a cup of tea. Then there is the problem of the commitments of other staff. You are a nurse by profession. The doctor, who is supposed to be responsible, works his official hours and goes away, he waits to be called. You are there, someone is bleeding, she needs to be operated, and you cannot help. There are no facilities. People are suffering, and the other staff are not on duty. The means to save this lady are not available. If someone is supposed to be on duty and is not there, what can you do as a nurse? There are no infusions, no emergency drugs. Relatives rush to send the sick person to hospital, then we are not in a position to save the patient.

Source: Mackintosh and Tibandebage 2004b (fieldwork notes, 1998).

---

low-income, low-status patients and individuals regarded as socially reprehensible.[26] There are also problems which nurses have to confront on a daily basis. Some of these are explained in box 8.1 by a matron in a maternity hospital in Tanzania.

Health sector liberalization appears to have widened the gap in wages and working conditions between doctors and nurses. Many doctors benefit from additional private practice, and the "going rate" for informal payments to doctors tends to be substantially higher than for nurses. Moreover, nurses have more contact with patients than doctors (one of the main points in box 8.1), and when the service falls apart they take most of the strain. This helps to account for the departure of many nurses abroad, with "pull" factors in the North converging with "push" factors in the South (see chapter 7). Typically, the bulk of incentives aimed at retaining health care staff in the home country are focused on doctors. Given that nurses and ancillary workers provide the backbone of health services virtually everywhere, rising out-migration has serious effects which ripple out to the health centres and clinics providing the primary provision on which many low-income women depend.[27]

Health sector reform in both high and low-income contexts has been presented by its promoters as a force for change, away from services run in the interests of staff, to services run in response to patient demand. But this can lead to losses in decent working conditions and wages, as recent International Labour Organization (ILO) research in Eastern Europe has demonstrated.[28] A different way of framing these issues is suggested by an approach which owes much to gendered considerations. The Health Workers for Change (HWFC) projects in Africa and elsewhere have built efforts to improve health care quality on the observation that the interpersonal aspects—such as respect and ability to listen to a patient—are important to care quality, and that these relational aspects are gendered. Female health workers have a different working style than men; women patients also have special needs, and in certain circumstances—sexually transmitted disease, for example—are fearful of discrimination and abuse. The HWFC projects have therefore built up collaboration between staff and patients, and sought to shift behaviour in gender-sensitive directions.

Unpaid care and the crisis of care

In most countries, women continue to assume a disproportionate share of unpaid work and caregiving. It has been estimated that activity worth US$16 trillion takes place every year without being recorded as part of the global economy, and that of this, 69 per cent (US$11 trillion) is the unnoticed contribution of women in households and the informal sector.[29] As women struggle to bear the increasing burden of both paid work and unpaid care in a relentless economic climate and, in rural areas, from a dwindling environmental resource base, their physical condition may suffer. Since the paid work they engage in is usually a survival strategy rather than an act of liberated choice, the irony of their entry into the workplace is that they may earn too little even to offset their extra physical needs. Meanwhile, health sector reforms propose a degree of devolution of health care activity onto the community.[30] This strategy fails to recognize that this means imposing a further burden, unpaid, onto volunteers who will invariably be women. Women, therefore, are being involuntarily landed with the social fall-out from service depletion brought about by reforms, as well as invisibly shouldering an extra economic burden.

The epidemics of HIV/AIDS which have overtaken many African countries have brought an existing crisis of health care into sharp relief. In 2001, of the estimated 40 million people in the world with HIV, 28 million or 70 per cent were in Africa. Africa also accounted for 90 per cent of the 58,000 children under the age of 15 who had died of AIDS. The vast nursing care burden represented by these figures has overwhelmingly fallen on women and girls. Since the economically active age group (15–49 years) suffers the highest levels of infection, much of the load has to be borne by the elderly. This includes care of and economic support for orphaned grandchildren, of which AIDS has produced over 12 million in Africa. In places where resources for health and welfare services are already extremely scarce, home-based care and "community care" are the fall-back policy response. Essentially, formal care-service structures have devolved responsibilities onto informal structures with the sanction of the neoliberal policy agenda, an echo from the earlier analysis of what has happened in the workplace (see chapter 5). Thus policy decisions about service delivery and drug regimens in the face of HIV have particular implications for women. The notion of "community care" appears gender-neutral; but within communities, the time, work and responsibilities of this care invariably default to women.[31]

Thus it appears that health sector reform has been built on a number of hidden or inexplicit gendered assumptions. These include assumptions that women's access to household resources or their external networks of mutual support are robust enough to find the money for fees; that women's work burdens can be expanded to include more responsibility for care; and that the needs of health-care staff (especially lower-level staff) and those seeking care are inherently contradictory. Further dubious assumptions include the notion that the governance structures established for decentralized health system management will inevitably reflect women's needs better than previously centralized systems. Another key issue is financing: whether the decentralization of responsibilities is accompanied by an adequate redistribution of resources from the central government; where decentralization is mostly a means for the central government to reduce expenditure, the outcome is likely to be growing disparity in the quality of the services between poorer and more affluent local communities. It is certainly not clear from the available evidence that any of these assumptions were warranted, even before the devastating impact of HIV/AIDS.

The gender implications of pension reform

Reform of public pension programmes has taken place in a large number of countries around the world over the last decade. In many developing and transition countries, pension schemes had been facing serious problems even before the economic crises of the 1980s and 1990s. In Latin America, for example, the maturing of pension systems had already led to a deterioration in the ratio of those contributing to those drawing pensions by the end of the 1970s. Both employers and employees, especially the self-employed, did not pay their contributions; pension schemes were also being drained by the heavy costs of privileged pensioners, for example, those in the military, and the high administrative charges paid to unaccountable bureaucrats running the schemes. These problems were aggravated when economic crisis struck. The shrinking of formal-sector employment produced a sudden decline in the number of contributors. At the same time high inflation meant that real wages declined and so did the real value of contributions. All of these factors created a perception of crisis in pension systems.[32] Thus their reform became an integral part of structural adjustment programmes, with significant input from the IFIs.

While there was a general consensus that existing systems were bankrupt and required urgent reform, there was no corresponding consensus on a desirable replacement model. In many countries IFIs and domestic reformers argued that privatization was the way forward. Their grounds included that privatization would ensure greater financial viability, closer links between contributions and benefits, reduced administrative costs and the promotion of capital markets. Significantly, issues of equity and redistribution—across generations, across class and across gender—were excluded from the debating positions of advocates of privatization.

A recent comparative analysis of pension reforms in eight Latin American countries shows that the neoliberal reformers were not strong enough to impose their preferred model in all countries.[33] Rather, the nature of reforms was shaped by the balance of power between the neoliberal reform coalition on the one hand, and its opponents—unions, pensioners and opposition parties—on the other. The full privatization model took hold in only two of the eight countries, namely Chile (regarded as the prototype) and Mexico; in four others—Peru, Argentina, Colombia and Uruguay—it was watered down, and in Costa Rica and Brazil it was strongly resisted. Pension reforms in three Central and Eastern European countries had a parallel experience.[34] Only one—the Czech Republic—was able to resist the pressure from IFIs for privatization, while the other two—Poland and Hungary—have chosen partial privatization and become front-runners of radical pension reform in the region.

In none of the debates surrounding the adoption of reforms in either region do concerns with gender equity appear to have surfaced. Yet the move towards privatization has major gender implications. The fact that pension benefits in privatized systems are strictly determined by the overall amount of money contributed by the insured person, and that women typically earn less money and work for fewer years than men, means that women receive considerably lower benefits. Since women's higher life expectancy is taken into account in most private systems, women's benefits are further comparatively depressed.

In public systems with defined benefits, there are generally similar gender discrepancies. But women's disadvantages are usually mitigated by generous minimum pensions, by the fact that life expectancy does not affect benefit levels, and by credits given for years spent caring for children. The last feature was particularly strong in the ex-socialist countries, where the "caring credits" were financed by cross-subsidy within the pension system. In both Poland and Hungary the rules with respect to "caring credits" have changed, with the result that those taking leave receive lower pensions than if they had stayed in employment. This is a retrograde step: credits given for caring are not charitable gestures but an acknowledgement that social and economic "contributions" can take different forms over a person's lifecycle.

The implications of these reforms are not the same for all women. The shift towards privatization and individualization works in favour of those women who are active in the labour market, earn high incomes, and do not take "leave" for care-related reasons. But for the majority of women who have a weaker labour-market position or intermittent careers because of care duties towards children or elderly relatives, the reforms mark a serious regression.

A larger point here concerning the values underpinning social policy, or in this case pension policy, is that redistribution and solidarity do not have much place in private fully funded pension schemes. Nor is the failure of the private system to provide equity and inclusion being compensated for by increased efficiency. In fact there is considerable evidence to show that the private system is less efficient than the public system it has replaced. While claims were made that pension privatization would reduce wasteful administrative costs, this has not in fact happened. Instead, the pressures of competition require large numbers of sales personnel working on commission and large advertising budgets, which appear responsible for driving administrative costs upward.[35]

While the move towards privatization of pensions has been strong in recent years, it is important to emphasize the diversity of ways in which countries provide old age security. South Africa's system of state social assistance to elderly people, which is discussed below, is one example of a non-contributory pension plan. In Brazil, the expansion of social insurance to workers in informal and rural employment has resulted in a large increase in coverage. These schemes demonstrate innovation in pension provision models in the developing world.[36]

Innovations in social protection for informal workers

Formal insurance schemes are beyond the reach of people working in the informal economy. Barriers to entry include high premiums, having to present a pay slip, and inflexible procedures such as being required to contribute exactly the same amount monthly year-round. There are, however, a variety of ways of building systems of social protection for informal workers. The ILO is making concerted efforts to extend existing social security benefits to new categories of workers. In the field of micro-insurance, the emphasis is on building grassroots schemes. There has been a great deal of experimentation with social insurance in general, and health insurance in particular. Many of these have attempted to reach women, and especially poorer women.

The following examples illustrate that it is possible to build schemes that reach many informal workers. While in practice there is great variability in the extent to which social protection schemes actually redistribute across generations, social classes and genders, the very idea underlying these schemes is that the state has a responsibility to provide social protection, and that this should facilitate at least some degree of redistribution. By extending the coverage of existing social protection programmes to new groups of informal workers, and by facilitating cross-subsidies, some valuable efforts are being made to increase the inclusion of existing social protection mechanisms. It is not surprising that more inclusive social systems are being forged in contexts where there has been a great deal of social struggle and soul-searching about social responsibility (Chile, Brazil, South Africa), and where there is an ideological commitment to social equity (Costa Rica).

SEWA's Integrated Social Insurance for women informal workers [37]

The Integrated Insurance Scheme (IIS) has been successfully built over 20 years by the Self-Employed Women's Association (SEWA) in Gujarat, India. A subsidy is provided by the Indian government to two large insurance corporations to offer some of their services to disadvantaged groups, including those belonging

to SEWA. SEWA has thus managed to build partnerships with government and the insurance industry on favourable terms, and has also been inspiring in its ability to continuously respond to members' needs. Today, IIS provides a comprehensive package of social insurance benefits to over 100,000 informal women workers.

SEWA attributes some of the success of IIS to the interaction between its different programmes: the SEWA Bank, into which annual premiums are paid; health education, which heightens members' awareness of health problems; and literacy training. SEWA does receive donor support to cover the scheme's administrative expenses, but SEWA's solidarity and unity also make a critical difference, with a large part of the administrative work being done by the members themselves.

Challenges include the fact that, although the scheme is oriented to poor women, some of SEWA's poorest members cannot afford the premiums, which have to be set at a rate that ensures viability over time. There is also concern that the health facilities to which the health insurance gives access are far from adequate.

Health benefits for women temporeras in Chile [38]

As already noted in chapter 6, there has been a striking growth in the export of horticultural products from Latin America in recent years, with increased employment of seasonal women workers or *temporeras*. In Chile, social protection benefits originally restricted to full-time workers have recently been extended to include them.

The majority of both men and women *temporeras* work at below the legal minimum wage; a few women earn high wages for a short period of the year, but the average earnings of women are lower than men's, with significantly more women in the lowest-earning group. Chilean workers can choose private or public health insurance, but affiliation requires them to pay contributions year-round. Temporary workers were not motivated to affiliate to either type of scheme, given this requirement. As a result, *temporeras* were only able to obtain care by applying to the health services as "indigents".

Over time, pressure from the *Servicio Nacional de la Mujer* (SERNAM) in Chile has led to a number of changes in the

---

Box 8.2   Extending coverage to domestic workers

Countries differ as to whether domestic work is classified as formal or informal work. In many, domestic workers are classified as "self-employed" despite the reality of an employment relationship. The vast majority of domestic workers are women, often still in their teens or younger, and living away from home; working conditions are characterized by long hours, low pay and lack of autonomy.

The relationship between employer and domestic worker is a complex mix of mutual dependence and matriarchal authority. Although the domestic worker has little say over her life, there may be voluntary measures of assistance such as with health costs, school fees or training if she is young, or the school fees of her children. These are not contractual obligations and depend on the whim of the employer. There is no long-term security.

Since they are dispersed in people's homes, domestic workers are very hard to reach or organize, and it is difficult to provide them with social protection. However, in certain countries, especially in Latin America, both informal and formal organizations have taken up their cause. In 2002, South African domestic workers (and seasonal agricultural workers) came under the scope of the Unemployment Insurance Fund. Their enjoyment of this insurance depends both on workers asserting their rights and making sure employers do not evade payments to the fund.

Source: Lund 2004.

---

working terms and conditions for women *temporeras*. These include the provision of childcare facilities for horticultural and other agricultural workers, and the establishment of four national commissions, on Health and Safety at Work, Childcare, Pesticides and Training, to deal at the policy level with conditions of temporary workers. In 2000 the regulations on health insurance were amended. The required contributory period for year-round coverage was reduced first to three months, and then to 60 days, to enable *temporeras* to participate.

Other examples where labour protection mechanisms have been extended to non-standard and informal workers include provisions for domestic workers, an extremely vulnerable and hard-to-reach group (see box 8.2).

Innovative health and pension provision for informal workers in Costa Rica [39]

An unusual example of a scheme initiated by government to bring informal workers who do not qualify for formal social security provision under the social security umbrella comes from Costa Rica. Unlike the statutory scheme for temporary workers in Chile, this is at present a voluntary scheme, covering access to health care and to a pension savings scheme.

Costa Rica has a long history of extensive social security coverage for its relatively small and homogeneous population, but demographic and labour market changes are presenting new challenges to social protection. These changes include a rapid growth of women's involvement in paid work and employment, mostly in the services sector and on poor terms relative to men. The expansion of the informal economy, which includes strong participation by women, has led to lack of social insurance coverage for an increasing proportion of the Costa Rican workforce. In the mid-1990s, the privatization of pensions was strongly resisted by civil society groups coming together under the auspices of the Forum of National Concertation. The outcome was a Law of Protection of Workers, which included a voluntary insurance scheme.

This scheme is open to independent workers, those who are self-employed, and those who receive no salary or wage, such as family workers, housewives and students. It is aimed at those who have never contributed to a health or pension plan, or who have done so only for too short a period to gain adequate benefits. All those from families with a per capita income lower than the basic basket of food products determined by the Statistics Institute are entitled to join. The state contributes

0.25 per cent of the reference income, while the independent worker contributes 7.25 per cent; the individual's contribution can vary downwards to 4.75 per cent.

At present the scheme is voluntary, but by 2005 it will become statutory and all independent workers will be required to enlist. This is intended to increase the numbers of those in contributory schemes: at present a remarkable 74 per cent of independent workers already contribute to the health insurance scheme, while only 24 per cent contribute to the pension insurance. This is partly because poor Costa Ricans are able to enjoy a non-contributory pension. A country with a good history of social provision is thus attempting to adjust to changes in the labour market in flexible ways, including establishing links between contributory and non-contributory schemes.

South African old age pensions [40]

This scheme evolved from a safety net pension for poor whites, later extended to coloured people in 1928 and Africans in 1944. The African population, however, faced more stringent means tests and received much lower pension benefits than whites during the apartheid era. The end of apartheid led to full parity in entitlements and to a rapid rise in take-up rates among Africans. Women at age 60 and men at age 65 become eligible to receive a monthly old age pension (OAP) from the state, if they qualify through an income-based means test.

These pensions have become recognized as making a distinct contribution to poverty alleviation, both for pensioners themselves, and for people in their households. A large proportion of older people in South Africa, especially in low-income rural areas, live in three-generational extended families. The pension is the individual entitlement of the pensioner, but there is extensive income pooling and a large part of it enters the common household purse. Thus ageing women workers in the informal economy, and other disadvantaged elderly women including retired domestics and widows, have a guarantee of partial economic security in their late years. This protects them in their own right against the vulnerabilities associated with old age, and gives them an earned place in the household. At present, the system reaches 80 per cent of the African elderly population and an insignificant number of whites.

Although the scheme is non-contributory and paid from general revenue, the OAP is judged to be sustainable and affordable. In fiscal terms, the government allocates an annual increase, which in the last few years has been an increase in real terms. Demographically, the numbers of ageing people constitute a small fraction of the population. The HIV/AIDS epidemic has reduced longevity, and proportionally fewer people are likely to reach eligible age. However, among those who already have done so, many are already taking on the responsibility for looking after and supporting children whose parents have died of AIDS. Thus the OAP has become for many a vital contribution to household security.

Learning from innovatory schemes

SEWA's IIS provides convincing evidence that social insurance for informal workers can be successful and sustainable. However, such robust examples are hard to find. A rare example from Africa is Umoja wa Matibabu katika Sekta Isiyo Rasmi Dar es Salaam (UMASIDA), an insurance scheme specifically for informal workers, men and women street vendors in Dar es Salaam, Tanzania. UMASIDA was initiated in 1995 following an ILO intervention, and rapidly grew to some 1,500 workers and 4,500 of their family members. It gave access to primary health care services at selected private facilities, and care for referrals at government hospitals. While UMASIDA is encountering some financial difficulties with the affordability of fees, it has been more successful in sustaining its membership than many other mutual health schemes.[41]

One of the secrets of success, notably with SEWA's IIS, is responsiveness to members' needs. Flexibility is also a hallmark of the Chilean and Costa Rican governmental approaches. In Chile, access to health insurance was extended to a formerly uncovered group of workers, the waged seasonal workers. Costa Rica built a voluntary insurance scheme for health and for old age pension for independent and unremunerated workers. However, both these schemes have been introduced relatively recently, and it is too early to assess their performance.

The extension of social protection to informal and dispersed workers necessarily involves additional administrative costs. Both Chile and Costa Rica grafted their innovations onto an existing administrative system for delivering social security, and both countries have relatively small populations. SEWA draws on the solidarity and unity that it has nurtured over many years, with a large part of the administrative costs being borne by the members themselves. None of the case studies looked at how employer contributions might be secured. In the absence of favourable organizational circumstances, financial sustainability may require a long-term subsidy.

The Costa Rican case shows that informal workers find it easier to insure against ill-health than to save for old age. SEWA also finds that its health insurance tends to attract older members who are more likely to experience illness than the average member—a common problem of insurance schemes. Another SEWA lesson is that the quality of the health care which will become accessible has to be considered when inviting people to join a scheme.

The examples of these innovatory approaches also show that the role of the state in being able to deliver to large numbers of people through existing and new institutions is likely to be critical. This is clear from the South African OAP, and the Chilean and Costa Rican schemes. So we need to revise the call for the state to "get back in", acknowledge how it is "already in", and look at ways of making these interventions even more effective. Finally, the provision of some kind of basic income—whether in the form of universal, or near-universal, flat-rate pension, or child allowance—can avoid stigma while reducing the opportunities for bureaucratic discretion. It can also have the additional advantage of being relatively simple and cheap to administer.

ANTI-POVERTY PROGRAMMES: "TARGETING" WOMEN BUT GENDER-BLIND?

Over recent decades, several governments and non-government organizations have implemented anti-poverty programmes specifically aimed at poor women. Micro-credit programmes

are the best-known. But less international attention has been given to a genre of poverty relief programmes directed specifically at poor women in their capacities as community members, mothers and carers. In Latin America, for example, the severe social crisis associated with structural adjustment propelled many low-income women into diverse community projects aimed at meeting the day-to-day needs of poor urban and rural families. These projects had their roots in a much longer history of community welfare associated with Christian philanthropy.[42] The success of some of these programmes during the 1980s attracted both donor and government attention and funding.

In the recent past and in the present, efforts have been made to incorporate the new emphasis on "participation" and "empowerment" currently fashionable in national and international policy circles into some of these programmes. Whether these features of democratization are merely rhetorical add-ons, or whether they have been successfully institutionalized, and with what implications for gender equality, are questions worth exploring in relation to many such schemes. However, only one appropriate state programme is examined briefly here: the *Oportunidades* programme, or *Progresa/Oportunidades* as it is often referred to, introduced in 1997, reorganized and extended since under the administration of President Vincente Fox which came to power in Mexico in 2000.

Progresa/Oportunidades is the most extensive programme of its kind in Latin America. It provides cash transfers and food handouts to approximately five million poor rural households, but on the condition that they send their children to school and visit local health centres on a regular basis. This targeted programme therefore attempts to combine short-term and long-term poverty reduction objectives, along the lines of the "social risk management" approach advocated by the World Bank. The emphasis is on "co-responsibility": in return for the entitlements provided by the programme, certain obligations are assumed by the participants. These are mothers from poor families who are expected to ensure the obligations of school attendance and health care usage.

The programme has been welcomed by some as positive in making the cash transfers directly to women, because they can be more trusted than can men to use them for family welfare purposes. But despite this effort to "empower" women, evaluations of the programme have identified various other gender problems.[43] These arise in addition to well-known problems associated with targeting: exclusion of some families who should be in the target group, stigmatization of those identified for assistance, and the creation of community divisions. In addition, there are concerns that the programme has intensified the women participants' unpaid workloads and has done little to strengthen their labour market skills. Because "they were paid by the government", the women were expected to perform community work such as cleaning schools and health centres, unlike those not in the scheme.[44]

Despite the focus on women, little effort has been made to bring in a gender equality angle into the programme, for example by involving fathers in some of the unpaid volunteer work, or in taking children to school and to local health clinics. Hence the programme is based on, and reinforces, traditional gender divisions by making its transfers conditional on "good motherhood"—a policy stance reminiscent of the 1920s and indicative of considerable continuity in social policy.[45] Women's active involvement in the design and management of the programme has not been sought, nor have opportunities been provided for collective action by members—organizational initiatives which would have substantiated a claim of fostering women's real "empowerment".

There are lessons to be learned from the *Progresa/ Oportunidades* experience. While government poverty relief programmes increasingly recognize the contributions that women can make to development, the benefits of such recognition to women themselves remain elusive. Despite the lip-service paid to gender equality, little attention is paid in donor evaluations to the way in which the interests of children may be pushed at the expense of their mothers. WDR 2004, for example, holds up *Progresa/Oportunidades* as an exemplary anti-poverty programme.[46] For all *Progresa/Oportunidades* has achieved by way of improvements in child nutrition and primary school attendance (especially of girls),—social objectives that are undoubtedly highly valued by many of the women involved in this programme—it has also had its blind spots and biases. There is not even a passing reference in the WDR to the way in which the

programme has built upon, endorsed and entrenched a highly non-egalitarian model of the family, where women effectively become a "conduit of policy"[47]—ensuring that resources channelled through them translate into greater improvements in the well-being of children and the family.

Not only are such programmes subsidized by women's unpaid work, but there is little recognition that many women in low-income communities are of necessity often working for cash, in jobs or self-employment. Programmes such as *Progresa/ Oportunidades* miss the opportunity of being transformative by responding to the expressed needs of many low-income women for affordable and reliable childcare facilities and job training to advance their autonomy and income security. In the absence of such measures, there is a real danger that care-centred and child-centred programmes will further entrench existing gender inequalities, and make it even more difficult for women to engage in paid work and pursue other options of their own choosing.

In assessing anti-poverty programmes, social protection schemes or government service delivery, a key question that must be asked is whether the expectations raised by the emphasis on participation, rights and citizenship are being fulfilled. Are women in particular able to acquire the presence and voice needed to ensure that their interests are fully integrated in policy making? Liberalization policies and the assault on the state explain some of the reasons for the persistence of biases against women. But there are also broader political questions about viewpoints and interests that triumph in politics, and in policy making and service design: political debates about what constitutes a healthy society and women's place within it, about what people's obligations are towards each other, and the state's obligations to its citizens. These issues are addressed in section 3 of the report.

Notes

1 See note in figure 8.1 for an explanation of what items are included under "social sectors".

2 Cornia et al. 1987.

3 MacPherson and Midgley, 1987:134 cited in Vivian 1995:21.

4 Vivian 1995.

5 IMF 1998 and 2000 cited in Mkandawire 2001.

6 World Bank 2001c; Holzmann and Jorgensen 2000:28.

7 UNDP 2003; ILO Socio-Economic Security in Focus Programme; UNRISD Programme on Social Policy in a Development Context; Globalism and Social Policy Programme (GASPP).

8 World Bank 2003a:133,60.

9 Devereux and Sabates-Wheeler 2004.

10 Mackintosh and Tibandebage 2004b:167; Huber 2002.

11 Baldwin 1990; Barr 1998; Mkandawire 2001; Lund 2004.

12 Mackintosh and Tibandebage 2004a.

13 Molyneux 2004.

14 Molyneux 2004.

15 Elson and Cagatay 2000.

16 See UNESCO 2003; other reports scheduled for 2005 are likely to cover this issue comprehensively.

17 Esping-Andersen 1990.

18 This subsection is based on Mackintosh and Tibandebage 2004a.

19 Jackson and Rao 2004 provide evidence for India.

20 Kutzin 1994; Walraven 1996; Ekwempu et al. 1990; Abdullah 2000.

21 Baru 2003.

22 Sen 2003.

23 Sources cited in Mackintosh and Tibandebage 2004b.

24 Tibandebage 2004.

25 Tibandebage and Mackintosh 2002.

26 Jewkes et al. 1998, cited in Mackintosh and Tibandebage 2004b.

27 Mensah 2004.

28 Afford 2003.

29 World Bank 1995 cited in Mackintosh and Tibandebage 2004b.

30 World Bank 2003a:144–5.

31 Lund 2004.

32 Huber and Stephens 2000.

33 Huber and Stephens 2000.

34 Steinhilber 2004.

35 Diamond and Valdes-Prieto 1994:309.

36 Barrientos 2004.

37 Chatterjee and Ranson 2003; ILO 2001, cited in Lund 2004.

38 Barrientos and Barrientos 2002.

39 Martinez Franzoni and Mesa-Lago 2003, cited in Lund 2004.

40 Ardington and Lund 1995; Case and Deaton 1998; Case 2001; Lund 2002.

41 Tibandebage 2004.

42 Jelin 1990; Molyneux 2004.

43 The evaluations are summarized in Molyneux 2004.

44 Molyneux 2004:29.

45 Molyneux 2004:36.

46 World Bank 2003a:30–1.

47 Molyneux 2004.

Section 3
Women in politics
and public life

WOMEN QUEUE WITH
THEIR VOTING SLIPS
ON ELECTION DAY.
JAVA, INDONESIA

The capacities of states to deliver on policy promises—to do with gender equality or anything else—are fundamentally shaped by politics, as are the outcomes of economic and governance reforms. As this has become increasingly evident, development analysts' interest in political dynamics has grown; but the full dimensions of how political processes affect gender equality and ongoing efforts to achieve it are not yet well studied or understood.

This section explores the interactions between the wider political sphere and efforts to promote women's rights and interests in public policy. In particular it examines the assumption that a greater presence of women in decision-making public bodies leads to more attention to gender concerns by the institutions of government, and more expenditure on meeting women's needs.

The first chapter, "Women in public office: A rising tide", looks at the encouraging trend which finds more women than ever before in elected national assemblies, and examines the related mechanisms and impacts. In the second chapter, "Women mobilizing to reshape democracy", the impact of women's movements around the world on public decision making is explored, together with questions surrounding women's other political identities, especially as members of faith or ethnic groups. The current reform agenda for "good governance" in national and local-level public institutions has crucial implications for women and for gender equality, but has it been designed with a proper degree of gender sensitivity? The third and fourth chapters—"Gender and 'good governance'" and "Decentralization and gender equality"—consider the impacts on women of a range of public-sector reforms designed to improve public accountability and to enhance popular participation in decision making.

Chapter 9
Women in public office:
A rising tide

One resolution in the Beijing Platform for Action to have enjoyed marked progress is that calling for women's greater access to public office. Even if governments have been uneven in their responses and there is still far to go, nonetheless the entry of more women to representative office is an achievement that deserves celebration as a contribution to deepening democracy around the world.

Although the average proportion of women in national assemblies has only increased from 9 per cent in 1995 to almost 16 per cent in 2004, a level far short of the Beijing call for equality, 16 countries have managed to put 30 per cent or more women into their national legislatures (table 9.1). In 2003, Rwanda achieved a world record with a parliament in which almost half of members (MPs) were women, a higher proportion than in the highest-ranking OECD country. In the same year Finland achieved the simultaneous tenure of a woman head of state (president) and head of government (prime minister)—another "first" for elected women in political life. However, such achievements remain exceptional. In the absence of measures such as affirmative action to boost numbers of female candidates, the level of women in politics worldwide remains low, increasing at the painfully slow pace of only 0.5 per cent a year.

As we saw in chapter 1 (figure 1.3), every region in the world except for Eastern Europe and Central Asia has seen a slow increase in the numbers of women in office. In the ex-socialist states in these two regions, women's share of seats in national legislatures plummeted by 50 per cent after 1989 when previous communist party quotas for women were dropped; but

during the late 1990s there was some recovery. This experience is a salutary indication of how easily efforts to increase women's participation in politics can be reversed.

The number of women to be found in formal politics is not the best indicator either of the intensity of women's political participation, or of its effectiveness in orienting policy making towards gender concerns. Nor is it necessarily a reflection of the level of civil society activism on women's issues. In the pre-1989 state socialist countries, the large numbers of women in formal politics bore no relation to the strength of women's movements; women's independent civil society activity was actually suppressed under these regimes.[1] A contrasting experience is found in India and the United States; these countries have the largest women's movements in the world in terms of number, variety of organizations and membership size, yet the presence of women in national office is among the lowest in the world.[2]

The numbers of women active in women's organizations, or even the numbers of active women's organizations in a country, might be a far better indicator of women's political participation than the level of formal female representation in elected bodies. But consistent cross-national data on the numbers and strength of women's associations and movements is not available. Women's political participation has to be understood more broadly than such figures would imply even if they were available: many women voice their interests and views through participation in a wide variety of political and civic associations.

Table 9.1 Countries achieving a "critical mass" (30 per cent and over) of women in national assemblies, April 2004

Country	Electoral system	Existence of Quotas [2]	% Women in NA 2004
Rwanda	Plurality: first past the post	YES Type 1: Constitution establishes quota for women. Type 2: 24 seats out of 80 are reserved for women in the National Assembly. Type 3: 20% district councilors are reserved for women.	48.8
Sweden	Proportional representation: list system	YES Type 4: 50% quota for women in the Swedish Social Democratic Labour Party, the Left Party and the Green Party of Sweden.	45.3
Denmark	Proportional representation: list system	NO Used to have Type 4. Quotas were abandoned around 1996.	38.0
Finland	Proportional representation: list system	NO N/A	37.5
Netherlands	Proportional representation: list system	YES Type 4: Labour Party has 50% quota for women; Green Left has a quota for women also (% not confirmed).	36.7
Norway	Proportional representation: list system	YES Type 4: 40% quota for women in the Socialist Left Party, the Norwegian Labour Party, the Centre Party, and the Christian People's Party.	36.4
Cuba	Majority: two-round system	NO N/A	36.0
Spain	Proportional representation: list system	YES Type 4: Spanish Socialist Workers' Party has 40% quota for either sex.	36.0
Belgium	Proportional representation: list system	YES Type 2: One third minimum quota for either sex; two top positions on party list cannot be held by members of the same sex Type 4: 50% quota for women in Flemish Socialist Party and French Socialist Party.	35.3
Costa Rica	Proportional representation: list system	YES Type 2: 40% quota for women in all public elections. Type 4: 40% quota for women in the National Liberation Party and the Christian-Social Unity Party; 50% in the Citizen Action Party.	35.1
Argentina	Proportional representation: list system	YES Type 1: Constitution establishes quota for women. Type 2: 30% of party's lists must include women in winnable positions. Type 3: The capital and provincial laws include quotas. Type 4: Most parties adopted a 30% quota for women.	34.0
Austria	Proportional representation: list system	YES Type 4: The Green Alternative has 50% quota for women; the Austrian People's party has 33.3% and the Social Democratic Party of Austria has 40%.	33.9
Germany	Proportional representation: mixed-member system	YES Type 4: The Party of Democratic Socialism and the Greens have 50% quota for women; the Christian Democratic Union has 33.3% and the Social Democratic Party of Germany has 40%.	32.2
Iceland	Proportional representation: list system	YES Type 4: The People's Alliance and the Social Democratic Party have 40% quota for women.	30.2
Mozambique	Proportional representation: list system	YES Type 4: The Front for the Liberation of Mozambique has a 30% quota for women.	30.0
South Africa [1]	Proportional representation: list system	YES Type 4: The African National Congress has a 30% quota for women. 50% quota for women on party lists at local level.	30.0

Notes: The rest of countries in the world have percentages of women in national parliaments below 30%.
(1) As of December 2003 (information as of April 2004 was not available).
(2) The following types of quotas are considered:
Type 1 = Constitutional quota for national parliament
Type 2 = Election law quota or regulation for national parliament
Type 3 = Constitutional or legislative quota for subnational government
Type 4 = Political party quota for electoral candidates.
Sources: IDEA 2002; IDEA and Stockholm University 2004; IPU 2004.

TOWARDS A "CRITICAL MASS"

In spite of the risks of reading too much into the growth in numbers of women in representative politics, their presence, numbers and visibility are important. Women's wider participation in formal electoral competition brings core issues of political structure to the fore. Reforms to electoral systems may be designed to progress towards equal gender representation; male-dominated political parties may be challenged; and the presence of more, and more visible, women among senior policy makers may improve responsiveness in both policy and practice to women's needs.

This idea is expressed in the notion that a "critical mass" of women can change the culture, practice and outcomes of politics. The metaphor of the critical mass was first used in the 1980s to explain the impact that the presence of large numbers of women in local and national government bodies in Scandinavian countries had managed to make on policy making and spending priorities; the proportion regarded as necessary for this critical mass is around 30 per cent.[3] The outcome of "critical mass" in Norway, for instance, was that measures were passed to increase subsidized childcare services, extend parental leave, introduce options for flexible working hours and improve pension rights for unpaid care work.[4] In South Africa, important new legislation on rape, domestic violence and abortion rights was introduced as a result of its promotion by women office holders: they constituted 25 per cent of the total in the 1994 government.[5]

Though effective as a mobilizing slogan, the notion of critical mass implies an automatic, even irreversible, causal sequence between increased numbers of women in politics and better policy outcomes for women. But many obstacles lie between women's greater access to politics—a challenging enough project on its own—and their capacity to influence decision making in any direction, let alone to bring about gender equity. These obstacles include entrenched male bias in political parties, and as importantly in the formal institutions of government; from the fiscal policy and budgetary systems whereby spending priorities are set, to the mechanisms for law

enforcement, justice and public accountability. It will require more than a rise in the numbers of women in politics to remove such obstacles as these.

WHY ARE WOMEN ABSENT?

A common-sense explanation for the low numbers of women in politics is that their resource endowments for public life—their education, spare time, employment, income and connections—are lower than those of men. However, as figures 9.1 to 9.3 show, it is difficult to establish a hard and fast correspondence between the levels of women's education or economic activity and their political participation. Countries and regions with similar levels of female net secondary and tertiary enrolment have very different levels of women's representation in formal politics. And the relationship between women's economic activity rate and numbers of women in office is as uneven. The evidence does not suggest that women's participation in formal politics simply increases in step with advances in their educational or employment status in comparison with those of men.

Evidence for this is confirmed in a study of 23 middle and low-income countries in Asia. The findings show little significant difference in the levels of women in formal politics regardless of whether there is near-universal education, as in the Republic of Korea, quite extensive female educational participation (as in Sri Lanka), or extremely low female literacy (as in Pakistan and Nepal).[6] This implies that there are other gender-specific influences at work to discourage female political participation, which may well include selection and treatment biases in political institutions.

National income influences women's access to formal politics, as shown in figure 9.4. Women in higher-income countries will tend to benefit from higher human capital, as well as from the fact that democratic institutions and accountability are better entrenched than in developing or transitional countries, and systems are more open. But averages such as these disguise considerable variation. For example, the world's wealthiest country, the United States, suffers from persistently low levels

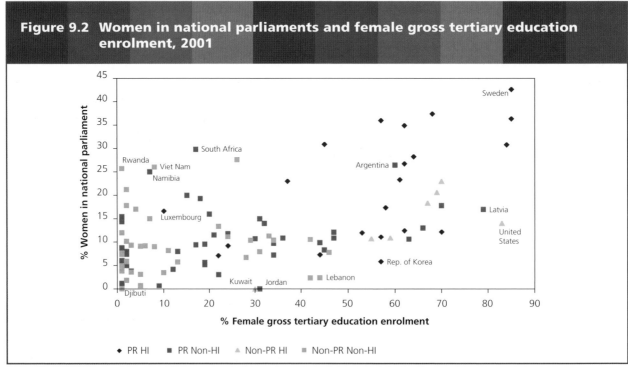

Figure 9.1 Women in national parliaments and female net secondary education enrolment, 2001

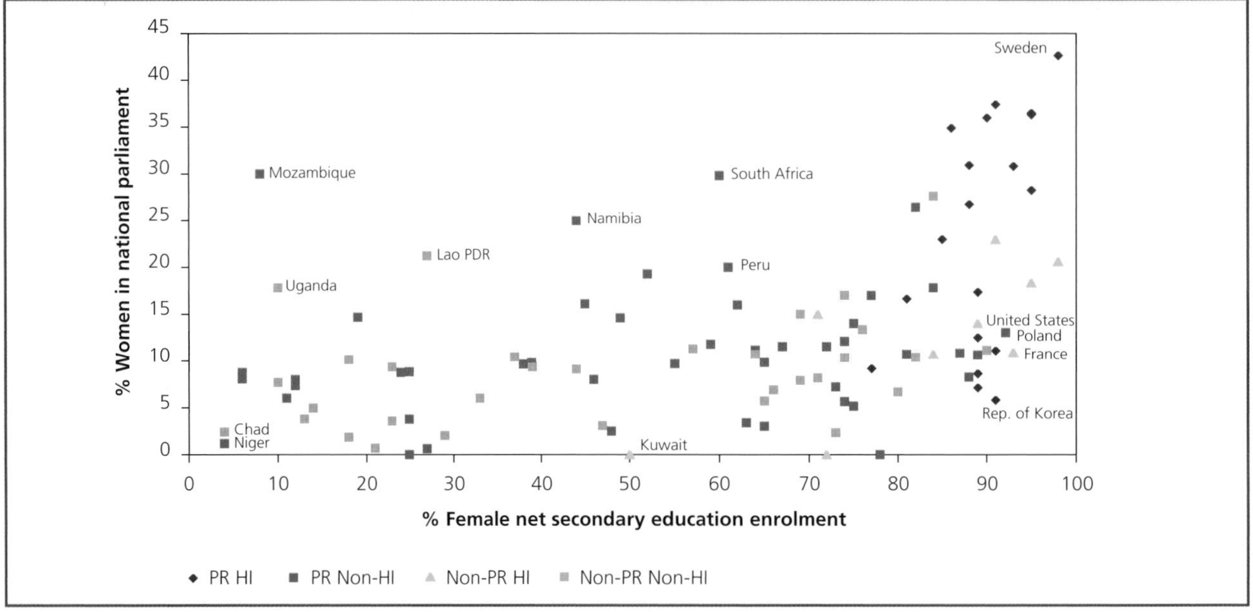

Notes: PR = Countries with a proportional or semi-proportional electoral system; HI = High-income countries
Sources: UN Statistical Division 2004; UNDP 2003.

Figure 9.2 Women in national parliaments and female gross tertiary education enrolment, 2001

Notes: PR = Countries with a proportional or semi-proportional electoral system; HI = High-income countries
Sources: UN Statistical Division 2004; UNDP 2003.

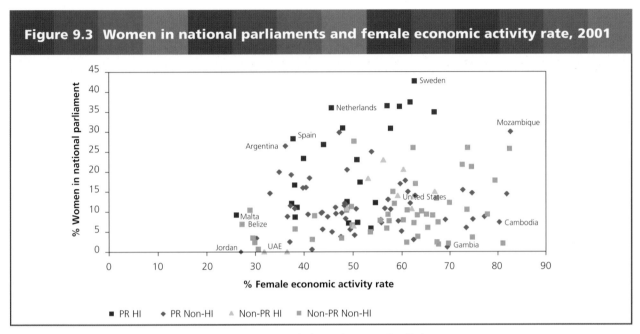

Figure 9.3 Women in national parliaments and female economic activity rate, 2001

Notes: PR = Countries with a proportional or semi-proportional electoral system; HI = High-income countries
Sources: UN Statistical Division 2004; UNDP 2003.

of female political representation; meanwhile some of the world's poorest countries, such as Rwanda and Mozambique, have high levels of women in politics.

Differences of culture plays an important role in determining levels of women's participation, as is demonstrated by data from the Indian states of Kerala and Rajasthan. Kerala has a matrilineal tradition, which endows women with more autonomy and mobility than in other parts of India, and they marry much

later than in other states. By contrast, communities in Rajasthan tend to be aggressively patriarchal and continue such traditional practices as child marriage. Female literacy rates in these two states are at the opposite ends of the spectrum: 86 per cent in Kerala in contrast with 20 per cent in Rajasthan, dropping to 12 per cent in rural areas. However, women's cultural and educational advantage in Kerala has not propelled them into politics in greater numbers than in Rajasthan. In neither state has the proportion of women in state legislative assemblies reached even 10 per cent, peaking at 9 per cent in Kerala in 1993–7, and 8 per cent in Rajasthan in 1985–90.[7]

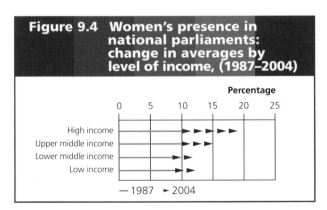

Figure 9.4 Women's presence in national parliaments: change in averages by level of income, (1987–2004)

Source: Calculated from IPU 2004; UN Statistical Division 2004; UN 2003.

ELECTORAL SYSTEMS AND WOMEN'S ENTRY

Kerala and Rajasthan may be culturally divergent, but they do share a common electoral system. The evidence shows that electoral systems—the way in which citizens' votes are assigned to seats in representative bodies—are the best predictor of the numbers of women in politics.[8] Regression analysis using both

Box 9.1   Gender implications of variations in electoral systems

Electoral systems vary chiefly in the electoral formula used for translating votes into seats in a representative assembly, in the ballot structure and in *district magnitude.*

There are two broad types of electoral systems: plurality/majority systems and proportional representation (PR).

Plurality/majority systems tend to use single-member districts, where voters chose a preferred candidate, and the candidate to secure more votes than anyone else wins. Some systems try to establish a majority preference through, for example, run-offs between the highest-polling candidates. But the most common formula, found in at least 70 countries, is the Westminster single-member, simple-plurality system.

In *PR systems,* voters select their preferred party, and seats in the relevant assembly body are assigned in proportion to the percentage of votes won by the party. Constituencies with PR systems tend to be multi-member, with more than one representative elected. The ballot structure in PR systems presents voters with a list of candidates; this may be an "open" list, enabling voters to select preferred candidates, or a "closed" list. In the latter case the party sends candidates to office in proportion to the percentage of votes won; for instance, with 40 per cent of the vote, the top 40 per cent of its listed candidates are successful.

Semi-proportional systems may combine PR lists and plurality/majority systems, for instance by giving voters a chance to select both a party (which will assign candidates based on the percentage of votes it gains) and an individual candidate for a given district. Alternatively they use the plurality principle but have multi-member districts.

regional and global data consistently produces the same results. Out of a total of 174 countries for which statistics were available in 2003, those with electoral systems based on proportional representation (PR) returned assemblies with an average of 16 per cent women politicians, while those without proportional systems (plurality/majority systems or semi-proportional systems—see box 9.1) returned assemblies with 11 per cent women politicians. The contrast is most striking in certain regions: in sub-Saharan Africa, countries with PR systems have legislatures in which women constitute on average 12 per cent of representatives, in contrast with 5 per cent in other systems.

The experience with PR illustrates the way in which variations in institutional rules can have gender-specific impacts, intended or otherwise. PR systems are designed to encourage the representation of diverse interests, and have proved more open to women's participation than are plurality/majority systems. In the latter, the one shot at office, all or nothing character of the electoral contest provides an incentive for parties to front the safest candidate, usually a representative of "the common man". In multi-member PR systems where a particular party is strong and can expect to see a number of its candidates elected, more women candidates tend to be fronted.

However, even under PR systems there is still considerable variation in the proportions of women elected to assemblies. Some countries with PR persistently return tiny proportions of women to their legislatures; examples are Israel and Greece. Just as inconsistently, a few countries with single-member, simple-plurality systems return substantial proportions of women: New Zealand and Canada, for example. Thus the choice of electoral system cannot alone provide sufficient explanation for different country experiences. This confirms that a number of variables influence women's electoral prospects, including the political culture and the nature of political parties.

AFFIRMATIVE ACTION: BOOSTING THE NUMBERS

Women quotas

During the last ten years, there has been considerable experimentation with the use of affirmative action or all-women quotas in order to meet the goal of gender parity in representative politics. Quotas on party electoral lists are the most common

Figure 9.5 Women in national parliaments, averages by level of income, electoral system and existence of quotas, 2004

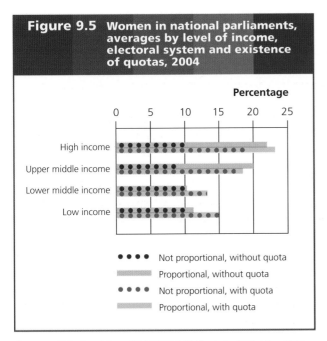

Sources: Calculated from IPU 2004; UN Statistical Division 2004; UN 2003; IDEA 2002; IDEA and Stockholm University 2004.

means of promoting women's political participation; today they are in use in over 80 countries. As shown in figure 9.5, they enhance the positive impact of PR systems on women's electoral chances, and help return more women to office in non-PR systems too.

Quotas may be adopted by parties following pressure from women members, or they may be a requirement mandated by law. In single-member, simple-plurality systems the application of quotas can be difficult where local party branches are closely involved in selecting their candidate: they may resist pressure to exclude men. Some parties in these systems have tried to encourage those members responsible for candidate selection to choose women, setting internal "targets" rather than strict quotas.

Quotas alone have not guaranteed better female representation: party commitment is also needed. Quota provisions are evaded when women candidates are demoted to the bottom of a closed list, where they are unlikely to be assigned seats in parliament unless the party's winning majority is overwhelming. Parties at local level will typically avoid applying quota provisions if there are no penalties for failing to implement them (see box 9.2). As a result, quotas in some countries have not

produced as significant an increase in elected women as had been hoped. For example, Brazil, Venezuela and Panama all have an official quota of 30 per cent women in the national assembly, but during their elections returned respectively 9 per cent, 10 per cent and 10 per cent.

Quotas are most effective where there are large electoral districts, and requirements that women are spaced evenly on lists: a "zipped" list, known as a "zebra" list in southern Africa, contains alternating women and men. Where there are also penalties for non-compliance, such as withholding of government campaign subsidies, co-operation is better assured. These conditions hold in Argentina, Bolivia, Uruguay and Costa Rica; Argentina has a 30 per cent quota and placed women in 31 per cent of seats at the last national election; with an electoral quota of 40 per cent, Costa Rica placed women in 35 per cent of assembly seats. In both these countries the legal mandate for the system requires that women are placed in winnable positions.

Reserved seats and constituencies

In single-member, simple-plurality systems, measures to reserve seats for women have been preferred over quotas of women candidates. These systems of reservation vary according to whether the seats are filled by a direct or indirect election process. For several decades, Tanzania, Pakistan and Bangladesh have filled seats for women in parliament by assigning seats for parties' own female nominees in proportion to the seats they have won. These reserved seats have simply been a way of further boosting government majorities, and have undermined the perceived legitimacy of the women who fill them.

Another example of seats filled by an indirect process comes from Uganda, where there is a special category of seat reserved for the "woman representative" of every district in the country. The majority of the women in parliament occupy such seats, and their selection is by district-level electoral colleges composed of local-government representatives, almost all of whom were men until very recently.

Box 9.2   Legal challenges to quota law violations in Argentina

In 1991, Argentina passed a quota law mandating that at least 30 per cent of electoral candidates must be women. During the 1993 elections for the Chamber of Deputies, party leaders in every political party and in every province failed to apply the law. Because the electoral judges at the time did not consider the quota law as a "public law", only the wronged candidates were eligible to challenge the lists. Highly organized women's groups, with the support of the state-sponsored *Consejo Nacional de la Mujer*, moved quickly to assist women from across the political spectrum in all 24 electoral districts to file legal challenges. These lawsuits produced rulings by the national electoral chamber and the Supreme Court certifying that the quota law was a public law and had to be enforced. A constitutional amendment granting women "equal opportunity ... for access to elective and political party office ... by positive action" was also approved. Today, women legislators hold more than one-third of the seats in both chambers of the Argentinean Congress, and party lists that do not comply with the 30 per cent minimum quota laws are rejected.

Source: Bouvier 2004.

An alternative affirmative method is the reservation of a percentage of territorial constituencies for all-female competition; this enables women to compete for the popular vote rather than lobby for nomination by a party elite. Under a 1992 constitutional amendment, one-third of India's local government seats are reserved for women, and these constituencies rotate in each electoral round, enabling—or obliging—a new set of constituents to chose a woman representative each time.

Impacts of affirmative measures

The design and application of quota and reservation systems influence the perceived legitimacy of the women politicians who fill them. They may also affect the relationships between women politicians and women's movements and organizations, and the politicians' desire or ability to promote gender-equity goals in the political arena.

As with any affirmative action system, the beneficiaries may be stigmatized. A candidate may be regarded as token and without representative credibility, especially if she has no geographical constituency. Where party executives determine which women to include on a list or place in reserved seats, aspiring candidates will be primarily accountable to the party leadership rather than to a potential gender-equity constituency. In

Uganda, selection for reserved assembly seats by a district-level electoral college has been known to prevent aspirants from advancing a feminist agenda or confessing links to the women's movement—this could be tantamount to electoral suicide if the electoral college is socially conservative.

Among affirmative-action measures, the voluntary adoption of party quotas for female candidates has probably been the most effective at normalizing women's engagement in politics. The struggle to establish these quotas has sometimes helped to strengthen a party's commitment to gender equity, and to forge connections between women politicians and women's organizations in the wider society. Where parties have followed others' examples—as has happened among conservative parties in continental Europe attempting to match leftist parties' success in fronting women candidates—an "inter-party contagion"[9] on the issue of women's representation can ensue, informing wider debates on gender-equity issues. Quotas work very well in closed-list systems, but there are democratic deficits in these systems. Closed-list systems tend to detach representatives from their constituents, making them accountable less to voters than to party bosses. This problem is exacerbated in highly centralized parties, which, as it happens, also tend to be the most effective at promoting women's participation: party command structures can overcome resistance to affirmative action and to gender equity itself.

Clearly therefore, entrenched cultural obstacles to women in political leadership are difficult to reduce with affirmative action measures alone. Without supportive action from national women's movements, affirmative measures may end up by populating representative fora with women elites who differ little in social background or political approaches from their male colleagues.

THE MYTH OF VOTER HOSTILITY

An enduring obstacle to the effective promotion of women candidates for office is that parties perceive women to be un-electable. However, there appears to be less resistance among voters to female candidates than there is among party bureau-cracies. A Vox Populis opinion poll carried out in Brazil in January 2000 showed that women were considered by voters to be more honest, trustworthy, competent and capable than male candidates; 84 per cent of the electorate claimed they would vote for a woman as mayor, 80 per cent for a woman as state governor, and 72 per cent for a woman president.[10]

This favourable attitude was echoed throughout the Latin American region. Fifty-seven per cent of respondents to a 2001 Gallup poll in five major regional cities believed that more women in politics would lead to better government; 69 per cent believed their country would elect a woman president in the next 20 years.[11] Prior to the 1988 local elections in Belgium, the law was changed to make it mandatory for candidates' first names to be printed on the ballots so that voters could more easily identify their gender. The result was an astonishing 26 per cent increase in the number of women elected.[12]

In India, figures show that although the number of women elected to the Lok Sabha (the lower house of parliament) has always been lamentably small, this owes much more to the reluctance of parties to field women candidates than to the reluctance of voters to elect women representatives. Since 1957, female candidates have enjoyed a consistently higher success rate than male candidates; on average a woman is twice as likely to be elected as a man.[13] Voter attitudes elsewhere, however, remain ambivalent or opposed to women exercising equal power with men. A 2001 survey of the Zimbabwean electorate found that 29 per cent of respondents were in favour of equal repre-sentation, and only 25 per cent were in favour of having more women politicians.[14] Eastern European voters have also been slow to accept women in public leadership positions and are still more likely than West Europeans to agree that "men make better political leaders than women do".[15]

WOMEN'S PRESENCE AND PERFORMANCE IN PUBLIC OFFICE

In the past 10 years, political systems have made significant changes to enable higher levels of female participation. Although this has not taken place without considerable campaigning effort by women's movements and organizations, the speed with which some of these changes have occurred suggests that pub-lic institutions can be highly responsive to social engineering. Experimentation with electoral systems and affirmative action has demonstrated that institutional design can have a profound impact on women's prospects of bringing weight to bear in decision-making councils. But easing women's access to office is just the beginning of the struggle to bring gender equity to state policy making. Their effectiveness in generating support for women's concerns, in ensuring new policies are translated into new patterns of service delivery, and in setting new stan-dards against which the actions of bureaucrats and officials can be judged, depends upon several factors. These include:

- the ideological climate and its openness to gender concerns
- the institutional leadership positions to which women are elected or appointed once in office
- the standing committees for debating legislation or reviewing government policy to which women legislators are assigned
- the responsiveness of political parties to gender-equity concerns
- the relationship between politicians and women's movements
- the capacity of public institutions to implement policies or to regulate private providers so that they respect national gender-equity goals

- the existence of an effective institutional base for promoting gender equity in government planning within the bureaucracy; gendered "national machinery" can consist of a Women's Ministry, an equal opportunities bureau, or an office on the status of women
- the gender-sensitivity of public accountability systems.

The changing ideological climate

The multiple and expanding roles played by women in political life depend to an extent on ideologies, especially on the association of specific political parties with feminist or anti-feminist views. Parties of the left have been more strongly associated than those on the right with the redistributive and social justice issues of concern to women's movements. They have also traditionally been more responsive to women's issues and more willing to support women candidates for office. This has been the case, for example, in Latin America, where left-of-centre parties have promoted ideas of gender equality and supported women's citizenship rights. Revolutionary groups such as the *Frente Sandinista de Liberacion Nacional* in Nicaragua, the *Farabundo Marti* or National Liberation Front in El Salvador, or Guatemala's *Unidad Revolucionaria Nacional Guatemalteca* have been particularly forceful on women's behalf.[16]

Historically, however, parties of the left have only shown more alacrity in fielding women candidates or addressing gender-specific concerns following concerted mobilization by women members. Labour-based parties drawing membership and resources from trade unions have often given rhetorical support to gender equity but been reluctant to promote women to leadership positions; women have made this complaint about the ruling *Partido dos Trabalhadores* (PT or Workers' Party) in Brazil. In Eastern European countries, ex-communist parties and socialist parties have only been marginally more effective than right-wing parties at putting up women candidates; some of the new, still small, conservative parties in countries such as Poland have prominent and numerous female candidates.[17]

"Left–right" ideological distinctions have recently become less meaningful given the global spread of neoliberal economic policies, and the simultaneous politicization of cultural and ethnic identities. In industrialized countries, political parties have typically campaigned on macroeconomic policies reflecting the interests of their principal class constituencies. Parties on the left have appealed to the working class, emphasized employment over inflation, promoted the taxation of capital, and fostered socially inclusive public services; parties on the right have associated themselves with corporate and landowning interests and pursued policies of the opposite stamp. But in developing and transitional economies, people's interests may be secured less by supporting a class position than by exploiting family connections, or through networks and identities determined by ethnicity, region, religion and race. Thus political parties may be formed around the interests of particular ethnic, religious, or in India, caste groups. Old-style leftist parties, with their inclusionist and secular traditions, have had to respond to this phenomenon; at the same time they have had to deal with the discrediting of state socialism accompanying the dissolution of the Soviet bloc, and the onslaught on organized labour represented by liberalization and adjustment.

Links between parties and women's movements

In these circumstances, parties of the left have set out to build alliances with social and popular movements, including women's movements. Those seeking to appeal to women voters are most common in contexts where women's movements have been strong and played a critical role in democratization; the most prominent examples are in Latin America and southern Africa. But these are not the only types of parties seeking to draw upon the vote-generating capacity of organized women. In South Asia this has been a notable trend amongst chauvinist Hindu, fundamentalist Islamic, and regional caste or ethnicity-based parties. Those representing lower castes, such as the Bahujan Samaj Party in Uttar Pradesh, have seen women not only as key bearers of caste or cultural identity, but as critical sources of electoral support. In regional parties such as the Telugu Desam Party (TDP) in Andhra Pradesh, appeals have been made directly to women voters through populist gestures, such as the distribution of fuel-gas canisters, or the rapid extension of women's self-help and micro-credit programmes at election time. Hand-outs to women have taken precedence over efforts to increase their numbers in leadership positions or revise party policy in women's favour. This factor may account for women's sudden and marked desertion of the TDP in the 2004 state elections.

The influence of women with a feminist agenda within parties and government administrations depends upon the sustained pressure they can bring to bear on the leadership. Party support for key legislation may be withdrawn at the last minute if more pressing priorities intervene. In South Africa's African National Congress (ANC), where feminists have a significant presence both in the leadership of the parliamentary party and among the grassroots membership, the party's commitment to gender equality can never be taken for granted. ANC women leaders had this lesson pressed home when, in 1998, the financial allocation for their Domestic Violence Bill was sidelined by the ANC in favour of a new arms deal.[18]

Figure 9.6 **Women in ministerial and subministerial positions, and national parliaments, regional averages, 1998**

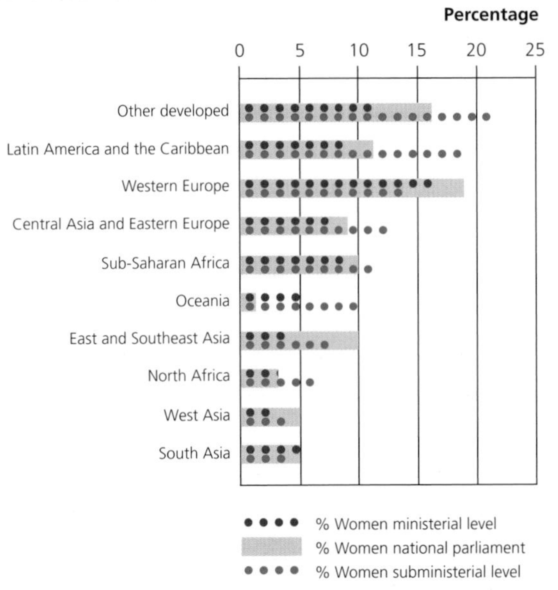

Sources: Calculated from UN Statistical Division 2004; UN 2000a.

WOMEN'S EXPANDING AND CHANGING POLITICAL ROLES

Women in leadership positions

As numbers of women legislators begin to increase, their participation in decision-making processes is constrained by their limited access to leadership positions. Figure 9.6 shows that women tend to be assigned to ministerial and subministerial executive positions roughly in proportion to their share of seats in parliament. This means that they constitute a minority of executive decision makers.

Women rarely become heads of state or government. More women are to be found as deputy heads, or as presiding officers of parliament (for instance speakers) of lower and upper houses—especially the latter, as these have less direct power than lower houses. Beyond this, the types of ministerial and subministerial assignments women legislators hold tend to be clearly gender-typed. Powerful ministries such as foreign affairs,

defence, home affairs, finance, trade and industry are still primarily the preserve of men, while women are found in ministries of environment, social affairs, health, education, family affairs, gender or women's affairs, and culture. Ministries of justice and labour are being assigned to more women than in the past (figure 9.7).

Caucusing and working in committees

Women parliamentarians in a number of countries have taken steps to raise the profile of gender issues in legislative debates. Some have formed women's caucuses to work across party lines and co-ordinate their work in legislative committees. Legislative decision-making processes are typically mediated by systems of standing committees. The gender composition of these committees clearly reflects the importance attached to their decisions. Women have struggled to be assigned to the most powerful committees: appointments, appropriations, ways and means, and finance or public accounts. But instead they tend to be assigned

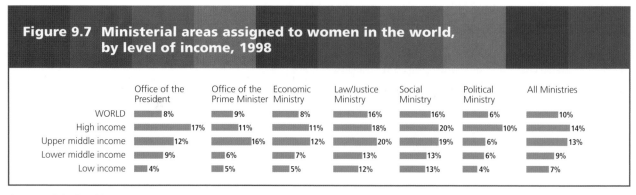

Figure 9.7 Ministerial areas assigned to women in the world, by level of income, 1998

	Office of the President	Office of the Prime Minister	Economic Ministry	Law/Justice Ministry	Social Ministry	Political Ministry	All Ministries
WORLD	8%	9%	8%	16%	16%	6%	10%
High income	17%	11%	11%	18%	20%	10%	14%
Upper middle income	12%	16%	12%	20%	19%	6%	13%
Lower middle income	9%	6%	7%	13%	13%	6%	9%
Low income	4%	5%	5%	12%	13%	4%	7%

Sources: Calculated from UN 2000a.

to committees dealing with health and welfare, youth, environment, culture, transport and consumer affairs, all of which are perceived as having jurisdiction over policy areas of direct interest to women.

Women legislators have sometimes sought to work against this pattern by creating standing committees on women's rights or on equal opportunities. One of the most successful of these is the South African Parliament's Joint Standing Committee on the Improvement of the Quality of Life and the Status of Women, initially set up to review the government's performance in relation to the Convention on the Elimination of All Forms of Discrimination against Women (CEDAW). This body was later permanently incorporated into the parliamentary committee system, and is charged with assessing the gender impacts of new legislation. It also works on institutional changes in parliament itself, challenging sitting hours inimical to family life and the lack of childcare facilities, thereby contributing to women MPs' increased effectiveness.

Although parliamentary committees on women's rights may not have automatic rights of review over fresh legislation, they can be influential in politicizing government business of relevance to women. There are, however, drawbacks to legislative committees on women's affairs, which can become ghettos for women legislators and women's issues. In the Philippines, both houses of Congress have committees on women's welfare; this means that labour measures affecting women are discussed there, not in the committee on labour. Similarly, women legislators are concentrated in "their"

committees, not in other more powerful ones such as those on foreign affairs or public accounts.[19]

THE MOBILIZATION OF WOMEN IN AND BY POLITICAL PARTIES

Political parties are the main gatekeepers to women's selection for office. They are also important arenas for debating policies, and are therefore key institutions through which to promote gender-equality concerns. Women's movements need to be aware of "the conditions under which political parties serve as institutional carrying agents for advancing women's interests and improving women's status".[20] But political parties have not been notable promoters of women's interests. Rarely have they anywhere assigned priority to gender issues or promoted women as candidates for office without prompting or obligation. Even though women are often key "foot-soldiers" in campaigning and fundraising, parties the world over appear hostile to women's decision-making participation, especially at top leadership levels. From the scant available data, it appears that few parties anywhere have women in party leadership and management positions in proportion to their grassroots membership.

Parties with clear rules and hierarchies, transparent selection procedures, a distinct and self-standing organizational structure, and strong discipline are thought best able to support women's participation.[21] But without internal democracy—and commitment—even well-institutionalized parties can be hostile to women's participation. In the Central Committee of the Chinese Communist Party, women's share of seats has never been high, peaking at 10 per cent in 1973 in the Maoist era, when seats were occupied by wives of prominent leaders. Since the 1980s, women's presence in the Central Committee has declined continuously, with only five women elected among the 198 seats contested in the 2002 elections.[22] In Eastern Europe, former communist parties likewise had few women on their central committees.

Parties in developing countries are often weakly institutionalized. Resources, seats and positions are determined by patronage, without reference to systems of transparency or internal accountability. Such parties often have highly personalized leadership systems based on family dynasties, and decision making is not open to internal challenge. One of the few routes open to women in such systems is to exploit their kinship connections to prominent male politicians to secure leadership positions. Where a woman has gained position within a party via such a route, there is less chance that she will seek connections with organized feminism or other expressions of women's concerns in civil society, or challenge the masculine party hierarchy by supporting gender causes. In the Philippines, a gendered familial political duty has almost become institutionalized. Male politicians' wives routinely step in to hold their husband's seat for the family while husbands take a legally required break to comply with regulations limiting consecutive terms in office.[23]

Women's party wings

Parties have sometimes created "women's wings" to help mobilize women voters and recruit women members. These, however, have often been captured by the spouses of male leaders and have not proven fertile arenas for the development of female party leadership or for promoting party policy on gender equity.[24]

In sub-Saharan Africa, even the ANC's Women's League, the largest and most militant women's wing of any party in the region, had difficulty in challenging the male party leadership

over women's representation on the National Executive Committee and quotas for women on party lists. Eventual success relied upon the actions of ANC women activists working outside the Women's League in concert with feminist civil society organizations. In West and East African countries, women's wings in dominant parties have sought to control and contain the wider women's movement, harnessing women's energies to support the president. Nana Konadu Agyeman Rawlings' 31st December Women's Movement in Ghana was a notorious example, but similar efforts by political spouses to monopolize international resources for women's development and to limit women's independent associational activity has made women wary of engagement with the state.[25]

Elsewhere in sub-Saharan Africa, the discrediting of one-party "big man" politics has led to challenges to female support structures for male party hierarchies. In Botswana women in the rank and file of the main political parties have exposed the conflict of interests that prevent spouses of male politicians from advancing women's interests, and are bringing new leadership and revamped structures to women's party wings. A feminist civil society organization, *Emang Basadi*, has held regular conferences inviting women's wings of parties to report on their progress in meeting quotas on party lists and in inserting women into the party leadership.[26]

Quotas for women in party leadership positions have been one means of breaking down party resistance to women at top levels, but they have been harder to introduce than quotas for women on party lists. In southern Africa, only the ANC has a quota for women in its National Executive Committee, and this was agreed at a later date than the hard-fought battle to ensure that 30 per cent of the party's lists were female. In Brazil four parties have internal quotas, and these are the only ones to have more than 10 per cent of women in their decision-making offices. Where there is marked resistance to women's participation, quotas become ceilings, not entry points. The *Partido dos Trabalhadores* (PT; Workers' Party) introduced its quota in 1993, and since then the proportion of women in the leadership has remained exactly the same at just under 30 per cent (figure 9.8), not even reflecting the 40 per cent proportion of the party's membership that is female.

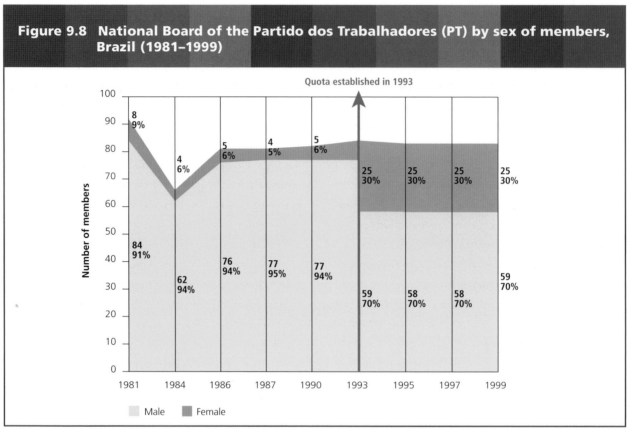

Figure 9.8   National Board of the Partido dos Trabalhadores (PT) by sex of members, Brazil (1981–1999)

Source: Sacchet 2004.

In some developing-country contexts, political parties are introducing a greater degree of internal democracy to give their branch-level membership a role in selecting candidates and internal party decision makers. For instance, in Mexico, the Institutional Revolutionary Party (PRI) was known in power for its centralized domination and lack of transparency in selection processes. In 2001, it responded to electoral defeat by introducing primaries—direct elections by members—enabling the party rank and file to elect about half the candidates. Other parties in Mexico have since followed suit.[27] In Brazil, the PT introduced similar direct elections for candidates in 2001. In Puerto Rico, the use of primaries by political parties for their nominating processes during the 1990s resulted in a greater number of women being selected by the rank and file than had previously been selected by the party leaders, particularly in the two parties that account for the majority of seats.[28] When primaries were introduced by the ruling party in Botswana in 1999 there was a dramatic upsurge in female candidates: 10 times more women competed for party nominations than the cumulative number for all past elections and parties combined. Opposition parties followed suit, resulting in a marked increase of numbers of women nominated to run for seats around the country.

The creation of women's parties

Women's frustration with the male bias of conventional political parties has occasionally led to the creation of women's parties. In fact these are not a new phenomenon, having provided a means for women to engage in politics in some Nordic countries since the early years of the 20th century. In Iceland for example, women's parties have been putting women into office since the Women's List won 22 per cent of the votes for the Reykjavik city council in 1908.[29] Women's parties have existed in the Philippines since the 1950s, and six women's parties contested the 1998 national assembly elections. Two women's parties contested the 1994 South African elections.

Revisions to electoral systems that enable non-government organizations to run for office, as in Armenia or the Philippines, can be helpful in giving certain social groups opportunities to gain electoral support when conventional parties will not embrace their interests. In the Philippines, the 1995 Party-List System Act reserved 20 per cent of seats in the House of Representatives for such groups. They campaign at a national, not local constituency level, appealing to cross-cutting interests all over the country, and are therefore able to appeal to a cross-national interest in gender issues.

Tough campaigning

Where political campaigns are regularly marred by crime or violence, women candidates may stand down because they are unwilling to engage in violence or seek strong-arm support from criminal networks. Much of the local "muscle" mobilized to intimidate opponents during elections is young and male, sometimes organized through party "youth wings". The example of Winnie Mandela's Soweto "football club" in South Africa shows that some women do access these kinds of support groups, but fewer women than men engage in this kind of politics.

The impact of corruption and violence on women's participation in politics is evident in Zimbabwe. Political repression and a general climate of insecurity have made it extremely dangerous to engage in opposition. Since the early 1990s women's participation in national and local elections has plummeted. In 1997, the Southern African Development Community agreed a target for women's representation in public office in all member countries. The Zimbabwean Women in Parliament Support Unit thereupon wrote to all political parties, reminding them of the need to increase women's participation at all decision-making levels. Few parties responded, but a spokesperson for the Movement for Democratic Change (MDC), the main opposition

party, explained that given the current political violence and intimidation faced by MDC candidates, his party was not encouraging women to stand: "Everyone knows the kind of political atmosphere we are operating in. Unless there is a change that allows candidates to campaign freely, without fear of harassment and intimidation, we will continue to see less women being nominated as candidates for local councils." [30]

Another serious problem is the generation of campaign finance. Open lists in PR systems and single-member constituencies are thought to exacerbate the problems women face in mobilizing funds. The focus on individual candidates creates incentives for personal campaigning and direct appeals to voters. This in turn encourages patronage practices, in which politicians seek alliances with powerful individuals who can mobilize their "clients" or dependents as "banks" of votes, in exchange for state resources.[31] Candidates also seek funding from their parties; however there is an impression among women candidates that parties spend more of their resources on financing the campaigns of "safe" male candidates.[32] Most of the countries that have achieved a "critical mass" of women in elected bodies have some form of government subsidy for political campaigns.

Reducing gender voting gaps

Political parties need to attract women's votes. This ought theoretically to promote better representation of women's interests on party policy platforms and better electoral accountability to women. But parties only respond to the need to attract women in this way if there is a discernible "gender gap" in voting behaviour.[33] Gendered voting gaps have only emerged recently in many Western democracies, after many decades in which there was either little difference in women and men's votes, or else a slight female preference for conservative candidates. This began to change in the 1980s in countries such as the United States, Canada and Australia, where women's support shifted to liberal or left-of-centre parties.[34] In many developing countries, awareness of the gender voting gap is a relatively recent phenomenon. Votes may not be tabulated according to gender, and awareness is usually contingent on whether feminist organizations have

---

Box 9.3   Chile: A case of votes rather than convictions

In 1995, the government of President Eduardo Frei Ruiz-Tagle in Chile introduced a progressive Plan for Equal Opportunities for Chilean Women. The plan was notable for its feminist language and the inclusion of goals such as expanded reproductive rights and the recognition of non-traditional partnerships: controversial measures in a conservative Catholic society. The plan also signalled a relaxation of controls on the ambitions of the national women's bureau, the *Servicio Nacional de la Mujer*, and an expansion of its budget.

The mystery of why President Frei's *Concertacion* party should have suddenly taken this feminist turn is explained by the long-standing existence of a marked gender gap in Chilean voting. In every presidential election since 1952, there has been a gap between votes cast by men and votes cast by women, ranging from 14 per cent in 1964 to 3 per cent in 1993. Women's voting clout has increased as they have reached and surpassed parity in voter turnout, constituting a majority (52 per cent) in the 1989 presidential elections.[35]

Therefore the plan's introduction seems to have been a bid to cultivate support amongst the country's female electorate, rather than a response to pressure from women's groups or an initiative of female legislators.[36] In Chile, women do not tend to vote more conservatively than men, and have only been truly decisive in one election (1958); but they are still seen as a crucial group of swing voters, and particularly decisive in relation to presidential choices. With the Beijing Women's Conference looming in 1995, the government needed to display feminist credentials to the women voters.

Source: Baldez 1997.

---

made efforts to measure and publicize a voting gap as a means of gaining political leverage. There are cases where the existence of a large gender voting gap has had a significant effect on policy choice (see box 9.3).

ASSESSING WOMEN'S POLITICAL EFFECTIVENESS

Do women politicians represent women's interests and gender-equity issues effectively? Like male politicians, women address the issues of concern to their constituents and their parties, and for those representing traditional social groups or conservative parties, gender equality may not be on their agenda. Given the way in which party selection systems may eliminate outspoken feminists as an electoral liability, it is not surprising to find women politicians who do not advocate these concerns. Their links with activist women's organizations may be weak or nonexistent. In Namibia, for instance, very few women MPs had been active in women's organizations before joining Parliament.[37] Where family-based hierarchies, identity politics,

and the prejudices of male-dominated selection systems put a lid on the numbers of women in leadership positions, women with an autonomous base in civil society will tend to be weeded out. Where those dynamics prevail, the arrival at the "critical mass" proportion of 30 per cent women's participation will not necessarily make a feminist difference to politics and policy making.

Women legislators are divided on a great number of issues, including those connected to their party, class, ethic group or religious affiliations, and their legislative impact in the area of gender equality can therefore be uneven. In the Philippines, women's participation in Congress has more than doubled between 1987 and 2001 to 18 per cent of members; but this jump has failed to translate into the tabling and approving of a greater number of bills addressing women's concerns.[38] On the contrary, deep divisions between women legislators on emotive issues such as abortion rights have served to stall advances in reproductive heath legislation. Late in 2003, women opponents of a reproductive rights bill in the House Health Committee loudly recited rosaries to disrupt discussions about the bill. The Catholic Church mobilized opponents of the bill and condemned its supporters in public. The consequence was a dramatic decline in the number of female or male legislators willing to support it.

Uneven progress

The assumption that a heightened presence of women in politics may eventually work in favour of greater gender equality in public decision making appears, to date, to be borne out by the experience of some industrialized countries. Case studies of the legislative programmes of women in office suggest this finding, although no systematic cross-national comparative data is yet available. Even when women's divergent party interests are taken into account, they do their best to introduce bills and pass legislation dealing with the expansion of women's citizenship rights. In the United States, Canada, the United Kingdom and Australia, this has been the subject of research for at least two decades. Studies of participation in legislative debates, and bills introduced by politicians, shows unambiguously that although women and men share the same top policy concerns (in Canada for instance, economy, social policy and jobs [39]), woman legislators are more likely than men to introduce bills that address issues related to women's rights, family or children.[40]

It is difficult to say what impact increased numbers of women in developing country governments have had on policy making. One reason is that, with the exception of socialist states, too few women have been in office for long enough to have had a discernible impact on policy making. Another limitation on the capacity of women legislators to influence policy making is the rather limited scope for policy innovation in states highly dependent on support from international financial institutions. Although the extent to which liberalization limits the range of policy options facing governments is often exaggerated, there is no question that straitened economic circumstances and aid dependence limit resources available for progressive gender-related policies, and tend to sideline social concerns in favour of promoting national economic growth and improving the investment environment.

Hard as it is to measure women's impact on policy making in different regions and in widely different circumstances, it is important to assess the validity of expectations that women in office will help advance gender equality. In time, relationships may become apparent between numbers of women in office and advances in women's status, such as lower maternal mortality rates, higher levels of female education, less gender-based violence, and more even distribution of asset ownership and wealth between women and men. Although causal connections between women's presence in office and such outcomes cannot yet be made, there is currently one arena in which a strong association between numbers of women in office and policy change is measurable: abortion rights (see box 9.4). The statistical association between women politicians and abortion rights, though much stronger than any other variable examined, does not indicate causality: it may be that socially progressive parties introduced abortion rights and this contributed to an environment in which it was easier for women to gain political office. Nevertheless, the association is striking.

In a different area—violence against women—one study finds, in contrast, only a weak and nonlinear relationship between proportions of women in the legislature and responsive policy outcomes.[42] The study concluded that focusing on the numbers or percentage of women in legislative bodies might well be the wrong lens through which to determine the ways in which women legislators influence public policy.[43] Although individual feminists or groups of women legislators are not unimportant as political actors in advancing women's rights, the study found that the presence of a strong, autonomous women's movement explained more about government responses to violence against women than the presence of women in the legislature.

Box 9.4   Women in politics: What difference does it make? An empirical assessment of the case of abortion laws

Currently, only about 28 per cent of countries have legal access to abortion on request (see figure 9.9). Although this situation has improved in the last 15 years, around 34 per cent of countries still consider abortion illegal under any circumstances.

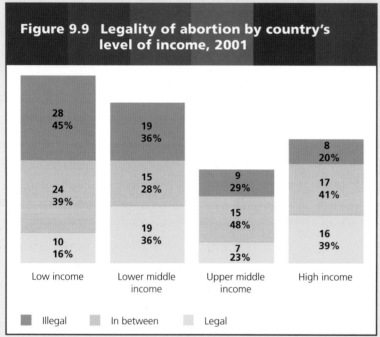

Figure 9.9 Legality of abortion by country's level of income, 2001

Low income: Illegal 28 45%, In between 24 39%, Legal 10 16%

Lower middle income: Illegal 19 36%, In between 15 28%, Legal 19 36%

Upper middle income: Illegal 9 29%, In between 15 48%, Legal 7 23%

High income: Illegal 8 20%, In between 17 41%, Legal 16 39%

■ Illegal   ■ In between   ■ Legal

Note: "Legal" includes only countries where abortion on request is allowed. "Illegal" includes only countries where abortion is not permitted under any grounds, though an exception is usually made when the woman's life is at risk. Such an exception does not exist in Malta, Chile and El Salvador. "In between" includes countries where abortion is neither "legal" nor "illegal" (abortion may be legal under certain circumstances such as when the woman's physical or mental health is at risk, amongst others).
Source: Calculated from UN 2000a.

What are the conditions under which some countries grant the right to abortion on request, while others refuse? To answer this question, an empirical logistic model was estimated using key variables such as the country's level of income, the extent of women's political and economic participation, female education, political regime and state religion. Countries were classified in three categories according to their abortion laws:[41]

- Abortion is legal on request ("legal").
- Abortion is legal under certain circumstances ("in between").
- Abortion is illegal in any circumstances (except when the woman's life is at risk ("illegal").

The results of the model are striking. Women's participation in the economy and in politics are the main variables explaining why abortion laws are granted in countries worldwide. A 1 per cent increase in either of these variables will increase (in a similar proportion) the chances of making abortion legal on request, and will reduce (in a slightly smaller proportion) the chances of having rigid laws that make abortion "illegal".

Variables such as the level of female literacy, national income and whether the country is Roman Catholic also play an interesting role. The probability of a country legalizing abortion on request is reduced if the country is low-income and increased if is classified as "nation in transit" or "not free".* Female literacy is only an important factor when there is a transition from a situation where abortion is never legal to one where it is granted under limited conditions. The probability of a country moving from a situation of no abortion under any circumstances to some limited abortion rights is reduced if the country is Roman Catholic and low or middle-low income.

It is important to add a world of caution. The empirical analysis shown here does not prove causality, but only reflects statistical relationships of the variables affecting the rigidity or flexibility of abortion laws.

Note: (*) Classifications used by Freedom House [www.freedomhouse.org]. Countries are "not free" according to a score obtained using a survey that measures political rights and civil liberties. "Nations in transit" is the term used for post-communist countries.
Source: Cueva 2004.

Notes

1   Molyneux 1994; Jie 2004.

2   Kenworthy and Malami 1999:254–5.

3   Dahlerup 1986; Beckwith 2002.

4   WEDO 2001.

5   Meintjes 2003.

6   Jayaweera 1997:421.

7   Narayan et al. 1999:2.

8   Matland 1999; Reynolds 1999; Yoon 2001.

9   Matland and Studlar, 1996.

10   CFEMEA 2000:2.

11   Inter-American Dialogue 2001.

12   Darcy et al. 1994:150.

13   Narayan et al. 1999.

14   Women in Parliament Support Unit 2001:4.

15   Wilcox et al. 2003, cited in Fodor 2004a:15.

16   Luciak 2001.

17   Fodor 2004a:21.

18   Selolwane 2004:72.

19   Sobritchea 2004:5.

20   Beckwith 2000:439.

21   Norris and Lovenduski 1993; Walyen 2000.

22   Jie 2004.

23   Sobritchea 2004:7.

24   Tsikata 2001.

25   Sow 2004; Tripp 2000; Tamale 1999.

26   Selolwane 1997, 1999.

27   Baldez 2004.

28   del Alba Acevedo 2000:19.

29   Bjarnhé_insdottir 1905.

30   Sunshine for Women 2004.

31   Nicolau and Schmitt 1995:144.

32   Sacchet 2004:13; Goetz 2003:134.

33   Mueller 1988:31.

34   Hayes and McAllister 1997:6.

35   Hayes and McAllister 1997:1.

36   Baldez 1997.

37   Bauer 2004:17.

38   Sobritchea 2004:7, citing Naz 2002:27.

39   Tremblay 1998:450.

40   Thomas 1991; Dodson and Carroll 1991; Kathlene 1994; McAllister and Studlar 1992; Vega and Firestone 1995; Norris 1996.

41   Usually, abortion laws are classified into seven categories: (i) legal on request, (ii) legal only for social and economic reasons, (iii) allowed on the grounds of foetal impairment, (iv) allowed in cases of rape or incest, (v) permitted to preserve the woman's mental health, (vi) permitted to protect the women's physical health, and (vii) illegal (with a exception in most countries when the woman's life is at risk).

42   Weldon 2002:chapter 4.

43   Weldon 2002:14.

Chapter 10
Women mobilizing
to reshape democracy

Women's activism in civil society is the main force behind women-friendly legislative change, and underpins the efforts of feminists in public office. A strong and autonomous women's movement can greatly magnify the influence of a women's caucus, providing "an external base of support and legitimacy to counterbalance internal government resistance to the enactment and implementation of feminist policies".[1] Politicians committed to gender equality need to take their cue from domestic women's movements. Their work would be much simpler if women's movements were united around a common agenda, or if political parties had greater incentives to respond to women's needs. Instead, gender concerns compete with many other priorities for women around the world, and may be subsumed by the requirement that they adhere to national or cultural codes whose versions of gender relations are decidedly inequitable.

Women are regarded as having low political efficacy because of their poor endowment in resources such as the time and money needed to create social and political influence, and because their interests diverge according to all manner of social cleavages.[2] Yet women are well mobilized in civil society associations and social movements almost everywhere. The globalization of communications has created new opportunities, enabling women to experiment with new means for bringing key players—governments, corporations and international organizations—to account. Global summits and conferences on a wide range of topics including trade, health and human rights have enabled women to network across countries and regions, and have conferred legitimacy on their own national and international movements as key participants in global policy debates.

Before the role of women's movements in political life is examined, the character of these associations needs to be understood. A useful general definition is that they can be "understood as female collective action in pursuit of social and political goals".[3] The collective action may take a distinct associational form, or may simply comprise a diffuse coalition of like-minded organizations and informal groups taking part in demonstrations. This definition does not insist that women's movements necessarily have as their core purpose the rebalancing of gender power relations, or that they define themselves as feminist; they simply have to be led by, and to mobilize, women. The dominance of women indicates that they are grounded in claims of gendered identity: women have mobilized explicitly as women and because they are women, thereby asserting a female gendered identity distinct from other possible identities.[4]

WOMEN'S MOVEMENTS AND FEMINIST POLITICS

Women's movements are not necessarily feminist. Feminist politics specifically object to patriarchy and seek to eliminate the subordination and discrimination stemming from male dominance.[5] Feminist groups within women's movements may therefore seek to challenge the conventional gender roles that may have been the basis for organizing in the first place.[6] The two types of movement should not be conflated; it cannot be assumed that female collective action is necessarily devoted to advancing women's rights and seeking gender justice. Indeed, certain forms of right-wing or conservative faith-based women's activism seek to do the opposite.

A significant amount of female mobilization and solidarity occurs outside women-dominated organizations. Trade unions, political parties, state-sponsored mass organizations, and civil-society groups with other agendas may advocate on behalf of their women members. These other forms of female mobilization constitute a large part, possibly the greater part, of female solidarity in the world.[7] Where female mobilization is not autonomous or independent, it may take the form of "associational linkages" with other social movements. This results in many parts of the world in strategic alliances between women's groups and other, sometimes more powerful, civil-society organizations whose principal agenda is in such fields as the environment, peace, trade liberalization, globalization and human rights.[8]

Alternatively, female mobilization may take the form of "directed mobilization"; here, it is under the control of another institutional authority, typically governments or political parties. Female mobilization directed by authorities in the name of collective, national or religious interests may not only exclude women's emancipation as a central goal; it may actually work to abrogate rights women have already gained, as in the case of some faith-based movements.[9] Women's participation in this form of collective action has been actively sought by conservative leaders to demonstrate the popular legitimacy of proposals to strengthen patriarchal interpretations of women's rights. A striking example was the participation of women in the Islamic revolution in Iran in 1979.

WOMEN'S ENGAGEMENT IN DEMOCRATIZATION

What has been described as the "third wave" of democratization[10] peaked in 1989–90 with the collapse of state socialism in the old Eastern bloc and their transition to open economies. In the remaining authoritarian states, there has continued to be movement towards democracy during the last 15 years, as well as the establishment of new democracies following

conflicts in the Balkans, and in Africa. Around the world, a number of countries are undergoing an extended process of democratic consolidation, in which legal systems are being amended to incorporate new constitutional rights, and political systems are being tested for their capacity to tolerate opposition. In Latin America, where the wave of revolutionary struggle and political liberalization peaked earlier than elsewhere, women have gone furthest in seeking constitutional and legislative changes which recognize their equality, followed by policy confirmation of these gains.

Women have played a central role in many democratization struggles, a role recognized as essential to their success, especially where conventional channels for political opposition have been closed. Where parties and trade unions have been banned, as in Chile under President Augusto Pinochet, or where the male leadership of national liberation movements was in exile or jail, as in South Africa, women's grassroots mobilization provided an arena in which oppositional politics could be sustained. This contribution to democratization has not always provided a springboard for women's subsequent engagement in politics. In Chile, for instance, during the slum-based protests of the late 1980s, decentralized organizations and diffuse leadership structures protected women activists, but did not generate women politicians able to gain leadership positions in the new democratic parties.

Patterns can be detected for women's involvement in the democratization process, some of which are echoed in different settings from around the world; others are regionally specific. In some cases where there has been protracted social discontent and a resistance movement, women have not only been active in the upheaval stage, but their representatives have been able to participate in negotiations over new constitutions. The contribution of the Women's National Coalition in South Africa to the constitution-writing process in the mid-1990s is the clearest case of a women's movement capitalizing on its previous role to assert its interests in the new environment. A similar process occurred in Namibia, Ethiopia, Eritrea, East Timor, the Philippines and Mozambique.

Backlash: The Eastern European experience

Where authoritarian states such as those in the ex-USSR and Eastern Europe based part of their legitimacy on their inclusive attitude towards women in the workplace and public life, subsequent democratization has brought a backlash against women's political participation. In Eastern Europe the role in public affairs previously assigned to women by repressive communist regimes encouraged women to downplay feminist interests; instead they sought to emphasize their role in the domestic sphere of family life as the guardians of privacy and family integrity. Dissident movements of the 1980s protested against invasive social engineering, and have been described as having an ideology of "anti-politics".[11] Women were not represented in the leadership of these movements; only 20 per cent of the signatories to Charter 77 were women, and although half of the members of Polish Solidarity were women, few held leadership positions.[12]

The demise of state socialism and the transition to democracy brought a collapse in the numbers of women in public office and stagnation in their involvement in civil-society activity. Feminist groups are today described as very weak in many Eastern European countries,[13] and even where there are a number of active feminist groups, as in Poland, these have been described as "more a curiosity than a real political force".[14] Some women's organizations align themselves with conservative ideologies, idealizing women in motherhood and domestic roles and actively opposing abortion and reproductive rights. The Hungarian Christian Democratic Party, with the strongest appeal to women voters and the highest proportion of women members, celebrates women's moral superiority and their responsibilities in a traditional Catholic household.

Paradoxes: North Africa and the Middle East

In some North African and Middle Eastern states, democratization has produced similar paradoxes. Where military,

one-party or monarchical regimes suppressed Islamic associations—as in Algeria, Egypt, Jordan and Morocco—they often substituted social development programmes for democracy as a source of their legitimacy, and took steps to enhance women's status.[15] The promotion of women's rights thus became linked to unpopular governments. Rapid top-down processes of political liberalization have been incomplete, and have seen few incumbents of the previous regimes unseated. The manifest bad faith demonstrated by the restrictions on effective political competition have discredited the political reform process.

In many of these countries, the only movements articulating coherent and credible opposition to the regime may be Islamic groups whose critique is grounded in antipathy to western democracy and consumer capitalism. The dilemma for women's movements is profound. In the ongoing conflicts in Israel/Palestine and Iraq, the legitimacy of secular governments has been eroded, and the Islamic critique made all the more credible to women. Women's movements do not have the social and political resources to contest powerful Islamist groups, and instead engage strategically with them. For many, this has meant working from within the Islamist camp, seeking to revise religious interpretations of women's roles in order to expand the space for women's political expression.[16]

Imposed democratization: Sub-Saharan Africa

In several sub-Saharan African countries, the political liberalization process set in motion in the context of structural adjustment and as a condition for external loans has been half-hearted; women's participation has been limited. Ruling parties accustomed to unchallenged power, as in Mali, Côte d'Ivoire, Guinea, Zambia, Tanzania, Burundi and Malawi, have tried to control democratization and contain the emergence of effective opposition. Traditional "big man" politics has had a tendency to limit women's political engagement to activities that were marginal and uncritically supportive of the national leader; when the political process opened up in the 1990s, women's movements were in weak positions to take part.

In 1995, for instance, the ruling party in Tanzania announced the resumption of multi-party politics and took the nation to the polls for the first time in 30 years. There was no opportunity to take stock of the past and renegotiate the rules of democratic politics. In Malawi, civil society was given only a few months to change the constitution in early 1994; in Zambia social upheaval and violent unrest in the mid-1990s provoked a hastily called multi-party election in 1996, with no opportunity for constitutional and institutional change. In post-civil-war Uganda, in contrast, a protracted transition enabled women to make a substantial contribution to constitutional debate, although this has taken place within constitutionally entrenched one-party rule.

As in North Africa, the slow rate of democratic consolidation in most sub-Saharan African states is shown by the absence of any significant change in governmental composition or leadership, although the encouraging exceptions of Ghana, Benin, Senegal and Kenya stand out. In some countries, opposition parties remain weak, and executives excessively powerful. This poses serious problems for women's movements, as they rely upon state support for gender-sensitive policy development. A familiar cycle is reappearing: executives legitimize themselves in part through their patronage of the women's movement, and this works to the discredit of the cause of gender equality. In yet other countries such as Angola, Burundi, Congo, Somalia, Sudan and Liberia , democratization remains a distant prospect as civil society tries to contain, or recover from, terror and war. Zimbabwe is an example of a country where the democratic process has lost ground in the face of violent state repression. In the run-up to the 2000 elections, women's political mobilization across the political spectrum was held in check by widespread intimidation.

Women's drive for constitutional change

Constitutional change has been a central focus of women's recent participation in democratization. The 1990s saw women's organizations around the world exposing the limits of basic civil and political rights that exclude the "private" sphere of marriage and family life from democratic scrutiny. Constitutional review has enabled women politicians to identify serious gaps in women's basic citizenship rights, and to address the problem of gender-biased customary/religious law in the jurisdiction of family matters. They have also set in place provisions designed to make women's access to public office easier in future, such as quotas or reservations in national and subnational governments.[17]

The importance of taking a strong position on women's rights within constitutional review processes has galvanized women's movements to unify, even if only temporarily, around constitutional change processes. In Uganda, women's participation in the Constituent Assembly created the basis for effective caucusing there and in the first National Assembly to which many were elected. Participation has sharpened the strategic abilities of women politicians, and broadened the political understanding and skills of women's groups that have tried to support and lobby women in office. Constitutional engagement represents a new front in the struggle for public accountability for gender equality: by insisting on participating in framing the rules of membership in the national community, and the rules on access to and exercise of power, women are suggesting that they will not be bound by political systems in which they have had no voice or representation.

Mobilizing for electoral gain: The 50/50 struggle

In the post-transition period, many countries have seen a demobilization of the women's movement. In Latin America and South Africa in particular, some prominent feminist pro-democracy activists have been absorbed into government. In many settings, the unity provoked by opposition to authoritarianism has dissolved and long-standing differences re-emerged. But however profoundly divergent women's positions are on many issues, there has been one patch of common ground on which the majority converge: the demand for gender parity in public office. Since the late 1990s, civil society campaigns for equal representation with men have gathered momentum, aided by the international "50/50" campaign of the Women's Environment and Development Organization. Women on all points of the political compass can agree to protest at the low numbers of women in politics and the poor take-up of their concerns by political parties.

The presence of growing numbers of women in office acts as a catalyst for a push to increase these numbers still further. For example, the growth in numbers of Ugandan women in politics has spurred a "new kind of political self-organization for Ugandan women":[18] gaining access to politics has become a common interest among diverse women's groups. In Namibia, an ethnically diverse and hitherto divided women's movement has come together around the same purpose: electing women to office. Launched in 1999, the Namibian Women's Manifesto Network, a coalition of groups backing a women's election manifesto, had as one of its main aims the achievement of a 50 per cent quota for women on lists of party candidates; these lists were to be structured "zebra" fashion with alternating women and men. This 50/50 campaign provoked country-wide mobilization to an extent unprecedented in Namibia, to the point that "politics is becoming the central point around which a new feminist consensus is emerging [in Africa]", and where "the pragmatics of women's political representation in the 1990s are shaping the emerging African women's movement".[19]

Latin America has seen a similar development. Since the 1990s the goal of increasing women's representation in formal political bodies has become a unifying theme of women's groups in the region. Many countries have passed laws mandating female quotas on party lists, and many parties still attempt to evade these requirements. In the circumstances, monitoring party compliance has become a shared concern of women's groups across the political spectrum: women in conservative parties are as interested in political seats as left-wingers.

However, proposals for affirmative action measures do not always unify women. In India, a constitutional amendment to reserve 33 per cent of seats in parliament for women has been stalled since 1996. Although the amendment is supported by many women's associations, this has not been a unifying issue

for women in the political climate of today. The reasons for this cut to the heart of Indian politics. The recent expansion of democracy in India has included the emergence of many small ethnic and caste-based parties at state level, whose role in the successful formation of coalitions at the centre is often decisive.[20] The rise of these parties reflects decades of affirmative action to support socially disadvantaged tribes and castes, through reserved places in schools, universities and public-sector jobs. Some of these parties oppose the 33 per cent women amendment on the grounds that it is a means of reasserting upper-caste dominance of national political institutions—which has been significantly eroded. The reservation bill does not make provisions for "quotas within quotas", to make sure that the women who reach parliament are not the educated, wealthy and upper-caste women most likely to have the connections and resources needed to run for office.[21]

WOMEN'S REACTION TO FAITH-BASED AND ETHNIC MOVEMENTS

While in many countries political liberalization has enabled secular women's movements to flourish, in some countries democratization has stalled or become mired in economic or political crisis. When the state in its modern and secular guise fails to deliver physical security or service improvement, its image sours. In some countries, the discrediting of modernity as a solution to social ills has stimulated the growth of conservative ethnic and religious movements, often in spite of official repression. Gender relations are matters of central importance to many of these groups, particularly where "women's liberation" is associated with failed or repressive modernization.

In a growing number of countries these groups have become important political actors, especially where they are effective at mobilizing socially marginal populations. Islamic groups in North African and Middle Eastern countries such as Tunisia, Morocco, Egypt and Jordan; in South and Southeast Asian countries such as Bangladesh, Malaysia and Indonesia; and in West African countries such as Senegal and Nigeria, may not win large numbers of seats in parliament. However, they have tremendous political leverage as brokers and kingmakers in ruling coalitions. In other countries such as the Philippines or Algeria, they remain banned but have an increasing capacity to disrupt. Both conservative and radical Christian groups around the world have also experienced a surge, for example as social animators of grassroots self-help activities in Latin America and Africa. The institutional church also retains its impact on high-level politics in many Latin American and African countries and in the Philippines. In India, Hindu chauvinist cultural and religious movements have polarized the electorate on Hindu–Muslim lines and contributed to the electoral success of the parties with which they are associated.

There is no evidence that women are more attracted than are men to conservative faith-based or culturally extremist groups, but there is evidence from around the world that these groups are gaining in strength. Women form an unspecified but visible component, both in membership and leadership. Women's deportment, mobility, dress and roles within the family are often central to the cultural revival or pious society envisaged by these groups; women's behaviour is upheld as a marker of authenticity and moral integrity. When constituted as political parties, conservative religious associations have not given women access to institutional power either within the party or in public office. But as social movements they have encouraged women to engage in public activism, and even to become militant in ways that violate traditional gender roles; for example, in inciting violence as did Hindu nationalist women in the anti-Muslim pogroms in Gujarat in 2002. At the same time, these women articulate cultural and social agendas that propose the restriction of women's rights. This simultaneous capacity of ethnic or religious groups to mobilize women while undermining their advancement is a matter of great concern to feminists. In particular, the growth of political Islam has made many feminists in Muslim societies reconsider the usefulness of a secular approach that can alienate women for whom religion is central, who may well constitute a majority.

Women in illiberal mobilization

There are many explanations for the appeal of conservative or extremist religious movements to women. A religious congregation can provide a socially acceptable arena in which women can express their concerns. Many faith or church-based movements provide a range of services that women need, and even support their gender-specific needs in a more credible and practical way than do progressive, but unimplemented, secular constitutional provisions. They appear to offer arenas of social approval, sexual safety, normative certainty and political agency, that have the advantage of inciting less resistance from husbands than does women's feminist activism.

In conservative societies, women may find social leadership roles available to them through religious movements, particularly when there are few respectable means of taking up politically prominent roles in environments where women moving about in society on their own can expect to face sexual harassment. In India, the Rashta Sevika Sangh, which is the women's branch of the militant Hindu cultural association the Rashtriya Swayam Sevak Sangh, even provides younger women with a means of postponing marriage while they make their contribution to the cause of Hindu nationalism through physical activity, social work, and training in the use of rifles and *lathis* (wooden batons). The Jamaat-e-Islami in Bangladesh and Pakistan gives its women recruits a distinctive *burqa* to identify them as Jamaat members to be defended by party activists from attack; this enhances their mobility.

Faith-based movements also have extensive resources and can provide social services where the state has failed. Islamic groups run *madrassas*—Koranic schools—for children in Bangladesh, Pakistan and other Muslim countries. Christian churches organize soup kitchens, schools and basic health services in low-income neighbourhoods in Latin American countries. Charity can be the only means of succour for women who fall out of the safety net of families and communities in societies with few state-provided services. In Bangladesh, when wives are arbitrarily divorced by husbands, have no property and no means of securing maintenance, the rural women's groups of the Jamaat may be the only source of shelter and financial support. Religious groups can also offer vigilante services where state security systems have failed.

Central to the appeal of contemporary religious movements is their critique of the state, society and the cultural invasion associated with globalization, coupled with the concrete rights that they advance for women. Across Latin America the Catholic Church has re-evaluated its alliances and sought to support the struggles of the poor against traditional elites. In Brazil, Chile and El Salvador, the protests of the church against human rights abuses have brought it into conflict with military regimes; in Brazil, its protests brought feminists into direct alliance with the Church on some matters. Islamist, Hindu and Christian movements articulate critiques of official corruption and of invasive Western cultural decadence, and lay claim to a moral high ground. The authentic cultures they wish to propose promote complementary social roles for women and men; this can be attractive in contexts where economic change has eroded men's breadwinning capacity, and women are stretching their time and energies between poorly paid employment and domestic work.

At the same time as offering an attractive critique of political regimes and of neoliberal economic policy, religious movements appear able to combine conservative views on gender relations with prominent roles for women leaders. Some even provide support for areas of women's empowerment and rights. One of the most striking features of Hindu nationalism in India is the fact that the movement's most successful orators are women, some unmarried, who do not conform to conservative prescriptions for women's behaviour. Two of these, Uma Bharati and Sadhvi Rithambara, were instrumental in goading mobs to destroy the mosque at Ayodhya in December 1992. Their anti-Muslim recordings inciting people to violence were so virulent they were banned by government. Exceptionally militant women leaders like these live and work with great independence; yet they advocate women's subjugation to domesticity and subordination to their husbands.[22] Nevertheless, the interests of the religious or nationalist programme outweigh in importance the fulfilment of traditional expectations to the extent that they inveigle women to abandon female modesty, engage in militancy and even take on suicide missions.

Socially progressive positions

Many religious groups have strong positions against violence against women, and against polygamy. They may also support women's inheritance rights, or oppose women's commercial sexual exploitation. Because women's social position and moral behaviour is of more importance to faith-based movements than to secular parties, some of them make great efforts to involve women and address their needs. Pentecostal groups in working-class areas of Brazil have put a particular emphasis on helping women tackle domestic violence.[23] In Bangladesh, where urban and rural women's mobilization around livelihood issues and women's rights is significant, the Jamaat-e-Islami clearly regards women's support as important to its electoral prospects and social legitimacy. Its 1996 election manifesto promised to increase women's (segregated) employment, end dowry payments, stop violence against women, and support their inheritance rights, using Islamic precepts on human equality to construct a socially progressive image.

In some countries women have sought to take charge of this faith-based agenda by attempting to define a feminist Islamist position and challenging the clerics' monopoly over the interpretation of Shari'a law. These efforts also represent a drive to establish greater consistency in interpreting women's rights; in many nominally secular countries—Egypt, Algeria and Jordan—religious law is used in a haphazard and inconsistent way to override women's constitutionally sanctioned rights. Similarly in Iran, where a dogmatic interpretation of Islam is used by an authoritarian theocratic state to restrict women's rights, there are few contexts where feminists can legitimately engage other than working within the Shari'a, offering new interpretations to justify an expansion of women's rights.[24]

The work of feminist Islamist theologians has shown that the Shari'a is capable of accommodating many of women's needs in matters of marriage, divorce and inheritance. Feminist Islam has had an important cultural impact, expanding women's knowledge of their rights in Shari'a law. However, the entire enterprise would not have advanced so far were it not for the fact that the Islamic Republic of Iran has provided a model of a contemporary theocratic state to which Islamists can aspire.

Contemporary Islamist feminism is also a reaction against the cultural stereotyping of Islam.[25] Thus the feasibility of Islamist control of the state, and contemporary vilification of the Muslim faith and its adherents, have made feminist Islam a credible option for women active in Muslim societies.

Secular feminists increasingly engage with women in faith-based groups, recognizing that they do have an interest in political openness, and that they do have space to challenge gendered inequality. In Malaysia, for example, Muslim women representing welfare-based Islamic bodies joined the Women's Agenda for Change (WAC), a group formed after the debacle of Prime Minister Mahatir Mohamad's persecution of his Deputy Prime Minister Anwar Ibrahim in 1998. The 80 non-governmental organization (NGO)-strong WAC is essentially a lobby for democratic reform in an authoritarian neoliberal state. Malaysian feminists are highly critical of the state's repressive practices but have few practicable arenas for political activism. Islamic parties offer an alternative to the government's repressive modernism. Both government and Islamic opposition see the value of appealing to women, and have begun to compete for their participation and allegiance. In 2001 the government set up a Ministry of Women's Affairs, co-opted women activists from the WAC wherever possible, and has since derided the Islamic opposition for avoiding debates on gender equality. In the run-up to the 2004 election, the Islamic opposition retaliated by claiming feminist ground, announcing it would field a woman candidate in every state.

TRANSNATIONAL WOMEN'S MOBILIZATION

Transnational female mobilization has helped lay the foundations of global civil society over the past century. Its notable achievements include opposition to war, articulating an international treaty on women's rights, and the politicization of violence against women.[26] The last 10 years have seen an unprecedented growth in transnational women's and feminist activism. The many UN conferences and summits of the 1990s, and the rounds of international negotiations on trade, environmental

regulation, crimes against humanity and a number of other issues important to women, galvanized a search for alliances and enabled women's movements to become increasingly sophisticated in their engagement with global institutions. The spread of Internet-based communication has helped women overcome in-built disadvantages relating to mobility and voice. The communications power and institutional strength recently shown by global civil society can boost the campaigning effect, making the kind of impact on national and international policy that domestic women's movements rarely achieve on their own.

There is, of course, no one unified international women's movement, nor is there any such thing as global feminism. Profound disparities of all kinds exist between women's associations in different regions and countries. Nevertheless, alliance building among them has made a powerful impact on global norm setting and policy making in such contexts as reproductive rights,[27] violence against women, and international criminal law. Women campaigning for economic justice have been closely associated with the loose-knit Global Justice and Solidarity Movement, which focuses on the negative implications of free trade and globalization for developing world populations, and whose base since 2001 has been the annual World Social Fora.[28] Women's peace groups were centrally involved in the largest one-day protest in history: the 15 February 2003 anti-war demonstrations in 800 cities involving 11 million people. The Women's Caucus for Gender Justice made an important contribution to the drafting and adoption of the International Criminal Court (ICC) Statute in Rome in 2000, and helped assure the appointment of seven women judges (out of 18) to the ICC in March 2003.

The effectiveness of transnational women's mobilization is limited by certain factors. Similar problems face all international civil society lobbies trying to influence those who make and implement national and subnational policies by demanding adherence to international norms and treaties. Transnational women's campaigns have targeted UN organizations and the international financial institutions (IFIs), joining in demands for greater willingness on their behalf to address the expressions of policy-making concern coming from civil society through representative NGOs. They have also used the occasions of their conferences and meetings as a staging arena for joint activism and an opportunity to develop cross-national positions. However, international treaties and resolutions do not necessarily lead to national enforcement, especially in states that are deeply conservative and opposed to a feminist agenda. Resolutions at international conferences are not binding, and rarely address deep structural problems in society. If changes are to take place at the national level, action is needed by women inside and outside government to hold states to account for their international commitments.[29]

A further problem arises from ambiguities of working at both national and international levels. The goal of much feminist and women's engagement with global institutions is to improve the accountability of individual states to female citizens. For instance, some recent "anti-globalization" activism has sought to strengthen the independent policy-making capacities of individual states in relation to bodies such as the World Trade Organization (WTO). Should the women's network look to the same international bodies as potential advocates and enforcers of their agenda as are currently decried as the key perpetrators of programmes that reinforce social injustice in low-income countries? If women join in efforts to undermine these institutions' importance, they may have even less hope of influencing national agendas in favour of women's equal opportunities, or of galvanizing support for domestic women's movements in anti-feminist states. Recently, US unilateralism has prompted transnational women's groups to push for the strengthening of multilateral institutions, without which their own endeavours would not have flourished.

Transnational women's activism is also in tension with itself, given the vast range of difference among and between movements in different parts of the world. The definition of problems, their prioritization, goals and targets, and strategies for reaching them may all be differently perceived. Some divisions are along classic divides such as North–South; others are grounded in ideological or religious dogma, and have no particular geographical association; yet others are culturally specific. The alliances into which transnational women's movements enter also inevitably involve a lack of coincidence between agendas of different groups. For example, a useful ally

in the international campaign to cancel debt (Jubilee 2000) has been the Catholic Church, whose current hierarchy is vehemently opposed to gender justice.[30] The umbrellas provided by rights regimes and other sets of international norms and treaty obligations by no means invariably succeed in bringing all viewpoints together.

Human rights as a unifying framework

The concept of human rights appeals to a common humanity and human equality, universal standards of justice and fairness, liberal concepts of the individual and the community, and a responsive democratic state. Although its application across different cultures can be controversial, the human rights framework has nonetheless provided an umbrella under which diverse women's movements have worked together for the last 15 years. The specific articulation of women's human rights has also helped to centre gender equality and women's rights in other global policy fields, including social development, humanitarian law, population and environmental protection.

The principal international women's rights instrument is the 1979 Convention on the Elimination of All Forms of Discrimination against Women (CEDAW). Due to increased mobilization by women's movements, ratification speeded up over the 1990s and many countries that had earlier registered reservations withdrew them.[31] The legitimacy of women's organizations as credible monitors of CEDAW compliance was recognized in its 1999 Optional Protocol, which empowers the CEDAW Committee (a body of 23 independent experts charged with monitoring CEDAW performance at national level) to consider complaints brought directly by individual women or groups. Seventy-five countries have signed the Optional Protocol, but it remains to be fully ratified by many; it is also still too early to see whether it will improve states' compliance. Women who have exhausted their options under national law, or who have found that "the application of such remedies is unreasonably prolonged or unlikely to bring effective relief", can now directly seek redress under the terms of the Optional Protocol. The protocol is a recognition that state reporting systems can suffer from the institutionalized male bias that normally inhibits reporting of women's rights abuses, and there should be a mechanism whereby women can bypass them.[32]

The International Criminal Court

The experience of mobilization around CEDAW and its enforcement mechanisms led to the creation of a special women's campaigning body in connection with the establishment of the ICC. The Women's Caucus for Gender Justice, set up in 1997, grew out of the non-governmental Coalition for an ICC formed in 1995, and drew on the strength and sophistication gained in earlier international activity. The Caucus lobbied for the appointment of women and gender experts throughout all the organs of the Court, and for its independence from traditional power structures.[33] The group also demanded better protection for victims of crimes, prompting the adoption of Article 15 of the Statute of the ICC. This empowers the ICC prosecutor to investigate allegations of crimes not only upon referral from the Security Council or individual states, but also on information from victims, non-governmental organizations and "any other reliable source".[34]

The Women's Caucus also demanded the inclusion of sexual violence as a crime against humanity (and a war crime). Thus all states that acknowledge ICC jurisdiction have a duty to co-operate with the ICC in the investigation and prosecution of these crimes, no matter where they are committed or by whom: sovereignty cannot be claimed as cover for domestic atrocities. Public actors responsible for sexual violence will now be held accountable to the global society, not just to citizens of their own countries. By insisting on women's position at the centre of global civil society and by ensuring that sexual violence is a serous crime, the Women's Caucus created a new instrument for making states more accountable to women for preventing and prosecuting the human rights violations from which they predominately suffer.

Polarized positions on sex work and trafficking

A context in which the human rights framework has failed to bridge ideological divides is over the issue of the trafficking of women and girls in the sex trade. In December 2000, over 80 countries signed the Protocol to Suppress, Prevent and Punish Trafficking in Persons, Especially Women and Children, sponsored by the UN Centre for International Crime Prevention, in Palermo, Italy. The definitions of trafficking and sex work, and disagreements about the nature and scale of the problem, were the subject of intense and deeply polarized debate between the key women's groups in two transnational lobbies, the International Human Rights Network and the Human Rights Caucus. Both laid claim to the feminist and "human rights" label as a legitimating tactic; both also highlighted their networks in developing countries, particularly South and Southeast Asia.

The International Human Rights Network had at its core an international NGO with an "abolitionist" perspective on sex work: the Coalition Against Trafficking in Women. This group views prostitution as a form of sexual violence which women would not undertake if given a meaningful and free choice, and therefore sees sex work as a human rights violation; in this view anyone who helps women to migrate in order to engage in sex work is a trafficker.[35] The opposing camp embraced the Global Alliance Against Trafficking in Women and the Asian Women's Human Rights Council as well as other sex workers' rights groups and human rights groups. Central to their position were the perspectives of the global sex workers' rights movement, in which sex work is recognized as labour, as a form of employment chosen by women, and as an expression of women's sexuality. Trafficking occurs in this perspective if women are forced to migrate for, or forced to engage in, sex work; official policies to deal with this problem must respect women's agency and determine whether they have consented to sex work and migration.

At issue were conceptions of female agency, sexuality, consent, and the coercive impact of state-level efforts to "protect" women. A member of the sex workers' lobby noted that historically, anti-trafficking measures have been used against sex workers themselves, rather than against "traffickers".[36] They argued that force or deception was a necessary condition in the definition of trafficking; also that "trafficking" and "prostitution" should not be linked in the Protocol, as men, women and children are trafficked for a large variety of services, including sweatshop labour and agriculture. However, ultimately the UN Trafficking Protocol did not make a distinction between forced and free migration for sex work, and the victim does not have to demonstrate that she has been forced; a human rights abuse is assumed.[37] This is seen by sex workers as feeding into contemporary anxieties about immigration and asylum seeking, and about female independence, where the socially accepted view is that women should be subjugated to the family (see also chapter 7).

Other instances where "human rights" have not proved inclusive

Similar problems associated with women's agency and sexuality have divided women's organizations and movements on issues of homosexuality, and abuses of people identifying themselves as lesbian, gay, bisexual, transgendered and intersexed.[38] Indigenous people's movements have challenged the individualistic basis of Western liberal human rights frameworks in contrast to notions of rights grounded in group identities, cultures and ways of being.

Another concern raised about the human rights approach in transnational feminism is that it privileges lawyers, and focuses on national laws and international treaties and their implementation. Critics argue that the stress on legality is misplaced,[39] and promotes standards of economic and social rights unattainable in many settings. Rights-based approaches presuppose a functioning and accountable state, where recourse may be had to the law by citizens or groups. In countries where legal systems are under-resourced or discredited through corruption, states may be less than efficient about prosecuting their own laws and bringing rights violators to book, let alone delivering on their international legal commitments. This

realization has intensified the efforts of domestic women's movements to improve national capacity to reform and implement legislation with a bearing on women's rights. Their ambitions and horizons have expanded, and they have gone on to develop a feminist critique of contemporary "good governance" reforms.

Economic justice: New feminist activism

Transnational women's movements have developed their own response to the impacts of the neoliberal macroeconomic policies of the 1980s and 1990s, particularly in the context of trade liberalization. A coherent feminist critique of market-driven and economic austerity policies emerged at the 1994 UN Social Summit in Copenhagen. At the Summit, the Women's Global Alliance for Development Alternatives linked regional networks of women's associations into a Women's Caucus that proposed far-reaching amendments to the Summit's Declaration and Platform for Action. These stressed the importance of regulating markets in the interest of reducing inequalities, preventing instability and expanding employment; sought the taxation of international financial speculative transactions and other politically destabilizing or environmentally harmful forms of profit seeking; and demanded that multilateral economic machinery such as the International Monetary Fund (IMF), the World Bank, and the WTO should be accountable to the United Nations Economic and Social Council (ECOSOC) and human rights treaty monitoring bodies.[40] Subsequent feminist critiques of free trade have successfully exposed its failure to contribute to poverty reduction.

Activism on trade and investment is a fast-growing area of transnational women's mobilization. Some groups focus upon creating new mechanisms to negotiate environmental and labour standards with international corporations, and monitor their compliance. The most visible activity is within the "anti-globalization" movement; here women's groups have taken up the task of critiquing the WTO's mandate and governance and examining regional trade agreements. The South-based International Gender and Trade Network focuses on the United Nations Conference on Trade and Development (UNCTAD), the WTO, and the Free Trade Area of the Americas as well as the Cotonou/African Caribbean and Pacific (ACP) Agreement. The Europe-based Informal Working Group on Gender and Trade is evolving into a permanent Women's Caucus at the WTO, using its Trade Policy Review Mechanism as an entry point through which to develop gender-sensitive impact assessment of trade policy. The Women's International Coalition for Economic Justice attempts to influence macroeconomic policy-making via the United Nations Commission on the Status of Women.

A major concern of transnational women's activism on trade issues is the way export-led growth may be premised on cheap female labour, and the way the ferocious competition involved in free trade can provoke a "race to the bottom" in labour standards (see chapter 3). Tactics to counter this, as well as the inequitable exemptions that rich countries are adept at negotiating through the WTO, have included putting pressure on the WTO to support sustainable development by employing existing "special and differential treatment provisions" to promote poverty reduction and gender equity in poor countries.

As in the broader anti-globalization movement there are several sometimes contradictory strands to women's economic justice movements. Cheap female labour in the South draws jobs away from women in the North; thus the economic interests of Southern and Northern women tend to conflict— a division mirrored within international activist movements. Campaigns on labour and environmental standards may have the effect of driving women in the South out of work, or into impossible-to-regulate informal employment or enterprise. Anxiety about the environmental consequences of aggressive trade-led growth is counter-balanced by anxiety that environmental controls deny poor countries the capacity to export their commodities and develop their industries as rich countries have already done. These conflicts of economic interest pose a challenge to coalition building. Transnational women's economic justice groups continue to debate whether their members should have a common agenda and critique, or whether they should simply act as solidarity networks to support members from the South.

Notes

1   Weldon 2002:97.

2   Randall 1987.

3   Molyneux 2001:3.

4   Beckwith 2004:4.

5   Beckwith 2001:372; Weldon 2004:3.

6   Baldez 2002:14.

7   Molyneux 2001:145.

8   Molyneux 2001: 146.

9   Molyneux 2001:146–52.

10 Huntington 1991.

11 Goven 1993, cited in Fodor, E. 2004a.

12 Einhorn 1993.

13 Adamik 1993; Einhorn 1993.

14 Fodor 2004:14, referring to Graf 2003.

15 Brand 1998; Salame 1994; Lazreg 2004:6.

16 Lazreg 2004.

17 Dobrowlsky and Hart 2003.

18 Tripp 2000:195.

19 Mikell 2003:14.

20 Jaffrelot 1996.

21 Menon 2000; Basu 2004.

22 Basu 1995.

23 Bouvier 2004:19.

24 Paidar 2002.

25 Lazreg 2004:27.

26 Rupp 1997; Boulding 1993.

27 Petchesky 2003.

28 Said and Desai 2003.

29 Silliman 1999:152, cited in Petchesky 2000:28.

30 Sen 2004:4.

31 Ackerly and D'Costa 2004:3.

32 CEDAW 1999, Article 4.

33 Spees 2003: 1.

34 Prakash 2002: 4115.

35 Doezema 2004:chapter 1.

36 Doezema 2004.

37 Sen 2003:140.

38 Ackerly and D'Costa 2004:15–18.

39 Sen 2003:145.

40 Petchesky 2000:28.

Chapter 11
Gender and "good governance"

Whether policy makers can take steps to reduce women's poverty or address gender injustice depends upon the implementation of policies on the ground. Signing up to international treaties and passing legislation—on issues such as women's rights, equal access to education, rape in marriage, and equal eligibility to credit and property ownership—is only a first step. Legislation and policy has to be translated into government directives, budgetary allocations, institutional arrangements, bureaucratic procedures and monitoring standards. The connection between political commitment and effective policy implementation is expressed in the concept of "governance". Programmes of governance reform have consumed considerable international and national attention in the recent past and present.

Definitions of "governance" range from a restricted view focusing on sound management of the economy, to an expanded view embracing such projects as the liberalization of politics and the reduction of social inequality.[1] Governance is described by the World Bank as "the manner in which the State exercises and acquires authority".[2] For policy purposes, governance is broken down into two broad components: the capacity of the state to exercise authority, and its accountability doing so.[3] "Capacity" encompasses the state's "hardware": its financial resources, the extent and effectiveness of its physical and administrative infrastructure for distributing public goods, the number and skills of its personnel, and the conduct of budgeting and policy-making processes. "Accountability" describes the "software": the system whereby certain actors have the power to demand answers of others, and whether and how malfeasance is detected and punished.

The concept of "good" governance requires normative judgments to be made about what constitutes the legitimate acquisition and efficient exercise of power. For some external support agencies and social activists, good governance implies democratic governance, and therefore implies an agenda of participation, human rights and social justice. For others, it simply means the management of national endowments in human and natural resources in such a way as to generate public goods (including security and justice), and to distribute them so as to create wealth and promote human development. The international financial institutions (IFIs) have taken this more restrictive view of governance; in their perspective "good governance" concerns the effectiveness of the state rather than the equity of the economic system or the legitimacy of the power structure.

THE CONTEMPORARY GOVERNANCE REFORM AGENDA

Contemporary governance reforms address problems of low capacity, inefficiency and poor accountability in budgetary, judicial, legislative and administrative institutions. Reforms include the creation of independent central banks and autonomous tax boards, and measures to improve budgeting and auditing (to contribute to sound macroeconomic management); protections for private property, and assertion of the rule of law and enforcement of contracts (to promote economic growth); merit-based public service recruitment, results-oriented management in the public sector, and civil service job cuts and retraining (to down-size inflated government); decentralization (to improve service delivery); oversight committees within parliament, and judicial reform (to combat corruption and improve accountability).

Critics suggest that although these reforms address issues of government legitimacy and the public participation of socially excluded groups, they are dominated by a narrower preoccupation: the use of "governance" reforms primarily to expand market activity and all its supporting institutions, especially the entrenchment of private property rights.[4] They point out that the reform agenda is based on assumptions about the relationship between capitalist economic activity, legal systems and governance institutions that are drawn from a Western experience, and which may have failed to take certain considerations into account. In the first place, it produces institutional "mono-cropping":[5] the imposition of imported, usually alien, one-size-fits-all institutional arrangements; and it supports institutional "mono-tasking":[6] an unbalanced preoccupation with contracts and property rights so as to facilitate and regularize commercial exchange.

Even more problematically, the narrow focus on "capacity" produces a technocratic approach that may deliberately set out to evade subjection to the messy process of political debate. Politics and politicians can be seen as problematic not only because they admit the entry of patronage and corrupt practice, but as far as policy is concerned, they tend to favour short-term incentives rather than long-term needs—such as lowering interest rates just before an election Thus reforms in banking systems or tax administration often seek to build autonomy and exclude unwelcome political interference; but they also thereby put the new arrangements beyond the reach of democratic control. A danger arises that the process of supporting "governance" will entrench the power of technocratic (sometimes externally influenced) elites, and reduce the exercise of power over economic instruments by those with quite different priorities; for example, the attainment of social goals. The panicked reactions of the Brazilian and Indian stock markets to the electoral victory of parties committed to redistribution and social justice illustrate the nervous response of markets to democratic support for this type of agenda.

GENDER EQUALITY AND GOVERNANCE REFORM

Efforts to place gender-equality legislation on the statute books and see it implemented must address gender-related capacity and accountability problems. Where they are narrowly preoccupied with market strengthening and property rights, governance reform programmes are not likely to be sympathetic to gender concerns, and may even undermine their prospects of advancement. For gender equality to be tackled strategically, programmes of reform must take into account from the outset the way in which the institutions, arrangements and procedures about to be restructured are shaped by unequal gender relations and will tend to reproduce gender-based inequality unless they are appropriately adjusted or redesigned during the reform process.

Gender equality has not been a fundamental concern of "good governance". In the World Bank's early statements concerning governance reform, women's participation was explicitly addressed only in discussions of decentralization and the use of participatory approaches; and gender equity only raised in the context of human rights.[7] Yet there are gender-specific capacity failures in all public institutions targeted for reform. Public expenditure management systems fail to acknowledge women's needs or distribute budgetary resources equally. The civil service or judiciary may be dominated by men antipathetic to gender equality. Women public-sector workers clustered at the bottom of state bureaucracies may be the first to be fired when cost-cutting efficiencies are introduced. "Rule of law" reforms, even if limited to the stabilization of the market for commercial activity, may limit women's scope to profit from informal private enterprise, or fail to enable them to secure assets over which they previously enjoyed customary rights. Legislative committees may be ill-equipped to conduct a gender analysis of the bills or accounts they review, and may therefore fail women in their oversight functions.

Recently a case has been made for increased participation of women in formal politics and public service on efficiency grounds: women, it is hoped, will prove more responsive and less corrupt as public sector managers.[8] Public opinion surveys and studies have suggested that women in parliament, in the bureaucracy or in the labour force are thought to be less inclined to engage in corrupt activity than are men.[9] However, such studies are not based upon observation of actual engagement in corrupt acts, but on public perceptions that draw upon idealizations of womanly virtue. There are some practical reasons that women might engage in fewer corrupt acts than men—in many contexts opportunities for corruption might be gender-specific, and might not always be open to women newcomers to public office. In other contexts, where illicit transactions are virtually institutionalized in public office, the gender of the office-holder is not likely, on its own, to have much effect.

A recent study of women leaders and councillors in villages in two Indian states showed that neither gender nor education had an impact on corruption. The factors determining the chances that a politician will be corrupt included the high cost of campaigns, the number of terms in office, and the extent to which women were serving as "proxies" for men, whether husbands or other local patrons.[10] Women—or their gender—ought not to be seen simply as possible agents of good governance. Instead, public-sector accountability to women must become an objective of "good governance" reforms.

GENDER AND ACCOUNTABILITY

In addition to gender-specific capacity problems in public institutions, governance debates should take account of gender-specific accountability failures. Power holders in the public sphere should be held to account for upholding laws and standards affecting gender equality. Accountability institutions are expected to act in an impartial, gender-neutral way, but even electoral institutions—which give citizens the means to demand answers of politicians, and to eject them from power if they are found wanting—contain hidden gender biases that fail to translate women's political preferences into the selection of representatives who will advance gender-equity interests. A number of institutions exist whose task is to maintain oversight regarding state actions; these include audit institutions, the judiciary, policy review committees and special anti-corruption or human

rights commissions. These too can reproduce gender and other biases in the standards they use for assessing probity in public action.

There are many informal accountability mechanisms, ranging from protest action and lobbying, to more structured efforts to engage citizens directly with state actors through public hearings, participatory planning exercises and social audits.[11] But there is a limit to the informal power of civilian groups to hold leaders to account. Social mobilization to put pressure on officials and to call authorities to account takes time and media skills, and is rarely an option for poorer and lower-status women. Lack of accountability except through these informal channels contributes to the weak political "voice" of women, and their inability to challenge inequalities in access to resources and social justice.

Gender-sensitive reforms to accountability institutions should enable women, individually or collectively, to secure representation within such institutions, and ensure that power holders are made accountable for supporting the principle of gender equity in their public actions. They need to be scrutinized in the following areas: the terms upon which men and women participate or are appointed, investigation methods, the use of evidence, and standards of probity and fairness. There should be a remit in their terms of reference or articles of establishment to answer to women as a group; and their standards of conduct and procedural methods should view gender inequities as unacceptable.

CIVIL SERVICE REFORMS

The starting point of many governance reform programmes in the 1990s was civil service cutbacks designed to trim the cost of the public sector payroll, promote efficiency in service delivery and eliminate corruption. However, radical "downsizing" reforms had only modest successes, and today's civil service restructuring programmes stress a package of "new public management" measures. These include the outsourcing of some public administration functions; encouraging better performance by changing incentives; and the introduction of performance monitoring to improve accountability. The IFIs now recognize that there are key areas of state action where the goal must be service improvement rather than state shrinkage. These are areas such as primary health care, education and social protection, in which markets do not offer the tools for achieving full coverage or reasonable minimum quality.[12]

So far there has been little interest in gender equity as a component of public sector reform. Some areas to be considered include the impact of civil service restructuring on the gender balance of staff at all levels, and how changes to incentive and accountability systems affect the interactions between state agencies and women citizens. Privatization, or "outsourcing" of key state services and amenities, also has an impact on gender equity, especially where cost recovery has required the introduction or increase of user fees. This tends to discriminate against women, especially in low-income groups, who represent a significant proportion of the clients (see also chapter 8).

Comparable cross-national data on women's share of public-sector employment, and on their position in public-sector hierarchies, are difficult to obtain; but evidence suggests that public bureaucracies display a marked gender asymmetry in their staffing patterns, with many more women at lower than at higher levels. International Labour Organization (ILO) figures show that women average less than 10 per cent of staff in "public administration, defense, and social security" around the world, and between 10 and 20 per cent in education and health.[13] Only in some state-socialist and transition countries, and in some Caribbean countries, do numbers rise significantly above these low averages. Downsizing may target areas where female employment is scarce but where overstaffing is chronic, such as mining or transportation. However, in countries where women's share of public-sector employment is high, such as was the case in Viet Nam, downsizing programmes have had a devastating impact. In the early 1990s, 70 per cent of the nearly one million employees laid off from state-owned enterprises were women.[14]

Where cuts are made at the lowest levels of public services, this can mean that the proportion of women losing their jobs is greater than that of men. A 2003 South African study into the effects on women of privatizing solid waste management in three municipalities found that women workers tended to suffer most because of the way in which collective bargaining took place. The jobs performed by most women were not protected by collective bargaining agreements, unlike those of men.[15] Among clients, poor black women also suffered most from the new arrangements because they tended to bear responsibility for solid waste disposal and have to pay for the new services. The trade-off is that solid waste management is the urban service that improved most in the last few years, with the number of households receiving an acceptable level of service increasing dramatically between 1996 and 2001.[16]

The experience in China

China has not been immune from pressures to downsize and streamline its public sector in order to promote better economic management. Throughout the 1990s various measures were taken to abolish or merge ministries, to modernize recruitment patterns, and to lay off public sector workers. In 2001 the size of some central government units such as the State Council had been reduced by 50 per cent.[17] It is not clear what proportion of those who left the civil service were women; women's share of public-sector jobs had been falling since the 1980s,[18] and by 1996, constituted just 19 per cent. Since the reforms, this proportion appears to have dropped.

In 1993, when greater transparency in recruitment and promotion within the civil service was introduced, the step was welcomed by women, who anticipated an improvement on the obscure party-controlled appointments of the past. Instead they appeared to be further disadvantaged, as their qualifications were inferior to those of male competitors. The Chinese President Jiang Zemin's 2001 announcement that business people would actively be preferred for government jobs has likewise worked against women, who represent just one-third of entrepreneurs, and tend to be clustered in the micro-enterprise and service sectors. Thus they lack the big business expertise the government is looking for.[19]

China has no quota system for women in the public sector, nor even an anti-discrimination clause in its new civil service regulations. This experience shows how concern for equal opportunities can be neglected in a control-oriented, fiscally constrained public-sector environment. There is a risk that the emphasis on short-term financial control that characterizes some public-sector reforms will undercut client responsiveness. Where market values dictate the allocation of resources and the shaping of preferences, women's requirements will invite a poor response from public services because of market and political failures in translating them into consumer demand.

Damaging impacts on education and health outcomes

If public-sector reforms are trimming women out of the public service or confining them to insecure contracts, this will inhibit the attainment of global goals on female education and health. Gender parity in public-sector recruitment has distributive consequences beyond equal working opportunities; it also positively affects the equitable distribution of public resources.[20] Case studies of interactions between public-sector workers and clients show that there are differences in the ways male and female staff interact with clients, with women staff showing greater sensitivity and responsiveness to women's problems.[21] The effect on service delivery is, however, only apparent where certain institutional factors overcome professional and cultural biases against women. These include supportive top-level leadership, a gender-equitable organizational mission, and at least 30 per cent women in the bureaucracy.[22]

Where the service is underfunded or low-status, where conditions are poor, or where women staff are in the lowest-level jobs, they may replicate male-biased service delivery patterns, identify with male superiors, or disavow connections with women clients. Demoralized, underpaid and poorly resourced staff, women or men, may seek to limit the demands clients place upon them by providing limited information, curtailing their contact with socially marginal clients, and enforcing rituals of deference to augment their own status in relation to clients.[23]

Incentive systems are probably more important than gender in shaping the way public-sector workers respond to their clients. Public-sector reforms have focused upon ensuring that incentives and performance measurement discourage corruption and promote efficiency, though there is an increasing interest in rewarding performance which assists poorer people.[24] But where reform is designed to promote a market-like response in public-service provision, there are few incentives to encourage staff to invest in the time-consuming activities for which no financial gain to the service or individual is apparent. To visit families to ensure girls' attendance at school or ante-natal check-ups at the health centre is time-consuming and requires strong motivation.

Performance measures for monitoring the work of public-sector staff need likewise to recognize gender-related achievements. Incentive systems often limit rewards to staff to delivering services more rapidly and cost-effectively. Another problem is that actions to promote gender equality are not always easily quantifiable; they may involve a long-term investment in gaining the trust of women clients, and engaging with them on matters not directly related to the service in question. A study of women community health workers in northeast Brazil, for instance, showed that one key to their excellent performance was willingness to spend time in non-health-related activities, helping women clients cook nutritious meals, bathe children, and so on.[25] But these efforts are not recorded or rewarded in official performance-related pay systems.

Tools for improving gender sensitivity

Women's associations and international institutions have prioritized several areas for gender-sensitive public-sector reform. These include recruitment quotas to ensure a stronger presence of women at all levels of the bureaucracy; the introduction of gender-equity concerns in performance measurement; consultation with women clients of public services, and measures to respond to their complaints. The creation of public services exclusively for girls or women—such as girls' schools or women's police forces—has been seen in some settings as a way of redressing gender bias.

Where there are no institutional channels for citizens to influence service providers directly, informal means such as social mobilization and media exposure are deployed to shame officials into remedy. Exposure of malpractice in the public administration tends to be confrontational, and in many settings carries personal risks: people may lose their jobs or suffer ostracism. In reasonably consolidated democracies, the route is more practicable and developed. Organizations in India have taken this approach, conducting "social audits" in which public-spending accounts are exposed to and reviewed by the very people meant to have benefited. In New Delhi, an organization called *Parivartan* (Change) has used Delhi's 2002 Right to Information Act in this way to secure service improvements from the city's water board, road works and street-lighting departments. On behalf of more marginal populations, *Parivartan* used the Act to obtain information about government support for primary schools in low-income neighbourhoods, and exposed the failure to deliver on spending promises.[26]

Gender budgeting

A tool increasingly used for monitoring government spending is the "gender budget" method pioneered in Australia and South Africa.[27] Gender budgets analyse the likely impacts of planned spending in order to make links between national gender-equity policies and actual spending allocations. These exercises by civil-society groups, sometimes undertaken in partnership with government departments, supply parliamentarians with gender-aware budgetary information in the hope that they will goad the executive into more appropriate spending patterns. In some places they have been highly effective in exposing the gap between government commitments to certain social policies, and actual spending. In South Africa, for instance, they revealed that government commitments to social equity were in danger of being overridden by arms procurement deals that threatened expenditures on social programmes. In the period since 1999, civil-society scrutiny of public accounts in the area of defence and intelligence has helped put pressure on the Finance Ministry to live up to its commitment to make savings in these areas and commit the resources instead to improving women's and children's well-being.

Although the South African gender budget analysis exercises have been notably successful, others have run up against constraints. Delays in producing these analyses are difficult to avoid since they can only be conducted after budget priorities are announced. And follow-up is limited: sympathetic parliamentarians are usually restricted to raising questions about gender-differential spending patterns, which may not lead to governmental action. A lack of access or even a right to information on government spending has been the main obstacle to producing evidence that can be used for the enforcement of social policy commitments. Even if this information were available, it is usually not gender-disaggregated. Data on gender differences in actual spending would equip critics with the means of illuminating and closing gaps between budgets and expenditures.

Recent gender budget initiatives have addressed some of these problems. In India, gender budgeting by civil-society groups has accessed audits of government expenditure to compare stated against actual spending. A focus on the outcomes of spending has enabled results-based gender budgeting activity in Rwanda to show publicly whether government spending is achieving its objectives. And in Mexico, gender budget analysts have been effective in briefing parliamentarians and making changes in budget appropriations.

GENDER AND THE RULE OF LAW AGENDA

Legal and judicial reform have always been major concerns for gender-equality activists because law and its enforcement play a central role in establishing people's access to resources, social status and basic rights. Legal systems around the world, both in the content of law and its enforcement, provide a particularly striking case of the internalization and reproduction of gender biases. Enforcement systems frequently fail women. For instance, they may fail to define violations of women's physical security as a crime, or fail to enforce legislation in this context, particularly if women have suffered violence at the hands of male relations. This is also a feature of informal justice systems governing the lives of many: systems of community rulings or religious law presided over by religious or tribal authorities such as councils of elders. The norms and standards prevalent in these informal institutions often infuse formal legal systems.

Box 11.1 Women's struggle over citizenship rights leads to improved representation

The Emang Basadi Women's Association in Botswana, founded in 1994, set out to remove the restrictive provisions in the county's Citizenship Act that denied citizenship rights to the children of women married to non-citizen men. Subsequently the movement has demanded legal reform in a number of other areas, particularly those that confer excessive power on husbands in marital relations, in matters concerning the control and ownership of family property, and consequent restrictions on women's capacity to engage in legal contracts and financial transactions.

After some time, Emang Basasdi's tactics changed from lobbying for policy change to promoting an increase in women's presence in the legislature. Before national elections, it developed a women's manifesto, the first of its kind in Africa. The manifesto set out demands for redress against measures that had depressed women's social and economic status, and established a framework against which government performance could be assessed and monitored.

Source: Selolwane 2004.

Formal and informal legal systems that subordinate women to men in the family, weakening women's citizenship rights and exposing them to violence and abuse, have served as powerful platforms upon which women of different political persuasions can unite. An example of a broad-based legal-rights struggle in southern Africa is discussed in box 11.1. But feminist legal-rights activism has been less effective in promoting gender equality in informal justice systems; and there has not been marked success in bringing gender equity into the contemporary "rule of law" reforms that address commercial issues and the business environment.

Legal pluralism and gender equality

Many feminist approaches to law reform take a "legal centralist" approach: they view the state as the central authority in legal systems and the ultimate unifying source of legal norms. The "rule of law" reform agenda promoted by IFIs also focuses mainly on formal legal systems, although there is recognition in the international donor community that non-state justice and security systems have much more impact on the lives of low-income groups and women than do formal systems.[28] Legal pluralism, where two or more orders co-exist, is the norm in

many developing countries where different communities' own systems for matters such as marriage or inheritance are respected. In some contexts, informal justice systems severely limit the province or the legitimacy of formal law, casting doubts on the effectiveness of a feminist focus on the state as the medium through which to enforce changed rules and norms in gender relations.[29]

The focus on formal law has also tended to create the impression that statutory law and formal judicial institutions are inherently more progressive than traditional legal institutions, which claim authority on the basis of their unchanging authenticity. But any legal system, conventional or customary, is an evolving reflection of social norms and power relations. Historical analysis has shown that "customary" law is often a reflection of colonial practices that have privileged certain social groups. Similarly, conventional or modern legal systems often reproduce profound gender biases, and modern judicial institutions sometimes resist feminist legal reform, limiting women's access to justice.[30] Feminists have become much more critical of legal universalism and modernism as a result.

When "universalism" and "uniformity" disguise gender and cultural biases, modern legal instruments can remain just as limited as customary law in promoting social change. This is illustrated by the case of India. Here, a uniform civil code to override customary variations on personal law was a goal of the secular independence movement, and was embedded in the constitution. Subsequently, the notion of uniformity has been seen by the minority Muslim community as a ploy to obliterate their special and different cultural status. In recent years, the greatest champions of a uniform civil code have been Hindu chauvinist associations that promote legal uniformity as a means of highlighting the "backwardness" of the Muslim community. Muslims argue that behind the notion of "uniformity" are versions of family relations and social life that reflect the majority culture.[31] Thus "uniformity" can disguise discrimination, instead of serving as the levelling or equalizing force originally, and usually, intended.

Informal justice systems

The enduring legitimacy and practical accessibility of informal justice systems, especially in the area of personal law, make them an important focus for gender-sensitive reform. These codes and their practitioners often reinforce gender and age-based hierarchies in their rulings, using normative frameworks at odds with constitutional rights. This gender bias is particularly pronounced in matters dealing with inheritance and other marital property issues, due to the deeply embedded perception of male heads of household as having the ultimate or sole authority to take major decisions concerning family property.[32]

Exemption clauses for informal systems remain intact in many countries in Africa and South Asia. In Nigeria, for instance, federal states are given discretion to apply personal laws with respect to family matters. Some northern Nigerian states have gone so far as to extend the application of Islamic Shari'a law to criminal matters, which has generated heated debate on gender biases such as dress-code restrictions on women, workplace discrimination against unmarried women, and severe penalties for alleged adultery.[33] The death sentences imposed on two women for adultery in 2000 illustrated the extent to which traditional authorities can act with impunity in imposing sentences declared unconstitutional by the federal government.[34] The two women eventually won appeals against their sentences in the High Court, supported by local and international protests.

However, in countries where the formal judiciary has inadequate reach, the authorities are increasingly dependent on these informal institutions to settle disputes and bring offenders to book, in a pragmatic choice of customary law rather than no law.[35] These mechanisms are accessible, cheap, and deliver judgments that may be seen by parties to disputes as more legitimate than those of distant courts using alien legal frameworks.[36] They can also be effective at negotiating reconciliation and restorative justice, especially needed in war-damaged communities (see chapter 14). Thus there is mounting political pressure from religious and ethnic minorities and indigenous groups in many countries to legitimize community justice practices. This has benefits in allowing communities to own their justice systems, but can also compromise the advancement of women's rights.

Proposals for the reform of traditional justice

Since women's subordination to men is a central principle in many informal justice systems, challenges to gender-biased norms may seem impracticable. A pragmatic approach argues for expanding whatever space there is for women's rights within traditional systems, particularly in the adjudication of family disputes, and otherwise opening these systems up to constitutional oversight. In some informal justice systems in sub-Saharan Africa, constitutional changes that give power to traditional leaders impose new accountability requirements upon them at the same time: they are enjoined to uphold constitutional principles on gender equality to the same level as any public body. This accommodative approach to traditional systems recognizes the legitimacy of customary laws, but insists that they do not override citizens' rights to voice their dissatisfaction and seek redress from the national legal system when practices justified on the basis of personal laws produce unjust results.[37]

There is often a marked gender imbalance in the staffing of informal justice systems, and a lack of interface with formal judicial institutions that could regulate their actions. Reform measures and proposals have included increasing women's representation, linkages to social welfare services, and oversight measures. It is mandatory, for instance, that one-third of the members of Uganda's local council courts are women, and in Tanzania, three of the seven members on each village land council are women. The Rwandan *Gacaca* tribunals—traditional grassroots dispute-settlement forums that have been revived to deal with the local aftermath of the 1994 genocide—would in the past have been composed of male elders. But the government promoted the election of women magistrates, with the result that about one-third of the judges currently hearing cases are women.

Because informal justice tribunals hear a far greater number of cases of gender-based violence than do the police and the formal courts, women's non-governmental organizations (NGOs) in some contexts work with them to provide support services. The Kenyan Coalition on Violence Against Women has proposed training for chiefs on how to use referral services such as the Child Welfare department, in order to improve the chances that victims of domestic violence are supported.[38] Most efforts to regulate and monitor informal justice systems are still only at proposal stage. In South Africa, where it is proposed that headmen's tribunals be given formal recognition as courts, the Law Commission has proposed that they should abide by minimum standards such as respecting the rights of litigants to appeal to higher customary or magistrates' courts if issues remain unresolved, or if they do not agree with the judgments made by traditional leaders.[39]

The formal justice system and gender

The "rule of law" element of the governance agenda contains underlying assumptions about the relationship between law, the economy and society. Critics suggest that the agenda promoted by the international development establishment is premised upon models of economic rationality and social activity that are highly mechanistic and unrepresentative of "real world" societies. This is especially pertinent for societies where informal institutions profoundly influence the practical workings of the judicial system and the enforcement of rulings.[40] The outcomes sought by the reforms overestimate the extent to which individuals alter their behaviour in relation to such

changes, and their core premise—that productive capitalism needs formal adjudication, scrupulously enforced contracts and inviolable rights—is regarded as exaggerated.[41]

The principal intention of these "rule of law" reforms is to improve the capacity of the law and its enforcement to insulate private property and market activity from public regulation. This intention restricts the extent to which gender issues are explicitly addressed, or can be raised. The reform programmes also address the chronic problems of inefficiency, incapacity and corruption suffered by the formal justice system in many developing countries. Here, women's interests in removing the obstacles to their access to justice can perhaps be served. Women's activists in southern Africa have highlighted the following problems: the geographical inaccessibility of courts and the high cost of fees and professional legal assistance; delays, lack of legal aid and low levels of legal literacy. The lack of women judges and magistrates in most countries is also acute. Many Muslim countries and those in sub-Saharan Africa have no women at all in the highest courts. In others women have only a token presence: 1.3 per cent of judges in Nepal, for example.[42]

While these problems are widely recognized, most "governance reform" packages are primarily concerned with the larger accountability role of the judiciary. The lending practices of the World Bank and the African Development Bank focus primarily on the role of law in creating a healthy environment for business transactions by guaranteeing the security of property rights and upholding contracts. Thus current lending activity for judicial reforms focuses on fiscal matters such as changes to tax administration systems, revision of commercial codes, and liberalization of the financial sector (banking regulation, bankruptcy law, corporate governance, insurance and securities regulation). Other areas include laws to facilitate privatization, the creation of markets in land through formal titling systems, and administrative and infrastructural improvements to judicial institutions such as courts, police and prisons.[43]

Reforms to property law, labour law, commercial contracts and banking law have important implications for gender equity, but the gendered impacts of these reforms have not received much attention. The case of land-tenure reform, which is of critical importance both to the investment environment and to the survival prospects of rural people, illustrates the problem (see chapter 6).[44] Land in Africa is held and used under plural legal arrangements; it may be subject to different rules about use and ownership at different times, depending on the actors involved. The fixation with the market advantages of formal titling systems risks eroding the land-use rights of family members with undocumented interests in land. These invariably include women, whose rights to occupy or farm land in many cases depend on marriage to their nominal "owner", and whose rights traditionally may be assumed to have lapsed if he dies or rejects her.

Land titling and tenure

The 1990s saw land-tenure reform introduced across sub-Saharan Africa, notably in Tanzania, Malawi, Uganda, Côte d'Ivoire, Niger, Namibia, Zimbabwe, South Africa and Ghana. Most of these programmes were originated to encourage the transition from family holdings to individually owned land parcels. In many African customary tenure systems, the needs of women agricultural producers are protected through community land-management rules that limit the power of a male head of household to alienate land. Formal titling programmes in practice, if not in intention, tended to result in the issue of titles predominantly in the name of male heads of household, and have created a new problem of female landlessness. In Kenya, where land titling has been under way since the 1950s, only 5 per cent of registered titles are held in women's names.

This is a classic instance of a modernization programme reinforcing traditional ideas of male dominance and ownership of family resources in such a way as to reinforce and formalize gender bias. In the late 1990s some land-reform programmes took stock of the problem. Both in Tanzania and South Africa, the virtues of customary tenure as far as women's rights were concerned were acknowledged, and steps were taken to ensure that women's rights in land could be defended in law. South Africa has also provided for the legal recognition of communal ownership in the form of common property associations, with strong measures to defend women's land access.

Gender bias in property ownership and in family legislation has significant follow-on effects for women engaging in market enterprises. The capacity of women entrepreneurs to finance investments is limited to their inability to offer land as collateral; yet reforms in the financial services industry take no cognizance of this factor. A study of financial-sector reforms in Uganda showed that they reinforced the biases of lenders against the agricultural and retail marketing sectors—those in which women entrepreneurs are concentrated.[45]

Land and financial services reform demonstrates the gendered distributive consequences of legal arrangements, and show that it is critical for gender-equity advocates to mount more systematic challenges to the market-derived priorities in legal-system reforms. A commentator points out that in sub-Saharan Africa, "arguments for gender equality have always encountered a hostile reception: now there is a dominant discourse that gives even more legitimacy to such contestation in official circles, some of it couched in apparently neutral terms such as efficiency and competing priorities in the face of resource constraints."[46] Bringing gender equality into market-focused legal reforms is essential for extending the reach and enjoyment of women's constitutional rights.

DEDICATED INSTITUTIONS TO REPRESENT WOMEN'S NEEDS

The importance of establishing a formal presence for the representation of women's interests in public administrations has long been recognized by activists, and has produced 30 years of experimentation. Different types of "national women's machinery" have been invented, ranging from dedicated ministries to bureaux in the office of the chief executive, or women's units in key line ministries such as agriculture, health or education. A recent comparative analysis of women's political effectiveness across Europe finds that the presence of these women's units has had a major influence in promoting gender-equity policies.[47] Studies in developing countries have been more equivocal, suggesting that women's units have very often been captured by ruling parties or subordinated to women's wings run by first ladies, and have been starved of resources and access to decision making.[48] Nevertheless, they can be effective in forwarding the cause of women, depending on their powers and capacities, and the extent to which they are legitimized and supported by national women's movements.

The *Servicio Nacional de la Mujer* (SERNAM) in Chile, whose executive head has a cabinet seat, is considered a successful example. It has worked through the Ministry of Planning to ensure that adequate resources are devoted to improving women's economic opportunities and reducing their poverty.[49] Although its connections to the women's movement have enhanced the impact of its efforts, these relations have not always been smooth. During the first post-Pinochet democratic administration, SERNAM was criticized for failing to tackle discrimination against women. In 1995, under a new administration, SERNAM surprised its critics by brining out a radical Plan for Equal Opportunities that firmly embraced many key feminist concepts and demands. This turn-around has been sustained, as evidenced by the passing of a gender-sensitive national health policy in 2004.

Overcoming constraints

Many national policy bodies for women—including SERNAM— lack formal oversight powers to review policy making in other sectors. They therefore have to rely on informal accountability controls such as popular pressure and public shaming.[50] To tackle these constraints, some women's bureaux rely upon women's associations as "whistle blowers", even recognizing this role by granting them formal status. The Commission for Gender Equality in South Africa offers accreditation to civil-society associations and rights of regular observation of its work, to both supply the Commission with information and act as a quality check.

A contrasting experience is that of the state-level women's commission in Kerala. Set up in 1996, its six commissioners were so starved of resources, and its recommendations so ignored that in late 1999 it took the government to the High Court to demand resources and legislative attention. In its first three years the commission had proposed a revised law on child custody, stronger laws on rape and harassment, an increase in alimony, proposed measures to improve implementation of the Dowry Prohibition Act, and pressed for increased numbers of women in public-service posts. Not one recommendation was tabled in the State Assembly. Although it continues to struggle for resources and attention, the commission gained the respect of feminist women's groups when, in 2000, it defended a senior woman bureaucrat who had been sexually harassed by a prominent state minister. While the government closed ranks around the offender, the commission reminded Chief Minister E. K. Nayanar that "it is the Government's responsibility to create conditions conducive for women to work with honour".[51] The offender was forced to resign.

The establishment of commissions and similar bodies to defend women's interests will undoubtedly continue and their ranks expand, under pressure from women's movements and feminist groups. Sustained social and women's mobilization is needed to obtain better accountability to women from public-sector actors. Also needed is the dissemination of basic information about decision making and policy implementation to enable civil-society groups to assess whether official commitments to gender equity are carried out. This is another area where the formal presence in government of a women's bureau or unit can work with women in the wider society, opening up opportunities for dialogue and consultation. There is a long way to go before meeting the needs of women citizens is universally accepted as a measure against which the performance of leaders and officials is assessed.

Notes

1 Santiso 2001:4.

2 Campos and Pradhan 2003:1.

3 Campos and Pradhan 2003:2.

4 Upham forthcoming.

5 Evans 2004.

6 Personal communication with Thandika Mkandawire, 6 July 2004.

7 World Bank 1992, 1994.

8 World Bank 2001a.

9 Swamy et al. 2001.

10 Vijayalakshmi 2002.

11 Goetz and Jenkins 2004.

12 World Bank 2003a.

13 ILO 2003.

14 Rama n.d.:7.

15 Samson 2003:95.

16 SACN 2004:79, cited in Beall 2004:24.

17 Jie 2004:11.

18 All-China Women's Federation 1998.

19 Jie 2004:13.

20 Keiser et al. 2002:553.

21 Thieleman and Stewart 1996; Goetz 2001; Simmons et al. 1993; Keiser et al. 2002; Rao et al. 1999.

22 Dahlerup 1986; Kanter 1977.

23 Lipsky 1980.

24 World Bank 2003a.

25 Tendler and Freedheim 1994.

26 *Times of India* 2003.

27 UNDP 2002:80.

28 DfID 2002.

29 Manji 1999:439; Nyamu-Musembi 2004; Dahl 1987; Smart 1989.

30 Mukhopadhyaya 1998.

31 Kapur and Cossman 1995; Mody 2003.

32 COVAW 2002; Byamukama 2001; Khadiagala 2001; Nyamu-Musembi 2002.

33 Abdullah 2002.

34 Sow 2004:43.

35 UNDP 2004:59.

36 Nyamu-Musembi 2002; Penal Reform International 2000; Barya and Oloka-Onyango 1994.

37 Nyamu-Musembi 2000, 2002.

38 Nyamu-Musembi 2004:34.

39 Nyamu-Musembi 2004:35–6.

40 Upham forthcoming; Ohnesorge forthcoming.

41 Upham forthcoming.

42 UNIFEM 2004a.

43 Nyamu-Musembi 2004:1–13; Islam 2003; Faundez 1997.

44 Whitehead and Tsikata 2003.

45 Kiiza et al. 2000.

46 Nyamu-Musembi 2004:46.

47 Squires and Wickham-Jones 2001.

48 Goetz 1995; Staudt 1995; Tsikata 2001.

49 Waylen 2000:787.

50 Waylen 2000.

51 *The Hindu* 1997, 2000.

Chapter 12
Decentralization and gender equality

Since the 1990s, an important focus of governance reform has been the strengthening of local government by the decentralization of powers, resources and responsibilities to municipal councils and other locally administered bodies. The intention is to improve the quality and efficiency of services, strengthen fiscal management, enhance private sector development and increase local participation in decision-making processes.[1] Decentralization is expected to produce these outcomes because, since government will be nearer to them, citizens will take a closer interest in how their taxes are spent, and will subject to closer scrutiny the actions of their local representatives than they do those who disappear to the capital, holding them accountable to local needs.

This part of the reform agenda has been more open than others to the active participation of women, both as elected local councillors and as the clients of local government services. Women generally, as well as low-income and other socially marginal groups, are expected to benefit from the accountability and service delivery improvements that government in close proximity should provide. This is particularly relevant where social programmes of importance to disadvantaged groups are to be developed and managed locally—programmes such as those for health outreach, primary schooling, employment and income generation, slum redevelopment, and low-cost water and sanitation services.

Local government is also regarded as a significant political apprenticeship arena for women. Barriers to their entry—such as the need to travel and spend time away from home, a large disposable income, a reasonable level of education, experience of political competition, and social connections—are lower at the local level. Local government is also regarded as appealing to women participants because of the focus on basic community services; women's engagement in informal community management is believed to make them attractive as local planners and managers.[2] Institutional innovations to broaden local participation in decision making, such as new participatory budgeting arrangements in Brazil and elsewhere, can also give women more incentive and better opportunities to engage in public debate.

The 1990s saw a number of legal and constitutional innovations around the world designed to enhance women's participation in local government; these included quotas and other measures to bring women into local office. These actions were supported and promoted by the International Union of Local Authorities, which in 1998 issued a Worldwide Declaration on Women in Local Government to encourage national support for affirmative action at the local level. The implication to be derived from analysing some of these experiences is that specific institutional engineering is indeed needed both to encourage women's participation in local government, and to make local governments accountable to female constituents. Women's participation in local government will not make its institutions more responsive to women's needs unless measures are put in place to counteract their capture by patriarchal elites.

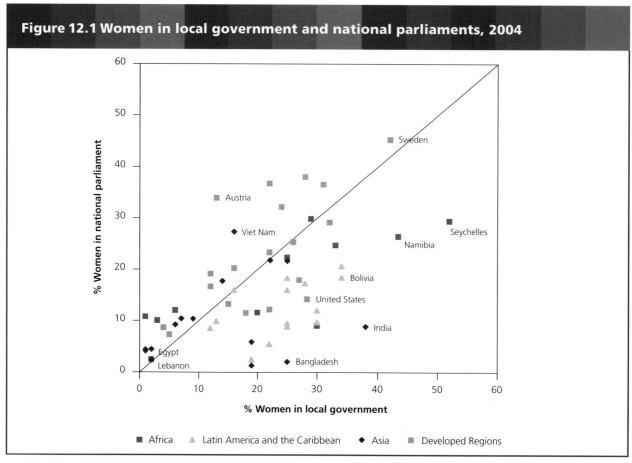

Figure 12.1 Women in local government and national parliaments, 2004

Sources: UCLG 2003; Drage 2001; Svara 2003; OSKa 2002; *Namibian* 2004; Evertzen 2001; UN Statistical Division 2004.

THE PREVALENCE OF WOMEN IN LOCAL GOVERNMENT

It is not possible to obtain globally comparable data on women's participation in local government. The International Union of Local Authorities does not offer such data; there is such wide variation in the demarcation of subnational governments that they are barely comparable. Nevertheless, using self-reported country data from a 2003 survey conducted by United Cities and Local Governments (UCLG), a global network supporting inclusive local government, a partial impression of the current proportions of women in local government can be obtained (see figure 12.1).

This data shows that with the exception of Latin America, in no region of the world is there a consistently higher proportion of women in local councils than in national parliaments. The survey found that the average proportion of women in local councils for the 52 countries reporting was just 15 per cent [3]—no different from the global average of women in national parliaments; and that in leadership positions, the proportions of women were even lower: for instance, 5 per cent of mayors of Latin American municipalities are women.[4] In many of the cases where there are more women in local than in national government, this is because quotas or other affirmative action provisions have been applied locally, but not, or not to the same extent, at the national level. This is the case for Namibia, Uganda, India, Pakistan, Bangladesh, France and many Latin American countries.

The implication of this data is that local government is not necessarily, or has yet to become, the attractive and positive arena for women's participation that has been assumed. It may even be the case, contrary to conventional thinking, that women actually face greater obstacles to political engagement at the local than national levels in some contexts because of the intensity of local patriarchal norms.

COUNTRY EXPERIENCES OF AFFIRMATIVE ACTION

Most of the countries with measures in place to promote women's presence in national parliaments have related measures at the local government level. Some states have used the local level for experimentation before applying affirmative action at the national level. Namibia's 1992 Local Authorities Act required that, depending on the size of the local authority, between one-third to one-half of candidates in local elections be women; the success of this measure led subsequently to voluntary quotas in some parties at the national level.[5]

In other contexts, local-level affirmative action has been something of an afterthought both for national administrations and for the women's movement, because so much attention was focused on improving women's rate of participation in national assemblies. In South Africa, for example, the relatively poor results for women candidates in the first local government elections prompted civil society action and legislative changes to boost their engagement in future rounds. Even though women's activism had been strongest at local levels during the anti-apartheid struggle, democratization drew many local women activists into national government, weakening their local participation.[6]

The case for affirmative action measures at local levels is best made by women's poor electoral performance in local and other subnational elections lacking such measures. In Namibia, contrasting outcomes are evident in different electoral systems. For both local council and national elections, a proportional representation (PR) system is used, with both formal and informal quotas of female candidates. For the regional elections for the upper chamber, the National Council, a single-member, simple-plurality system with no affirmative action is used. The numbers of women elected show striking differences. For the local authorities, the 1992 elections produced 32 per cent of women, rising to 41 per cent in 1998. At the national level, the main political party, the South-West African People's Organization, applies formal quotas, with the result that the proportion of women in parliament has grown from 8 per cent in 1989 to 29 per cent in 2003. However, in the regional elections only 3 per cent of those elected for the national council in 1992 were women, rising only to 4 per cent in 1998.[7]

In South Africa the closed-list PR system that proved so successful in sweeping women into national office in 1994, 1998 and 2004, was not applied wholesale to local council elections. Only 40 per cent of seats at the local level are selected through a PR system; a ward system with only one representative per ward and the winner decided by simple plurality is used for the rest. The African National Congress (ANC) did not apply the national quota of 30 per cent women in its candidate lists for the first local government elections in 1995; nor did other parties. As a result just 19 per cent of elected local councillors were women. In 2000 women did much better, thanks to a provision in the Municipal Structures Act urging parties to ensure that half of their candidate lists are made up of women, while women also competed more successfully for the ward seats, capturing 28 per cent of local government seats overall.[8]

Reservation systems

India's local government elections, which are ward-based, apply a different affirmative action method: the reservation of a percentage of wards for all-female competition. A 1992 constitutional amendment reserved one-third of local government seats for women, and in addition reserved seats for socially excluded caste groups in proportion to their numbers in the local population. This system, designed to overcome social resistance to the public participation of previously excluded groups in local affairs, has been celebrated for its success in putting about a million women in local government at any particular point in time. However, there are some disadvantages. The location of the reserved territorial constituency rotates after each election, and this can discourage parties from investing in women's political capacities. Women may also be seen as short-term participants in politics: after one term of office the constituency is released for open competition and the incumbent woman representative usually stands little chance of re-election. But since a portion of constituents are obliged to vote for women and to be represented by a woman, the attitudes towards their participation should change over time.

An alternative reservation method has been used in Uganda, where the 1997 Local Government Act reserves 30 per cent of local council seats for all-female competition. But these are added seats, not a portion of existing seats. New wards are created for women to represent, cobbled together out of clusters of two to three existing wards, in effect at least doubling the constituency size which women represent, compared with regular ward representatives. Instead of giving women an advantage in political contest with men, new public space is created for women's exclusive occupation. The elections for the women's seats are held around two weeks after the ward elections. In the 1998 local elections, voter fatigue and irritation with this drawn-out procedure led to a failure to achieve quorums in the elections for women all over the country. After several attempts to re-run the ballots, the results from poor voter turn-outs were accepted.[9] This undermined the legitimacy and credibility of Ugandan women as local councillors. The system also undermined their efforts to compete with men in ward lections. Voters told them that their turn would come later, in the special women's elections.[10]

RESISTANCE FROM TRADITIONAL AUTHORITIES

One of the important factors inhibiting women's participation in local governance systems is the endurance of traditional institutions for running community affairs, and women's previous role—or lack of one—within them. Where local elites dominate existing systems, decentralization is likely to entrench

them, with not very promising prospects for women. Local elites are often drawn from groups who held power traditionally, for example tribal authorities, religious councils or groups of clan elders. These were often groups created or co-opted by colonial authorities to extend their power over community affairs to the extraction of revenue or labour for public works. Their traditional roles included the adjudication of family life and property, including extending or refusing approval of marriage unions, assigning responsibility for widows and orphans, and settling land disputes. These mechanisms of community self-government derive resilience from the local respect and legitimacy they enjoy.[11]

These institutions, sometimes called "ascriptive" or "first-tier" institutions, are the source of substantive norms that remain deeply meaningful to participants, enabling them to survive when formal institutions suffer decay or discredit. Where civil conflict and social disruption prevail, they may remain the only source of functional authority. They also, importantly, control access to resources: to land, water and livelihoods; to arbitration mechanisms over disputes; and to informal services such as education and health. These are of key importance to the survival prospects of people whose government-run services and employment prospects are shrinking, and where services and amenities are commercialized. Traditional authority institutions in most parts of the world are deeply patriarchal, offering little space for the independent authority of women (and also excluding youth and the socially disadvantaged). They make women's participation contingent on conformity with the policy and spending preferences of masculine hierarchies.

The devolution of formal political and administrative powers to the local level may reinvigorate these systems and confer on them a new lease of life. The local chief or ruling group of landowning families typically assumes leadership positions or exercises patronage control over elected councillors. The continuity of power-holding may occur intentionally, when traditional rulers are politically powerful and demand protected space for their own authority, to exercise their traditional functions, for example in imposing order and enforcing security locally, and in the jurisdiction of petty local disputes.

Experiences in India

In Indian local government, where reservations in local government as already described are made for women and for representatives of scheduled castes and tribes, the old lines of authority may operate indirectly. A study of women elected to local councils in West Bengal found that 17 per cent of the women in reserved seats were married to men who had previously held the seat, in contrast to just 2 per cent of the women who held an open, unreserved seat.[12] Another study of women councillors in the first term of office after the reservation system had been installed in Rajasthan, Madhya Pradesh and Uttar Pradesh, found that one-third of these women were stand-ins for husbands and sons.[13] Thus some women in office act as proxies for influential male leaders in the locality who, had these wards not been reserved for women, would expect to have occupied these positions themselves.

Similar attempts are made to prevent certain members of scheduled castes and tribes from gaining seats on the council or being elected as *sarpanch* (council chairperson); where this position is reserved, traditional leadership groups often ensure that their own choice of candidate is elected. The prevalence of these "proxy politics" methods have delayed the erosion of traditional local power and patronage systems.[14] Campaigns continue to be waged not on programmes and policies but on appeals to caste and community loyalty.[15] Women councillors may be routinely denied access to records, knowledge of accounts, and even the right to sit with the male council members. In Rajasthan, where the traditional patriarchal system is deeply entrenched, there have been cases where women councillors and *sarpanches* (local council chairpeople) miss council meetings because they are not informed of them, and thereby can be removed from office for nonattendance at several consecutive meetings. No-confidence motions have unseated

Box 12.1   Ousting a Rajasthani women leader

Chaggibai was elected *sarpanch* of Rasulpura *panchayat* (council) in 1995, a position in this case reserved not just for a woman but for a member of a scheduled caste or tribe. Chaggibai was a member of the Bhil tribal group, and was encouraged to run for the position by members of the Rawat caste that made up over 60 per cent of the population in this Rajasthani constituency.

An independent-minded woman, Chaggibai was literate, had worked as a school administrator, and was known in the area as a participant in the national-level *Mahila Samakhya* (Women's Equality) programme, and was therefore a surprising choice as a proxy candidate. But she had long ago separated from her husband and was seen therefore as more easy to manipulate than a married woman would be.

At the first village assembly after her election, the local Rawat strongman—who had always run the local council from the confines of his house—refused to allow Chaggibai to speak. She had assembled over 400 women and scheduled caste and tribal people to attend, but they were all ordered to go home. During the next months, Chaggibai mobilized the downtrodden groups in the community to support her efforts. She held open meetings to discuss local development plans, initiated construction projects concerning drains, school buildings and roads, and saw that the council office building was completed so as to accommodate open sessions.

When Chaggibai led local women in demonstrations against an illegal liquor store run by the deputy *sarpanch*, the Rawat community leaders counter-attacked, locking the council office doors against her, hiding files containing illicit transactions, and attempting to assault her. Subsequently, nine of the 12 council members including two women met privately and passed a vote of no confidence against her.

Chaggibai's case was taken up by the People's Union of Civil Liberties and by Rajasthan's women's movement, and a petition was filed against her removal in the Jaipur High Court. But she was never reinstated. She commented several years later: "They simply couldn't tolerate a woman, especially a Bhil. If I had been their puppet, as they expected me to be, none of this would have happened."

Sources: Weaver 2000; S.B. Civil Writ Petition 1998.

a number of lower-caste women *sarpanches* in Rajasthan, a case of which is described in box 12.1.

Not only may women councillors be silenced or undermined, but gender-equity proposals and policies emanating from the state or national level may be rejected. In 1995 the *sarpanches* of Bassi block, also in Rajasthan, unanimously passed a resolution condemning *saathins* (the word means "friend"), the women workers of the state's Women's Development Programme. The *saathins* were expected to engender a critical consciousness of gender relations amongst rural women, not simply to deliver development resources. Their work was therefore controversial in such a conservative society, and provoked the boycott by the *sarpanches* of Bassi. This in turn provoked the following observation: "As long as *sarpanches* of the Bassi type continue to dominate the panchayats, the women members will be bypassed, or even harassed, if they dare to oppose the male patriarchs of their villages".[16] Since the time of these incidents, there has been progress in the exercise of influence by women councillors and *sarpanches*; they have been able not only to articulate local women's preferences regarding local services, but to change spending priorities in some areas.

Experiences in South Africa

In South Africa, some traditional bodies have been assigned direct powers, either in competition with, or directly over, democratically elected local councils. Under white rule, indirect rule in the black-designated apartheid territories was delegated to tribal authorities to help contain and depoliticize rural populations. When apartheid rule ended, these authorities fiercely resisted the loss of the considerable local power they had amassed.[17] Both they and conservative Afrikaner associations have subsequently manoeuvred for as much local autonomy as possible. One of the democratization challenges in post-apartheid South Africa has been to undermine the racial and ethnic divisions that were previously exploited to help maintain political control.

The reorganization of local government in South Africa has proceeded in several difficult stages since the first round of local government elections in 1995/6. First came the merger of racially segregated areas to end the skewed distribution of public goods and services. Middle-class white ratepayers in cities put up most resistance, but traditional leaders also objected when new municipal boundaries cut across rural districts and tribal land.

The need to juggle the demands of various interest groups led to extensive negotiation and uncertainty between 1994 and 2000 over the ways local government should be constituted. Traditional leaders were able to use this period to entrench their already considerable local influence.[18] Represented by the Congress of Traditional Leaders of South Africa (Contralesa) and supported by such powerful ethnically based political parties as the Inkatha Freedom Party (IFP) in Kwa-Zulu Natal, in 2000 the traditional authorities demanded the reservation of 50 per cent of local authority positions, in response to the ANC government offer of 10 per cent. The compromise agreement was a 20 per cent reservation for hereditary leaders, which by definition excluded women.

Not only are unelected traditional authorities given space on local councils, but in some areas where state service delivery systems are weak, they have been designated the gatekeepers of access to key public goods. New government-sponsored "traditional development centres" are presided over by local chieftaincies and serve as one-stop shops dispensing pensions, HIV/AIDS awareness services, small business advice, as well as providing sites for mobile clinics. It may well be the case that in the more remote rural areas where the apparatus of administration is thin, traditional routes are the only effective means of delivering these services. One observer has commented: "It is ironic that government closest to the people is occurring within the context of a system dominated by non-elected, patriarchal structures. The flurry of compromises aimed at placating traditional leaders has … in turn compromised rural women's access and position, through the elevation of hereditary chieftainship to a privileged and protected position within local governance".[19]

GENDER-SENSITIVE INSTITUTIONAL INNOVATIONS IN LOCAL GOVERNMENT

Wherever women's access to local government has been promoted through affirmative action measures, non-governmental organizations (NGOs) have rushed to offer training programmes to build women leaders' capacity to engage in local decision making. These programmes make a valuable contribution to women councillors' assertiveness and ability to analyse policies; but they need to be complemented by a matching programme of institutional reorientation. A minimum programme for institutional reform in local government to enhance the capacities of women councillors might include:

- systems to ensure that the voice of women and other socially marginalized groups is weighted effectively against the interests of more powerful groups
- safeguards on poverty-sensitive or gender-sensitive spending
- effective means of enabling women councillors and women local residents to engage in participatory budgeting, planning and auditing, to see that funds that have been committed for gender-equity and pro-poor efforts are spent properly
- incentives to encourage bureaucrats and elected officials to respond to the concerns of disadvantaged groups and women.

Any such programme would presuppose that decentralization has devolved to local authorities a degree of financial autonomy, access to sufficient revenue to make an impact on local development, and planning powers. However, this might not be the case. Local governments have access to revenue from local sources (such as taxation, service charges and duties), and other sources (state or central government grants, and sometimes external aid); but there is tremendous variation across countries and within federal states in the levels of revenue that local governments enjoy. In many cases, their decision-making powers over local spending are severely constrained. Local governments also vary in their mandates to design spending plans for local services, amenities and social programmes.

There is also considerable variation in the degree of control that local authorities have over lower-level personnel in line ministries.

ENABLING WOMEN'S VOICES TO BE HEARD

The extent to which local governments acknowledge unequal participation by women and other marginalized groups and try to compensate for it varies very widely around the world. In the Indian system of local government, the *gram sabha*, or village assembly, is the arena for participation in planning. Indian states differ in their regulations for membership and quorums in these assemblies, but some have tried to remedy deficits in women's participation. In Madhya Pradesh, a quorum at a *gram sabha* meeting is not reached until one-third of the people assembled are women. In Rajasthan, a similar provision requires that women must be present in the village assembly in the same proportions that they are found in the local community—that is, at least 50 per cent.

Women may be present in councils and village assemblies yet may not feel free to voice their views. The Indian state of Kerala has instituted additional measures to elicit women's views on local planning. About 10 percent of the local budget is ring-fenced for "Women's development", and decisions about the allocation of these funds must be taken by all-women subgroups in the special *gram sabha* annual planning meeting. A further measure is designed to make local planning fora less intimidating and more accessible to women. Legal recognition has been given to smaller assemblies, both at ward level and among even smaller neighbourhood units of around 50 households. These are somewhat better suited to women's participation than the much larger *gram sabhas*; they are less intimidating and address locality-specific problems, enabling women to take active decision-making roles.

Reviews of local spending

In decentralization processes everywhere, the function or power most weakly institutionalized is that of monitoring and auditing local spending. In India, each state's Local Government Act has made some provision for the "watchdog" role of the village assembly in supervising and monitoring the village *panchayat*. In most states village assemblies are empowered, on paper, to examine annual statements of accounts and audit reports. But this audit function is vague: there is no assertion of the power of village assemblies to audit actual spending through certification of expenditure or to ensure propriety in financial dealings. Thus there are few known cases of the gram sabha seriously challenging spending decisions.

A more structured approach to participatory reviews of spending has evolved in Brazilian municipalities. This was pioneered in 1988 when the *Partido dos Trabalhadores* (PT) introduced participatory municipal budgeting in Porto Alegre and Belo Horizonte. Participatory municipal budgeting gives citizens' neighbourhood associations a direct say in how local funds are spent. Their roles in monitoring the execution of public works, and in reviewing expenditures, are both institutionalized. The annual budgeting exercise involves citizen representation on sectoral committees in their neighbourhoods to establish spending priorities for amenities such as paved roads, drainage, sewerage and school construction. Two huge open assemblies are held annually, one to review spending on the previous year's budget, the second to elect representatives from each city zone to the Participatory Budget Council. Members of this Council, which includes senior municipal officials, are responsible for compiling the municipal budget.

During the 1990s participatory budgeting produced much greater equity in the distribution of public funds.[20] Between 1989 and 1996 the proportion of households in Porto Alegre with access to piped water rose from 80 to 98 per cent; those served by the municipal sewerage system rose from 46 to 85 per cent, and the number of children enrolled in public schools doubled.[21] Levels of popular participation have grown over time, with previously powerless and marginal groups making up at least half if not more of the regional assemblies. However, women are still not represented at the top decision-making levels of the neighbourhood committees that they otherwise dominate.[22]

Gender budgeting at local level

Gender-sensitive local budget analysis is a new tool with which feminist groups have recently been building the capacities of local councillors. Its use at local level is still in its infancy, not least because many local governments rely upon transfers from the centre to finance essential services, and therefore make few spending decisions of their own. In Uganda and South Africa gendered local budget analysis is pursued through feminist NGOs: the Forum for Women in Democracy in Uganda and the Women's Budget Initiative in South Africa.[23] Some progress has been made in South Africa towards raising awareness of the impact of local government spending on programmes relating to women. This has involved informing women about local government revenues and expenditures, and highlighting the types of resource allocation that promote gender equality.[24]

Gender-sensitive local budget analysis has exposed a key constraint on building accountability to women in rural areas: the perception that women contribute little to local revenues and therefore deserve little say in their expenditure. In Uganda, a form of poll tax, a vestige of the colonial "hut tax", is collected from men, although the payments may actually be taken from the income earned by women in the household. Other methods for raising local revenue, for instance in service cost recovery, have gender-specific impacts. User fees for health, education or water supply connections affect women if they are the family members chiefly responsible for generating funds to pay for basic services.[25] Low-income women are particularly affected by the imposition of licences and taxes for informal entrepreneurial activity, such as street trade or market stalls. Although in urban areas African women see themselves as taxpayers and as entitled to know how their taxes are used, in rural areas women may not be seen as taxpayers in their own right. Efforts by women to ensure that revenue is collected and spent in certain ways may not be accepted as an appropriate focus for women's participation.[26]

Innovations in local governance should amplify women's voice in local deliberations, support spending on women's needs, and build the capacity of women councillors to uncover fraud or failure to match commitments with spending. However, insufficient attention has been paid to entrenched attitudes among local government bureaucrats. Village accountants, land registration officials, officials in charge of local common property resources such as forests and water, tend to resist the transfer of authority from their line ministries to elected local councillors; these may seem to them to be socially inferior, technically ill-equipped for decision making, and to be assuming responsibilities rightfully their own. In some contexts these officials reserve special contempt for women councillors, whose authority they may undermine by refusing to co-operate with them.

WOMEN'S IMPACT ON LOCAL DECISION MAKING

In spite of the significant obstacles to women's local political effectiveness, there is evidence from decentralization experiments around the world that women councillors and residents do manage to articulate priorities in local planning and decision making that differ from those of men. In Rajasthan, women councillors and leaders have been increasingly vocal in articulating women's perspectives in matters such as access to water, fuel and health care.[27] They are also active over such practices such as the illegal privatization of the commons by encroachment and tree-felling; these are often important sources of illicit

"rents" for *panchayat* officials. Evidence from a few all-women *panchayats* in Maharashtra, Karnataka, Madhya Pradesh and West Bengal shows that women have introduced shifts in local spending, prioritizing land transfers to women, water supply issues, and toilets for women in low-caste areas.[28]

Two systematic studies of the relationship between women's stated priorities and actual spending patterns in village councils led by women in West Bengal and Rajasthan suggest that, despite the handicaps they may face in terms of education and prior experience, and the preconception that they will provide weak leadership, women have a real impact on policy decisions.[29] These studies found an unambiguous association between women's stated spending priorities—drinking water and roads—and changed levels of spending, as shown in figure 12.2. In both states, women expressed more interest in drinking water facilities than men, and spending shifted—even if only a little in the Rajasthan case—to reflect their priorities. Another review, this time of the quality of services under the supervision of *panchayats* led by women, found that drinking water supply services were generally better, and that women councillors were less likely to demand bribes from contractors. Unfortunately, the review also found that residents in these *panchayats* were less likely to be satisfied with the service.[30] Even when objective measurements demonstrated the superiority of councils run by women in delivering certain services, they were held to harsh standards of performance.

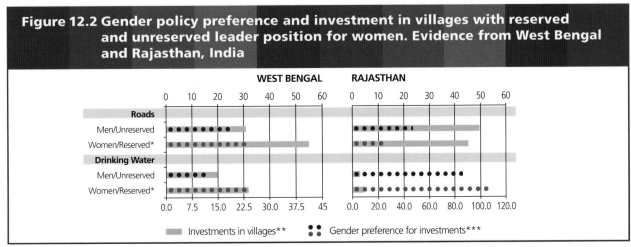

Figure 12.2 Gender policy preference and investment in villages with reserved and unreserved leader position for women. Evidence from West Bengal and Rajasthan, India

Notes: * Villages (*gram panchayats*) with leader position (*Pradhan*) reserved for women. ** For the year 2002. The indicators for investment used were: for roads, condition of roads (100 if good); for drinking water, number of drinking water facilities built or repaired (bottom axis). *** Percentage of issues raised in the previous six months (among the total number of issues raised by women or by men); information collected in 2000 (top axis).
Source: Chattopadhyay and Duflo 2004.

POLITICAL REPRESENTATION: THE PROMISE FOR WOMEN

Local government will be the political arena of women's participation to watch over the next decade. In spite of the formidable obstacles women face in gaining a presence in local government bodies and gaining a hearing for their major concerns, there is no question that in some contexts they are having an impact, and that this impact is being reflected increasingly in local spending patterns. Conflicts over local resource access may well intensify in coming years, but the numbers of women councillors defending women's interests will increase also.

There is ample evidence to show, as the studies drawn upon have done, that women-responsive politics and policy making require changes to the conduct of politics and systems of governance that reach beyond simply putting more women in office. Strong and autonomous women's movements are needed to debate priorities, to legitimize feminist policy demands, and press them upon political parties and government leaders at both national and transnational levels. Public institutions such as social service bureaucracies, public expenditure, audit and judicial systems have still a long way to go in developing sensitivity to women's needs and to gender equity. Women legislators alone cannot compensate for gender-specific accountability failures in governance systems.

There is still much research to be done on the policy impact of women in pubic office in developing countries. Although

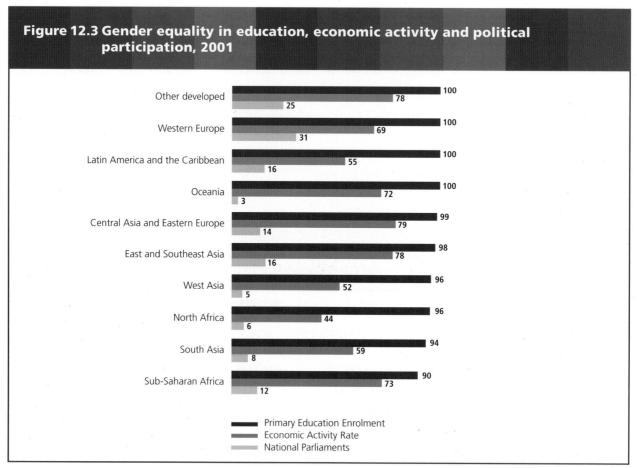

Figure 12.3 Gender equality in education, economic activity and political participation, 2001

Region	Primary Education Enrolment	Economic Activity Rate	National Parliaments
Other developed	100	78	25
Western Europe	100	69	31
Latin America and the Caribbean	100	55	16
Oceania	100	72	3
Central Asia and Eastern Europe	99	79	14
East and Southeast Asia	98	78	16
West Asia	96	52	5
North Africa	96	44	6
South Asia	94	59	8
Sub-Saharan Africa	90	73	12

Notes: All indicators are measured as female to male ratios, including "National Parliaments", where the ratio calculated was the number of female to male members. Hence, a ratio of 100 means perfect equality among genders.

Sources: Calculated from UN Statistical Division 2004; UNDP 2003.

male bias in governance institutions can act as a counterweight to the efforts of women in office, the main drivers of gender-equity policy agendas around the world have been women's political engagement and civil society activism. This is reason enough to pursue gender parity in politics with more vigour. A lot remains to be done. Whereas gender disparities in primary education and economic activity have been substantially reduced, gender disparities in formal politics remain striking, as figure 12.3 shows.

Figure 12.3 is a sobering reminder that the successful integration of larger numbers of women in politics remains exceptional; these are inspirational cases that do not yet indicate a trend. Finding ways of increasing women's participation in public life—as elected representatives, as executive appointees, and in the rank-and-file of public service bureaucracies, from the police to the education system—remains a priority. And even then, it will not on its own necessarily result in women-friendly public policies. The accountability of public and private power holders to women must be improved, and institutional frameworks reshaped to be more responsive to the needs of women and to the expression of demands by women activists inside and outside the formal machinery of government and political life.

Notes

1 Molyneux 2004:16.
2 Beall 2004:4.
3 UCLG 2003.
4 Massolo 2004:25.
5 Hubbard 2001:11; Bauer 2004.
6 Beall 2004:15.
7 Bauer 2004.
8 Beall 2004:17.
9 Ahikire 2003.
10 Tamale 1999.
11 AnanthPur 2004.
12 Chattopadhyay and Duflo 2004:984.
13 Buch 2000.
14 Vijayalakshmi 2002:18.
15 Vijayalakshmi and Chandrashekar 2001.
16 *EPW* 1995:5335.
17 Beall 2004.
18 Mbatha 2003.
19 Beall 2004:19–20.
20 Avritzer 2000:19.
21 World Bank 2001b.
22 Abers 1998:530; Avritzer 2000:14–15.
23 Beall 2004:31.
24 Budlender 1999; Coopoo 2000; Beall 2004:31.
25 Budlender 1999:21.
26 Beall 2004:31.
27 Mayaram 2000.
28 Kaushik 1996: 93–6.
29 Chattopadhyay and Duflo 2004: 984.
30 Topalova 2003.

Section 4
Gender, armed conflict and the search for peace

A WOMAN SALVAGES
BELONGINGS FROM THE
WRECKAGE OF HER HOUSE
DESTROYED DURING CONFLICT.
GROZNY, CHECHEN REPUBLIC,
RUSSIAN FEDERATION

Some of the armed conflicts and states of pervasive violence that proliferated unexpectedly after the end of the Cold War have abated in the 10 years since 1995, but others continue in as brutal a form. To these are added the acts of multilateral military intervention under US leadership which, since 9/11, have been justified within the framework of a worldwide "war on terror". These new types of war, associated less with formal battlefield confrontations than with the breakdown of order, livelihood systems and social norms have particular impacts for women, both in their persons and in their socially constructed roles.

During the past 10 years, the recognition in the early 1990s of sexual assault as a weapon of war and a crime against humanity has been further concretized in international humanitarian law; a few cases have even been successfully prosecuted in postwar tribunals associated with Rwanda and former Yugoslavia. At the same time, increasing attention has focused on women's roles in conflict resolution and peace building, and in helping bring into being the transitional or "new" institutions of state emerging in the postconflict environment. Much needs to be done to consolidate a "gender-friendly" peace, so that women are not forced back into the very roles and disadvantages that were part of the social and political circumstances out of which armed confrontation originally emerged.

The first chapter in this section, "The impacts of conflict on women", examines the multiple and sometimes contradictory ways in which women are affected by armed conflict, while the second chapter, "After conflict: women, peace building and development", looks at the challenges of postwar peace building as well as the potential for positive change in women's ability to seek justice and exercise rights.

Chapter 13
The impacts of conflict on women

Ten years after the Beijing Conference, the world is still enduring an epidemic of armed violence, with 19 major conflicts[1] and many more smaller-scale violent confrontations ongoing in different parts of the globe. Although the number of major conflicts is lower than in most of the years since the end of the Cold War, the decline in armed confrontation and warfare optimistically anticipated at the beginning of the 1990s has never effectively materialized. Some wars have ended; however, not only do many continue, but the changed circumstances wrought by the 11 September 2001 attacks on the United States and the subsequent "war on terror" appear to have left the world more prone to unpredictable armed violence than before. The problems of addressing the causes and implications of conflict in the lives of ordinary people, including and especially women, have accordingly become more complex.

The end of the Cold War saw changes in the forms and arenas of armed violence. Some conflicts or armed political confrontations earlier fuelled by the global competition for strategic allies between the two superpowers of East and West came to a negotiated end. However, new wars were also unleashed by the relaxation of controls held in place by the long era of superpower stand-off, such as those in the former Yugoslavia. Several ongoing conflicts—Kashmir, Sudan, Democratic Republic of Congo (DRC)—are holdovers from the postcolonial period, continuing in new mutations. Yet others derive from internal contest over territory or resources between local clan or ethnic leaders, as in Burundi, Somalia and Indonesia; or are armed insurrections against the state, whose fortunes ebb and flow but which fail to reach a conclusive end, as in Sri Lanka, Chechen

Republic and Colombia. Most of these conflicts are internal or "civil" wars: only two of the 19 major conflicts underway in 2003 were interstate (the US/UK-led invasion of Iraq, and India–Pakistan over Kashmir); but interference or involvement from external powers or interests is common (see figure 13.1).

The dissolution of the Union of Soviet Socialist Republics (USSR) led to a reduction in the prospects of mighty clashes between organized national armies using sophisticated aerial, battlefield and nuclear weapons; this was the image of war which dominated most of the 20th century, with guerrilla warfare emerging more strongly in the Viet Nam war and African liberation struggles. Subsequent geopolitical developments, including the rise of US unilateralism, have opened the door to new kinds of external military interventions: onslaughts from the air against a nonconformist or outcast state, or military invasions whose nominal purpose is to end gross violations of human rights or restore order. The complex crises of the 1990s and early 2000s have witnessed the evolution of comprehensive external interventions, often under the rubric of UN peace building. Their objectives—peace, stability, development and accountable governance—have become steadily more ambitious, wide-ranging and trusteeship-like than in the past; the 2002 intervention in Afghanistan is a classic example.[2] These interventions, often with the involvement of forces from many nations in military and nonmilitary roles, is yet another important element in the confusing picture of today's conflict and postconflict situations.

At stake in today's wars are not only territories, but ethnic and religious identities, control over natural resources such as oil and minerals, and control over lucrative and sometimes illicit

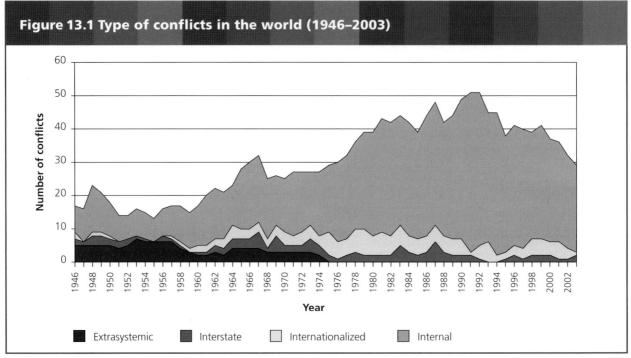

Figure 13.1 Type of conflicts in the world (1946–2003)

Note: Extrasystemic armed conflict occurs between a state and a non-state group outside its own territory. Interstate armed conflict occurs between two or more states. Internationalized internal armed conflict occurs between the government of a state and internal opposition groups with intervention from other states. Internal armed conflict occurs between the government of a state and internal opposition groups without intervention from other states.

Source: UCDP/PRIO 2004.

trade, such as in drugs and arms. Tensions have been exacerbated by economic crises and their accompanying social distress; growing wealth gaps between regions and nations; and the weakness of state institutions in the face of impoverishment and civil unrest. A common feature is the assertion of ethnic, religious and racial allegiance, overlaying political and economic malaise. In a world in which the balance of power is lopsided, and where many people feel economically or politically vulnerable, these bonds of common identity often provide a powerful mobilizing force.

In the playing-out of these forces, women's role is subsidiary to that of men, since their influence over power structures and decision-making leadership is minimal. They occasionally gain an emblematic prominence in exceptional guises, such as suicide bombers or "mothers of martyrs" (the two may even be combined). But as a group, women's explicit role in waging war and influencing military outcomes is marginal, even if a few have exercised important influences on their commander-spouses,

privately, behind the scenes. They have also been important as cheerleaders, challenging men to behave courageously in battle, and helping to shape notions of honour and masculinity by conferring female approval on the warlike male.

WARFARE AND WOMEN

When contrasting today's wars with those of previous generations, it is common to cite the statistic that whereas 80–90 per cent of casualties in the First World War were military, around 90 per cent of the victims of today's conflicts are civilian, of whom the majority are women and children.[3] Although the accuracy of these statistics is questionable, and it is probable that there is some confusion between "casualties" and "victims", they do indicate important changes in the way war is experienced by ordinary people, by men and women alike but especially by women (see box 13.1).

The distinction between a "war front" on some distant battlefield exclusively occupied by men, and a "home front" where women carry on daily life as closely as possible to "normal", if it was ever accurate, has eroded.[4] No longer is there a separate sphere where women are kept away from hideous sights, carefully cocooned with children and dependants to mind the hearth while husbands, fathers and sons face the heat of battle. War can permeate whole areas and embrace their entire populations, or can persist in alternating high-intensity and low-intensity forms as "fronts" move unpredictably through contested terrain. These situations may last years or even decades, waxing and waning as different parties enter the fray or different armed groups achieve temporary ascendancy.

Conflict zones in today's wars embrace homes, markets, cafés, workplaces, trains, theatres, temples and schools: almost nowhere can be considered a reliable safe haven. Just as the venue of war has become diffuse, so have the actors. National armies—in which women are present in numbers that are small but larger than they used to be—still play an important role, especially in external interventions. But many wars are fought by informal fighting forces rather than organized armies. Their active perpetrators comprise a variety of state and nonstate actors, including private militias, paid mercenaries and criminal groups, indicating a "privatization" of violence.[6] For example, in the battle for autonomy in the state of Kashmir in India, at least a hundred different groups are now engaged in fighting the Indian State, some also fighting each other.[7]

The degree to which women play a role in these informal fighting forces varies greatly; but the idea of their total absence from the battlefield is now discredited. Feminist researchers have identified active participation by women in wars historically, not only as camp followers, carers and providers, but as

---

Box 13.1 Data on women affected by armed conflict

There is relatively little sex-disaggregated data on the impacts of armed conflict; and indeed the difficulty of collecting data in any conflict zone means that there is usually little dependable data at all. A recent review of conflict-associated mortality and injury data by World Health Organization (WHO) experts and others points out that information services break down during warfare, and uncertainty prevails concerning death and disability statistics.[5] Situations are fluid, populations ebb and flow rapidly according to events, security is limited, and priorities for relief personnel lie elsewhere. For these reasons, surveys cannot be undertaken; those that do exist are limited to particular populations in special circumstances, and do not form a reliable basis for extrapolation. Reported figures of deaths from conflict or conflict-related causes are therefore always estimates and may be biased; all data of this kind is politically charged and may have been developed for propaganda purposes. Statistics such as that 80 per cent of camp populations are women and children, or that indirect deaths from war are in a ratio of 9:1 to direct deaths, are not based on empirical evidence and should be treated with caution.

WHO is now attempting to improve methods of assessing mortality, disability and morbidity in conflict and postconflict environments. UN bodies, as well as human rights organizations, are trying to assess levels of sexual violence against women, and to collect data among the populations of camps for the displaced and refugees. There is a growing recognition that women refugees have different needs and vulnerabilities than men, and that sex-disaggregated data, and information about female-headed households and family dependency within refugee populations, are important. The UN High Commissioner for Refugees (UNHCR) and key emergency relief non-governmental organizations (NGOs) attach a higher priority to refugee registration and documentation than in the past; without registration, refugees have no rights, effective protection and assistance is difficult to offer, and families cannot be reunited. WHO has also set up a database on violence against women and its effect on women's health, and is conducting a multicountry study, but the emphasis here is primarily on domestic violence.

Source: United Nations 2000b:156–7, 162–3.

combatants. More recently women have trained and fought as "freedom fighters", in Nicaragua, Viet Nam, Sri Lanka, South Africa and southern Sudan.[8] They also play important subsidiary roles in resistance movements and insurrections, acting as couriers and spies, providers of refuge and care for the injured. Sometimes they are acting in these supplementary military roles under coercion, but many female participants also sign up to a military life voluntarily.

Fighting methods

The means of fighting the wars of today also have strong social repercussions. Aerial bombardment invariably involves "collateral" deaths—of unarmed civilians, even if deliberate civilian onslaught from the air is now less common than in the first half of the 20th century. The spread of conflict has also been fuelled by the proliferation and bourgeoning worldwide trade in small arms. Around 1,250 companies in more than 90 countries (predominantly Europe and the United States) are currently producing small arms and light weapons.[9] Stockpiles of government-purchased small arms are vulnerable to looting and dispersal among the population, and may be sold on very cheaply. In 1997, the loss of control over Albanian arsenals led to an increase in the fighting in neighbouring Kosovo and Macedonia.[10] In 1991 in Somalia when the government collapsed, hundreds of thousands of firearms found their way into the hands of warring clans. In Iraq, in the wake of Saddam Hussein's defeat, civilians took possession of an estimated seven to eight million small arms; every household in Basra had up to four guns.[11]

The profusion of weapons makes possible the rise and sustenance of militias and gangs; these use them not only for shootouts, ambushes and obvious acts of war, but for criminal purposes, to settle old scores or carry out revenge killings. Where order has collapsed and the police force is unable to function, civilians are exposed to personal insecurity. Rape in wartime and related contexts often occurs under the threat of a gun.

Meanwhile some 100 million landmines are thought to be endangering life in different conflict terrains around the world. Not only do these cause death and maiming, they also put large

areas of agricultural and grazing land out of bounds. This means that women and girls going to the fields for work, or to collect fuel or water, are put at risk.[12] Terror tactics which create widespread fear, render land and homes unusable or uninhabitable, and which destroy sacred buildings and monuments, are all deployed in the new wars, made easier by the ready availability of small arms and explosives.[13]

The infestation of violence helps to foster fear, hatred and insecurity, brutalizing attitudes and damaging interpersonal relations. Ethnic or faith groups previously intermingled within communities and neighbourhoods, and within families by marriage across clans, communities or religions, are often forced by the diktat of local "commanders" into warring camps. The emotional hurt and psychological trauma stemming from the experience of atrocities at the hand of previous neighbours and friends reaches a level which is very difficult to cope with when "peace" is restored.[14] The descent into internecine clan war in Somalia forced many women who had married out of their clan to leave their husbands and children, and travel long distances to their fathers' or ancestral home areas for safety.[15] Relationships so sundered may be impossible to repair. Many mothers in exogenous marriages have lost their children for good, and as a result marriage in Somalia today is more often within the clan.

WOMEN AS DIRECT VICTIMS OF WAR

The violence of war and conflict affects everyone in its vicinity. These impacts are differentiated by many factors, in which age and gender loom large. While women are seldom among the instigators of wars and conflicts, they rank high among their victims, both in their own persons and in their socially constructed or gendered roles. Their experience of conflict tends to be markedly different from that of men, in the contexts of both agent and victim.

Until recently there has been a tendency to emphasize women's victim roles and downplay their agency; but the changing nature of conflict and the evaluation of contemporary warfare from a feminist perspective have begun to fill in a far more

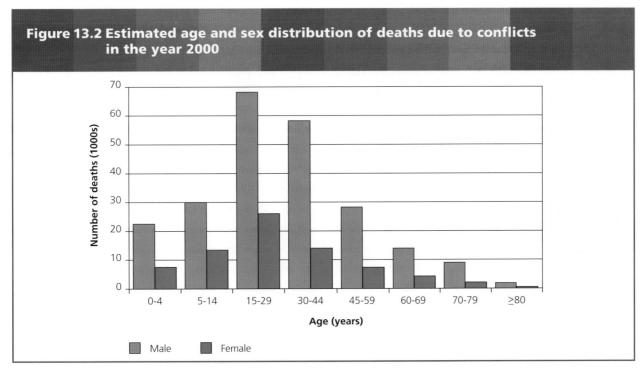

Figure 13.2 Estimated age and sex distribution of deaths due to conflicts in the year 2000

Source: Murray et al. 2002.

complex picture of women's activity in war and its implications for them. They are, in this view, both more actively involved and associated with defending the society at war and sustaining its fabric, and more openly exposed to its brutality, and sometimes complicit in it. The recognition that mass rape may be used as a "weapon of war", and that sexual assault is routine as a corollary of the fighting culture, has emphasized the direct vulnerabilities faced by women in situations of pervasive insecurity. These phenomena can be seen as symptoms of the generalized exposure to violence of entire populations.

Far from being protected or "immunized" by their feminine status, women may be especially targeted in the endemic violence that engulfs many theatres of fighting. In wars arising from social and economic inequality, identity or religious difference, women are assigned involuntarily to the side of the dispute to which they are deemed to belong by family, kin or faith, whether or not this reflects their personal sense of identity. The targeting of wives and children of fighting leaders for kidnap or assault has been routine historically. Cases have recently been reported in eastern DRC of women being buried alive by local villagers, ostensibly because they were believed to be witches, but actually because they provided food and medicine to armed groups the villagers did not support.[16] In conflict zones in sub-Saharan Africa and elsewhere, women face personal danger every day, as they scour the environment for food, water and fuel. In eastern DRC, a UN official reported to independent experts from the United Nations Development Fund for Women (UNIFEM): "Women take a risk when they go out to the fields or on a road to a market. Any day they can be stripped naked, humiliated and raped in public. Many people no longer sleep at home. Every night there is another village attacked, burned and emptied.... always they take women and girls away."[17]

Mortality and loss

The number of deaths among men is higher than those among women, as is shown by figure 13.2. However, deaths among women from injury are higher than might be expected. In 2000 alone, conflicts are estimated to have resulted in 310,000 deaths by injury, with more than half taking place in sub-Saharan Africa, one-fifth in Southeast Asia, and the rest in the Balkans, Central Asia and the Middle East.[18] While the highest mortality rates were among men aged 15–44, a quarter of direct mortality was among women, with the highest number being among women between the ages of 15–29 (26,000 dying of direct causes).

Thus the region where women suffered worst was in sub-Saharan Africa; in this region, where the brutal and vicious forms of violence experienced by rural people has been exceptional and a cause of special concern,[19] sudden raids and attacks on villages are a common pattern. This puts women especially at risk, as times when the men are absent may be chosen deliberately as good moments to launch an assault. This is indicated by the testimony of many survivors of attacks on villages in West Darfur, Sudan in a study undertaken by Amnesty International in early 2004. One stated: "Only women and children were in the village, the men were with the cattle a bit further north, closer to the hills. When the attack occurred, men ran up the hills in order to see and the women ran into the village to take their children and flee south of the village." [20]

A high proportion of deaths also transpire as a consequence of flight and population disruption. As was noted earlier, one estimate of deaths in war suggests that there are nine indirect deaths for every direct death, among which women and children constitute a high proportion; however, like almost all war-related statistics, there is no empirical basis for this figure.[21] These are deaths from hunger, exposure, exhaustion, infection or epidemic disease, or some combination of these exacerbated by injury or trauma. The mortality rate among war-torn populations is much higher than usual. When civil war restarted in Congo in late 1998, a third of Brazzaville's population—about a quarter of a million people—fled into the forests, where they remained trapped for several months without access to aid. Their death rates soared to five times the level regarded as the emergency "alert threshold".[22]

Estimates by the International Rescue Committee in DRC show that between August 1998 and April 2001, there were 2.6 million excess deaths in the five eastern provinces where armed groups were attacking one another. Of these, 350,000 were directly caused by violence, 40 per cent of which were among women and children; the remaining excess deaths were from disease and malnutrition.[23]

Widowhood

While their survival chances from injury may be higher, women have to absorb the loss of husbands, fathers and sons with all the attendant emotional and psychological pain, and cushion the effects of loss for other dependent family members, including children. Demographic estimates suggest that up to 30 per cent of the population in war-torn societies may be widows.[24] The predicament of war widows can be acute. They are strongly associated with the increase in female heads of household common during war;[25] but they can face particular difficulties compared with those whose male partners or household members have temporarily departed to fight, or have disappeared or been detained. Support from the family may traditionally depend on reassignment as an extra wife to a brother or other family male; a life at the economic margins may be the only alternative. In places where widows can own or access land they may be forced to sell it if they are cash-constrained and thus unable to hire labour and purchase inputs. Issues relating to female land ownership and access are highly significant in postwar settlements (see chapter 14).

That there is such a large number of widows in a population engulfed in conflict may relieve the individual effects of stigmatization, where that is traditionally felt; widows may even manage to change social attitudes towards them and wring concessions from the authorities. However, widows' needs for economic and social support might not be met willingly. Even in countries where pensions and benefits are theoretically in place, they might be denied or difficult to access. In situations where the husband has disappeared without trace, this problem can be compounded. In the northern Indian state of Kashmir, there are large numbers of women who are known as "half widows". These women are not able to produce proof of a vanished male provider in the form of a dead body or some other formally accepted evidence. In such cases the woman is not technically considered a widow, a status that would qualify her to receive certain kinds of state assistance.[26]

The experience of war widows is not invariably negative. Tamil war widows in Sri Lanka have shown a courageous independence of action and become a "liberated" group within a highly conservative society. A Sri Lankan study describes a generation of widowed women as: "challenging conventional Hindu constructions of widowhood as a negative and polluting condition which bars their participation in many aspects of community life." [27] These women have redefined what it means to be without a spouse in the South Asian context; many have sought a newfound independence, access to the public world, and to employment if urban opportunities are within reach. Here is another example of the contradictory experience of war for some women: a triumph of social transformation stemming from predicaments of extreme distress.

Targeted sexual assault

I was sleeping when the attack on Disa started. I was taken away by the attackers, they were all in uniforms. They took dozens of other girls and made us walk for three hours. During the day we were beaten and they were telling us: "You, the black women, we will exterminate you, you have no god." At night we were raped several times. The Arabs guarded us with arms and we were not given food for three days.

A refugee from West Darfur Sudan, interviewed in Goz Amer camp, Chad, May 2004 [28]

The use of sexual violence in armed conflict has been recorded since ancient times, but it has recently gained a much higher profile. Evidence exists for sexual assaults on a wide scale in postcolonial conflicts. During the Partition of the Indian subcontinent into India and Pakistan in 1947, an estimated 100,000 women were raped, abducted and forcibly married. [29] Rape was also used strategically in Korea during the Second World War, and in Bangladesh during the 1971 war of independence. [30] However, it was not until the mass rape of women in Bosnia and Herzegovina received worldwide media attention in 1992, followed by that of between 250,000 and 500,000 women

during the Rwandan genocide in 1994, that rape was acknowledged as a weapon of war. Subsequently, far more official and unofficial reporting of war has focused on the issue of sexual violence, and it has emerged as a characteristic of hostilities in Afghanistan, Algeria, East Timor, Liberia, northern Uganda, Sudan, DRC, Somalia and elsewhere. Rape seems to be on the increase in conflict, [31] but such is the silence that has previously surrounded the issue that trends are difficult to assess.

The circumstances and forms of sexual violence are many and can be extreme. They include the rape and torture of women in front of their husbands; the use of rifle barrels and knives; attacks on pregnant women and their unborn foetuses; the mutilation of breasts and genital areas; and other horrors which women are barely able to confide. Some women and girls have endured repeated gang rapes; some have survived "rape camps" where they were imprisoned and suffered systematic sexual assault. [32] Rape used in this way demeans and humiliates not only the woman herself but the people or clan to whom she belongs. In Rwanda and the former Yugoslavia, rape was used as a strategy to subvert community bonds and even as a tool of "ethnic cleansing". [33] The violation of women's bodies, and of their sexuality and reproductive functions, in this way becomes an extension of the battlefield.

For the women victims, the impact might not only be physically and psychologically devastating, but lead to divorce, family rejection or social ostracism. In many cultures rape is deeply shameful for the woman and polluting for her family. Somali women do not confess to having been raped because social rejection and divorce will follow. Palestinian women resistance fighters who have been imprisoned have been rejected by their communities upon release, whether or not they have actually been violated. Some Iraqi women victims of rape, or women who have been imprisoned and assumed to have been violated by their captors, have subsequently been divorced or even killed. [34]

A study in Sierra Leone carried out by Physicians for Human Rights estimated that war-related sexual violence had been suffered by 11 per cent of female household members; 8 per cent reported rape, but a number of others reported abduction, and/or became pregnant or experienced vaginal bleeding, pain, swelling or had some kind of sexually-transmitted infection

Box 13.2   Rape as a tool of Somali clan conflict

Between 1991 and 1994 thousands of Somali women were subject to rape and assault as a component of interclan conflict. These atrocities were unprecedented in Somali history. Traditionally, feuding and conflict in Somali pastoral society were bounded by social codes which protected women, the elderly, the sick and children from attack, or at least ensured retribution. These rules were abandoned during the conflicts which erupted in 1991, in which women and other nonfighters were attacked with impunity by militias and individuals, a cause of profound and lasting shock to Somali women.

Many women escaped to Kenya where sexual violence continued in the refugee camps in which they took shelter. Here, since they constituted 80 per cent of camp populations, they were insecure and exposed to attack by marauding groups of Somali gunmen (*shifta*). Human rights activists uncovered assaults on a large scale, and UNHCR undertook a full investigation. The following is an excerpt from one of the interviews conducted in the camps with 192 rape survivors.

In July 1992 nine *shifta* (bandits) with guns came into my house at night. They were wearing black trousers, black jackets and hats pulled low. I did not know them. They all had guns and big boots like soldiers. They pulled my arms behind my back and tied my hands. They told me not to scream and pushed knives into my upper arms and head. They kicked me with their boots. They told me to give them all the money I had. I traded at the market during the day and they must have followed me to know where I stay. After they tied and cut me I gave them the money which I had buried in a safe place. Then three of the men caught me and dragged me into my house and raped me. One man raped me while another held a gun at my head and told me he would kill me if I made a noise. My daughter of 10 years woke up and cried and they beat her on the head with guns. Up to today she has [mental] problems. I tried to shout but the *shiftas* shot in the air and so people ran away.

Source: Musse 2004.

(STI), indicating coercive sex to which they did not admit for fear of stigma. Most of these victims had been raped and one-third had been abducted; some had been forcibly married, and a few had become pregnant.[35]

According to a report commissioned by the Reproductive Health for Refugees Consortium, estimates of war-related rape and sexual assault in Kosovo ranged from 10,000 to 30,000. However international health and human rights organisations including the Centers for Disease Control, the Organisation for Security and Cooperation in Europe and Human Rights Watch have been unable to verify the actual number.[36] Such is the "metallic silence" and taboo on rape that very few cases were ever reported. It is common for such pregnancies to come to term without medical help, in Kosovo as in Liberia, Bosnia and Sierra Leone; many mothers are subsequently outcast by their families, as are the children.

Forced marriage and sexual slavery

Populations in areas ravaged by war, where previously strong social norms of protection for the defenceless can no longer be relied upon, are very conscious of the threat to women's honour. In Afghanistan, where civil war has continued for over two decades, households which previously sent young daughters away to marry a kinsman in another region because of fear of possible abduction or forced marriage by the Taliban, have adopted this course of action as a protective strategy against the predations of young armed men forcibly taking brides.[37]

There is evidence from other conflict zones that parents try to pre-empt sexual assault on their daughters by marrying them off at a very early age; or they may resort to the "sale" of a young daughter into marriage as assets become depleted.[38] In camps for the displaced in Burundi, for example, surveys showed that

55 per cent of girls married at an earlier age than before; in the troubled countryside, the figure was 18 per cent.[39] Somali refugees from minority communities reported that girls as young as 13 were forcibly abducted, and married to militia "commanders"; such marriages may be arranged with families as the price of a family's "protection".[40] The UN Special Rapporteur on violence against women reported in 1998 that forced marriage and forced prostitution were among the human rights violations perpetrated by the Indonesian security forces in East Timor.[41]

Sexual slavery, or keeping women in captivity to provide sexual services to soldier combatants, is another abuse of women during conflict. "Comfort women" were forcibly recruited from Malaysia, Indonesia and Korea by the Japanese army during the Second World War, and have since unsuccessfully sought reparations from Japan. In northern Uganda, a systematic campaign of abduction and kidnap of girls by the Lord's Resistance Army (LRA) has been underway since the mid-1990s. The abductees are known as "wives" or "helpers", but are used as sexual and domestic slaves. They are allocated to soldiers as a reward for good performance, a source of prestige and a proof of status: the higher the rank within the LRA, the greater the number of allocated "wives". When those who escaped were medically examined, nearly 100 per cent had STIs.[42]

Other sex-associated vulnerabilities

All conflict zones show a marked increase of STIs and often of HIV/AIDS. The high rate of STIs is caused by the sexually predatory behaviour of soldiers, local marauders, militiamen and also of peacekeeping forces. The Joint United Nations Programme on HIV/AIDS (UNAIDS), which focuses on soldiers as one of many groups at risk of STIs including HIV, states that STI infection rates among armed forces are generally two to five times higher than in civilian populations, but that in time of conflict, the difference can be 50 times higher or more.[43] There are many instances where HIV has appeared on an epidemic scale in a civilian population after the presence of an army in the vicinity, either encamped or passing through. In Rwanda in 1992, infection patterns of HIV were high in urban areas (27 per cent of pregnant women attending antenatal clinics) but only 1 per cent in rural areas. By 1997, the demographic upheaval following the 1994 genocide had led to near-equivalence of urban and rural rates.[44] Since health data are difficult to collect in conflict zones, the association between HIV spread and conflict is difficult to show categorically, but it is fairly widely accepted. In Rwanda, infection with HIV during rape was an expressed intention of some Interahamwe militias.[45]

Box 13.3 Abducted girl mothers and babies

In Northern Uganda and Sierra Leone, girls who have been kidnapped to be used as forced wives of bush "commanders", and become mothers of their babies, are highly vulnerable when they return to their communities. The children themselves are often stigmatized, lack basic health care, food, shelter and clothing; their mothers have difficulty providing for them, and attachment disorders between mothers and babies can affect their ability to thrive. On their return to their communities, the stigma involved in having given birth to the child of a rebel commander—a stigma even greater than that of having suffered sexual abuse—may lead the girls to hide and avoid attendance at clinics and programmes where their situation would be revealed. The babies may not be accepted in the communities, or even by the mothers: they are seen as the "rebels of tomorrow". A UNICEF/Government of Uganda psychosocial assessment team recorded many statements confirming these attitudes: "The young mothers do not like the unwanted babies; many of these mothers are young and want to go to school but they can't because of the kids. Flashback of their attacks torment many of these young mothers" (young man in Adjumani, northern Uganda, 1998).

Source: McKay and Mazurana 2004.

The problem of STIs in women is exacerbated by the prevalence of rape, and by the number of women who sell sex during times of severe distress as a means of survival. The demand for sexual services, especially in the presence of external armies or UN peacekeeping forces with money to spend, rises just at a time when there is acute need to find the wherewithal to live and keep a family going. A workshop on the social consequences of the peace-building process in Cambodia held in Geneva in 1992 pointed out that the growth of the "rest and recreation" industry had impacted on both women and children, with children increasingly being drawn into the sex trade.[46] The independent experts of UNIFEM, reporting in 2002, described this as a phenomenon in several conflict zones they visited, including DRC, Sierra Leone, Cambodia and former Yugoslavia. Radhika Coomaraswamy, the former UN Special Rapporteur on violence against women, has called on the United Nations to take active steps to prevent peacekeepers' involvement in sexual violence against women and punish it where it occurs.[47]

Although the definition of trafficking remains controversial, situations of war and conflict seem to be associated with an increase in trafficking of people, especially women and girls. This is partly because social upheaval and lack of functioning legal systems or law enforcement provide good cover for this lucrative trade; there is also an association between the destruction to economic life and the penury to which families are reduced, and their resort to drastic means of survival by trading themselves or their children. The lack of proper border controls during conflict has helped create an environment in which the trafficking of women has flourished.[48] The rate of trafficking is estimated to have risen 50 per cent between 1995 and 2000. Much of it derives from countries subject to turmoil and its attendant economic stress; the majority of trafficked persons are thought to be women, many destined for prostitution, according to the International Organization for Migration (IOM).[49] In war-torn Colombia, just as one example, an anti-trafficking organization believes that as many as 50,000 women are being trafficked annually out of the country (see also chapters 7 and 10 for an elaboration of the controversies surrounding human trafficking).[50]

WOMEN AS MILITARY PARTICIPANTS

Although armed violence is commonly regarded as a male preserve, women have long taken on active military roles in wars and revolutions. Their active role as fighters has received more attention in the recent past, especially since the advent of woman suicide bombers among the Liberation Tigers of Tamil Elam (LTTE) in Sri Lanka, in the Palestinian intifada, and among Chechen insurgents. Women performed as freedom fighters in the African liberation struggles of the 1970s and 1980s in Mozambique, Zimbabwe and Namibia; also in Nicaragua, Viet Nam, and in South Africa where they were trained and fought along with men in the African National Congress (ANC) forces.[51] Some women combatants are coerced into carrying arms or working for military commanders; yet others are inspired by identification with the cause in which war is being waged by kin and identity groups. Their participation is not limited to revolutionary and radical causes: chauvinist or nationalistic movements include women among their active members and principal cheerleaders. Women's agency in conflict situations can grow in a variety of different political contexts—democratic, revolutionary and authoritarian—and in strong as well as weak states.

A considerable amount of attention has been given in recent years to the recruitment and use of "child soldiers", both in organized forces and in militia bands. This has been made much easier by the development of light-weight, easy-to-use automatic weapons. Most of these child (under-18) soldiers are boys, but by no means all. Between 1990 and 2003, girls belonged to fighting forces in 55 countries, and took part in fighting in 38 of these countries where internal armed conflicts were underway.[52] Many were abducted and forced to serve as fighters, or in other roles; in the internal wars of Africa where girls' presence in armed groups is most common, the idea that many participate voluntarily is disputed since they may have no realistic alternative.

Women played a role as combatants and political supporters in the civil conflicts in the Central American countries of Guatemala, El Salvador and Nicaragua. At the height of the Sandinista effort to topple the regime of President Anastasio

Somoza in Nicaragua from 1977–9, women made up 25–30 per cent of the combatants;[53] in subsequent years, they continued to play a central role in the transition from armed struggle to governance. In El Salvador, where better statistics are available, the United Nations Observer Mission (ONUSAL) estimated that women made up 29 per cent of the combatants, and 37 per cent of the political cadres. In Guatemala, the Guatemalan *Unidad Revolucionaria Nacional Guatemalteca* (Guatemalan National Revolutionary Unity, or URNG) data show that women made up 15 per cent of the combatants and 25 per cent of the political cadres (see figures 13.3 and 13.4). Interestingly, women in Guatemala did better out of the peace settlement than did those in El Salvador, partly because the settlement came six years later and reflected the growing awareness of women's rights as well as civil society pressure.[54]

In the ongoing Maoist armed rebellion in Nepal, one-third of the guerilla cadres and around half of the middle-level leadership are believed to be female.[55] These figures are based on interviews with the Maoist leadership and anecdotal evidence and cannot be confirmed, but appear likely. Nepal is a poor, rural and mountainous country and the Maoist rebels are based in the poorest and most remote areas. Most rural areas contain few men, since they have migrated either to the capital, Kathmandu, in search of work, or to other towns and cities across the Indian border. Women are left behind to farm, maintain the family and somehow make ends meet. The state is virtually absent, and in many communities the Maoists are the only providers of administration, services or security that people know. It is therefore no surprise that their ideology is attractive, and that women, facing grinding poverty and hardship, enter the guerilla cadres and make a significant contribution to their numbers.

Cases of women participating in warfare as active supporters and provocateurs of fighting forces have also been reported from a number of countries, including northern Uganda and western Sudan. One example is the al Hakkamat of Darfur, who have a traditional role as praise-singers and cultural performers, as do women's groups in many countries of the region. In recent attacks carried out by the Janjaweed militia on local villages, Hakkamat have been reported as accompanying the male fighters, ululating and singing songs to encourage them,

declaring that local African villagers will be driven out and "our cattle will be in their land". According to testimonies collected by Amnesty International, Hakkamat women play the role of communicators during attacks and, although not actively involved in combat, participate in acts of looting; in some instances, they have been known to watch their men while they rape other women.[56]

WAR'S EFFECTS ON WOMEN AS SOCIAL ACTORS

During their course, and as a consequence of changes in ruling authorities and power relations, war transforms the way societies function in fundamental ways. Especially if they continue for a long period, they destroy the economy in the area they pervade, and alter its key structures, including the modes of livelihood, means of survival and active providers. These changes have important ramifications on gender relations. Women may on the one hand lose professional and business occupations and be plunged into poverty, as happened in Bosnia and Herzegovina; they may lose access to land, or to workable land, as in many African conflicts such as Angola, Rwanda and Uganda. On the other hand their efforts to survive may lead them into new ventures, and even—in the context of the international and non-governmental relief aid effort—give them training and access to jobs as teachers, health and social workers. Many feminist observers have pointed to a pattern of gaining social, economic and even political rights for the first time, even if this comes with the shouldering of burdens which are barely supportable.

In their caring roles as social providers, women also have to assume extra levels of responsibility; these come from the fact that they may be separated from their homes, and from other family members, especially men who normally act as principal providers, protectors and heads of household. Additional burdens may also derive from the collapse of services, especially of health services, in the fighting vicinity. The impacts of service loss may affect them personally, but it is primarily in their roles of carers for their children, for the elderly and infirm, for orphans or other family members entrusted to their care because of death or injury,

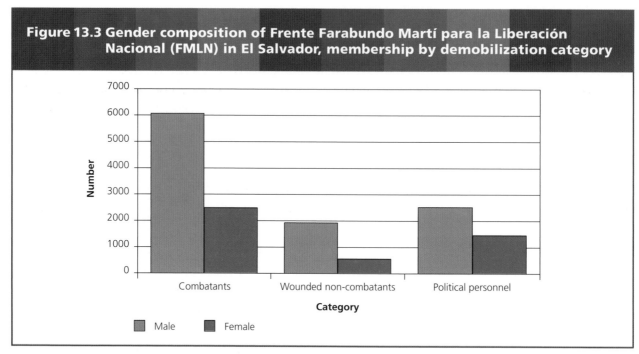

Figure 13.3 Gender composition of Frente Farabundo Martí para la Liberación Nacional (FMLN) in El Salvador, membership by demobilization category

Source: United Nations Observer Mission in El Salvador (ONUSAL) cited in Luciak 2004.

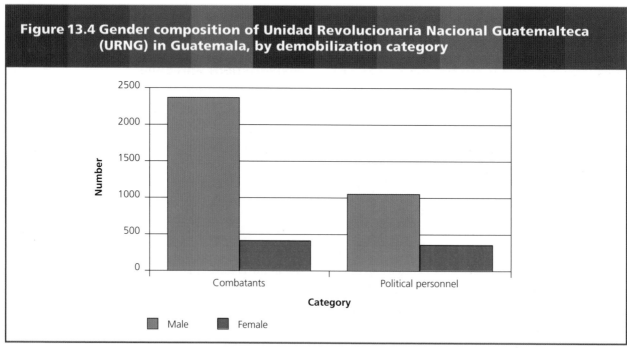

Figure 13.4 Gender composition of Unidad Revolucionaria Nacional Guatemalteca (URNG) in Guatemala, by demobilization category

Source: URNG 1997 cited in Luciak 2004.

that the lack of support mechanisms for daily life is particularly stressful. Epidemics of infectious disease or shortages of nutritious food cause the most havoc in small children; women and their older daughters have to carry the burden of disease and hunger in the family, seeking out relief feeding programmes and taking the children in; or else sustaining the responsibility for their loss.

The impact on health and health services

Women's own health is put at risk from heightened exposure to STIs, physical and psychological damage from rape, and from lack of reproductive care. They may have to give birth without medical assistance or in conditions of extreme distress, such as flight. The care of children and other family members who are sick or infirm is more difficult even than usual, and they also have to tend the injured. These functions often have to be carried out in circumstances where clinics have been destroyed and looted, health professionals have vanished, there is a general lack of medicine and equipment, and fighting may have put medical assistance beyond reach. A 1992 UNICEF report on the situation of Afghan women and children described how "A few women of the poor neighbourhood had assembled on the rooftops and were discussing health care facilities in the area.… The women were distraught with their daily problems of survival and were not able to talk about anything else." [57]

Their caring and family provision roles exert pressures on women which may have additional implications for their health. There is strong evidence that women frequently reduce their own food intake to protect the nutritional status of other family members, such as able-bodied men or children, depending on cultural norms. [58] In some conflict areas or in the exigencies of camps for the displaced, foods known as "famine foods" which are only consumed at times of severe food insecurity may be introduced into the diet. Such "famine crops" as cassava (eaten in West and Central Africa) have a poor nutritional content and require extra time and labour spent on preparation to ensure that toxicity is not a threat.

Doctors and medical personnel often flee as their conditions of work become dangerous. In Bosnia and Herzegovina, 40 per cent of physicians and 30 per cent of nurses left the country during the war. In Rwanda, over half the health workers were killed during the genocide, the infrastructure was destroyed and administrative capacities disrupted. [59] In Uganda, between 1972 and 1985 half of the doctors and 80 per cent of the pharmacists left the country. [60] In such circumstances, women are forced to devise their own health care systems and apply whatever remedies they know. Those who have had minimal experience as traditional birth attendants are called upon in refugee camps to assist in deliveries, and many become involved in trying to establish basic health facilities and other social services, such as children's feeding centres, psychosocial counselling services, and schools. [61] UNIFEM's independent experts enquiring into the consequences of war for women found a number of ways in which their sex and gender additionally compromised their state of health and access to services. [62]

Displacement and exile

We received an official document for refugees. They explained to us our status, rights and how to get help. That's the moment when I became aware of my loss. I lost my homeland and my personality.

A Bosnian woman refugee [63]

Populations are often forced to move en masse when violence and insecurity escalate. These moves, both internal, within the borders of the same country, or external, across national boundaries initially to neighbouring countries, are often devastating for those involved and put huge pressures on host populations and authorities. Those who move within their own countries are known as "displaced"; those who leave their countries and cross borders are designated "refugees". In some parts of the world, notably in parts of sub-Saharan Africa where national borders divide ethnically contiguous people, these designations are more bureaucratic than real. The figure of 80 per cent has been commonly cited as the proportion of women and children in refugee and displaced populations; recent analysis shows that the proportions of men and women above the age of 18 are approximately equal.[64] However, women make up a smaller proportion of asylum applicants: many are young males who leave refugee camps or their country of origin, leaving women to follow later.

According to UNHCR the numbers of those currently designated refugees rose from 2.4 million people in 1975 to 14.4 million people in 1995. By the end of 2003 the global refugee population had gone down to 9.7 million people.[65] The US Committee on Refugees, however, which includes the internally displaced in its calculations, estimated a rise from 22 million in 1980 to 38 million in 1995, of whom around 50 per cent were displaced.[66] One estimate of trends suggests that the number of refugees per conflict has roughly doubled since 1969, from 287,000 per conflict to 459,000 per conflict in 1992. The increase in internally displaced persons is higher, from 40,000 per conflict in 1969 to 857,000 per conflict in 1992.[67] UNHCR estimates that about half the world's refugees are women, and that they represent a higher proportion in the older age groups [68] (see figures 13.5 and 13.6).

Statistics mask the extent of human suffering endured by families broken apart, homes and belongings lost, older and younger family members unable to survive long and dangerous journeys, and lives repeatedly disrupted and remade. "In 1984 we were forced to flee. Myself, I took nothing thinking that we would return next day to peace and quiet. However, it lasted for months and months. In the country where we sought refuge, we suffered terribly—no house, no food, almost everyone was sick. Children were dying day by day," reported a refugee from Chad.[69] Refugees and the displaced are usually accommodated in camps, where conditions are cramped and unhygienic, food, water and medical assistance may be in short supply, and schooling and other services may not be available. However, it can also be the case that the camp is the first encounter for women in extremely poor countries, such as Afghanistan and Somalia, with modern medical and reproductive services,[70] and that women gain in literacy and personal empowerment:[71] the displacement experience cuts both ways.

The trauma of loss, anxieties concerning people, property and lands left behind, and the psychological effects of having witnessed slaughter and destruction, can take a heavy toll. The experience of being a refugee, with its inevitable dependency and sense of personal disempowerment, can cause serious depression. Camps for the displaced are also breeding grounds for disaffection and rage. They provide recruitment opportunities for agents of violence and terrorist groups; they can also lead to tension and conflict with host populations. Where women and children predominate in the camps, as is common in most African conflicts, women are also vulnerable to attacks from external bands of marauders, or from security personnel or refugee "commanders" within them. Their predicament was brought to international attention in 1993, when sexual atrocity on a shocking scale in camps sheltering Somali refugees in northern Kenya was brought to light by international human rights organizations and the UNHCR.[72] The need of women and girls for personal security in all refugee camps is now treated much more seriously.

The lack of privacy, the difficulties of managing children in camp conditions and of maintaining family health, the lack of hygiene and the personal insecurity exacerbate the difficulties of the refugee experience for women. Health-related problems can be compounded. A study of Somali refugees indicated that up to 70 per cent of women of reproductive age were anaemic, probably because of a lack of iron in the diet, or because of malaria which depletes the body's stores of iron.[73] Epidemics of diarrhoeal disease due to poor sanitation and inadequate water supplies are also common among camp populations. For example, among the 500,000 Rwandans who fled into DRC (then Zaire) in 1994, almost 50,000 died in the first month from diarrhoeal infections. The death rates were highest among children under five, and among women.[74]

Providers and workers

Within camps, the supply of food and other basic necessities is rarely regular or sufficient, and women may need to supplement it by selling keepsakes or establishing some kind of petty trading

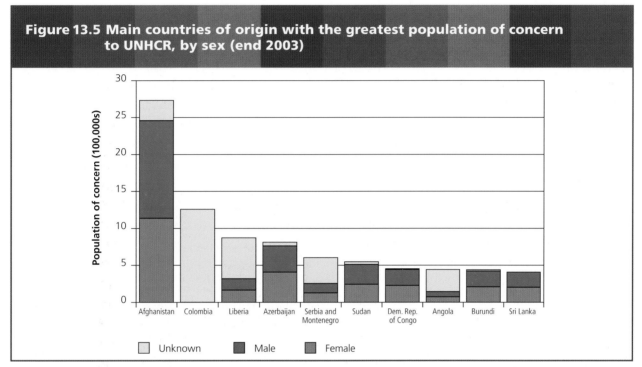

Figure 13.5 Main countries of origin with the greatest population of concern to UNHCR, by sex (end 2003)

Note: Population of Concern to UNHCR includes the 6 following categories: Refugees; Asylum-seekers; Returned refugees; Internally displaced persons (IDPs); Returned IDPs; Others of concern to UNHCR; Refugees/asylum-seekers; Various/unknown. The total population of concern from the main countries of origin does not necessarily represent their actual total number because data regarding some of the countries of residence are not available.

Source: UNHCR forthcoming.

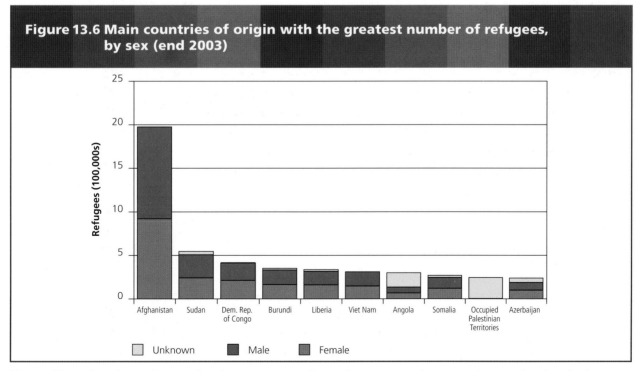

Figure 13.6 Main countries of origin with the greatest number of refugees, by sex (end 2003)

Note: The total population of concern from the main countries of origin does not necessarily represent their actual total number because data regarding some of the countries of residence are not available.

Source: UNHCR forthcoming.

concern. Women may also collect fuel or water for sale to others. There are many situations when local authorities—whether legal or de facto rulers—inhibit women's mobility and activities, or deny access to international organizations providing relief. In 1998, for example, the National Movement for the Total Independence of Angola (UNITA) launched a campaign of violence specifically intended to provoke civilian displacement from the countryside into the main cities; having herded over a million villagers into the cities of Huambo, Kuito and Malange, UNITA then cut off their access to food.[75] The war in Angola lasted for 27 years, ending only with the death of UNITA's leader, Jonas Savimbi in February 2002; the long narrative of warfare was studded with episodes of famine, civil distress and displacement, and women were driven to their limit in trying to provide for their families.

During the Soviet occupation of Afghanistan from 1979 to 1989, insurgency and counter-insurgency in the countryside ruined the rural economy, and—aided by the inducement of politically motivated humanitarian aid—led to the flight of millions of citizens to camps across the Pakistan border and in Iran. Between 1979 and 1992, an estimated six million people—more than one-fifth of the population, fled their places of origin to become refugees or internally displaced in Afghan towns and cities. The transformations within society, and of the rural economy, had contradictory repercussions on women's roles, on gender relations, and on the assertion of patriarchal controls. As in other turbulent settings, communities sending out male combatants burdened women with new types of responsibilities in the day-to-day management of their households.[76]

The absence of men, who are away taking part in fighting, loads on to women temporary headship of the family, and the burden of ensuring food provision whether it is possible to farm, travel, find any kind of paid work, or not. There is a shift of economic and social responsibilities within households and communities from men to women, despite the many different contexts in which conflicts occur. In rural areas they become responsible for agriculture and livestock; in towns, they are more likely to resort to self-employment or casual wage labour. Even when overt warfare is over, and the situation has become merely tense and unsettled with sporadic violence, as in southern Somalia, men's

will or capacity to provide for the household may have disintegrated: "Now we obey our women. Women sell tomatoes, maize, etc., and men are supported by their wives. They are taking us through this difficult time.... That is how we are living," was how an elder from the beleaguered coastal town of Brava described life to a researcher in a study conducted by the Agency for Co-operation and Research in Development (ACORD).[77]

Responsibilities for family provision also extend in some situations to very young women: in postgenocide Rwanda, an estimated 45,000 households were headed by children, 90 per cent of them girls.[78] For some women, the changes into which they are forced may be embraced as a liberation from the old social order. Some find work with NGOs in relief camps, or develop their own self-help groups. The opportunity for opening up "political space" and pushing the social boundaries are frequently present in times of social crisis, and wars are no exception.[79] Many women in refugee camps, or in the diaspora created by conflict, have gained from education programmes and exposure to the wider world. They bring to the establishment of peace and "normal life" a desire for expanded educational opportunities for girls, and experiences of earning independent incomes and making other choices in life, which were previously unthinkable in the culture in which they were raised.

WOMEN AND THE SEARCH FOR PEACE

In the past decade, considerable interest has developed among researchers and organizations working for peace in the potential and actual role of women in bringing an end to conflict. The conventional view is that women find war and violence intrinsically antipathetic, and that femaleness or femininity can automatically be equated with an urge for peace. This assumption, disputed by recent feminist critique, appears oversimplistic in the light of the active role some women take in conflicts or in supporting the fighting cause. However, the view prevails that women—whether for biological or socially constructed reasons—have a stronger motivation for peace than men, and special capacities for conflict resolution. International Alert's 1998 Code of Conduct states: "We explicitly recognize the particular and distinctive peace-making roles played by women in conflict-afflicted communities. Women and women's organizations are often reservoirs of important local capacities which can be used in peace-building activities".[80] This perception has led to a range of recent international activity to explore and promote women's peace-building initiatives.

One interpretation of the "warrior" instinct displayed by some women is that it is an attempt to reduce violence rather than increase it. Many examples exist of women courageously resisting violence, or putting themselves in the way of armed assault. Women in the Palestinian territories, for example have frequently confronted Israeli soldiers in their homes and neighbourhoods, showing equal or even superior bravery to men.[81] In northern Somalia, women have staged cultural sit-ins to forestall hostilities between warring clans. Many of these spontaneous actions can be seen as attempts to reduce day-to-day carnage or protest about its effects in the midst of ongoing wars, rather than as efforts to bring warring parties to settlement. Protests such as that of the Mothers of the Plaza de Mayo in Argentina during the crisis of the "disappeared" in the late 1970s and early 1980s may start spontaneously and then continue over many years. They contribute to the idea of the peace-making woman and her iconic role in re-establishing a social order with moral and compassionate values at its core.

Undertaking action in the midst of war

Many activities undertaken by women at the peak of fighting are measures to provide relief assistance in their neighbourhoods or communities. In these contexts, women may act within a church or faith group, or as members of some existing voluntary organization for women. While they may confront acute political and military difficulties, having to cross fighting lines, face down militia leaders trying to co-opt their supplies, and be as strategic in their operating tactics as any commando unit,

these efforts are usually labelled "charitable", "humanitarian" or "social", and their political significance is ignored.[82]

The lack of acknowledgement of their significance does not extend to those whose interests these programmes cross. Rajani Tirangana of Sri Lanka, a poet and writer who wrote powerfully against the violence of conflict, was one of a group of women who set up the Poorani Women's Centre in Jaffna, the Tamil stronghold. Poorani provided shelter to victims of the war, including victims of rape and their children. In 1989, Rajani was killed because her activities threatened perpetrators of the conflict.[83] Political engagement and risk is a precondition of all such activities. In Mogadishu, Somalia, between 1991 and 1993, when indiscriminate fighting led to famine in many parts of the country, women activists were similarly threatened. They risked their lives to run food kitchens under targeted attack from gunmen. By moving food about in small quantities to nearly 1,000 locations, and cooking it immediately, thus devaluing it as a commodity, they thwarted warlords trying to steal their supplies. This programme saved over one million lives, but the safety of its co-ordinator became so jeopardized that she was forced into exile.[84]

Other women's groups have come together to assist those suffering from assault, rape or bereavement, opening up hotlines, and refuges or centers where women can jointly address common problems. A large number of such organizations sprang up in Bosnia-Herzegovina and Croatia in the early 1990s, especially in response to the widespread problem of sexual assault, and have subsequently remained in existence, protecting women victims and actively opposing war, violence and nationalist extremism.[85] The dividing line between relief and protesting war or militarism can be extremely thin. In Russia, the Mothers of Soldiers organization has demonstrated in the streets, lobbied among officials of state institutions and employed other peaceful means to recover youths from the Russian army before they are socialized into a culture of violence.[86] Among the NGOs formed by urban and educated Afghani women in exile was the controversial Revolutionary Association of the Women of Afghanistan (RAWA), founded in 1977. RAWA engaged in political campaigning and advocacy, alongside humanitarian assistance for women and children.[87]

The creation by women of grassroots NGOs whose work straddles humanitarian, social and educational activities in the midst of armed struggle, alongside the promotion of peace, has an important role in establishing women as civil-society actors, with implications for women's later claims for enhanced participation in the postconflict society. When war-affected women in Afghanistan, the former Yugoslavia, Somalia, Colombia, Sri Lanka or elsewhere have joined with others similarly affected and taken on such roles, they have developed strength and an unexpected capacity for setting goals and undertaking action to reach them, without male guidance or control.

Women's informal peace initiatives

From community-based action on behalf of the war-affected, to participation in action to end war itself, only a small conceptual step is required. A recent study of individual and collective initiatives for peace in Sri Lanka shows how, since the early 1970s, women have repudiated the ethnic divide over which the civil war was fought, and worked hard to create the conditions for peaceful democracy and support for human rights.[88] Many examples exist of women's efforts, in societies that have long been in a state of tension overlapping into war, to build ideas of peaceful co-existence across religious and cultural divides, and take positive actions to support this purpose. Such community-based movements exist in Palestine, Indonesia, former Yugoslavia, Mozambique, Israel and other settings. The importance of these initiatives has been acknowledged in a number of UN reports, which have also underlined the contribution women make to peace as educators within their families and societies.[89]

Women's peace activism may encounter fewer difficulties in expressing concerns about conflict than do men. This is not to decry the courage that is required, or the strategic and political understanding: such acts as peace rallies, or non-violent obstructionism, are far from disingenuous. A women's march in Sierra Leone in May 2000 set the stage for a march of parliamentarians and civil-society organizations a few days later.

Without the women's demonstration that peaceful action against the conflict was possible, the second march would probably have incited a violent reaction.[90]

Another little-known example is the Naga Mothers' Association (NMA) in one of India's northeastern states, home to a long-running insurgency. Set up in 1984, the initial focus of the NMA was on development work. Gradually, the group intervened in the conflict. Adopting a two-pronged strategy, NMA members walked miles into Myanmar, where the leaders of one of their factions were located, and attempted to persuade them to initiate dialogues for peace. They then began a campaign called "Shed no more blood" in which they appealed as mothers—both of fighters and martyrs—to the Indian security forces and the militants to end rivalry and bloodshed, both among the militant factions and with the army.[91] The women have subsequently maintained pressure for peace and for negotiations among the Naga factions to create the environment for a settlement.

The visibility of women in such initiatives has recently become more prominent. One example is that of the Women in Black (WIB) international network, with chapters in over 12 countries. The Serbian group was credited with a role in the overthrow of the regime of President Slobodan Milosevic. Members of Women in Black demonstrated outside government offices for years, calling for peace and denouncing the government's military adventures. Stones were thrown at the women, they were beaten up and arrested, and every effort was made by the regime to isolate the group and alienate its support. As members of an international network, their strategy was to build networks of solidarity "combining feminism and anti-militarism".[92]

Colombia has recently seen the establishment of a National Movement of Women against the War. The independent experts collecting evidence on women's participation in war for UNIFEM describe taking part in a peace march of 20,000 women in Medellin, in which the principal slogan was: "We won't give birth to more sons to send to war". Examples of cross-border initiatives by women searching for peace include the Mano River Union Women's Network for Peace, which contains members from Guinea, Liberia and Sierra Leone. The network claims to have been instrumental in resolving the conflict in Sierra Leone, and in helping start negotiations between the Mano River countries; its own origins lie in the membership of one of its key activists in the national Women's Forum in Sierra Leone before the war began there in 1991. The Women's Forum already had a voice and powerful contacts at the national level, and was able to reach out regionally and internationally.

Women and formal peace negotiations

The processes surrounding the search for peace vary according to the circumstances of war, and these circumstances are more or less propitious for women's involvement. Some wars are relatively short, and consist of a military campaign which ends in the victory of one side over the other (for example, Tanzania's 1979 invasion of Uganda); in such a case, the victor usually dictates the terms of peace. In other cases, a long-term or short-term insurgency or multiple insurgencies within a country can lead to external intervention of some kind, and the parties may be brought to the table under the pressure of larger national powers or the international community (for example, Cambodia 1967–91, Kosovo 1999 and Somalia 1991–2004). The creation of a new state by a national or ethnic subgroup seeking independence is a further variation (for example, Bangladesh in 1971 and Eritrea in 2000), and here the settlement involves the establishment of a whole new set of government institutions. In yet another kind of situation, a long period of armed resistance has aided a country's "liberation" from repressive or colonial regimes (for example Viet Nam, Nicaragua, Namibia and South Africa); the establishment of a new government similarly involves a transition or transformation of structures.[93]

Where women have taken part in a liberation struggle as fighters or active supporters, it may be easier for women to demand places at the settlement table.[94] The creation of a new state or the emergence of a new liberal and democratic state, as in South Africa and Namibia, also offers opportunities for women's organizations previously active in the struggle to demand a role in negotiations for new constitutional provisions and governmental structures. Women are often aware that if they do not manage to gain a place in negotiations and help to shape the new governance framework, the upheaval of war, the trials, tribulations, losses and distress endured in the name of fighting for a "better society" may leave them in the same disadvantaged positions as before the war took place, or even worse off (see next chapter).

Thus women's desire to sit at the peace table is motivated by many considerations, among which is the determination to create better livelihood circumstances and not simply contemplate the carve-up of power over government offices, patronage and budgetary resources. Women are often anxious that socioeconomic predicaments arising out of war should be addressed (see box 13.4). Some feminist critiques of standard peace processes have pointed out that unless the underlying causes of conflict, including gross poverty and inequity, are addressed in the course of their attempted resolution, peace will be neither long-lasting nor "gendered".[95] In this perspective, efforts to secure peace settlements or resolve conflicts definitively cannot afford to regard gender considerations as peripheral to the peace-seeking quest—as tends still to be the case. Where an "ungendered" peace is secured, it may be a peace in which the widespread violent conflict associated with war has ended; but it is likely to be a peace in which social violence (against women), structured violence (against minorities or other seriously discriminated groups), and gross violations of human rights continue to occur.

At the peace table
Significant attention at the international level has recently been given to the difficulties women face in gaining actual places at the negotiating table. On the exclusion of women from the post-Oslo peace discussions between Israel and Palestinians, a female commentator wrote:

"How ironic it was that high-ranking Israeli generals, who spent a good proportion of their lives waging war, have now become the ultimate voices of authority of peace, while the perspectives and experience of women peace activists have been rendered trivial".[97]

Box 13.4 The end of conflict in Cambodia

Women account for nearly two-thirds of the population of Cambodia and head a third of all households. With the breaking up of old social structures and relationships as a result of the long years of war, genocide and upheaval, the old pattern of mutual assistance and community interaction that once characterized Cambodian society gave way to individualized, monetized relations.

More women and children have been pushed into the "rest and recreation" industry, and increasing burdens have been imposed on returnees (an estimated 370,000 refugees), among whom are many women, especially widows. A 1995 survey of the reintegration of this population showed that up to 40 per cent were not managing economically.

The pressure on agricultural land, especially where it is mined, affects livelihoods in a society that remains primarily agricultural, in particular those women running households on their own. The UN Transitional Authority in Cambodia (UNTAC) noted that at the village level, many disputes arose over ownership of land. The breakdown of traditional systems of conflict resolution also meant that with the return of peace, women and children found themselves at the receiving end of heightened levels of violence.[96]

In such circumstances, a peace settlement that fails to address the predicaments affecting women will fail to address the underlying circumstances which foment insecurity and violent upheaval.

Source: Curtis 1998.

There were no women at the Dayton peace talks that ended the war in Bosnia and Herzegovina; the examples are too many to name. Whatever the credibility of women in grassroots organizations and traditional community and caring roles, they are marginalized from negotiations at the peace table. Their relative lack of education and experience at senior levels in public life compound their difficulties in seeking a voice.

However, a number of international organizations now try to provide women with fora in which they can develop positions which can be placed before peace negotiation delegations. In the case of the Somali conflict, the ongoing negotiations between the warring clans which have been attempted in different venues over the past 10 years have admitted a women's representative delegation, even if its role has been restricted to observer status. Women were credited by former US Senator George Mitchell for having made an important contribution to the Northern Ireland peace negotiations. "The two women who made it to the table had a tough time at first. They were treated quite rudely by some of the male politicians.… Through their own perseverance and talent, by the end of the process they were valued contributors."[98]

Postwar transitional arrangements and interim administrations, such as those in Afghanistan and Iraq, have made significant gestures in the direction of female inclusion. The Bonn Agreement of 2001 ending the Afghan war offered a clear commitment to mainstreaming gender and redressing past injustice; and after discussions in Kabul in 2002, a Ministry of Women's Affairs and a Gender Advisory Group were established. A number of international organizations have offered training to women so that they have the leadership and negotiating skills to participate effectively in peacekeeping activities and interim governmental institutions. All such efforts help to avoid a situation in which women and the issues that are of most importance to them do not become relegated to the sidelines once peace has begun to prevail. However, it is also the case that effective modalities for women's inclusion where social cleavages in the society have been acute and there can be no one "women's voice", are still in their infancy.

There has been a similar recognition by some international peace-keeping operations that gender issues should receive attention. The "peace-keeping environment" is not necessarily one that favours women, who face continued, sometimes enhanced, levels of violence in the postconflict situation, and are lured by need into flourishing "rest and recreational" industries, including prostitution and trafficking. In East Timor, the UN Secretary-General's Representative was originally opposed to the creation of a gender affairs unit in the UN Transitional Authority, but later agreed he had been mistaken. The first regulation passed by the Transitional Authority guaranteed human rights standards, including the Convention on the Elimination of All Forms of Discrimination against Women (CEDAW), as a foundation of all new government institutions. Women thereafter participated in negotiations surrounding the establishment of new institutions of democratic governance. The gender affairs unit worked with women throughout East Timor to make the acceptance of a human rights regime into a reality. As a result, the subsequent elections for the Constituent Assembly produced a relatively high number of women representatives.[99]

The international climate

In recent years international and donor organizations have given increasing recognition to the impact of conflict on women, and to the necessity of taking account of women's specific needs in the transition to peace. Two programmes—the International Fellowship for Reconciliation's Women and Peacemaking Programme launched in 1998, and International Alert's Gender Campaign launched in 1999—have been established specifically to promote women's contribution to peace. The US Agency for International Development (USAID) has carried out a two-year investigation of gender issues in postconflict societies (Bosnia and Herzegovina, Cambodia, El Salvador, Georgia, Guatemala and Rwanda).[100] The Asian Development Bank (ADB) has held internal seminars on "Gender and post-conflict reconstruction" in which it has looked at how women's voices can be integrated in peace negotiations, and in the allocation of resources and monitoring of human security in postconflict situations.

Thus it is fair to say that, since the Beijing Conference, the international climate has become more open to engaging with women and addressing their specific predicaments in conflict situations, as well as consulting them during the transitional phase leading out of conflict towards peace. Considerable progress can similarly be seen to have been made in the development of international humanitarian law. Much has been done to correct the historic impunity enjoyed by perpetrators of sexual violence against women during war, and to recognize women's and girls' special needs for protection during conflict, and in areas in transition from states of war to states of peace. These developments were stimulated by the international publicity given to mass rapes in Bosnia and to the experiences undergone by women during the Rwandan genocide, tragedies regarded as having had a catalytic effect on advancing international gender justice.[101] But the new respect accorded to women in landmark provisions of international law was also a response to prolonged efforts of women activists to attain legitimacy for their cause.

The first milestone came in January 1992, when CEDAW adopted Recommendation 19 to add to its existing provisions, declaring violence against women a form of discrimination. In 1993 the World Conference on Human Rights in Vienna stressed women's rights as "an inalienable and indivisible part of human rights" in its Declaration and Programme of Action, and called for an end to all forms of violence against women. Shortly thereafter the UN General Assembly adopted the Declaration on the Elimination of Violence Against Women (DEVAW) and in 1994 came the appointment of a Special Rapporteur on violence against women by the Office of the United Nations High Commissioner for Human Rights (OHCHR). These developments were precursors to the emphasis given in the Beijing Platform for Action to the need to curtail violence against women, especially during war, and obtain enforcement of human rights instruments and redress against perpetrators of violations. The passage by the UN Security Council of Resolution 1325 in 2000, urging member states to ensure increased representation of women in decision-making mechanisms for the resolution of conflict, is the high-water mark of many post-Beijing advances. These are examined in chapter 14.

The application of international instruments to resolve problems of gender injustice experienced on the ground can never prove an adequate corrective in situations where gender inequality is a prevailing norm. This is not to suggest that changes to international law are not worth pursuing: on the contrary, they help to legitimize new normative frameworks, and can be used in advocating legal and social change. However, their limitations are real. The call to uphold international human rights for women and all those facing gross violations is at its least efficacious in situations of conflict, where the rule of law has broken down and insecurity is at its worst. But once peace building begins to take serious hold, the fact that there has been a recognition of the need for women's voices to be heard in creating a real and effective peace ought to yield further dividends in years to come. Nothing, however, can be taken for granted while armed conflicts and the "war on terror" remain pervasive in so many parts of the world.

Notes

1 SIPRI 2004:summary of chapter three.

2 Kandiyoti 2004:2, quoting Donini et al. 2004.

3 Nordstrom 1992:271, cited in Turshen and Twagiramariya 1998.

4 Afshar 2003:149.

5 Murray et al. 2002:346.

6 Turshen and Twagiramariya 1998; Kaldor 1999.

7 Butalia 2004.

8 Afshar 2003:178–9.

9 Small Arms Survey 2004.

10 Small Arms Survey 2004.

11 Jadwa 2003.

12 UN Secretary General 2002: 26.

13 Kaldor 1999.

14 Mamdani 2001.

15 Gardner and El Bushra 2004:162.

16 Rehn and Sirleaf 2002:10.

17 Rehn and Sirleaf 2002:11.

18 Murray et al. 2002:346, using WHO data.

19 Mkandawire 2002.

20 Amnesty International 2004:14.

21 Murray et al. 2002.

22 Legros and Brown 2001.

23 Rehn and Sirleaf 2002:33.

24 Sørensen 1998:38.

25 UN Secretary General 2002:23.

26 Butalia 2002.

27 Rajasingham-Senanayake 2001:122.

28 Amnesty International 2004:1.

29 Butalia 2004.

30 Krug et al. 2002:156.

31 Pankhurst 2003:159.

32 Gardner and El Bushra 2004:70.

33 Krug et al. 2002:156.

34 IWRC 2003; Harding 2004.

35 Physicians for Human Rights 2002:44–51.

36 Ward 2002.

37 Kandiyoti 2004.

38 UNICEF Innocenti Research Centre 2001.

39 World Vision International 1996:14.

40 Minority Rights Group International 1997:26.

41 United Nations 2000b:158.

42 Amnesty International 1997.

43 UNAIDS 1998, quoted in Rehn and Sirleaf 2002:53.

44 Rehn and Sirleaf 2002:50.

45 Rehn and Sirleaf 2002:52.

46 UNRISD 1993:24.

47 Coomaraswamy 1998.

48 Williams and Masika 2002, quoted in Rehn and Sirleaf 2002:12.

49 IOM 2001, quoted in Rehn and Sirleaf 2002:12.

50 IOM 2001, quoted in Rehn and Sirleaf 2002:12.

51 Afshar 2003:179.

52 McKay and Mazurana 2004.

53 Luciak 2004.

54 Luciak 2004; Ertürk 2004.

55 Gautam et al. 2001.

56 Amnesty International 2004:24.

57 Quoted in Sørensen 1998:33.

58 UNIFEM 2004a:25.

59 OAU 2000:176.

60 Krug et al. 2002.

61 Sørensen 1998:33.

62 Rehn and Sirleaf 2002.

63 Cited in Bennett et al. 1995:14.

64 UNHCR quoted in United Nations 2000b:162.

65 UNHCR 2004.

66 Kaldor 1999.

67 Weiner 1996, cited in Kaldor 1999.

68 UNHCR 2004.

69 Watson 1996:49.

70 Kandiyoti 2004; Gardner and El Bushra 2004.

71 El Bushra 2003:259; Holt 2003:229.

72 Gardner and El Bushra 2004:70.

73 Centers for Disease Control 1992:16.

74 *Lancet* 1995, quoted in Rehn and Sirleaf 2002:35.

75 Save the Children 2000:45.

76 Kandiyoti 2004:9–10.

77 Quoted in El Bushra 2004.

78 UN Secretary-General 2000, para 35.

79 Pankhurst 2003:159.

80 International Alert 1998:6, quoted in Pankhurst 2003.

81 Afshar 2003:181.

82 Sørensen 1998:6.

83 Samuel 2004.

84 Gardner and El Bushra 2004:179.

85 Center for Women War Victims 2003.

86 Sørensen 1998:7.

87 Kandiyoti 2004:10.

88 Samuel 2004.

89 Rehn and Sirleaf 2002.

90 Rehn and Sirleaf 2002.

91 Banerjee 2001.

92 Rehn and Sirleaf 2002; Women in Black 2004.

93 UNRISD 1993.

94 Corrin 2003; UN Office for Coordination of Humanitarian Affairs 2003, 2004.

95 Pankhurst 2003:156–7.

96 Curtis 1998.

97 Sharoni 1995, quoted in Sørensen 1998.

98 Rehn and Sirleaf 2002:79.

99 Rehn and Sirleaf 2002:61.

100 USAID Office of Women in Development 2000.

101 Walsh 2004.

Chapter 14
After conflict: Women, peace building and development

The lack of separation between the "war front" and the "home front" which characterizes so many of today's armed conflicts has important implications for the onset of peace. This rarely derives from a climactic defeat or victory by military forces, yielding to a state of tranquillity in which the regular apparatus of the state reassumes control. Formal hostilities may end because military commanders flee or capitulate, or peace accords are signed; but armed violence continues within disputed terrain, urban neighbourhoods and even in households. The hold and reach of the civilian authorities may be weak, and their legitimacy may continue to be challenged by groups unready to accept a final outcome. In these circumstances, the insecurities and deprivations experienced during conflict may continue, and their pattern remain as unpredictable as during actual war.

Thus the postconflict environment cannot be characterized as one in which life for women invariably returns to "normal"—even if a return to previous patterns of gender and social relationships, as if no war had occurred, were desirable or even possible. The upheaval of war, in which societies have been transformed and livelihood systems disrupted, in which women have assumed certain roles for the first time or come into contact with new ideas, has its own impact on intrapersonal relationships and societal expectations. But beyond these well-established historical patterns, evidence emerging from gendered analysis of postwar situations in the former Yugoslavia, sub-Saharan Africa, Cambodia, East Timor, Colombia and elsewhere[1] shows that women not only face a continuation of aggression endured during the war, but may also face new forms of violence.

Furthermore, in the design of policies for postwar reconstruction, women's needs may be systematically ignored, and even deliberately marginalized. This may carry forward echoes of past situations and power relations, but there can also be a new edge of aggression against women. Together, the continued and new forms of violence, and the attacks on women's newly assumed rights and behaviours, constitute what frequently amounts to a postwar backlash against women.[2]

THE CONTINUATION OF VIOLENCE AND SEXUAL ASSAULT

In the aftermath of war, women are still exposed to abuse and violence at home, on the way to collect water, to work in the fields, in the urban workplace and when they go to the police station for help—sometimes by those whose responsibility it is to safeguard and protect them in the "at peace" environment. In camps for refugees and the displaced, and in areas where livelihood systems have collapsed, they continue to be forced to sell sex as a means of economic survival. In addition, it is normal for domestic abuse to increase in the postwar setting, both from partners returning home from the war, and from partners who remained together.[3]

The apparent rise in postconflict domestic violence may result from a number of interrelated processes. In the aftermath of war, men may experience trauma and dislocation derived from the culture of violence experienced as combatants. They

Box 14.1   Domestic violence increases after war

Recent research indicates that many combatants have difficulty making the transition to peacetime non-violent behaviour after returning home. In the United States in 2002, four Special Forces soldiers at Fort Bragg in North Carolina killed their wives within a period of six weeks. Three of the four had recently returned from overseas duty in Afghanistan, although some commentators believe it is not the experience of conflict but the culture of violence and masculinity that permeates military forces that causes soldiers to be violent in civilian life. Studies in Cambodia in the mid-1990s indicated that many women—as many as 75 per cent in one study—were victims of domestic violence, often at the hands of men who have kept the small arms and light weapons they used during the war.

Source: Rehn and Sirleaf 2002.

may also feel intense dissatisfaction with their lives, whether they have returned with little support or have benefited from demobilization, development and reintegration policies.[4] There are often no effective constraints against men behaving violently to their partners; existing community sanctions may have broken down, and women may not find it possible to go to the police where the routine practice is to treat women unfairly and even abuse them.

The backlash women experience may extend to a public outcry, dominated by male voices, against women who are perceived as having moved away from their assigned positions in society during the war; as a result, rights or spaces to which they have gained access are removed.[5] These outcries can be accompanied by violent assaults on women; even their arrest[6] and murder.[7] Women can be targeted for having gained economic independence from men, having been employed in "male" roles, or for having adopted urban and educated lifestyles in predominantly rural societies. There are calls for them to be forced "back" into kitchens and fields, even if they were not so occupied before the war. It is usually unclear whether these outcries are spontaneous reactions from individual men, or whether they are orchestrated by the state or government.[8] In either case, at both social and individual levels there are forceful attempts to define women's roles and rights as secondary to those of men.

For instance, in the immediate aftermath of the ceasefire agreement in Sri Lanka, codes and behaviours were imposed on women which amounted to restrictions of their rights. Married Tamil women were called upon to wear the sari; unmarried Tamil women were adjured to follow certain behaviour patterns and restrict their movements at night; Sinhala military widows were carefully "policed" with regard to their sexual activities; Muslim women were encouraged to wear the veil and had their movements restricted within their communities.[9] Such instances of backlash were also experienced with bitterness by women active in earlier liberation struggles, for example in Algeria, El Salvador, Eritrea, Mozambique, Nicaragua, Viet Nam and Zimbabwe; some of the women concerned had even risen to senior military rank.[10]

THE REDUCTION OF "SPACE" AND LIFE CHOICES

Many women who were active in war find that they have to adjust to a new situation in peacetime in which they have less political space to challenge gender relations than they did during wartime, or even beforehand. They are subject to violence and censure if they do not want to return to old ways of living. In the face of such obstacles, many women prioritize the restoration of peaceful relationships with men, rather than continue to fight for greater rights themselves.[11] For instance, in Namibia it was noted that "Women accustomed to leadership in exile were soon observed to suppress their skills so as to achieve community acceptance."[12] The consequent increase in divorce adds to the overall postwar context of heightened gender tensions.[13]

Women commonly find their contributions to the war and peace efforts marginalized in both official and popular accounts of war immediately afterwards, as happened in Europe after the Second World War. There seems to be an attempt to deny that shifts in gender relations were required for women to take on their wartime roles, or that such shifts will ever, by implication, actually be possible.[14] The ideological rhetoric is often about "restoring" or "returning" to a state of gender relations that resembles something associated with peace in the past, even though the proposed "restoration of normality" may undermine women's rights even further. The "restored" balance of gender politics will, in effect, unambiguously favour men. This is often accompanied by imagery of the culturally specific notions of "tradition", motherhood, and peace.[15] The challenge to gender relations experienced during war seems to become too great for patriarchal societies to maintain in times of peace.

Protests by women against such behaviour are often castigated as being "Western-influenced".[16] In such an intense and sometimes violent moment, the state can bring to bear many of the policies used in "normal times" to intervene in gender politics, or weight the "sex war",[17] in favour of men. The state becomes instrumental in enforcing controls over women's sexuality; fails to increase, or prevent a decline in, women's personal security; imposes or supports restrictions on women's movement, access to housing, jobs and property (especially land); and marginalizes women's health needs. In many cases such official policy outcomes are reinforced by the practices of international organizations which do not actively seek the opinions of women, or fail to promote their interests where this might be "culturally insensitive".

TENSIONS BETWEEN WOMEN

In this difficult postwar situation, the differences between women often reassert themselves, especially in countries where women are divided by a strong ethnic or regional identity.[18] New divisions can occur as a result of the different experiences women have endured, or their different allegiances, during the war; for example, whether they were on the side of "victors", "perpetrators" or "collaborators", and whether they have given birth to children of "the enemy" after rape. Such issues can determine who qualifies for aid and other support,[19] as can women's marital status, and whether or not they still live with their husbands, or are widowed, abandoned or divorced. Marital status is highly significant in situations where women do not have strong legal rights (such as in land and property titles or access to credit).

Where the majority of the surviving population is female (as in Rwanda, where around 70 per cent was female), this can lead to competitions between women over men and resources. Tensions also exist between women over whether or how their children survived the war. For many reasons, it is not unusual for there to be very little trust between women as a group in the postwar period, as is the case between many mixed groups of conflict survivors. These types of difference and tension between women make it very difficult for them to articulate common needs, which adds to the silencing effect of the backlash against them. Peace-building strategies do not usually address this tension between common experience and major differences and divisions between women, but rather tend either to focus on women as a homogeneous category, or assume their existence as genderless members of other groups.

POTENTIAL FOR POSITIVE CHANGE: OPPORTUNITIES GLIMPSED AND REAL

This negative picture is alleviated by the potential for positive change in some postwar circumstances which arise where the nature of the conflict creates new opportunities. Some wars end in an atmosphere pervasive with the desire to build a new type of society, particularly where some kind of liberation struggle was fought and won.[20] Where gender issues were raised as part of the political agenda of the conflict (for example, in Uganda), or where the situation of women received a lot of attention during the conflict (for example, Afghanistan), there may be a greater potential for improving women's legal rights beyond the prewar situation, although the realization of these gains might be more elusive.

Other factors may favour women's assertion of their rights or the consolidation of temporary gains. Where many women gained sufficient confidence to articulate their needs during the conflict, they may be more effective campaigners and activists. Where the postwar period heralds a greater openness to learning from similar circumstances in other countries, governments may see more clearly the efficacy of supporting women. If unprecedented amounts of international funding become available from intergovernmental and non-governmental organization (NGO) sources, as is often the case in poor countries following a conflict, there may be external pressure for policies that support women, and funds may be directly available to women's organizations.

If women are to benefit from such opportunities, it is important to identify the strategies to promote and the issues to be given priority. These are bound to vary. Postwar contexts pose confusing dilemmas about the extent to which they require special approaches, or merely represent normal challenges of social development. Where considerable devastation has been wrought to production and communication, and where large numbers of people have fled their homes, for instance, the need for "exceptional" approaches to macropolicies for "recovery", "rehabilitation" and "reintegration" is commonly perceived. In the political arena, there may likewise be "exceptional" requirements: for example, for voter registration and the establishment of machinery to hold elections, and increasingly for some kind of exceptional judicial or "truth and reconciliation" process.

THE GENDER-WEIGHTED PEACE INDUSTRY

Such exceptional and urgent activities may receive new streams of international funding and be given high priority by all parties, to be conceived and implemented outside any normal planning process. And in the immediate postwar stage, these exercises are even more difficult to implement effectively than usual since the state, so recently contested, is politically weak and its apparatus

damaged or barely intact. Weakened state capacity tends to lead to outcomes that are detrimental to women's interests, thus adding to the cards stacked against them. In the absence of an effective state, the exercises in question are largely controlled and determined from outside the country, as part of what has become known as the "peace industry".[21]

Steps taken at moments of emergency, and periods immediately following a conflict, often have serious implications for the longer term. Yet in such climates, the sense of urgency itself tends to eclipse such considerations as gender analysis; women's needs are usually overlooked, or at least misunderstood. For instance, despite women's activism and the important role they had played in the war in El Salvador, gender was not a priority for the *Frente Farabundo Martí para la Liberación Nacional* (FMLN). In the words of one activist: "Before the negotiations we [women's groups within the FMLN] had already elaborated women's demands but it was not possible to introduce them into the process. They [the FMLN leadership] did not even bother to read the document."[22]

Postwar policies need to be able to bring in key lessons from a gender analysis of the processes of economic, social and political development. There are a number of highly significant policy areas to be considered for postwar situations, although the particular mix is bound to vary from one context to another. A selection is reviewed here, with special attention to the potential opportunities for reducing the gender bias inherent in the way many authorities tend to behave, and therefore for breaking many of the persistent inequalities and injustices facing women after wars.

MACROECONOMIC AND MACROSOCIAL POLICIES: IMPLICATIONS FOR WOMEN

Macro-level policies for the postwar context tend to ignore the constraints and realities of women's lives. For instance, many women continue with wartime economic strategies involving small-scale trade in the informal economy. However, in a bid to increase meagre revenues, governments may attempt to

Box 14.2   Women excluded from postwar planning

"It is really amazing", said one Kosovar woman, "… that the international community cared only about Kosovar women when they were being raped—and then only as some sort of exciting story. We see now that they really don't give a damn about us. What we see here are men, men, men from Europe and America, and even Asia, listening to men, men, men from Kosovo. Sometimes they have to be politically correct so they include a woman on a committee or they add a paragraph to a report. But when it comes to real involvement in the planning for the future of this country, our men tell the foreign men to ignore our ideas. And they are happy to do so—under the notion of 'cultural sensitivity'. Why is it politically incorrect to ignore the concerns of Serbs or other minorities, but 'culturally sensitive' to ignore the concerns of women?"

Source: Rehn and Sirleaf 2002: 125.

formalize the "grey economy" by introducing regulations, fees and income tax. Without the means to comply with regulations, such measures often serve to deprive women of their livelihoods. This was the experience of women in Mozambique.[23] Similarly women also often attempt to rebuild or maintain primary education and primary health-care services themselves as state services collapse, but these efforts are not generally built on after the war. The women are pushed aside in favour of bringing in qualified professionals, who tend to be men.[24]

Policy initiatives at the macro level need to build gender analysis into peace-building policy processes, alongside "special" policies specifically geared towards women; this has been accepted as appropriate by key international organizations for some time.[25] At its simplest, a gender-aware approach requires people to apply the question: "Does this policy affect women and men differently?" If the answer is in the affirmative, then policy makers need to explore what can be done to prevent or correct women's disadvantages.[26] Posing this question should lead in some cases to a complete rethink in the way a policy is developed and implemented; in others, relatively minor adjustments would be required.

In postwar emergency situations in poor countries, it may be difficult to apply a gender-aware approach. Not only are resources scarce and infrastructure weak, but new governments are often constrained in their spending by the conditions attached to multilateral and bilateral loans, which place strict limitations on budget deficits. A growing lobby supported by some eminent economists

argues that such conditions ought to be loosened in postwar economies, since they severely undermine the chances of economic recovery. The needs of women and other vulnerable groups should be given a higher priority than macroeconomic probity.[27]

Applying a gendered approach

If there is political willingness to take the gender implications of policy seriously, the analytical tools already exist to undertake the necessary data collection, analysis, monitoring and evaluation. In some postwar environments, as was the case in Uganda after 1986, the political will to do this may be strong. Where such opportunities occur, it might be possible to develop some elements of a top-down gender-aware approach to a range of policies. It has now become usual in postwar circumstances to attempt a bottom-up approach of at least some support for women's organizations as the most obvious way to support women. International links between women's organizations have been expanded in recent years, and are greatly facilitated by the IT revolution.

Such a positive political environment cannot by any means be guaranteed; indeed, in the atmosphere of backlash already described, the political will for changing gender relations may be completely absent, or at best ambivalent. For various reasons, women themselves may not be in a position to press for positive change. Nonetheless, the contrasting political postwar contexts mean that opportunities can arise. Some general economic and social policies have more acute implications for women than others, and significant change could be supported by focusing on a few key areas.

Specific contexts determine both what is possible and what ought to be prioritized. For example, where the majority of the surviving population relies on agriculture as the main source of livelihood, land reform is often key. Where levels of urbanization and education are higher, employment issues are of far greater significance. In all contexts however, it is normal at the end of war to find women dominating the most marginalized sections of society. They are the returnees with access to the fewest resources, the ex-combatants who tend to be overlooked, the heads of household with least support. Women tend to predominate in the most stigmatized and disadvantaged groups: rape survivors, orphans, disabled people and widows (who may constitute up to 30 per cent of the surviving postwar population).[28] They generally tend to be the least well trained and educated, whether in urban or rural areas, and have specific health needs that are overlooked. How can these challenges be addressed?

AGRICULTURE AND LAND REFORM

Agricultural economies, where the majority of the population still mainly depend on cultivation and raising of livestock for their food supply, are normally characterized by a strong gender bias in favour of men. Women typically receive less of the income generated from their labour, and have less access to other people's labour and less control over their own, than do men. As a result, many women seek opportunities to sell their labour to others for very poor returns to guarantee some minimum resources for household needs.[29] In places where women are unable to get access to sufficient land to farm, as in Rwanda, Cambodia, Zimbabwe and Sri Lanka, they hire themselves out as casual workers.[30]

During periods of violent conflict, agriculture becomes important as a source of food, even for people whose livelihoods were previously non-agrarian. Where men are away fighting, or are injured or dead, women often take up the burden of agricultural production even where they did not do this previously. War also disrupts established systems of land tenure. Men take land by force as social regulation breaks down and people move away from their homes into new areas. Landmines restrict the use of fields and grazing land, putting great pressure on the remaining accessible areas. Soldiers use land for camps, often killing wildlife and stripping vegetation and soil. Traders and soldiers negotiate tenure deals with local leaders for mining or natural resource extraction, as in the Democratic Republic of Congo (DRC), and even buy and sell land.

All this may take place without reference to local custom or law relating to ownership and use of land, which leaves a confused postwar land rights legacy. This happened in Mozambique, even though existing communal land tenure arrangements made the sale of land illegal.[31] It is rare to find that there is agreement, let alone a written record, of land transactions during the war; nor is there a clear understanding of who the rights should pass to in the event of the landholder's death. Previously accepted land-tenure systems break down or become superseded because of new land shortages, the absence or removal of local leaders, and the collapse of local government institutions.

Land tenure and women's rights

The more severe the land shortage, the more the pressure on women's rights. In many places women may be the majority of postwar adult survivors in the countryside, and there may also be many women-only households, as in Mozambique, desperate for land to grow food.[32] Nonetheless, discriminatory legal practices or entrenched social attitudes can still prevent them from taking possession of family lands. In Rwanda, large numbers of men were killed during the genocide; but women were barred from claiming lands under customary law, even though under the constitution they have the legal right to inherit. Some revisions were made to inheritance laws to try to address this problem, but these still do not provide women with secure tenure.[33]

Many other examples can be cited to reinforce a picture of women's rights or access to land gained during conflict receding in the postconflict period. The United Nations Transitional

Authority in Cambodia (UNTAC) found that many disputes arose over ownership of land at the village level, while the simultaneous breakdown of traditional systems of conflict resolution meant that women and children found themselves at the receiving end of heightened levels of violence.[34] In postwar Eritrea, men protested against women having access to land even though the majority of households were probably headed by women. While in exile, Guatemalan refugees had given women a voice in political structures; on returning home, when women tried to claim equal rights to land, they were attacked by local people for having "overstepped the acceptable limits … prescribed for women".[35]

At the end of a conflict, there is often pressure to "sort out" land tenure and land use from several directions. Land and agrarian reform may be seen as a means of speeding up the process of recovery and "normalization"—part of a modernization agenda that takes on a keener urgency in the postwar context. Many countries emerging from conflict in the last decade have predominantly agrarian economies; systems of land tenure are seen as central to recovery. The World Bank identifies certain types of land reform with a "market friendly environment", particularly in Africa, and promotes this model in postconflict contexts. Land reform also figures as part of peace deals because land is often an issue in the conflict itself, even in wars that appear to be primarily about other issues (as in El Salvador, Nicaragua, Guatemala, Zimbabwe and Namibia). The nature of the land reform contained in the agreement reflects the view of what the postconflict society should be like and the future role of agriculture within it. It may involve negotiations with international donors expected to underwrite its costs, who are often themselves highly influential in determining the outcomes.

The land reform promoted by international lending organizations is almost universally in favour of privatized, individual land-tenure arrangements. The outcome of land reforms with this principle at their core has universally been that women emerge with rights no stronger than previously, and frequently find them drastically reduced (see also chapter 6).[36] There are a few exceptions where an effort has been made to correct this imbalance—as in El Salvador—by building on existing, more flexible approaches which had more capacity to protect women's land

rights; but in the postwar context none of these lessons are typically brought on board. Planners tend to ignore the fact that many men who have been fighting have not been farming for a long time, and those who joined military forces as boys have barely any farming skills at all. By contrast, women have been planning and managing scarce resources under difficult conditions, and are often better informed about the particular local ecological conditions and trading opportunities.

Title to land discriminates against women

Where there is an attempt to codify and modernize previous systems of land use, there is a tendency to overlook the ways in which women accessed rights as daughters, aunts, wives, widows and mothers, and even as independent women where they are able to negotiate with local leaders, even if their access was typically more limited than that of men. New land titles tend to be granted almost exclusively to men,[37] and even where there is no legal impediment to women purchasing such rights, and women have the resources to do so, men in their families and communities may actively discourage them from taking them up, as in Guatemala.[38]

Even where women have some access in their own right, this is usually less secure than men's and often dependent on their marital status. There may also be a conscious prejudice on the part of planners involved in land allocations and titles, who may characterize rural women as poorly educated, more "backward" than men, and therefore not as able to take advantage of land-reform opportunities. Inequalities are compounded by the fact that postwar rehabilitation of agriculture (usually involving the distribution of seeds, tools and livestock) is usually organized on a per household basis in which the man is always the head, even where it is clear that women's agricultural production is important for food security and small-scale business.[39]

Undermining women's land rights, and marginalizing them in agrarian reform, are not likely to improve food security where women retain the main responsibility for meeting household food needs, especially where conflict has left them as heads

Box 14.3   Women losing land: Postwar land reform in Africa and Latin America

Mozambique from 1997: Women's relatively secure access to land under customary law was eroded by the social disruption of war. In the increasingly market-based economy women are more disadvantaged than men. The government encouraged people to "go back to the land", but with competition over the best land, the new political and business elites made claims on huge tracts of land, putting extra stress on smallholders. Women went back to farming food out of necessity, but have great difficulty inheriting land, even in matrilineal parts of the country, where control is still vested in men. The 1997 law stipulates that women have equal rights with men, but implementation is weak and long-standing local practices often work against women.[40]

El Salvador from 1992: the need for land in El Salvador was ignored in postwar agreements, despite the efforts of women activists in the FMLN.[41] Subsequent reintegration programmes introduced a gender perspective and improved the situation for women, particularly ex-combatants. However, policy guidelines were subverted by local officials, denying women access to land. Land was allocated on a household basis with the title vested in the male household head; where women were assigned some land in their own right, it tended to be of poor quality. Extra requirements for receiving land included the ability to read and write, as well as the possession of documentation such as birth certificates and voter registration cards. Women were among those unable to fulfil such requirements.[42]

Guatemala 1990s: Women had a say in the peace agreements which facilitated legislation promoting land rights for women returnees and ex-combatants, at least on paper. Nevertheless, the objectives set up in the Guatemalan Peace Accords were not backed up by clear guidelines for implementation.[43] Consequently, many women were not able to exercise their rights because of "traditional male structures".[44]

Nicaragua 1990s: Deals were struck between Sandinistas and Contras over land that specifically excluded women's land ownership.[45]

of households. Thus in postwar settings, the standard approach to land reform reinforces the likelihood of food insecurity. Land and agrarian reform can, on the other hand, be used to support women's postwar roles. The political significance of land reform and the strong donor influence in postwar situations ought to present positive opportunities; international donors have at their disposal many reports that highlight the potential dangers of undermining women's land rights and the advantages of supporting them. If the political context is one where it is widely acknowledged that women played key roles during the conflict as farmers, and as managers of household resources, donors could be reasonably expected to highlight the advantages of their continuing to do so, although they rarely do.

URBAN EMPLOYMENT

The postwar context provides an opportunity for states to consider employment strategies afresh, rather than merely seek to recover the prewar situation and "reintegrate" returnees into a shattered economy. This is particularly important where towns and cities did not offer sufficient job opportunities before the war. Where wars are fought in the countryside, people tend to flee to urban areas, even while formal employment is severely constrained because of the disruptions of war. The public sector often collapses, creating problems similar to those in countries suffering retrenchment under public-sector reforms. The private commercial sector also experiences difficulties due to the destruction of infrastructure, including transport, communications, currency controls, security and other services.[46]

As recovery takes place, a prolonged shortage of male workers (caused by death or absence) may lead to women taking up key positions and becoming a significant part of the workforce. However, this is unusual; the norm is for returning men to take up the best employment opportunities—for which on average they have better education and training.[47] Cultural arguments about women's roles are often used to prevent women from trying to enter the formal sector. In some cases women's legal rights of access to employment may actually be curtailed by the state in the postwar context.[48] An International Labour Organization (ILO) document confirmed that in Namibia, some 60 per cent of women remained unemployed even two years after they had returned to the country.[49]

Women ex-combatants, even where they have held very responsible positions during a war, as in Eritrea, frequently find it harder than men to make a life in their rural homes, and so seek a living in town.[50] In the context of a backlash, they are particular targets for censure and may find getting work very difficult indeed. Cultural constraints or newly coined political versions of them also keep women away from employment. In Afghanistan, for example, the Taliban had very specific restrictions on women working, and many women nurses, teachers and other professionals were forced to leave formal-sector jobs. The change of government has so far produced no clear signs that this situation will change. The lack of adequate childcare can also be an obstacle to taking up jobs, as female ex-combatants in Eritrea found.[51]

The informal economy

For women and men, earning in the aftermath of war often means relying on the informal economy. Women's peacetime employment is predominantly in the informal economy anyway, based on trade in fruit and vegetables from the countryside, cooked food, beer, scarce goods from long-distance trade, and handicrafts. These goods offer relatively quick returns for small investment and do not require access to land. In war-ravaged societies where formal trade has not yet recovered—if it had ever developed—these activities may keep society provisioned. Women entrepreneurs are often able to meet local urban demands for cheap food which governments cannot provide.

In Somalia, for example, women have taken over men's traditional roles and sold livestock; in Mozambique, they took to marketing fruit, fish and vegetables, and beer. In many countries women take on long-distance and cross-border trade, as in Chad, Eritrea and Sierra Leone.[52] A survey of Somali refugees carried out by UNHCR in 1994 notes that in the absence of men, women have become increasingly involved in economic activity, and have acquired a virtual monopoly of the barter trade in food, clothing and a number of other items.[53] Yet none of these trading and retailing activities are supported by postwar governments—or ever given their due economic policy credit for that matter.

As part of the postwar "backlash" against women, their retailing can actually be curtailed. Successful women may be socially castigated, their entrepreneurial activities treated as undesirable and even declared illegal. In Zimbabwe, women have created informal trade networks that span several countries in an attempt to supplement family incomes. However, this transgressing of social boundaries has resulted in their being branded as prostitutes and harassed at international borders.[54] Increasingly, however, the international donor community is recognizing the growth potential among women entrepreneurs and is investing heavily in micro-credit programmes. Still, research from Bosnia showed that programmes targeting women tend to be at the lower end of the loan market whereas male borrowers are able to access significantly larger amounts of credit.[55] As they have become more successful economically, male-dominated state institutions have brought in regulations to undermine them. An alternative approach would be to investigate such activities and identify ways to support their development: many women's businesses fail because of insufficient capital and skills in business management. Relief and development organizations increasingly seek to work with women in the postwar context, and are also able to offer sources of income, either as direct employment or to support women's organizations. In the postwar countries of former Yugoslavia, women were very effective at coming together to establish new organizations so as to take advantage of this opportunity.

Selling sex to survive

The last resort for women without other gainful employment is often prostitution.[56] In postwar contexts formal and informal selling of sex flourishes, particularly where there is an international market, such as from international peacekeepers and international tourism.[57] Postwar countries may see very fast growth in the numbers of women involved, because of their lack of other opportunities, the presence of foreign, therefore moneyed, clients, and the degree of dislocation in social relationships.

The dilemmas faced by postwar authorities in managing prostitution are therefore even more complex than usual. The most effective strategy for limiting the numbers of women involved would be to support their alternative endeavours in small-scale production and trade, through the provision of training and small loans, and to ensure that they are included in general opportunities for training and education appropriate for formal-sector employment. This plea has featured in major reports for many years, but there are still many women who find they have little choice but to risk their lives in this way. Even those who are lucky enough to undergo training or education have to find ways to eat in the meantime.[58]

HEALTH, WELFARE AND EDUCATION

At the end of most wars, health services are very run-down and may even have collapsed entirely. Even where there have been valiant attempts to keep some kind of health provision going for children, that for adult civilians has usually been undermined. This is dramatically illustrated by the fact that women's mortality tends to worsen at a faster rate than men's during war, because of the indirect impact of war on mortality via health service collapse, food shortages and lack of professional obstetric assistance, rather than as a direct impact of fighting.[59] High morbidity and mortality levels in a population from avoidable disease constitute a serious development cost;[60] however, expenditure on health has not been given adequate weight by international financial institutions and major donors in the terms for loans and investments for postconflict reconstruction. Leading economists have called for public entitlements to health and education to be sustained during and after wars, particularly as primary health and education only take a fraction of social expenditure.[61]

Virtually every report on women and conflict highlights the need for health programmes to be geared specifically towards women, including ex-combatants, as a precondition for social recovery. Neglect of women's health needs during pregnancy, childbirth, and for rape injuries tends to be common; this neglect has a multiplier effect on their difficulties in meeting the needs of dependants and other community members, as well as undermining their ability to participate in public life. Instead, women are subject to gender bias against their interests in the ways that many health and welfare policies work during "normal" times. Injured women may not be able to access even the most basic elements of community support where they are stigmatized as a result of surviving their assaults, and/or being pregnant, and/or having HIV/AIDS.

Neglect of women's basic needs has an impact throughout society, as they tend to be the main carers at home. An alternative approach prioritizing women's welfare requirements would have positive knock-on effects throughout society during peace building. This requires imaginative and innovative approaches to budget allocations which are unlikely to become commonplace in the future.

In the immediate postwar setting, special measures are often put in place to provide support for ex-combatants before, during and after the processes of "demobilization, development and reintegration". It is still common for women (and child, especially girl) ex-combatants to be relatively marginalized, if not completely neglected in such programmes,[62] in spite of this having been highlighted for nearly a decade.

One of the most challenging areas in postwar healthcare is the need to address psychosocial trauma. Alcoholism, anxiety, violent and aggressive behaviour, even suicide, are common as a result of wartime experiences and difficulty in coming to terms with the postwar situation. Trauma counselling receives insufficient attention, and where resources are available, may be poorly designed. Research suggests that the employment of western medical approaches to treat such problems, by focusing on the individual, is not appropriate for all cultural contexts. In many predominantly rural societies the ways in which people experience trauma not as isolated individuals, but within a socially constructed context, mean that support has to take this into account, if not actually be provided through social relationships. Awareness is growing that culturally specific healing processes can be more effective in such societies.[63] Where women have roles in the rituals and practices associated with such healing, they could be given support.

Perhaps surprisingly, education is often seen by survivors of wars as a key part of recovery. This is partly because of a need to "return to normal", but also because people recognize that for children, and even adults, education can play an important role in conflict prevention. Women often attempt to re-establish primary education themselves during and after wars, rather than wait for the state to do it. In spite of its having this high priority in people's minds, government spending on education is restricted by the same budgetary constraints as health, and so rarely meets expectations.

In many countries, girls participate in education to a lesser degree than boys. Although this can be reversed during wars when boys may be away from home, the process of rehabilitating educational provision usually finds the proportion swing back again once boys return.[64] There are many ways in which unequal access to education reinforces gender inequalities, and this is therefore a useful point of intervention to foster future positive change. The education of girls and women is vital if women are ever going to be able to participate effectively in peace negotiations, postwar planning and public life. Even where women are included in peace negotiations, they are at a strong disadvantage where they do not even have primary education, while most other key players have been at least to secondary school.

Where peace education is taken seriously as part of the new curriculum, this frees women from what might be seen as a private responsibility (that of educating their children for peace) and makes it a public activity in which men can also play a part. Where peace education also contains explorations of gender issues, this can have a long-term impact on the overall transformation of gender relations in ways connected and unconnected to war.

WOMEN'S RIGHTS AND POSTWAR POLITICAL CHANGE

As well as trying to rebuild economies and societies, postwar administrations face the challenge of trying to (re)build respect for human rights and for rights-based behaviour in the population at large, among former fighters, members of the security forces, and in the justice system. Despite significant improvements, women are still able to access fewer political rights than men in the postwar context, as in most others.

Nurturing a human rights culture in the postwar context is complicated because all too often many of the perpetrators of human rights abuses during the war are still at large; they may even be members of the government, the police or the armed forces. Even where the necessary legal framework and evidence against suspects are available, a relatively small number of perpetrators tend to be prosecuted.[65] Furthermore, attempts to (re)establish the rule of law in postwar contexts have proved to be extremely difficult in most places, even where extraordinarily large sums of money are invested, as was the case in Latin America.[66]

The most common focus in immediate postwar situations is on the behaviour of the state, whether in a new or a changed form, to ensure that military and police personnel no longer act outside the law through arbitrary arrest, detention and torture. This attracts plaudits from the international community, even though achieving real change can remain elusive for many years. All too often however the (re)establishment of some degree of law and order simply means that men are not suffering such serious abuse at the hands of those holding power.

Children's rights have been taken more seriously over the last decade, with the plight of former child soldiers receiving a great deal more attention and increasing international support, but the focus still remains on boys' war experience rather than girls. Many experiences of girls, such as sexual abuse by peacekeeping forces in Mozambique,[67] remain hidden.

Women's human rights are sadly still not automatically considered with the same degree of importance as men's, even while they suffer forms of abuse identified above as part of the postwar backlash. In contexts where transitional systems of justice are used as part of a process to rebuild the rule of law, women's human rights are not given priority. For instance, the police tend to operate with a strong gender bias, even where postwar reform and political change means that men are no longer subject to arbitrary arrest and torture. It is not uncommon for there to be immense postwar social pressure on women not to report abuse by men, particularly if the men are members of key political movements, the government, or where there is a shortage of men available for marriage. Where rape was widespread during war, and wartime rapes are not effectively prosecuted afterwards, it is extremely difficult to bring prosecutions for rape in the postwar setting, an issue that remains as much of a problem as when it was highlighted over a decade ago in the United Nations.[68]

Violations of women's rights

Until relatively recently, women's rights in the postwar context seem to have been breached almost with complete impunity. In recognition of their persistent abuse in all stages of war, the UN Security Council passed a landmark resolution in 2000, UN Security Council Resolution 1325. Although this was an important achievement, Resolution 1325 has not escaped criticism.

Initial reviews speak of gaps in its conceptual framework, failures of implementation,[69] and a lack of proper guidelines for practical application in the field. However, to women in conflict zones, such initiatives can mean a great deal. This was evidenced by the story of women from Afghanistan, Kosovo and East Timor, who came together to testify before the Security Council in October 2001 to honour the Resolution's first anniversary.[70]

The immense international publicity about rape during war has had the effect of channelling additional resources into women's concerns in the postwar context, although these are by no means successfully mainstreamed into health or development policies. International agencies and human rights organizations offer support to local human rights organizations; but women's rights are still typically not centre-stage and such organizations are only now beginning to have an effect on women's lives. Women are increasingly forming human rights organizations themselves, and there are several that have taken on the challenge of retraining the police, judiciary and other institutions to contest the discrimination, culture and practices that are so deeply entrenched in the institutions of law and order.[71]

Increasingly, good practices with regard to helping women to report and record information, and to prevent the representation of postwar domestic violence as "cultural", are being

---

Box 14.4   UN Security Council Resolution 1325

Resolution 1325 urges member states to ensure increased representation of women at all levels of decision making in national, regional and international institutions and mechanisms for the prevention, management and resolution of conflict. It calls on:

> all actors involved, when negotiating and implementing peace agreements, to adopt a gender perspective, including, inter alia:
>
> (a) the special needs of women and girls during repatriation and resettlement and for rehabilitation, re-integration and postconflict reconstruction;
>
> (b) measures that support local women's peace initiatives and indigenous processes for conflict resolution, and that involve women in all of the implementation mechanisms of the peace agreements;
>
> (c) Measures that ensure the protection of and respect for human rights of women and girls, particularly as they relate to the Constitution, the electoral system, the police and the judiciary.

Source: UN Security Council 2000

Box 14.5   Talking about sexual assault and rape

"I have a question", Mirha Nurka begins, standing confidently in front of the 15 male judges. "Who had sex last night, and how was it?" There is an awkward stir in the room. The men shift in their chairs, or frown in distaste. Several clear their throats. One bursts into laughter. "I'm serious," Nurka continues. "We'd like each of you to share the details with the group." The judges have gathered in Zenica ... for the second day of a workshop on gender-based violence in the district. Mirha Nurka, their trainer, is a member of Medica Zenika, an NGO that is using their research on violence against women to change the way judges, prosecutors, police and health and social service providers respond to abused women. She waits until the silence is almost painful. "You don't need to answer. But can anyone tell me why you think I asked the question?" The men, relieved, begin to talk. They spend the next several hours trying to grasp how survivors of sexual assault and rape must feel when they are asked to describe their humiliating experiences in detail, again and again, to a judge and jury.

Sources: Spindel et al. 2004.

shared. Significant advances have taken place with regard to the prosecution of abuses against women during war, and it is to be hoped that further improvements in this area will assist those organizations that are also trying to work to prevent its occurrence in the postwar setting. However, as a recent report by the UN Secretary-General observes: "the facts on the ground point to our collective failure in preventing such violence and protecting women and girls from the horrors of gender-based violence and heinous violations of international human rights, criminal and humanitarian law. Sexual and gender-based violence has been recently reported in Afghanistan, Burundi, Chad, Côte d'Ivoire, the Democratic Republic of the Congo and in Darfur, the Sudan."[72]

SEEKING JUSTICE FOR WAR RAPE AND SEXUAL VIOLENCE

In spite of the large number of internal conflicts and of the existing international humanitarian legislation as governed by the Fourth Geneva Convention and Protocol II, historically few prosecutions of war crimes have occurred; fewer still have involved gender-based violence. Although these legal instruments have been available since 1949, they have not been implemented effectively and have proven to be limited. Amnesty

for war criminals is an important tool in peace negotiations, but its use may preclude their prosecution, as happened in a recent peace negotiation in Burundi.[73]

The past decade, however, has seen dramatic developments in, and enforcement of, international humanitarian law primarily through the creation of the ad hoc war crimes tribunals for Yugoslavia and Rwanda, the International Criminal Courts as well as the tribunals set up in Sierra Leone and East Timor.

Engendering the international legal framework [74]

Prior to 1994, the international legal framework governing armed conflict prohibited violence against women and in particular sexual violence. However, these provisions were considered inadequate and indeed inferior to the protection offered to men. Under the pressure of women's international organizations and of the political changes that occurred at the national and international levels throughout the 1990s, a new perspective on gender-based violence was established and violence against women has increasingly become a priority in the international agenda.

The dramatic atrocities in the Bosnian conflict and in the Rwandan genocide, and their media coverage, urged the international community to take serious measures to enforce women's rights. The massive scale of gender-based crimes and their systematic use as weapons of war prompted the international community into action. Here began the process of expanding a more gender-aware protective legal framework and enforcement. The UN Security Council set up the International Criminal Tribunal of Yugoslavia (ICTY, Security Council Resolution 827/93) and the International Criminal Tribunal of Rwanda (ICTR, Security Council Resolution 955/94) to prosecute these war crimes. Both the ICTY and ICTR Statutes explicitly mentioned rape only under crimes against humanity; this left it open to the tribunals to determine the precise standing of rape and other sexual offences in international law. Despite initial disappointment that the definitions were so limited, both tribunals were successful in establishing historic legal precedents, breaking new legal ground and expanding international jurisprudence. The cases of Tadic, Akayesu and Kunarac were landmark cases where perpetrators of violence against women in wartime were prosecuted for the first time.

Cases of prosecution of rape as a war crime [75]

The first case dealt by the ICTY—the prosecution of Dusko Tadic—illustrates a number of initial problem areas encountered. First, evidence of sexual violence had not been treated as seriously as other crimes. It was only when the female member of the Trial Chamber, Judge Odio Benito, challenged the Prosecutor upon receipt of submissions from women's organizations that a more robust view was taken in prosecuting these crimes. The case further raised the importance of protective measures for witnesses, leading to the establishment of guidelines set down by the Trial Chamber presided over by Gabrielle Kirk MacDonald. However, Tadic was never prosecuted for rape as the complainant decided not to testify.

The case of Akayesu in Rwanda establishes a remarkable number of historic precedents related to the definition of rape as well as to its conviction. Like the Tadic case, no charges related to sexual violence appeared at the initial stage of the trial. Only later, as the female judge Pillay drew out evidence of sexual violence from one of the witnesses' testimony, was Akayesu prosecuted and convicted for rape as a crime against humanity. Without

any precedent, sexual violence was punished by an international court in an internal conflict, with a pioneering definition of rape as "a physical invasion of a sexual nature, committed under circumstances that are coercive". Even more importantly, for the first time rape was punished as an act of genocide aimed at destroying a group, as it was found to be a constituent element of genocide "causing serious bodily or mental harm".

Equally, the Kunarac or "Foca" case constitutes a pioneering conviction of perpetrators of rape, for it redefined rape as a violation of sexual autonomy. More, this judgement acknowledged rape as an element of torture causing severe physical and mental pain and suffering, as well as of enslavement as a crime against humanity. It was also the first indictment brought to an international tribunal exclusively on the basis of a crime of sexual violence against women.

The International Criminal Court

Gender-based crimes are also now codified in humanitarian law in the International Criminal Court (ICC) Statute. This specifically mentions rape, sexual slavery, enforced prostitution and enforced sterilization as war crimes and crimes against humanity. It goes one step further in allowing any other forms of sexual violence as a grave breach of the Geneva Conventions. Persecution on the basis of gender is also now admitted in the definition of crimes against humanity. Further, by providing definitions of rape, enslavement and sexual violence, case law has helped to advance understanding by establishing that rape and other forms of sexual violence can constitute war crimes, crimes against humanity, and genocide.

In 1997 a Women's Caucus for Gender Justice was formed within the ICC, which brought together many groups and individuals who worked to ensure the centrality of a gender perspective in the procedures and functioning of the court. Among its other provisions, the ICC ensures protection for victims, and it requires that both male and female judges have legal expertise on specific issues, including violence against women.[76] However, the ICC has many limitations, not least that its jurisdiction only applies in signatory states; and it has no power to locate war criminals, execute arrest warrants, search homes and buildings, or compel witnesses to attend trial.

Box 14.6   Prosecuting sexual crimes in Sierra Leone's UN Special Court

The court was set up to hold accountable those most responsible for the atrocities committed during the Sierra Leonean civil war. Despite having significantly fewer resources and staff than the ICT for Rwanda, Prosecutor David Crane ensured that the prosecution strategy incorporated sexual crimes. With only 10 investigators in the team, two competent and experienced female investigators were immediately dedicated to sexual assault investigations (in contrast to the 1–2 per cent of a team of 100 working for the Rwandan tribunal). After only one year, all the indictments included sexual violence, before the court had even begun to hear cases. Crane also tasked a trial attorney to develop the prosecution plan for sexual crimes, and is planning not only to bring rape charges but to fully prosecute sexual violence, and to broaden the existing interpretation of international law. David Crane has shown that political will by the prosecutor can make all the difference, even when working under constrained conditions. On 7 May 2004 the Special Court of Sierra Leone announced that a new count of "forced marriage" will be added to the indictments against six defendants. It is the first time that forced marriage is prosecuted as a crime against humanity under international law.[78]

Source: Nowrojee 2004:13,23.

In Sierra Leone, political will and a commitment to learning from the mistakes of the ICTR enabled much faster and more effective prosecution of war crimes against women to take place, even without there being a majority of women judges or significant extra resources earmarked for special activities relating to women.[77]

This growing body of experience also helps people to campaign for their own countries to follow suit.[79] The ICC framework has also proved useful for highlighting crimes against women in several other contexts. It was incorporated into regulations of the special panels in East Timor and the Extraordinary Chambers in Cambodia. In Cambodia this was particularly important as there was no other reference to gender or sexual violence in the founding documents of the courts established to try Khmer Rouge leaders.

Slow and dilatory progress

Despite this progress, the majority of crimes against women during wartime still go unpunished. In the case of the ICTR, Judge Goldstone made it clear at the beginning that he intended to take crimes of sexual violence seriously, but then failed to develop the capacity of the investigations team to collect evidence; failed to include rape charges in most of the early indictments; and allowed there to be no consideration of this in the prosecution strategy.[80] Women survivors of such abuse are still stigmatized to a far greater degree than male survivors of human rights abuses, and are still at risk of being targeted again by perpetrators.[81] It is therefore not surprising that most women find it very difficult to take legal action and give evidence. Women are also still unlikely to receive compensation for such abuses, even where prosecutions are successful.

Wartime prosecutions tend to be painfully slow: "We will be dead before we see any justice," commented a woman seeking redress through the ICTR.[82] Ten years after the genocide, there have only been two successful prosecutions for rape and one acquittal. For many women, the process of justice—of revealing truths and validating people's stories, of showing up perpetrators in the open—is often at least as important as the outcome. Yet such prosecutions are ineffective as mechanisms to bring out and record narratives: the stories contain much more than comes to court. Rwandan women survivors' own accounts of rape and violence during the genocide reveal the extent to which the ICTR cannot be "left to tell the story".[83] These women are still waiting for an official announcement that what happened to them was wrong and that their survival does not signify collusion with their attackers. They also want support and better treatment as witnesses—at least the same level of healthcare and treatment for HIV/AIDS as the defendants awaiting trial. At present it seems unlikely that their requests will be met.

POSTWAR TRUTH PROCESSES, RECONCILIATION, AND WOMEN'S STORIES

The linking of "truth" and "reconciliation" has become very popular over the last decade. The most common understanding of "reconciliation" is that it is about restoring good relationships and involves some level of forgiveness; but different people mean different things, some focusing on what happens to individuals, some on groups, and some on society as a whole.[84] There is considerable national and international discussion about whether and how reconciliation might be possible,[85] but there has been virtually no discussion about "gender reconciliation". Women are often expected to identify themselves with reconciliation and peace-building interventions, in the same way as the idea of women's inherent peacefulness may be co-opted or deployed to reduce hostilities during wartime.[86] Some of these interventions could be interpreted as being about reconciliation between women and men.[87]

The issue of amnesty and truth-telling remains controversial; where amnesty is offered in return for truth-telling, the sense of being deprived of justice could provoke further violence. For this reason, when the El Salvadorian Truth Commission released its report, the government passed an amnesty law within a few days, fearing that the findings could fuel further conflict. In general, Truth Commissions do not have the power to prosecute, although some of them do grant amnesty; the South African Truth and Reconciliation Commission for example was empowered to grant amnesty to individual perpetrators in exchange for testimony if they could prove that their crimes were politically motivated. However, this can also create problems for anyone who would prefer a prosecution.

There have been 25 Truth Commissions in different parts of the world since 1974. Official Truth Commissions (TCs) take many different forms, seeking sometimes to find out information about "the disappeared", as in Argentina, Uganda and Sri Lanka; at other times to work towards "truth and justice" as in Haiti and Ecuador, or "truth and reconciliation" as in Chile, South Africa, the Federal Republic of Yugoslavia, East Timor and Peru. Box 14.7 summarizes the most common characteristics and purposes of TCs, but these are very difficult to achieve and most do not achieve them.

TCs can also be created by NGOs. When the government of Brazil refused to institute a formal enquiry into human rights abuses under Brazil's military regime, the Archbishop of Sao Paulo was assisted by the World Council of Churches in his own investigation. The Catholic Church in Guatemala also established a truth process.[88]

Difficulties of speaking out

The most common abuses under-reported to TCs are those suffered by women, as indeed are those least prosecuted. Women may find it impossible to speak out. In the most famous Truth and Reconciliation Commission (TRC), that in South Africa, although women constituted the majority of witnesses for acts of violence committed against others, only a few initially spoke about acts of sexual violence committed against themselves. After prompting from women activists, the TRC tried to create an enabling environment where women could feel safe to speak out; but even then few could find the words or courage to speak publicly of sexual violation. Some women-only hearings were then held, which many women regarded as successful in addressing the problem.[89] When women who have survived rape go on to enter public office, as has happened in South Africa[90] and Latin America,[91] they may strongly wish to avoid public exposure.

The development of good practice in encouraging women to come forward, in which women's organizations have played a key role, continues with tribunals and truth processes. The physical location of hearings is important where it is culturally or practically difficult for women to travel out of their homes; for this reason the Commissioners of the Guatemalan Commission for Historical Clarification[92] chose to travel to remote areas to reach out to the indigenous population. The Truth and Reconciliation Commission for Sierra Leone (2003) ensured that its 73 statement takers—who included regional and district co-ordinators—were first trained in taking statements; they then fanned out all over the country to talk to people who had been affected. The

Box 14.7	Characteristics and purposes of Truth Commissions

Four main characteristics:

- They focus on the past, and often on the recent past, but are not ongoing bodies such as human rights commissions.
- They investigate a pattern of abuse over a set period of time rather than a specific event. The mandate of TCs is time-bound, and specifies the types of abuse the Commission can look at.
- TCs are usually temporary bodies, operating over an average period of six months to two years at the end of which they submit a report. Sometimes their time period can be extended if necessary.
- They are officially sanctioned, authorized and empowered by the State; also sometimes by armed opposition groups as part of a peace negotiation. In theory this allows them access to information, and should also ensure that their recommendations and findings are taken seriously.

Source: Hayner 2001:14.

Six main purposes:

- To clarify and acknowledge truth.
- To respond to the needs and interests of victims / survivors.
- To contribute to justice and accountability.
- To outline institutional responsibility and recommend reforms.
- To promote reconciliation and reduce tensions resulting from past violence.
- To meet the rights of victims/survivors and society to the truth.

Source: Hayner 2001:28–31.

Sierra Leone Commission also established a Women's Task Force to work towards creating an enabling environment for women to be able to testify.

La Comicion de la Verdad y Reconciliacion—TRC—of 2001 in Peru looked at the conditions which accounted for 20 years of violent conflict, and formulated proposals to suggest how victims of violence could regain their dignity and humanity. From the beginning, the Commission incorporated a gender perspective as a central tenet, explicitly rejecting "the gender blind belief that the human rights of women and men are violated in the same way and with similar consequences".[93] The Commission put in place a gender programme to raise awareness of gender issues in the work of the Commission's interviewers and the rest of its officials in order to ensure that a gender perspective would be present in all its work. The programme developed training and communication materials, set up links, offered suggestions on how to carry out investigations in remote areas

and ensured that information was shared with different communities. Workshops were held in different areas on subjects such as disappearances, and educational materials were provided to help raise gender issues. This strategy of proactive engagement with women and the broader community ensured that gender concerns were given a hearing. The Commission's report stated that gender concerns were central to peace building, and needed to be taken into account if future human rights violations were to be prevented.

Recounting of war stories

The ideal of a gender-aware truth process is not only to avoid omitting the particular sufferings of women, but also to integrate into the conflict narrative their experiences as fighters, survivors of attack and torture, household managers and community leaders. To release such stories may require a different kind of truth process than a national commission. For example, in 2000 women's groups in Japan and neighbouring countries came together to hold a War Crimes Tribunal to look at the issue of sexual slavery by the Japanese army during the Second World War.[94] Set up by women's groups, this tribunal had no official status; but even though more than half a century had passed since they experienced being sexually abused, the women who came forward to testify felt keenly the need for public acknowledgment of what they had lived through. While reluctant to accept culpability, the Japanese government did eventually acknowledge the issue of sexual slavery, which had earlier been denied; however, the women's demand for compensation from the State was rejected. A few women accepted compensation from a special private fund, but many refused; it was important to them that the Japanese State itself make reparations and apologize.[95]

"Traditional" conflict resolution systems

In Africa, people are increasingly turning to local processes as a means of coming to terms with what happened during conflict. This coincides with a growing fashion among donors for promoting so-called "traditional" methods of conflict resolution (ending of organized violence) and postconflict mediation and reconciliation. Increasing funds are being applied to these, with multiple objectives and much confusion about whether justice, truth processes and/or reconciliation are being sought. These mechanisms include rituals, and transfers of property and labour (individual and collective), intended to achieve a range of outcomes including retribution, compensation, forgiveness and building of trust. Some of these systems are in regular use; others are being resurrected from the memories of elderly people and reinvented; yet others are actually being invented. These activities may co-exist in the same country—even in the same communities—but they are increasingly being packaged under the rubric of peace building, not least in order to access funding from international donors.[96]

These processes tend to reflect highly gendered local political and power relations, and by no means belong to a value-free

traditional culture. Women are normally completely marginalized in their practice, and their needs are not given any priority. Some even have cultural roots in such practices as exchanging women as wives between different groups by way of compensation and repairing community relations, as in Afghanistan.[97] In postwar contexts where there is a backlash against women, the revival of "traditional" practice can form part of the process of putting women back "in their place". On the other hand, where gender awareness is incorporated, it can be used to help build a new society. A notable example of this is the use of *Gacaca* in Rwanda. The Rwandan government revived an old system of dispute resolution that had largely fallen into disuse, to assist with hearing genocide cases. *Gacaca*, in its new form, has incorporated important roles for women (see also chapter 11). Among many other fundamental changes is the participation of women as judges, although it is too early to evaluate what difference this might make to the outcomes.

CIVIL AND POLITICAL PARTICIPATION

Where there is a perception that women "earned" new rights because of the roles they played during wartime, there may be a new awareness in the postwar environment of what women can contribute politically, and of the moral imperative to let this happen. The chances of such perceptions influencing political structures are greater where there is a conscious attempt to build a "new" society after a "liberation".[98] It is less likely when the postwar context is dominated by a political ideology that does not recognize women's contribution to, or potential for, public life.[99] In Kashmir, northern India, for example, it is unlikely that women will anticipate a moment of liberation. There, years of syncretism and a healthy mix of Islamic, Hindu and Sufi traditions had ensured a liberal space for women in society. With the deepening of the conflict and the growing hold of fundamentalism among insurgents, the imposition of restrictions on women has forced them to submit to rigid patriarchal mores.[100]

However, even in deeply conservative environments such as Kashmir or Somalia, there can also be recognition during wartime of the ways women exercise old forms of influence as power. In private, they may guide men's decisions; they may perform in public as singers or poets; they may give direction as elders or leaders in cultural activities, or act as informal negotiators while visiting kin or engaging in trade. From such gradual accretions of responsibility, the opportunity may emerge for basic legal and political rights to be developed in a postwar setting.

The chances of political participation

In the feverish postwar environment, new constitutions and laws with radical provisions can come speedily into being; even though they initially exist only on paper, they may well be more progressive than if there had been no war or upheaval. For example, after the war of liberation in Zimbabwe, women's legal status was much improved. In Namibia women were given clear rights in the constitution, as they were in Eritrea. The establishment of formal legal rights for women is, however, only one step towards their being able to exercise them. In postconflict settings, particularly where war has been prolonged, illiteracy is widespread and access to the law may be confined to a handful of the elite. So even if the population is aware of women's new rights they cannot easily be realized.[101] Moreover, the existence of such political rights does not protect women from the "backlash" explored earlier.

Even where the political and legal apparatus is in place to allow women to take part in political life, their level of political participation tends to remain lower than men's. They may be discouraged by the educational requirements for voter registration, or the long distance needed to travel in order to vote, as shown in a number of elections. Practical or cultural constraints, or family and community pressure, can bar women from exercising their right to vote, or standing in elections. In Algeria, men routinely vote on behalf of women. Similarly, attempts to encourage civil-society organizations to participate in public debate, or consult with government, may marginalize the views of women if they are dominated by men. Special activities to involve women may still be required, and may not be put in place even though they have long been proposed at the international level.

In situations where women are experiencing a backlash, it is extremely difficult to implement any measures that would increase their participation, even where there is the political will. For example, in Afghanistan, women are being excluded from democracy-promotion projects.[102] In postwar Central America, women ex-combatants who became politically active were ostracized by their families, and many faced sexual abuse from high-ranking officials within their own parties.[103]

The issue of how to increase women's representation in politics remains challenging, as discussed earlier in the report. The Beijing Platform for Action called for a 30 per cent minimum representation of women in decision-making bodies; UN Security Council Resolution 1325 urges the appointment of women in peace processes and subsequent political structures. There have been some striking successes in using these international frameworks to increase the representation of women. In postwar settings in particular there are sometimes opportunities for pushing forward reforms and innovative approaches, where there is a coincidence between the desires of international donors and local women's groups.

Where women have gained stronger political voice through the experience of conflict, they may be able to leapfrog stages that elsewhere remain protracted. For instance in South Africa, the majority of ANC leaders at the transition to democracy were men, even though gender equality was much discussed. Women fought for representation achieving the 30 per cent of seats in the National Parliament. Similarly in Eritrea, the government ensured that the postwar administrative system involved women; it was agreed that women would have a 30 per cent quota in regional and subregional councils and could contest any of the remaining 70 per cent of posts.[104] Even in Afghanistan, the Constitutional Loya Jirga ensured that at least 19 per cent of the 500 seats went to women, who actually gained 20 per cent.[105]

Sometimes measures to assist women's representation have been introduced postwar that would not be implemented in donor countries promoting this agenda.[106] For instance, the United Kingdom has legally rejected the use of women's quotas for political parties; but the reservation of seats for women in local and national government structures in Uganda was supported by the UK government.[107] Many such issues are felt

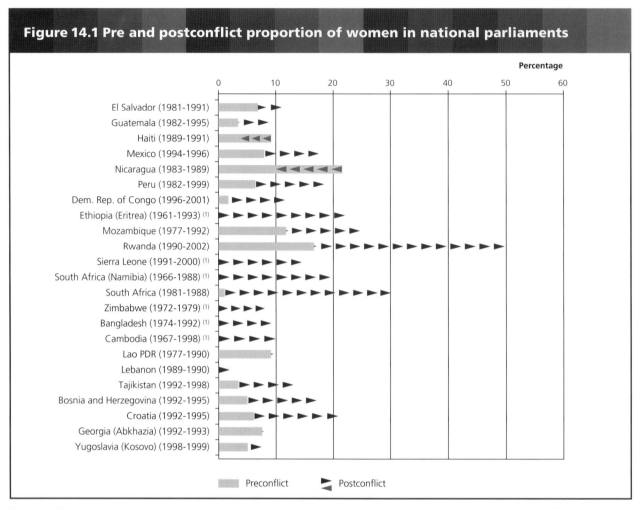

Figure 14.1 Pre and postconflict proportion of women in national parliaments

Notes: The years mentioned refer to the time range of the conflict considered. (1) Countries for which no data on pre conflict elections are available.
Source: IPU 2004; UN 2000a; UCDP/PRIO 2004

across the world as women try to increase their engagement in formal politics, but in postwar societies where the conditions are ripe, change can happen at an unprecedented rate. Rwanda offers a very striking example. Here, elections to the national assembly in 2003 delivered 49 per cent of the seats to women, a higher proportion than in any OECD country. This does not indicate a Rwandese revolution in gender relations, but rather reflects the high proportion of women among genocide survivors. Nonetheless this massive change was by no means demographically inevitable, and will have consequences for political life in Rwanda that are as yet too early to judge.

Visibility is not enough

For more than a decade, the United Nations has proclaimed that women's needs deserve greater attention in the postwar context. Yet the problems, rights abuses and programme shortcomings documented in many reports remain commonplace.[108] The plight of women during war, particularly the scale of their sexual violation, has attracted international attention, and is often used to characterize the barbarism of mankind or brutality of particular "enemy" groups. Women's roles in working to end conflicts are increasingly celebrated—even if other roles are downplayed. As a consequence, women participants in postwar peace building have been thrust into unprecedented prominence by certain international organizations. Yet for all this visibility, women usually remain marginal, as a group or as individuals, in peace negotiations, in consultations about postwar strategies, and in the public life of postwar societies.

The persistent reluctance of many analysts and advisers to take on board lessons about gender analysis and its incorporation into policy processes in the postwar setting needs to be recorded, and further effort is needed to overcome this thoughtless, or deliberate, resistance. This can itself be seen as part of the backlash against women, helping to allow, if not facilitate, the playing out of intense gender politics in households, communities and the wider polity. Feminist histories of conflict, and feminist studies of development, provide a rich store of relevant experiences, positive and negative. These have been collated and analysed for several years and comprise a significant literature; but they are still not taken sufficiently seriously by many of the key international actors in the context of postwar activity.

In the future it is to be hoped that international agencies and donors will be better prepared to take opportunities to put these lessons about how to mitigate injustices for women centre-stage when advising and supporting postwar recovery programmes—in the economic, social, political and governance spheres alike. As more successes are achieved, it is also to be hoped that postwar governments will more readily see the advantages in developing polices that not only support women's efforts to survive, but enable them to fulfil their potential in helping rebuild their societies in the image of gender equality and gender peace.

Notes

1 Rehn and Sirleaf 2002.

2 Pankhurst 2003:11; Pankhurst and Pearce 1997

3 Spindel et al. 2004; Rehn and Sirleaf 2002; Sørensen 1998.

4 Kandiyoti 2004: 25.

5 El Bushra 2004.

6 Jacobs and Howard 1987.

7 Luciak 2004:28.

8 De Abreu 1998; Luciak 2004.

9 Samuel 2004:6–7.

10 Sørensen 1998:37; Luciak 2004:23.

11 Sørensen 1998:39; Luciak 2004:23; El Bushra 2004.

12 Preston 1994:262, cited in Sørensen 1998:37.

13 El Bushra 2004.

14 Kelly 2000:62.

15 Pierson 1989.

16 El Bushra 2004.

17 Pankhurst 2003.

18 Korac 1998:39–46.

19 Turshen and Twagiramariya 1998:9.

20 Sørensen 1998: 41–2.

21 Pankhurst and Pearce 1997.

22 Yanira Argueta, cited in Luciak 2004:6.

23 Chingono 2001:116.

24 Sørensen 1998.

25 UN 1995a:para 141.

26 Elson 1995.

27 Stewart and Fitzgerald 2001:240.

28 Sørensen 1998:38.

29 UNIFEM 2001; Sørensen 1998:20.

30 Sørensen 1998:19.

31 UNIFEM 2001:45–53.

32 Chingono 2001: 95.

33 UNIFEM 2001:38–44.

34 Zimmerman 1994, cited in Curtis 1998.

35 UNIFEM 2001:58–62.

36 Davison 1998.

37 UNIFEM 2001; Davison 1998.

38 UNIFEM 2001:63.

39 Sørensen 1998:20; Chingono 1996.

40 UNIFEM 2001:45–53.

41 Yanira Argueta, cited in Luciak 2004:6.

42 Luciak 2001.

43 Luciak 2001.

44 UNIFEM 2001:66.

45 Pankhurst and Pearce 1997:161.

46 Stewart and Fitzgerald 2001.

47 Sørensen 1998.

48 Kelly 2000:62.

49 Date-Bah 1996, cited in Sørensen 1998.

50 Sørensen 1998:26.

51 Abreha 1996, Klingeblel 1995, both cited in Sørensen 1998.

52 Sørensen 1998:20, 22.

53 UNHCR 1994.

54 Cheater and Gaidzanwa 1996:191, cited in Sørensen 1998: 22.

55 Walsh 2000:10.

56 Coomaraswamy 2001, Add.2:20.

57 Sørensen 1998:24.

58 Rehn and Sirleaf 2002.

59 Stewart et al. 2001:93.

60 Stewart and Fitzgerald 2001:236.

61 Stewart and Fitzgerald 2001:237.

62 Farr 2003.

63 Sørensen 1998:34.

64 Stewart et al 2001:103.

65 Brownmiller 1975, and others cited by Walsh 2004:6.

66 Sieder 2003.

67 Nordstrom 1997:15–19.

68 For the example of Afghanistan see Kandiyoti 2004:27–8.

69 UNIFEM 2001.

70 Samuel 2004.

71 Spindel et al. 2004:85.

72 UN Secretary-General 2004:16.

73 Human Rights Watch 2003.

74 This subsection draws on Walsh 2004; Nowrojee 2004; ICC 1998.

75 This subsection draws on Walsh 2004.

76 UNIFEM 2001.

77 Nowrojee 2004:13,23.

78 See Special Court for Sierra Leone 2004.

79 Rehn and Sirleaf 2002: 88–97.

80 Nowrojee 2004:10.

81 Nowrojee 2004:24.

82 Nowrojee 2004:7.

83 Nowrojee 2004.

84 Pankhurst 1999

85 Bloomfield et al. 2003.

86 Pankhurst 2003.

87 On former Yugoslavia see Žarkov et al. 2004:11.

88 REMHI 1999.

89 Goldblatt and Meintjes 1998:29.

90 Sørensen 1998.

91 Luciak 2004.

92 REMHI 1999.

93 Mantilla 2003.

94 Chinkin 2001.

95 Vanderweert 2001:141.

96 Pankhurst 2002, 2003.

97 Kandiyoti 2004:26.

98 For example in Nicaragua in the 1980s, southern Africa in the 1970s and 1980s, the 'new' South Africa in 1990s, and possibly Iraq in 2004.

99 Sørensen 1998; on Afghanistan, Kandiyoti 2004:32.

100 Butalia 2004.

101 See Batezat et al. 1988 on Zimbabwe, Bentley 2004 on South Africa.

102 Kandiyoti 2004:32.

103 Luciak 2004.

104 Tsefai 1996, Fessehassion 1989, Marcus 1996, all cited in Sørensen 1998.

105 Kandiyoti 2004:19–20.

106 Rehn and Sirleaf 2002: 81.

107 Tamale 1999.

108 For instance see UN 1995a, 1996, 1997, 1998.

Concluding remarks

Women's agency is today increasingly visible and impressive in women's movements around the world, in organizations of civil society, in the state and political society, and in the international development establishment. Processes of democratization, to which women's movements contributed, have altered the terms under which women's groups engage in political activity. Despite some initial setbacks and loss of momentum, strategies have been adapted and revised to help women gain political power under the democratic rules of the game. The entry of more women into national legislatures as well as municipal councils and other locally administered bodies has contributed to the deepening of democracy around the world, while providing valuable openings for women representatives and councillors to articulate different priorities in national and local decision making.

Dovetailing with the vociferous demands of women's movements, "femocrats" from within the state and women legislators have worked hard to make national laws responsive to women's reproductive health and rights, and to prohibit violence and discrimination against women, no matter where these violations occur and who their perpetrators are. Landmark international prosecutions against sexual assault in war as a crime against humanity now mean that public actors responsible for sexual violence are beginning to be held accountable not just to the citizens of their own countries, but to global society.

These explicit policy and legislative moves have combined with long-term processes of social change in families and cultural practices to bring more women into the public domain. A decade on from Beijing there is indeed much to celebrate.

But there is also much at risk. On the tenth anniversary of the Beijing Conference women's movements will be pondering not only the continued dominance of neoliberalism in some important arenas of policy making, but the challenges thrown up by the recent shifts in geopolitics and new forms of religious-identity politics played out at the global, national and subnational levels. Women's ambitions for social change risk taking a back seat to concerns with security. Unilateralism is eroding the multilateral framework within which transnational feminist networks have painstakingly nurtured a global women's rights regime over the years. In a polarized ideological climate where security concerns loom large and internal dissent is discouraged, sustaining autonomous spaces where women's groups and movements can address critical and controversial issues of gender equality and liberal freedoms will require political agility and alliance building with other social movements, political parties and states.

ECONOMIC LIBERALIZATION

In reflecting on the achievements of the 1990s, the report has paid particular attention to the contribution that development policy can make in accentuating or diminishing women's subordination. It has suggested that among the reasons for the persisting gender inequalities has been the prevailing policy orthodoxy with its emphasis on monetary and fiscal restraint.

Economic liberalization has never been smooth or uncontested, and there have always been spaces for policy experimentation and heterodoxy, whether with respect to macroeconomic policies or social policies. Where policy makers have followed orthodox prescriptions—whether under pressure from Washington or of their own volition—the outcomes have been disappointing, even in the estimate of their designers. Rural livelihoods have become more insecure (as well as more diversified) in contexts where cutbacks in state support to domestic agriculture have coincided with increasing exposure to competition from large subsidized producers. At a time when global commodity markets have been volatile and depressed, large numbers of people have been trapped in poverty, hunger and even famine.

Insecurity is also etched into the growth of informal economies across the world, where "flexibility" has come to mean a weakening of labour standards rather than creating a better balance between work and life. With weak public health and welfare programmes, fragile infrastructure and thin social protection mechanisms, the provision of unpaid care by women and girls has been intensified—to intolerable degrees in sub-Saharan Africa, where the HIV/AIDS epidemic is taking a staggering toll of lives. At the same time taking on paid work has become ever more necessary for all household members—whether male or female, young or old—to make ends meet in increasingly commercialized contexts.

However it is important to underline that the economic policy agenda that has been so deeply adverse to many women and men around the world has also provided new opportunities to some social groups, including some low-income women. Jobs in export-oriented manufacturing firms and capitalist farms producing "high value" agricultural export crops around the world, no matter how fragile and short-lived, and how low the pay and unfavourable the conditions of work, have benefited some women: giving them their first discretionary income, new social contacts beyond the confines of kinship and neighbourhood, the chance to postpone marriage at a young age, maybe save for a better future, invest in their children's education, or have a greater say in how household resources are allocated. This may not have ended women's subordination and dependence on male protection, but it has given some women at least the tools with which to whittle away at the pillars of patriarchy. For those who command more capital and resources, liberalization of markets has provided opportunities to trade and invest, to purchase land and housing in their own name, and bequeath it to their offspring or siblings, perhaps in return for the promise of protection and security in old age.

For the vast majority of women, however, gender equality will remain a distant dream as long as the market calculus remains the principal arbiter of policy. Attaining gender equality requires the strengthening of publicly accountable systems of mutual assurance against entitlement failure. This means investing in areas that orthodox prescriptions cannot countenance: well-functioning and accessible public health and education services, labour standards and rights that protect women's employment and conditions of work, and investment in public provision of a range of complementary services (clean water, sanitation, electricity, paved streets, childcare) to support the care economy.

To have substantive rights and entitlements implies access to an accountable process where access to a resource is not at the arbitrary discretion of a public official, dependent on the favour of a patron or the goodwill of a husband, or the price-fixing power of a monopoly supplier.[1] Genuine empowerment is about having meaningful institutional alternatives to dependence on familial and conjugal relations, on markets and employers, and on public and non-state actors when the terms of any of these relations become unacceptable. It means decent jobs with employment rights, and fair allowances for lifecycle contingencies such as old age, ill-health, disability and periods of intense care. It also means a more equal sharing of unpaid care between men and women, and thus a redefinition of full-time work.

EMBEDDING LIBERALISM?

In response to widespread discontent with the liberalization agenda, more attention is now being given to social policies and governance issues. There is the view in some policy circles that if globalization is to stay on course, then it must be "tamed" or "embedded" through social policies and political reforms.[2] However, the full potential of these positive moves is vitiated by the persistent dominance of "market fundamentalism" in some of the most influential arenas of policy making.[3]

The social distress and inequalities that are being unleashed by current economic policies are far more extensive than the remedies that are suggested. Such prescriptions thus risk replicating the by now well-rehearsed limitations of minimal safety nets in the era of structural adjustment. In the context of liberalized trade (which reduces import and export taxes), and the pressures from mobile capital (which reduce corporate taxes, capital gains and income taxes) it is very difficult for governments to raise the kind of revenues needed to finance public services and transfers that can meet the casualties of economic policies. In sum, there is a lack of affinity and complementarity between sectoral and macroeconomic policies.

It is now more widely recognized that effective governance is not about shrinking the state. The neoliberal reform agenda is criticized by some of its own architects for its failure to unpack the different dimensions of "stateness" and distinguish between state scope and state strength.[4] Even on the restricted versions of governance, as seen by the international financial institutions (IFIs), the nimble, responsive state that regulates private industry and commercialized social services is a pretty high-capacity state. That means training, salaries and incentives.

It is also increasingly clear that the view of the modern state envisaged in governance reforms—with lean and clean bureaucracies and judiciaries creating the conditions for unfettered market competition, inviolable and individual property rights, well-enforced contracts—never actually existed in any historical version of the development of capitalism.[5] The "blueprint" versions of institutional reform that are being pushed on developing countries in order to foster growth will not necessarily promote vibrant private sectors, at least if history is to be taken as the guide. The dangers of institutional "monocropping"[6] mean that governance reforms are likely to run into as many problems as economic reforms, as they encounter the unruly reality of developing-country institutions.[7]

Nevertheless, there is an increasingly coordinated assault on domestic market and state institutions to make them resemble this abstract model. In this ideal state and market, gender equality hardly figures. Instead, the "abstract market" and "rational-legal" state are based on the notion of the rational, unencumbered, free-choosing individual. As the analysis in this report suggests, women do not fit this model. They have dependants and care burdens. Their political "voice" can be muffled by gender-biased institutions and the restricted notions of participation that some governance reforms entail.

TOWARDS A GENDER-EQUITABLE POLICY AGENDA

Any proposal for alternatives must eschew prescribing a "one-size-fits-all" solution in the manner that orthodox approaches have done, given the immense institutional, historical, social and political diversities among countries.[8] Charting gender-equitable macroeconomic policy is in a sense an art, for which there is no simple recipe. There are certain guiding principles however that macroeconomic policies need to observe: avoiding deflationary policies that sacrifice growth and employment creation, placing equality as a central objective at the heart of policy making along with macroeconomic stability, and ensuring affinities and complementarities between sectoral and macroeconomic policies. As a leading economist puts it:

"Financial conservatism has good rationale and imposes strong requirements, but its demands must be interpreted in the light of the overall objectives of public policy. The role of public expenditure in generating and guaranteeing many basic capabilities calls for attention; it must be considered along with the instrumental need for macroeconomic stability. Indeed, the latter need must be assessed within a broad framework of social objectives".[9]

While economic growth provides the necessary conditions for escaping poverty, improving standards of living, and generating resources for redistributive policies, it is not sufficient for gender equality. The widely praised East Asian growth trajectories may have produced relatively egalitarian societies in terms of asset and income distribution between social classes and households, but they were far from egalitarian when it came to gender relations and outcomes. This is not to suggest that growth is inherently inimical to gender equality, but to underline the point that some growth trajectories may indeed coincide with, or be premised upon, a highly inegalitarian gender order. High rates of economic growth, for example, may draw more women into the labour force, but this can coincide with persistent gender segmentation in labour markets. What this suggests is that more specific policies are needed to make growth and gender equality compatible: social regulation of all labour markets to erode gender-biased social norms and remove discriminations that account for the persistence of gender segmentation, together with removal of structural constraints on women's ability to take up widening labour-market opportunities.

Similarly, higher rates of growth together with taxation policies that generate higher levels of government income do not necessarily lead to a more gender-equitable use of these resources. To ensure that public expenditure is actually reaching women and girls equitably, for example, and that women benefit from mechanisms promoting social security, gender-policy objectives have to be set and mechanisms put in place to guarantee that public expenditures are channelled to these areas, and to the provision of infrastructure and services that contribute to a reduction in women's unpaid labour time.

The feminization of national parliaments and local governments in some parts of the world will not necessarily mean that women politicians will use gender budget initiatives—or indeed other mechanisms—to advance women's interests. The responsiveness of women in public office to the gender-equality cause will depend upon a number of factors, including whether their means of access to politics enjoins them to respond to a female constituency, and whether their political resources include the capacity to ensure that political parties place gender equality on their platforms. The effectiveness of women politicians as gender-equality advocates will also depend on whether the institutions of governance—the judiciary, the audit systems, the legislature, the public administration—can be reformed to make social justice and gender equality a measure of excellence in public service.

As the preceding paragraphs have argued, where economic and governance reforms do not pay heed to the protection of human rights and do not contribute to building meaningful opportunities for participation and deepening democracy, it

will remain difficult to enshrine gender justice as a measure and objective of performance in the public sector. Indeed, if the privatization of core state functions in some places, and the limitations imposed on domestic policy making by economic globalization in others, are heralding the demise of the proactive state capable of "governing markets",[10] then the capacity of women in public office to bring gender equality into public policy will be greatly diminished.

It is far too early to mourn the demise of the state, however. The many contradictions in the liberalization agenda are forcing a reassessment of policies for market and state reform that have proven destructive for secure livelihoods and for national stability. Democratization and globalization have also raised citizen expectations about the role of the state. In diverse contexts there are growing popular expectations that principles of greater accountability, transparency and openness should apply not just to commercial transactions, but across all institutions, public and private. Globalization has meant that the jurisdictions for rights-based struggles have multiplied: no longer limited to the state level, but evident at both supra and subnational levels. It is now possible for women's justice struggles to find an international audience through global justice institutions, and new local audiences through new institutions of local government.

These efforts to advance women's access to resources and to justice can support the efforts of gender-equality advocates at national levels to create and enforce progressive legislation on women's rights. This kind of multiple-jurisdiction strategy is evident today in, for instance, efforts to deal with sexual and domestic violence in Rwanda.[11]

The central instrument for the protection of rights has been, and must remain, the state, even if its own practices and institutions need to be thoroughly democratized to deliver gender justice.[12] Where market fundamentalism has reduced the legitimacy of the state as the maker of national rules about the obligations and rights of citizens, the utility of the state as the most important mechanism for promoting social change and enforcing standards of gender equality is diminished.

Fragile, failing or conflict-ridden states present acute challenges to the project of pursing gender equality, challenges that will demand increasing international attention over the years to come. Where core state functions, such as the provision of basic social services, are offloaded onto humanitarian and international aid organizations, where the processes of state building and peace consolidation are themselves subject to blueprints laid out by international players, and where domestic women's movements are weak, it is extremely difficult to build a national consensus for gender justice.[13]

On the contrary, when people seek social protection from traditional or informal social institutions, because of state failure to provide services or a sense of national purpose, conservative scripts for gender relations may enjoy a revival (or be invented from scratch). The resilience of these informal institutions, their ingenuity in substituting for state services, and their enduring effectiveness at providing members with dignity and social purpose, mean that these institutions must be recruited to the task of rebuilding social cohesion in post-conflict situations or in failing states.

It may be difficult to insert gender-equality concerns (or broader social equality concerns) to these processes, where traditional institutions have a patriarchal character,[14] but it is not impossible. South Africa provides a model of holding traditional institutions to basic constitutional standards of social equality. The South African case underlines the need for the state to uphold gender equality across all social institutions, and this will remain a challenge in fragile or failing state contexts.

What this shows is that good governance and equality projects are costly—they require strong states—but they are essential for building secure states and societies capable of tolerating diversity and difference. Neoliberal prescriptions for market and state reform avoid issues of inequality. In the short term inequalities, including gender-based inequalities, may facilitate rapid growth, but in the long term they deeply undercut the contribution of growth to poverty reduction, they erode social cohesion, and they can foster extremist political activity and instability.

Notes

1   Elson 2002.
2   ILO 2004d; Ruggie 2003.
3   Molyneux 2002.
4   Fukuyama 2004.
5   Upham forthcoming.
6   Evans 2004.
7   Mkandawire 2004.
8   Rodrik 2004.
9   Sen 1999:141.
10 Wade 1990.
11 Goetz and Jenkins 2004:chapters 2, 4.
12 Molyneux and Razavi 2002b.
13 Kandiyoti 2004.
14 Kabeer 2002.

Background papers

Ackerly, Brooke and Bina D'Costa. **Transnational Feminism and the Human Rights Framework.**

Basu, Amrita. **Women, Political Parties and Social Movements in South Asia.**

Basu, Rasil. **Gender and Local Government in India.**

Beall, Jo. **Decentralizing Government and Centralizing Gender in Southern Africa? Lessons from the South African Experience of Local Government.**

Berik, Günseli. **Growth and Gender Equity in East Asia.**

Bisnath, Savitri. **Trading to Equality? Gender and Trade Liberalization.**

Bouvier, Virginia. **Crossing the Lines: Women's Social Mobilization in Latin America.**

Boyd, Monica and Deanna Pikkov. **Gendering Migration, Livelihoods and Entitlements: Migrant Women in Canada and the United States.**

Braunstein, Elissa. **Foreign Direct Investment, Development and Gender Equity. A Review of Research and Policy.**

Butalia, Urvashi. **Gender and Conflict in South Asia.**

Cortes, Rosalia. **Gendered Patterns of Informalization in the Latin American Urban Labour Market: The 1990s.**

Deere, Carmen Diana. **The Feminization of Agriculture? Economic Restructuring in Rural Latin America.**

Diop, Ngoné. **Gender and Macroeconomic Policy in Rwanda. How to Make the PRSP Implementation Pro-Poor and Gender Responsive?**

Doraisami, Anita. **The Gender Implications of Macroeconomic Policy and Performance in Malaysia.**

Ekine, Sokari. **Women's Responses to State Violence in the Niger Delta.**

Espino, Alma and Paola Aznar. **Changes in Economic Policies in Uruguay from a Gender Perspective (1930–2000).**

Eyben, Rosalind. **The Road not Taken: International Aid's Choice of Copenhagen Over Beijing.**

Fejic, Goran and Rada Ivekovic. **Women and Armed Conflict.**

Fodor, Eva. **Women and Political Engagement in East-Central Europe.**

Fodor, Eva. **Women at Work: The Status of Women in the Labour Markets of the Czech Republic, Hungary and Poland.**

Gallin, Dan and Pat Horn. **Organizing Informal Women Workers.**

Ghosh, Jayati. **Informalization and Women's Workforce Participation: A Consideration of Recent Trends in Asia.**

Goetz, Anne Marie. **Gender and Good Governance at the National Level: Do Growing Numbers of Women in Public Office Produce Better Public Sector Accountability to Women?**

Guhathakurta, Meghna. **The Chittagong Hill Tracts (CHT) Accord and After: Gendered Dimensions of Peace.**

Hardy, Chandra. **The Political Economy of Development, 1945 to Date.**

Jackson, Cecile and Nitya Rao. **Understanding Gender and Agrarian Change under Liberalization: The Case of India.**

Jie, Du. **Women's Participation in Politics in the Transition to a Market Economy in China: Progress at High-Level Politics since 1995.**

Kandiyoti, Deniz. **The Politics of Gender and Reconstruction in Afghanistan.**

Kapur, Ratna. **Women's Equality and the Indian Constitution: Transformative or Truncated Justice.**

Kofman, Eleonore. **Gendered Migrations, Livelihoods and Entitlements in the European Union.**

Kwan Lee, Ching. **Livelihood Struggles and Market Reform: (Un)making Chinese Labour After State Socialism.**

Laky, Teréz. **Gender Equality in Employment in Hungary and in Some Other Eastern European Countries.**

Lazreg, Marnia. **Political Liberalization, Islamism and Feminism in Algeria, Egypt and Jordan.**

Li, Zongmin. **Gendered Impacts of Changes in Property Rights to Rural Land in China.**

Luciak, Ilja A. **Joining Forces for Democratic Governance: Women's Alliance-Building for Post-War Reconstruction in Central America.**

Lund, Frances. **Informal Workers' Access to Social Security and Social Protection.**

Mackintosh, Maureen and Paula Tibandebage. **Gender and Health Sector Reforms: Analytical Perspectives on African Experience.**

Manjoo, Rashida. **The South Africa Truth and Reconciliation Commission – A Model for Gender Justice?**

Massolo, Alejandra. **Local Governments and Women in Latin America: New Changes and Challenges.**

Moghadam, Valentine. **Women's Livelihood and Entitlements in the Middle East: What Difference has the Neoliberal Policy Turn Made?**

Msimang, Sisonke and Cecile Ambert. **Outputs Versus Outcomes: Gender, Culture and HIV/AIDS in Southern Africa.**

Nowrojee, Binaifer. **"Your Justice is Too Slow". How the ICTR Failed Rwanda's Rape Victims.**

Nyamu-Musembi, Celestine. **For or Against Gender Equality? Evaluating the Post Cold-War 'Rule of Law' Reforms in Sub-Saharan Africa.**

Packard, Le Anh Tu. **Gender Dimensions of Viet Nam's Comprehensive Macroeconomic and Structural Reform Policy.**

Peng, Ito. **Social Policy Responses to Post-Industrial Pressures in Japan, South Korea, and Taiwan.**

Reddy, Rita. **Conflict Situations in Southeast Asia and the Response of Women and Women's Organizations with Specific Focus on Indonesia, Myanmar and Mindanao, Philippines.**

Sacchet, Teresa. **Political Parties and Gender in Latin America.**

Samuel, Kumudini. **Doing Peace Versus Talking Peace. Making Visible the Invisible.**

Seguino, Stephanie. **Gender, Well-Being and Equality: Assessing Status, Progress and the Way Forward.**

Selolwane, Onalenna. **Gendered Spaces in Party Politics in Southern Africa: Progress and Regress Since Beijing 1995.**

Sen, Gita. **Reproductive Rights and Gender Justice in the Neoconservative Shadow.**

Sen, Sunanda. **India: A Country Paper on Gender and Development.**

Sobritchea, Carolyn Israel. **Filipino Women's Participation in Politics and Governance.**

Sow, Fatou. **Mobilisation Politique des Femmes en Afrique de l'Ouest (Women's Political Mobilization in West Africa).**

Steinhilber, Silke. **The Gender Implications of Pension Reform. General Remarks and Evidence from Selected Countries.**

Subrahmanian, Ramya. **Gender Equality in Schooling: A Global Review.**

Todaro, Rosalba. **Chile Under a Gender Lens: From Import Substitution to Open Market.**

Tsikata, Dzodzi. **Economic Liberalization, the Informalization of Work and Urban Women's Livelihoods in Sub-Saharan Africa since the 1990s.**

Walsh, Martha. **Gendering International Justice: Progress and Pitfalls at International Criminal Tribunals.**

Whitehead, Ann. **The Gendered Impacts of Liberalization Policies on African Agricultural Economies and Rural Livelihoods.**

Yamanaka, Keiko and Nicola Piper. **Feminized Cross-Border Migration, Entitlements and Civil Action in East and Southeast Asia.**

Žarkov, Dubravka, Rada Drezgic and Tanja Djuric-Kuzmanovic. **Violent Conflicts in the Balkans: Impacts, Responses, Consequences.**

Bibliography

Abalu, George and Rashid Hassin. 1999. "Agricultural productivity and natural resource use in Southern Africa." *Food Policy*, Vol. 23, No. 6, pp.477–490.

Abdullah, An-Na'im. 2002. "Religion and global civil society: Inherent incompatibility or synergy and interdependence?" In M. Glasius, M. Kaldor and H. Anheier (eds.), *Global Civil Society 2002*. Oxford University Press, Oxford.

Abdullah, H. J. 2000. "Gender and adjustment in Nigeria's manufacturing sector." In Dzodzi Tsikata and Joanna Kerr (eds.), *Demanding Dignity: Women Confronting Economic Reforms in Africa*. Renouf Publishing, Ottawa.

Abers, Rebecca. 1998. "From clientelism to cooperation: Local government, participatory policy, and civic organising in Porto Alegre, Brazil." *Politics and Society*, Vol. 26, No. 4, pp.511–538.

Acero, Liliana. 1995. "Women's work in Brazilian and Argentinian textiles." In Swasti Mitter and Sheila Rowbotham (eds.), *Women Encounter Technology: Changing Patterns of Employment in the Third World*. Routledge, London and New York.

Ackerly, Brooke and Bina D'Costa. 2004. *Transnational Feminism and the Human Rights Framework*. Background Paper for UNRISD Report on Gender Equality: Striving for Justice in an Unequal World.

ActionAid. 2004. *Gender and Trade Liberalisation in Tanzania*. ActionAid UK, London.

Adamik, M. 1993. "Feminism and Hungary." In N. Funk and M. Mueller (eds.), *Gender Politics and Post-Communism*. Routledge, New York.

Adams, J. 1991. "Female wage labour in rural Zimbabwe." *World Development*, Vol. 19, No. 2/3, pp.163–177.

Afford, C. 2003. *Corrosive Reform: Failing Health Systems in Eastern Europe*. International Labour Organization (ILO), Geneva.

Afshar, Haleh. 2003. "Women and wars: Some trajectory towards a feminist peace." *Development in Practice*, Vol. 13, Nos. 2&3, pp.178–188.

Agarwal, Bina. 2003. "Gender and land rights revisited: Exploring new prospects via the state, family and market." *Journal of Agrarian Change*, Vol. 3, Nos. 1&2, pp.184–225.

—. 1994. *A Field of One's Own*. Cambridge University Press, Cambridge.

—. 1990. "Social security and the family in rural India: Coping with seasonality and calamity." *Journal of Peasant Studies*, Vol. 17, No. 3, pp.341–412.

Agarwal, Bina, Jane Humphries and Ingrid Robeyns (eds.). 2003. "A special issue on Amartya Sen's work and ideas: A gender perspective." *Feminist Economics*, Vol. 9, Nos. 2&3, pp.1–335.

Ahikire, J. 2003. "Gender equity and local democracy in contemporary Uganda: Addressing the challenge of women's political effectiveness in local government." In Anne-Marie Goetz and Shireen Hassim (eds.), *No Shortcuts to Power: African Women in Politics and Policy-Making*. Zed, London.

All-China Women's Federation (ACWF). 1998. *An Outline of the Women's Political Participation Since Liberation*. China CCP History Publishing House, Beijing.

Allan, Helen and John Aggergaard Larsen. 2003. *"We Need Respect": Experiences of Internationally Recruited Nurses in the UK*. Royal College of Nurses, London.

Amnesty International. 2004. *Sudan: Darfur: Rape as a Weapon of War: Sexual Violence and its Consequences*. http://web.amnesty.org/library/pdf/AFR540762004ENGLISH/$File/AFR5407604.pdf, accessed on 20 July 2004.

—. 1997. *Uganda, Breaking God's Commands: The Destruction of Childhood by the Lord's Resistance Army, AI Index: AFR 59/01/97*. Amnesty International, London.

Amsden, Alice H. 1989. *Asia's Next Giant: South Korea and Late Industrialization*. Oxford University Press, Oxford.

AnanthPur, Kripa. 2004. *Rivalry or Synergy? Formal and Informal Local Governance in Rural India*. Institute of Development Studies (IDS) Working Paper No. 226, IDS, Brighton.

Anker, R.H. 1998. *Gender and Jobs: Sex Segregation of Occupations in the World*. ILO, Geneva.

Anker, R., H. Melkas and A. Korten. 2003. *Gender-Based Occupational Segregation in the 1990s*. ILO Working Paper No. 16. Focus Programme on Promoting the Declaration on Fundamental Principles and Rights at Work, ILO, Geneva.

Anner, Mark and Peter Evans. 2004. "Building bridges across a double divide: Alliances between US and Latin American labour and NGOs." *Development in Practice*, Vol. 14, Nos. 1&2, pp.34–47.

Arabsheibani, G. Reza, Francisco Carneiro and Andrew Henley. 2003. *Gender Wage Differentials in Brazil: Trends over a Turbulent Era*. World Bank Policy Research Working Paper No. 3148. World Bank, Washington, D.C.

Ardington, Elisabeth and Frances Lund. 1995. "Pensions and development: social security as complementary to programmes of reconstruction and development." *Development Southern Africa*, Vol. 12, No. 4, pp.557–577.

Arizpe, L., F. Salinas and M. Velásquez. 1989. "The effects of the economic crisis on the living conditions of peasant women in Mexico." In UNICEF (ed.), *Poor Women and the Economic Crisis. The Invisible Adjustment*. Americas and the Caribbean Regional Office, UNICEF and Alfabeta Impresores, Santiago de Chile.

Asia Watch and Women's Rights Project. 1993. *Modern Form of Slavery: Trafficking of Burmese Women and Girls into Brothels in Thailand*. Human Rights Watch, New York.

Asis, Maruja Milagros B., Shirlena Huang and Brenda S.A. Yeoh. 2004. "When the light of the home is abroad: Female migration and the Filipino family." *Singapore Journal of Tropical Geography*, Vol. 25, No. 2, pp.198–215.

Avritzer, Leonardo. 2000. *Civil Society, Public Space and Local Power: A Study of the Participatory Budget in Belo Horizonte and Porto Alegre*. Report for the IDS/Ford Foundation project "Civil Society and Democratic Governance". Unpublished mimeo, IDS, Brighton, UK.

Baden, Sally. 1996. *Gender Issues in Financial Liberalization and Financial Sector Reform*. Topic paper prepared for the Directorate General for Development (DGVIII) of the European Commission. Bridge, Development-Gender, IDS, Brighton.

Baden, Sally and Anne-Marie Goetz. 1998. "Who needs (sex) when you can have (gender)?" In Cecile Jackson and Ruth Pearson (eds.), *Feminist Visions of Development: Gender Analysis and Policy*. Routledge, London.

Baffes, John. 2002a. *Tanzania's Coffee Sector: Constraints and Challenges in a Global Environment*. Africa Region Working Paper Series No. 56. World Bank, Washington, D.C.

—. 2002b. *Tanzania's Cotton Sector: Constraints and Challenges in a Global Environment*. World Bank, Washington, D.C.

Bailey, B. 2003. *Gender-Sensitive Educational Policy and Practice: The Case of Jamaica*. Background Paper for the EFA Global Monitoring Report 2003/04. UNESCO, Paris.

Bakker, Isabella (ed.). 1994. *The Strategic Silence: Gender and Economic Policy*. Zed, London.

Balakrishnan, Radhika (ed.). 2002. *The Hidden Assembly Line: Gender Dynamics of Subcontracted Work in a Global Economy.* Kumarian Press, Bloomfield, Conn.

Baldez, Lisa. 2004. "Elected bodies: Gender quota law for legislative candidates in Mexico." *Legislative Studies Quarterly,* Vol. 29, No. 2, pp.231–258.

—. 2002. *Why Women Protest.* Cambridge University Press, Cambridge.

—. 1997. *Democratic Institutions and Feminist Outcomes: Chilean Policy toward Women in the 1990s.* Working Paper No. 340. Washington University, Department of Political Science, Seattle.

Baldwin, P. 1990. *The Politics of Social Solidarity: Class Bases of the European Welfare State, 1875–1975.* Cambridge University Press, Cambridge and New York.

Banerjee, Paula. 2001. "Between Two Armed Patriarchies: Women in Assam and Nagaland". In Rita Manchanda (ed.), *Women, War and Peace in South Asia,* New Delhi, Sage.

Bangura, Yusuf. 2004. *Technocratic Policy Making and Democratic Accountability.* UNRISD Research and Policy Brief No. 3. UNRISD, Geneva.

—. 2000. *Public Sector Restructuring: The Institutional and Social Effects of Fiscal, Managerial and Capacity-Building Reforms.* Geneva 2000 Occasional Paper No. 3, UNRISD, Geneva.

—. 1994. *Economic Restructuring, Coping Strategies and Social Change: Implications for Institutional Development in Africa.* Discussion Paper No. 52, UNRISD, Geneva.

Barr, N. A. 1998. *The Economics of the Welfare State.* Stanford University Press, Stanford, Conn.

Barrientos, Armando. 2004. "Comparing pension schemes in Chile, Singapore, Brazil and South Africa." In Peter Lloyd-Sherlock (ed.), *Living Longer: Ageing, Development and Social Protection.* UNRISD/Zed Books, Geneva and London.

Barrientos, Armando and Stephanie Barrientos. 2002. *Extending Social Protection to Informal Workers in the Horticulture Global Value Chain.* Social Protection Discussion Paper Series No. 0216. World Bank, Washington, D.C.

Barrientos, Stephanie. 2001. "Gender, flexibility and global value chains." Issue on *The Value of Spreading the Gains from Globalisation, IDS Bulletin,* Vol. 32, No. 3, July, pp.83–93.

Barrientos, Stephanie, A. Bee, A. Matear and I. Voger. 1999. *Women in Chilean Agribusiness: Working Miracles in the Chilean Fruit Export Sector (Women Studies at Work Series).* Macmillan, London.

Baru, R. 2003. "Privatisation of health services: A South Asian perspective." *Economic and Political Weekly,* Vol. 38, No. 42, pp.4433–4437.

Barya, J.-J. and J. Oloka-Onyango. 1994. *Popular Justice and Resistance Committee Courts in Uganda.* Centre for Basic Research, Kampala.

Basu, Amrita. 2004. *Women, Political Parties and Social Movements in South Asia.* Background Paper for UNRISD Report on Gender Equality: Striving for Justice in an Unequal World.

—. 1995. "Feminism inverted: The gendered imagery and real women of Hindu nationalism." In Tanika Sarkar and Urvashi Butalia (eds.), *Women and the Hindu Right: A Collection of Essays.* Kali for Women, New Delhi.

Batezat, E., M. Mwalo and K. Truscott. 1988. "Women and independence: The heritage and the struggle." In Colin Stoneman (ed.), *Zimbabwe's Prospects: Issues of Race, Class, State and Capital in Southern Africa.* Macmillan, Basingstoke.

Battistella, Graziano and Maruja M.B. Asis (eds.). 2003. *Unauthorized Migration in Southeast Asia.* Scalabrini Migration Center, Quezon City.

Bauer, Gretchen. 2004. "The hand that stirs the pot can also run the country: Electing women to parliament in Namibia." *Journal of Modern African Studies,* Vol. 42, No. 4, December.

Beall, Jo. 2004. *Decentralizing Government and Centralizing Gender in Southern Africa: Lessons from the South African Experience of Local Government*. Background Paper for UNRISD Report on Gender Equality: Striving for Justice in an Unequal World.

Bean, Frank D. and Gillian Stevens. 2003. *America's Newcomers and the Dynamics of Diversity*. Russell Sage Foundation, New York.

Beckwith, Karen. 2004. *Mapping Strategic Engagements of Women's Movements*. Paper presented at Annual Meeting of the International Studies Association, Quebec, Canada, 17–20 March.

—. 2002. *The Substantive Representation of Women: Newness, Numbers, and Models of Representation*. Paper presented at Annual Meeting of the American Political Science Association, Boston, USA, 29 August–1 September.

—. 2001. "Women's movements at century's end: Excavations and advances in political science." *Annual Review of Political Science*, Vol. 4, pp.371–390.

—. 2000. "Beyond compare? Women's movements in comparative perspective." *European Journal of Political Research*, Vol. 37, No. 4, pp.431–468.

Beneria, L. and M.S. Floro. 2004. *Labour Market Informalization and Social Policy: Distributional Links and the Case of Homebased Workers*. Paper prepared for the UNRISD Project on Social Policy and Gender, Mimeo, Geneva.

Bennett, Olivia, Jo Bexley and Kitty Warnock. 1995. *Arms to Fight, Arms to Protect: Women Speak Out About Conflict*. Panos, London.

Bentley, Kristina. 2004. "Women's human rights and the feminisation of poverty in South Africa." *Review of African Political Economy*, No.100, pp.247–261.

Berik, Gunseli. 2004. *Growth and Gender Equity in East Asia*. Background Paper for UNRISD Report on Gender Equality: Striving for Justice in an Unequal World.

—. 2000. "Mature export-led growth and gender wage inequality in Taiwan." *Feminist Economics*, Vol. 6, No. 3, pp.1–26.

Bhagwati, J. 2002/3. *Why Free Capital Movements may be Hazardous to your Health: Lessons from the Latest Financial Crisis*. Remarks prepared for the National Bureau for Economic Research (NBER) Conference on Capital Controls, Cambridge, Mass.

Bhattacharya, Debapriya and Mustafizur Rahman. 1999. *Female Employment under Export-Propelled Industrialization: Prospects for Internalizing Global Opportunities in Bangladesh's Apparel Sector*. Beijing Occasional Paper No. 10, UNRISD, Geneva.

Bigsten, Arne, Jorgen Levin and Hakan Persson. 2001. *Debt Relief and Growth: A Study of Zambia and Tanzania*. Paper presented at World Institute for Development Economics Research (WIDER) Development Conference on Debt Relief, Helsinki.

Bijlmakers, L., M. Bassett and D. Sanders. 1996. *Health and Structural Adjustment in Rural and Urban Settings in Zimbabwe at a Time of Structural Adjustment: A Three-Year Longitudinal Study*. Nordic Africa Institute Research Report No. 101, Nordic Africa Institute, Uppsala.

Blackden, C.M. 1997. *All Work and No Time: The Relevance of Gender Differences in Time Allocation for Agricultural Development in Zambia*. World Bank, Washington, D.C.

Blackden, C.M. and C. Bhanu. 1999. *Gender, Growth and Poverty Reduction: 1998 Africa Poverty Status Report*. World Bank for the Special Program of Assistance for Africa, Washington, D.C.

Bloomfield, David, Teresa Barnes and Luc Huyse (eds.). 2003. *Reconciliation After Violent Conflict: A Handbook*. International Institute for Democracy and Electoral Assistance (IDEA), Stockholm.

Boulding, E. 1993. "States, boundaries and environmental security." In Dennis J.D. Sandole and Hugo van der Merwe (eds.), *Conflict Resolution Theories and Practice: Integration and Application*. Manchester University Press, Manchester.

Bouvier, Virginia. 2004. *Crossing the Lines: Women's Social Mobilization in Latin America*. Background Paper for UNRISD Report on Gender Equality: Striving for Justice in an Unequal World.

Boyd, Monica. 2001. "Gender inequality: Economic and political aspects." In Robert J. Bram (ed.), *New Society: Sociology for the 21st Century*, 3rd edn. Harcourt Canada, Toronto.

—. 1992. "Gender issues in immigration trends and language fluency: Canada and the United States." In Barry R. Chiswick (ed.), *Immigration Language and Ethnic Issues: Public Policy in Canada and the United States*. American Enterprise Institute, Washington, D.C.

Boyd, Monica and Pikkov Deanna. 2004. *Gendering Migration, Livelihood and Entitlements: Migrant Women in Canada and the United States*. Background Paper for UNRISD Report on Gender Equality: Striving for Justice in an Unequal World.

Boylan, Delia M. 1998a. *Holding Democracy Hostage: Central Bank Autonomy in the Transition from Authoritarian Rule*. Paper presented at 56th Annual Meeting of the Midwest Political Science Association, Palmer House Hilton, Chicago, 23–25 April.

—. 1998b. "Preemptive strike: Central bank reform in Chile's transition from authoritarian rule." *Comparative Politics*, Vol. 30, No. 4, pp.443–462.

Brand, L.A. 1998. *Women, the State, and Political Liberalization: Middle Eastern and North African Experiences*. Columbia University Press, New York.

Braunstein, Elissa. 2004. *Foreign Direct Investment, Development and Gender Equity: A Review of Research and Policy*. Background Paper for UNRISD Report on Gender Equality: Striving for Justice in an Unequal World.

Breman, Jan. 1996. *Footloose Labour: Working in India's Informal Economy*. Cambridge University Press, Cambridge.

—. 1985. *Of Peasants, Migrants and Paupers: Rural Labour Circulation and Capitalist Production in West India*. Oxford University Press, Oxford.

Bruno, M. and W. Easterly. 1996. "Inflation and growth: In search of a stable relationship." *Federal Reserve Bank of St. Louis*, Vol. 78, No. 3, pp.139–146.

Bryceson, Deborah Fahy. 2002. "The scramble in Africa: Reorienting rural livelihoods." *World Development*, Vol. 30, No. 5, pp.725–739.

—. 1999a. *African Rural Labour, Income Diversification and Livelihood Approaches: A Long-Term Development Perspective*. ASC Working Paper No. 35, African Studies Centre, Leiden.

—. 1999b. *Sub-Saharan Africa Betwixt and Between: Rural Livelihood Practices and Policies*. ASC Working Paper No. 43, African Studies Centre, Leiden.

Buch, N. 2000. *Women's Experience In New Panchayats: The Emerging Leadership of Rural Women*. Occasional Paper No. 35, Centre for Women's Development Studies, Calcutta.

Budlender, Debbie. 1999. *The Fourth Women's Budget*. Institute for Democracy in South Africa (IDASA), Cape Town.

Busse, Matthias and Christian Spielmann. 2003. *Gender Discrimination and the International Division of Labour*. HWWA Discussion Paper No. 245. Hamburg Institute of International Economics, Hamburg.

Butalia, Urvashi (ed.). 2002. *Speaking Peace: Voices of the Women of Kashmir*. Kali for Women/Zed Books, Delhi/London.

Butalia, Urvashi. 2004. *Gender and Conflict in South Asia*. Background Paper for UNRISD Report on Gender Equality: Striving for Justice in an Unequal World.

Byamukama, E. 2001. *Population Dynamics of Vectors of SPVD in Uganda*. MSc dissertation, Makerere University, Kampala, Uganda.

Cagatay, Nilüfer and Korkut Ertürk. 2003. *Gender and Globalization: A Macroeconomic Perspective*. Mimeo, University of Utah Department of Economics, Utah, USA.

Cagatay, Nilüfer and Süle Ozler. 1995. "Feminization of the labour force: The effects of long-term development and structural adjustment." *World Development*, Vol. 23, No. 11, pp.1883–1894.

Caldeira, T. 2004.

—. 2000. *City of Walls: Crime, Segregation and Citizenship in Sao Paulo*. University of California, Berkeley.

Campos, J. Edgardo and Shilpa Pradhan. 2003. *A Framework for Studying Governance Reforms at the Country Level*. Mimeo, World Bank, Washington, D.C.

Cardelle, A. 1997. *Health Care in the Time of Reform: Emerging Policies for Private-Public Sector Collaboration on Health*. North South Centre publication, Vol. 6, No. 1.

Case, Anne. 2001. *Health, Income and Economic Development*. Paper presented at the ABCDE Conference, World Bank, Washington D.C., May.

Case, Anne and Angus Deaton. 1998. "Large cash transfers to the elderly in South Africa." *Economic Journal*, Vol. 108, pp.1330–1361.

Castles, Stephen. 2003. "Towards a sociology of forced migration and social transformation." *Sociology*, Vol. 37, No. 1, pp.13–34.

Center for Women War Victims. 2003. *Women Recollecting Memories: Center for Women War Victims Ten Years Later*. Center for Women War Victims, Zaghreb.

Centro Feminista de Estudos e Assessoria (CFEMEA). 2000. "Balanço Legislativo de 1999." *Jornal Fêmea*, No. 85, February. pp.1–12.

Chang, Kai. 1995. "Female employees' working conditions in medium and large state-owned enterprises." *Sociological Research*, Vol. 3, pp.83–93.

Chant, S. and S. Radcliffe. 1992. "Migration and development: The importance of gender." In S. Chant (ed.), *Gender and Migration in Developing Countries*. Belhaven Press, London and New York.

Chatterjee, Mirai and M. Kent Ranson. 2003. "Livelihood security through community-based health insurance in India." In Lincoln Chen, Jennifer Leaning and Vasant Narasimhan (eds.), *Global Health Challenges for Human Security*, Harvard University Press, Cambridge.

Chattopadhyay, Raghabendra and Esther Duflo. 2004. "Impact of reservation in Panchayati Raj: Evidence from a nationwide randomised experiment." *Economic and Political Weekly*, Vol. 39, No. 9, pp.979–986.

Chen, Martha, Jennefer Sebstad and Lesley O'Connell. 1999. "Counting the invisible workforce: The case of homebased workers." *World Development*, Vol. 27, No. 3, pp.603–610.

Chen, Shaohua and Martin Ravallion. 2001. "How did the world's poor fare in the 1990s?" *Review of Income and Wealth*, Vol. 47, No. 3, pp.283–300.

Chhachhi, A. and R. Pittin. 1996. *Confronting State, Capital and Patriarchy: Women Organizing in the Process of Industrialization*. Macmillan, Basingstoke.

Chin, Christine B.N. 2003. "Visible bodies, invisible work: State practices toward migrant women domestic workers in Malaysia." *Asian and Pacific Migration Journal*, Vol. 12, No. 1–2, pp.49–73.

Chingono, Mark. 2001. "Mozambique: War, economic change and development in Manica Province, 1982–1992." In Frances Stewart and Valpy Fitzgerald (eds.), *War and Underdevelopment*, Oxford University Press, Oxford/New York.

Chinkin, Christine. 2001. "Women's International Tribunal on Japanese Military Sexual Slavery. Editorial comment." *American Journal of International Law*, Vol. 95, pp.335–341.

Chiriboga, M., R. Grynspan and L. Pérez. 1996. *Mujeres de Maíz*. Banco Interamericano de Desarrollo (BID)/Instituto Interamericano de Cooperación para la Agricultura (IICA), San José.

Cho, Hyoung, Ann Zammit, Jinjoo Chung and In-Soon Kang. 2004. "Korea's miracle and crisis: What was in it for women?" In Shahra Razavi, Ruth Pearson and Caroline Danloy (eds.), *Globalization, Export-Oriented Employment, and Social Policy: Gendered Connections*, Palgrave, Basingstoke.

Coalition on Violence Against Women (COVAW-Kenya). 2002. *In Pursuit of Justice: A Research Report on Service Providers' Response to Cases of Violence Against Women in Nairobi Province*. COVAW - Kenya, Nairobi.

Collins, Catherine. 2004. "Turkey orders sermons on women's rights; Reforms preached in 70,000 mosques." *Chicago Tribune*, 9 May, p. 3.

Collins, Joseph and Bill Rau. 2000. *AIDS in the Context of Development*. Social Policy and Development Occasional Paper No. 4, UNRISD, Geneva.

Commission on Human Security. 2003. *Human Security Now: Protecting and Empowering People*. Commission on Human Security, New York.

Convention on the Elimination of All Forms of Discrimination against Women (CEDAW). 1999. *Optional Protocol to the Convention on the Elimination of All Forms of Discrimination Against Women*. Article 4. United Nations, New York.

Cook, Sarah and Susie Jolly. 2001. *Unemployment, Poverty and Gender in Urban China*. Research Report No. 50, IDS, Brighton, UK.

Coomaraswamy, Radhika. 2001. *Report of Special Rapporteur on Violence against Women, Mission to Sierra Leone 21–29 August 2001*. United Nations E/CN.4/2002/83.

—. 1998. *Report of the Special Rapporteur on Systematic Rape, Sexual Slavery and Slavery-like Practices During Armed Conflict*. United Nations E/CN.4/sub/2/1998/13, 22 June.

Coopoo, S. 2000. "Women and local government revenue", in Parliamentary Committee on the Quality of Life and Status of Women, *Women's Budget Series: 2000 issue*, Cape Town: Parliamentary Committee on the Quality of Life and Status of Women, CASE and Idasa.

Corner House. 2004. *Briefing 31: A Decade After Cairo: Women's Health in a Free Market*. http://www.thecornerhouse.org.uk.

Cornia, Giovanni Andrea. 1996. *Labour Market Shocks, Psychological Stress and the Transition's Mortality Crisis*. Research in Progress No. 4. United Nations University (UNU)/ WIDER, Helsinki.

Cornia, Giovanni Andrea, Tony Addison and Sampsa Kiiski. 2004. "Income distribution changes and their impact in the post-second World War Period." In Giovanni Andrea Cornia (ed.), *Inequality, Growth, and Poverty in an Era of Liberalization and Globalization*. Oxford University Press, Oxford.

—. 2003. *Income Distribution and Changes in their Impact in the Post-World War II Period*. WIDER Discussion Paper No.2003-28. UNU/WIDER, Helsinki.

Cornia, Giovanni Andrea, Richard Jolly and Frances Stewart (eds.). 1987. *Adjustment with a Human Face: Protecting the Vulnerable and Promoting Growth*. Clarendon Press, Oxford.

Corrin, Chris. 2003. "Developing Policy on Integration and re/construction in Kosovo." *Development in Practice*, Vol. 13, Nos. 1&2, pp.189–207.

Cueva, Hanny. 2004. *Women in Politics: What Difference does it Make? An Empirical Assessment on the Case of Abortion Laws*. MPhil Development Studies (MP 27), Institute of Development Studies, Brighton, UK.

Curtis, Grant. 1998. *Cambodia Reborn? The Transition to Democracy and Development*. Brookings Institution Press and UNRISD, Washington and Geneva.

Da Corta, Lucia and Davuluri Venkateshwarlu. 1999. "Unfree relations and the feminization of agricultural labour in Andhra Pradesh, 1970–1995." *Journal of Peasant Studies*, Special Issue, Vol. 26, No. 2/3, pp.71–140.

Dahl, Marilyn. 1987. *The Cultural Production of the Disabled Role Identity in Contemporary Canadian Society*. MA thesis, Simon Fraser University, Burnaby, BC.

Dahlerup, D. 1986. "Is the new women's movement dead? Decline or change of the Danish movement." In D. Dahlerup (ed.), *The New Women's Movement: Feminism and Political Power in Europe and the USA*, Sage, London.

Darcy, R., Susan Welch and Janet Clark. 1994. *Women, Elections and Representation*. University of Nebraska Press, Lincoln.

Das Gupta, Monica and P.N. Mari Bhat. 1998. "Intensified gender bias in India: A consequence of fertility decline." In Maithreyi Krishnaraj, Ratna M. Sudarshan and Abusaleh Shariff (eds.), *Gender, Population and Development*, Oxford University Press, New Delhi.

David, M., Beatriz de A., C. Morales and M. Rodríguez. 2001. "Modernidad y heterogeneidad: Estilo de desarrollo agrícola y rural en América Latina y el Caribe." In Beatriz David, C. Morales and M. Rodríguez (eds.), *Desarrollo rural en América Latina y el Caribe. La construcción de un nuevo modelo?* Economic Commission for Latin America and the Caribbean (ECLAC) and Alfaomega, Santiago de Chile.

Davison, Jean (ed.). 1998. *Agriculture, Women and Land: The African Experience*. Westview Press, Boulder, Colo.

De Abreu, Alcinda António. 1998. "Mozambican women experiencing violence." In M. Turshen and C. Twagiramariya (eds.), *What Women Do in Wartime: Gender and Conflict in Africa*. Zed, London.

de Soto, H. 2000. *The Mystery of Capital: Why Capitalism Triumphs in the West and Fails Everywhere Else*. Random House, New York.

Deedat, H. 2003. *Women Workers in the Leather and Footwear Industry in South Africa*. Research Report TWN-Africa, Accra North.

Deere, Carmen Diana. 2004. *The Feminization Of Agriculture? Economic Restructuring In Rural Latin America*. Background Paper for UNRISD Report on Gender Equality: Striving for Justice in an Unequal World.

—. 2003. "Women's land rights and rural social movements in the Brazilian agrarian reform." *Journal of Agrarian Change*, Vol. 3, Nos. 1&2, pp.257–288.

Deere, Carmen Diana and Magdalena Leon. 2003. "The gender asset gap: land in Latin America." *World Development*, Vol. 31, No. 6, pp.925–947.

Deininger, K. and P. Olinto. 2000. *Why Liberalisation Alone has not Improved Agricultural Productivity in Zambia: The Role of Asset Ownership and Working Capital Constraints*. Working Paper No. 2302, World Bank, Washington, D.C.

del Alba Acevedo, Luz. 2000. *Expanding the Boundaries of Citizenship: Women in Puerto Rico's Legislature*. Paper presented at International Political Science Association, Quebec City, Canada, 1–5 August.

Department of Homeland Security, United States. 2003. Office of Immigration Statistics. Unpublished tabulations 1990–2000, accessed January 2004.

Department for International Development (DFID). 2002. *Safety, Security and Access to Justice for All: Putting Policy into Practice*. DFID, London.

Deshmukh-Ranadive, J. 2003. "Placing gender equity in the family centre stage: Use of 'Kala Jatha' theatre." *Economic and Political Weekly*, Vol. 38, No. 17, pp.1674–1679.

Deutsche Gesellschaft für Technische Zusammenarbeit (GTZ). 2004. *Migration and Development*. GTZ, Eschborn.

Devereux, Stephen. 2002. "The Malawi famine of 2002." *IDS Bulletin*, Vol. 33, No. 4, pp.70–78.

Devereux, Stephen and R. Sabates-Wheeler. 2004. *Transformative Social Protection*. Working Paper, IDS, Brighton, UK.

Diamond, P. and S. Valdes-Prieto. 1994. "Social security reforms." In P.B. Bosworth, R. Dornbusch and R. Laban (eds.), *The Chilean Economy: Policy Lessons and Challenges*. Brookings Institution, Washington, D.C.

Dijkstra, A. Geske. 2002. "Revising the UNDP's GDI and GEM: Towards an alternative." *Social Indicators Research*, Vol. 57, No. 3, pp.301–338.

Directorate General of Budget and Statistics. 2003. *Yearbook of Earnings and Productivity, Directorate General of Budget and Statistics*, Taiwan.

Dobrowolsky, Alexandra and Vivien Hart (eds.). 2003. *Women Making Constitutions: New Politics and Comparative Perspectives*. Palgrave Macmillan, Basingstoke.

Dodson, D. L. and S.J. Carroll. 1991. *Reshaping the Agenda: Women in State Legislatures*. Center for the American Woman and Politics, New Brunswick, N.J.

Doezema, J. 2004. *Sex Slaves and Discourse Masters: The Historical Construction of Trafficking in Women.* DPhil thesis, Institute of Development Studies, Brighton, UK.

Dolan, Catherine S. 1997. *Tesco is King: Gender and Labour Dynamics in Horticultural Exporting, Meru District, Kenya.* PhD thesis, State University of New York at Binghamton. Available from UMI Dissertation Services, Ann Arbor, Mich.

Dolan, C. and K. Sorby. 2003. *Gender and Employment in High-Value Agricultural Industries Agriculture and Rural Development.* Working Paper Series No. 7, World Bank, Washington, D.C.

Dollar, David and Roberta Gatti. 1999. *Gender Inequality, Income, and Growth: Are Good Times Good for Women?* Policy Research Report on Gender and Development, Working Paper Series No. 1, World Bank, Washington, D.C.

Drage, J. 2001. *Women in Local Government in Asia and the Pacific. A Comparative Analysis of Thirteen Countries.* http://hdrc.undp.org.in/APRI/Rsnl_Rsrc/comparative_report.pdf, accessed May 2004.

Dwyer, D. and J. Bruce (eds.). 1988. *A Home Divided: Women and Income in the Third World.* Stanford University Press, Stanford, Calif.

Eade, Deborah. 2004. "Editorial overview." *Development in Practice,* Vol. 14, Nos. 1&2, pp.5–12.

Economic Commission for Latin America and the Caribbean (ECLAC). 2004. *Panorama Social de América Latina 2002–2003.* ECLAC, Santiago de Chile.

—. 2002. *Latin America and the Caribbean: Selected Gender-Sensitive Indicators.* Demographic Bulletin No. 70 (July), ECLAC, Santiago de Chile.

Economic and Political Weekly (EPW). 1995. "Panchayats: The dark side." EPW, Bombay, 18 March.

Economic Research Forum for the Arab Countries, Iran and Turkey (ERF). 1998. *Economic Trends in the MENA Region.* ERF, Cairo.

—. 1996. *Economic Trends in the MENA Region.* ERF, Cairo.

Ehrenreich, Barbara and Arlie R. Hochschild (eds.). 2003. Global Woman. *Nannies, Maids and Sex Workers in the New Economy.* Metropolitan Books, New York.

Eichengreen, Barry and Michael Mussa. 1998. "Capital account liberalization and the IMF." *Finance and Development,* Vol. 35, No. 4, pp.16–19.

Einhorn, Barbara. 1993. *Cinderella Goes to Market: Citizenship, Gender and Women's Movements in East Central Europe.* Verso, London and New York.

Eisenstein, Zillah. 1993. "Eastern European male democracies: A problem of unequal equality." In Nanette Funk and Magda Mueller (eds.), *Gender Politics and Post-Communism: Reflections from Eastern Europe and the Former Soviet Union.* Routledge, New York.

Ekwempu, C.C.D., M B. Maine, B.E. Olonkoba, and M.N. Kisseka. 1990. "Structural adjustment and health in Africa," Letter. *The Lancet,* 7July, pp.56–67.

El Bushra, Judy. 2004. "Fused in combat: Gender relations and armed combat." In Haleh Afshar and Deborah Eade (eds.), *Development, Women and War.* Feminist Perspectives. Oxfam, Oxford.

—. 2003. "Fused in combat: Gender relations and armed combat." *Development in Practice,* Vol. 13, Nos. 1&2, pp.252–265.

Elbers, Chris and Peter Lanjouw. 2001. "Intersectoral transfer, growth, and inequality in rural Ecuador." *World Development,* Vol. 29, No. 3, pp.481–496.

Elgie, Robert. 1998. "Democratic accountability and central bank independence: Historical and contemporary, national and European perspectives." *West European Politics,* Vol. 21, No. 3, pp.53–76.

Ellis, Frank. 2000. *Rural Livelihoods and Diversity in Developing Countries.* Oxford University Press, Oxford.

Ellis, Frank and Ntengua Mdoe. 2002. "Livelihoods and rural poverty reduction in Tanzania." *World Development,* Vol. 31, No. 8, pp.1367–1384.

Elson, Diane. 2002. "Gender justice, human rights, and neo-liberal economic policies." In Maxine Molyneux and Shahra Razavi (eds.), *Gender Justice, Development and Rights*. Oxford University Press, Oxford.

—. 1999. "Labour markets as gendered institutions: Equality, efficiency and empowerment issues." *World Development*, Vol. 27, No. 3, pp.611–627.

—. 1998. *Sector Programme Support*. collection of papers prepared for OECD/DAC-WID. Graduate School of Social Sciences, Genecon Unit, University of Manchester, Manchester.

—. 1995. "Male bias in macroeconomics: The case of structural adjustment." In Diane Elson (ed.), *Male Bias in the Development Process*. Manchester University Press, Manchester.

Elson, Diane and Nilüfer Cagatay. 2000. "The social content of macroeconomic policies." *World Development*, Vol. 28, No. 7, pp.1347–1364.

Epstein, G. 2002. *Alternatives to Inflation Targeting: Monetary Policy for Stable and Egalitarian Growth*. PERI Working Paper No. 62, University of Massachusetts at Amherst Department of Economics, Massachusetts.

Eriksson M. & Wallenstein P. 2004. "Armed Conflict 1989-2003" *Journal of Peace Research* 41:5 625-636 (P). Sage Publications

Ertürk, Korkut and Nilüfer Cagatay. 1995. "Macroeconomic consequences of cyclical and secular changes in feminization: An experiment at gendered macromodeling." *World Development*, Vol. 23, No. 11, pp.1969–1977.

Ertürk, Yakin. 2004. Paper presented at the meeting Affirmative Action and SC Resolution 1325: CEDAW General Recommendation 25 and women's participation in conflict prevention and resolution, organized by OHCHR and the Government of Germany with the collaboration of the (Congo) Committee on the Status of Women and OSAGI/DAW, 5 April 2004, United Nations, Geneva.

Esping-Andersen, Gøsta. 1990. *The Three Worlds of Welfare Capitalism*. Princeton University Press, Princeton, N.J.

European Commission (EC). 2003. *Migration and Social Integration of Migrants: Valorisation of Research on Migration and Immigration Funded under 4th and 5th European Programmes of Research*. Paper presented at Proceedings of a dialogue workshop organised by DG Research (RTD) with DG Employment and Social Affairs (EMPL) and DG Justice and Home Affairs (JAI), Brussels, Belgium, 28–29 January 2002.

—. *The European Union and the Issue of Conflicts in Africa: Peacebuilding, Conflict Prevention and Beyond*. EU SEC(96) 332. http://europa.eu.int/comm/development/body/theme/prevention/communication-1996.htm, accessed on 29 November 2004.

Evans, P. 2004. "Development as institutional change: the pitfalls of monocropping and potentials of deliberation." *Studies in Comparative International Development*, Vol. 38, No. 4, pp.30–53.

Evertzen, A. 2001. *Handbook on Gender and Local Governance*. SNV Netherlands Development Organisation. http://www.kit.nl/gcg/html/links_gender_and_local_governm.asp, accessed May 2004.

Farr, Vanessa. 2003. "The importance of a gender perspective to successful disarmament, demobilization and reintegration processes." *Disarmament Forum: Women, Men, Peace and Security*, Vol. 4, pp.25–36.

Faundez, Julio. 1997. *Good Governance and Law: Legal and Institutional Reform in Developing Countries*. St Martin's Press, New York.

Ferreira, Francisco H.G. and Peter Lanjouw. 2001. "Rural nonfarm activities and poverty in the Brazilian Northeast." *World Development*, Vol. 29, No. 3, pp.509–528.

Floro, Maria Sagrario and Gary Dymski. 2000. "Financial crisis, gender and power: An analytical framework." *World Development*, Vol. 28, No. 7, pp.1269–1283.

Fodor, Eva. 2004a. *Women and Political Engagement in East-Central Europe*. Background Paper for UNRISD Report on Gender Equality: Striving for Justice in an Unequal World.

—. 2004b. *Women at Work: The Status of Women in the Labour Markets of the Czech Republic, Hungary, and Poland.* Background Paper for UNRISD Report on Gender Equality: Striving for Justice in an Unequal World.

Fodor, Jerry. 2004. "Having concepts: A brief refutation of the twentieth century." *Mind and Language*, Vol. 19, No. 1, pp.29–47.

Folbre, Nancy. 1994. *Who Pays for the Kids? Gender and the Structures of Constraint.* Routledge, London.

—. 1986. "Hearts and spades: Paradigms of household economics." *World Development*, Vol. 14, No. 2, pp.245–255.

Food and Agriculture Organization of the UN (FAO). 2004. *FAOSTAT.* http://faostat.fao.org/faostat/collections?subset=agriculture, accessed on 6 August 2004.

Freedman, Jane. 2003a. *Gender and Insecurity: Migrant Women in Europe.* Ashgate, Aldershot.

—. 2003b. "Selling sex: Trafficking, prostitution and sex work amongst migrant women in Europe." In Jane Freedman (ed.), *Gender and Insecurity: Migrant Women in Europe*, Ashgate, Aldershot.

Freeman, Carla. 2000. *High Tech and High Heels in the Global Economy: Women, Work, and Pink-Collar Identities in the Caribbean.* Duke University Press, Durham, N.C.

Fukuyama, F. 2004 'The imperative of state-building.' *Journal of Democracy*, Vol.15, No. 2, pp.17–31.

Fultz, Elaine, Markus Ruck and Silke Steinhilber (eds.). 2003. *The Gender Dimension of Social Security Reform in Central and Eastern Europe: Case Studies of the Czech Republic, Hungary and Poland.* ILO, Hungary.

Gallagher, Anne. 2001. "Human rights and the new UN protocols on trafficking and migrant smuggling: A preliminary analysis." *Human Rights Quarterly*, Vol. 23, No. 4, pp.975–1004.

Galli, Rosemary and Ursula Funk. 1995. "Structural adjustment and gender in Guinea-Bissau." In Gloria Thomas-Emeagwali (ed.), *Women Pay the Price: Structural Adjustment in Africa and the Caribbean.* Africa World Press, Trenton, N.J.

Gallin, D. 2004. "Workers in the informal economy." *International Union Rights*, Vol. 11, No. 2.

Gallin, D. and P. Horn. 2004. *Organizing Informal Women Workers.* Background Paper for UNRISD Report on Gender Equality: Striving for Justice in an Unequal World.

Gangoli, G. 2003. *Sex Work, Poverty and Migration in Eastern India.* Paper presented at International Conference on Gender and Migration in Asia, New Delhi.

Gardner, Judith and Judy El Bushra (eds.). 2004. *Somalia—The Untold Story: The War through the Eyes of Somali Women.* Catholic Institute for International Relations (CIIR)/Pluto Press, London.

Gautam, Shobha, Amrita Banskota and Rita Manchanda. 2001. "When there are no men: Women in the Maoist insurgency in Nepal." In Rita Manchanda (ed.), *Women, War and Peace in South Asia: Beyond Victimhood to Agency*, Sage, New Delhi.

Gelleny, Ronald, David Richards and Shawna Sweeney. Forthcoming. "Economic globalization and women's rights: Oppression or opportunity?" *World Development*.

Ghosh, Jayati. 2004a. "Globalization, export-oriented employment for women and social policy: A case study of India." In Shara Razavi, Ruth Pearson and Caroline Danloy (eds.), Globalization, *Export-Oriented Employment and Social Policy*, Palgrave, Basingstoke.

—. 2004b. *Informalization and Women's Workforce Participation: A Consideration of Recent Trends in Asia.* Background Paper for UNRISD Report on Gender Equality: Striving for Justice in an Unequal World.

—. 2003a. "Exporting jobs or watching them disappear? Relocation, employment and accumulation in the world economy." In Jayati Ghosh and C.P. Chandrasekhar (eds.), *Work and Well-being in the Age of Finance*, Tulika Books, New Delhi.

—. 2003b. "Where have the manufacturing jobs gone? Production, accumulation and relocation in the world economy." In Jayati Ghosh and C.P. Chandrasekhar (eds.), *Work and Well-being in the Age of Finance*, Tulika Books, New Delhi.

Gill, K.K. 2001. "Diversification of agriculture and women's employment in Punjab." *Indian Journal of Labour Economics*, Vol. 44, No. 2, pp.259–267.

Goetz, Anne Marie. 2003. "Women's political effectiveness–A concept framework." In Anne-Marie Goetz and Shireen Hassim (eds.), *No Shortcuts to Power: African Women in Politics and Policy-Making*. Zed, London.

—. 2001. *Women Development Workers: Implementing Rural Credit Programmes in Bangladesh*. Sage, New Delhi.

—. (ed.) 1995. *Getting Institutions Right for Women in Development*, IDS Bulletin, Vol. 26, No. 3.

Goetz, Anne Marie and R. Jenkins. 2004 *Reinventing Accountability: Making Democracy Work for Human Development*. Palgrave, Basingstoke.

Goetz, Anne Marie and R. Sengupta. 1996. "Who takes the credit? Gender, power and control over loan use in rural credit programmes in Bangladesh." *World Development*, Vol. 24, No. 1, pp.45–63.

Goldblatt, Beth and Sheila Meintjes. 1998. "South African women demand the truth." In Meredith Turshen and Clotilde Twagiramariya (eds.), *What Women Do in Wartime: Gender and Conflict in Africa*, Zed, London.

Goodman, John B. 1991. "The politics of central bank independence." *Comparative Politics*, Vol. 23, No. 3, pp.329–349.

Gore, Charles. 2003. "Development partnerships for escaping the global poverty trap." *Development Policy Journal*, March, pp.107–126.

Goven, Joanna. 1993. "Gender politics in Hungary: Autonomy and anti-feminism." In Nanette Funk and Magda Mueller (eds.), *Gender Politics and Post Communism: Reflections from Eastern Europe and the Former Soviet Union*, Routledge, New York.

Grown, Caren and Geeta Rao Gupta. Forthcoming. *Taking Action: Achieving Gender Equality and the Empowerment of Women*. Final Report of United Nations Millennium Project Task Force on Education and Gender Equality, International Center for Research on Women, Washington, D.C.

Grunberg, Isabelle. 1998. "Double jeopardy: Globalization, liberalization and the fiscal squeeze." *World Development*, Vol. 26, No. 4, pp.591–605.

Gulati, L. 1993. *In the Absence of their Men: The Impact of Male Migration on Women*. Sage, New Delhi.

Gupta, Nabanita Datta. 2002. "Gender, pay, and development: A cross-country analysis." *Labour and Management in Development Journal*, Vol. 3, No. 2, pp.1–19.

Harding, Luke. 2004. "After Abu Ghraib." *Guardian*, 20 September.

Harriss-White, Barbara. 2000. *Work and Social Policy with Special Reference to Indian Conditions*. Paper presented at UNRISD Conference on Social Policy in a Development Context, Tamsvik, Sweden, 23–24 September.

Hart, Gillian. 2004. "Reworking apartheid legacies: Global competition, gender and social wages in South Africa, 1980–2000." In Shahra Razavi, Ruth Pearson, and Caroline Danloy (eds.), *Globalization, Export-Oriented Employment and Social Policy: Gendered Connections*, Palgrave, Basingstoke.

—. 2002. Reworking Apartheid Legacies. Global Competition, Gender and Social Wages in South Africa, 1980–2000. Social Policy and Development Programme Paper No. 13, UNRISD, Geneva.

—. 1995. "Gender and household dynamics: Recent theories and their implications." In M.G. Quibria (ed.), *Critical Issues in Asian Development*, Oxford University Press, Oxford.

Hartmann, Heidi. 1981. "The unhappy marriage of marxism and feminism: Toward a more progressive union". In Lydia Sargent (ed.), *Women and Revolution: A Discussion of the Unhappy Marriage of Marxism and Feminism*, South End Press, Boston, Mass., pp.1–42.

Hauge Byberg, Ingvild. 2002. *Immigrant Women in Norway: A Summary of Findings on Demography, Education, Labour and Income*. Statistics Norway, Oslo.

Hayes, Bernadette and Ian McAllister. 1997. "Gender, party leaders and election outcomes in Australia, Britain, and the United States." *Comparative Political Studies*, Vol. 30, No. 1, pp.3–26.

Hayner, Priscilla B. 2001. *Unspeakable Truths: Confronting State Terror and Atrocity*. Routledge, London.

Heinen, Jacqueline and Stéphane Portet. 2002. "Political and social citizenship: An examination of the case of Poland." In Maxine Molyneux and Shahra Razavi (eds.), *Gender Justice, Development and Rights*, Oxford University Press, Oxford.

Heinz, James and Robert Pollin. 2003. *Informalization, Economic Growth and the Challenge of Creating Viable Labor Standards in Developing Countries*. PERI Working Paper No. 60, University of Massachusetts at Amherst Department of Economics, Amherst, Mass.

Hélie-Lucas. 1993. "Women's struggle and strategies and the rise of fundamentalism in the Muslim world: From entryism to internationalism." In Haleh Afshar (ed.), *Women in the Middle East: Perceptions, Realities and Struggles for Liberation*. St Martin's Press, New York.

Hernandez Castillo, R. Aida. 2002. "National law and indigenous customary law: The struggle for justice of indigenous women in Chiapas, Mexico." In Maxine Molyneux and Shahra Razavi (eds.), *Gender Justice, Development and Rights*, Oxford University Press, Oxford.

Heston, Alan, Robert Summers and Bettina Aten. 2002. *Penn World Table Version 6.1*. Center for International Comparisons at the University of Pennsylvania (CICUP), Philadelphia (October).

Hewitt de Alcántara, Cynthia. 1993. "Introduction: Markets in Principle and Practice". In Cynthia Hewitt de Alcántara (ed.), *Real Markets: Social and Political Issues of Food Policy Reform*. Frank Cass in association with EADI and UNRISD, Geneva.

Heyzer, Noeleen. 1996. *Gender, Population and Environment in the Context of Deforestation: A Malaysian Case Study*. UNRISD and APDC, Kuala Lumpur.

Hindu, The. 2000. "Nalini moves panel, Nadar on his way out." The Hindu, 12 February.

Hindu, The. 1997. "High Court to be moved for redressal." The Hindu, 27 October.

Hochschild, Arlie. 2000. "Global care chains and emotional surplus value." In Will Hutton and Anthony Giddens (eds.), *On the Edge: Living with Global Capitalism*, Jonathan Cape, London.

—. 1989. *The Second Shift: Working Parents and the Revolution at Home*. Viking, New York.

Holt, Martha. 2003. "Palestinian women, violence and the peace process." *Development in Practice*, Vol. 13, Nos. 1&2, pp.223–238.

Holzmann, R. and S. Jorgensen. 2000. *Social Protection Sector Strategy Paper: From Safety Net to Trampoline*. World Bank, Washington, D.C.

Hong Kong Census and Statistics Department. 2002. *2001 Population Census*. Special Administrative Region, People's Republic of China, Hong Kong.

House of Commons UK, International Development Committee. 2003. *The Humanitarian Crisis in Southern Africa*. House of Commons papers 2002-03 116, The Stationery Office, London.

Hsiung, P.C. 1996. *Living Rooms as Factories: Class, Gender, and the Satellite Factory System in Taiwan*. Temple University Press, Philadelphia.

Huang, Shirlena and Brenda Yeoh. 2003. "The difference gender makes: State policy and contract migrant workers in Singapore." *Asian and Pacific Migration Journal*, Vol. 12, Nos. 1–2, pp. 75–97.

Huang, Yinyin and Pan Wuanming. 2003. "Female sex workers in the labour market of Northeastern China." *Sociological Research (Shehuixue Yanjiu)*, Vol. 3.

Hubbard, D. 2001. *50/50: Options for Namibia*. Namibian Women's Manifesto Network, Windhoek.

Huber, Evelyne. 2004. *Gendered Implications of Tax Reform in Latin America: Argentina, Chile, Costa Rica, and Jamaica*. Background Paper for UNRISD programme on Gender and Social Policy, UNRISD, Geneva.

—. 2002. "Conclusions: Actors, institutions and politics." In Evelyne Huber (ed.), *Models of Capitalism: Lessons for Latin America*. Pennsylvania State University Press, University Park PA.

Huber, Evelyne and John D. Stephens. 2000. *The Political Economy of Pension Reform: Latin America in Comparative Perspective*. Geneva 2000 Occasional Paper Series No. 7, UNRISD, Geneva.

Hugo, Graeme, Dianne Rudd and Kevin Harris. 2003. *Australia's Diaspora: Its Size, Nature and Policy Implications*. Committee for Economic Development of Australia (CEDA) Information Paper No. 80, CEDA, Canberra.

Human Rights Watch. 2003. *Everyday Victims: Civilians in the Burundian War*. Human Rights Watch/Africa, New York.

Huntington, Samuel P. 1991. *Democracy's Third Wave*. University of Oklahoma Press, London.

Institute for Democracy and Electoral Assistance (IDEA). 2002. *Database of Electoral Systems*. Electoral System Design Project. http://www.idea.int/esd/data/world.cfm, accessed in May 2004.

—. 1997. *The International IDEA Handbook of Electoral System Design*. http://www.int-idea.se, accessed in May 2004.

IDEA and Stockholm University. 2004. *Global Database of Quotas for Women*. http://www.quotaproject.org, accessed in May 2004.

Institute for Labor Studies of the Ministry of Labor and Social Security of China. 2002. *Chinese Employment Report*.

Inter-American Dialogue. 2001. *Women and Power in the Americas: A Report Card*. Inter-American Dialogue, Washington, D.C.

Inter-Parliamentary Union (IPU). 2004. Archive of statistical data. http://www.ipu.org/wmn-e/classif.htm, accessed May 2004.

International Criminal Court. 1998. *Rome Statute of the International Criminal Court*. UN Doc. A/CONF.183/9. ICC, Rome. www.icc-cpi.int/library/basicdocuments/rome_statute(e).pdf/, accessed on 4 May 2004.

International Development Economics Associates (IDEAS). 2002. *Globalisation and Income Inequality: A Survey*. http://www.networkideas.org/feathm/aug2002/ft19_Globalisation_Survey.htm, accessed on 22 November 2004.

International Labour Organization (ILO). 2004a. *Economic Security for a Better World*. Socio-Economic Security Programme, ILO, Geneva.

—. 2004b. *LABORSTA*. http://laborsta.ilo.org/, accessed on 29 November 2004.

—. 2004c. *Millennium Indicators System 11*. http://millenniumindicators.un.org/unsd/mi/mi_series_results.asp?rowId=722, accessed on 18 November 2004.

—. 2004d. *NATLEX Database*. http://www.ilo.org/dyn/natlex/natlex_browse.home?p_lang=en, accessed on 15 August 2004.

—. 2004e. *Report of the World Commission on the Social Dimensions of Globalization*. ILO, Geneva.

—. 2004f. *Towards a Fair Deal for Migrant Workers in the Global Economy*. Report VI, prepared for the International Labour Conference, 92nd Session, ILO, Geneva.

—. 2003. *Key Indicators of the Labour Market*. 3rd edn. CD-ROM. ILO, Geneva.

—. 2002a. *Home Work Convention, 1996*. www.ilo.org/public/english/employment/skills/recomm/instr/c_177.htm, accessed in August 2004.

—. 2002b. *Women and Men in the Informal Economy: A Statistical Picture*. ILO, Geneva.

—. 1999. *Key Indicators of the Labor Market 1999*. ILO, Geneva.

International Monetary Fund (IMF) 2004. *World Economic Outlook April 2004: Advancing Structural Reforms*. IMF, Washington, DC.

—. (various years). Government finance statistics. www.imf.org, accessed various dates.

International Organization for Migration (IOM). 2004. *Migration for Development in Africa (MIDA)*. http://www.iom.int/MIDA/#mida, accessed in September 2004.

—. 2001. *Trafficking in Migrants Quarterly Bulletin*, No. 23, April.

Iraqi Women's Rights Coalition (IWRC). 2003. *Newsletter*, No. 6, 15 August.

Islam, R. 2003. *Do More Transparent Governments Govern Better?* Working Papers No. 3077, World Bank, Washington, D.C.

Islamic Republic of Iran (IRI). 1997. *Iran Statistical Yearbook 1375 [1996]*. Statistical Center of Iran, Plan and Budget Organization, Tehran.

—. 1993 [1372]. *Amargeeriye Jariye Jamiat 1370, Natayeje Omoumi, Kole Keshvar*. Statistical Centre of Iran, Tehran.

Jackson, Cecile. 2003. "Gender analysis of land: Beyond land rights for women", *Journal of Agrarian Change*, Vol. 3, No.4, pp.453–480.

Jackson, Cecile and Nitya Rao. 2004. *Understanding Gender and Agrarian Change Under Liberalization: The Case of India*. Background Paper for UNRISD Report on Gender Equality: Striving for Justice in an Unequal World.

Jacobs, Susie and Tracey Howard. 1987. *"Women in Zimbabwe: Stated policy and state action."* In Haleh Afshar (ed.), Women, State and Ideology: Studies from Africa and Asia, Macmillan, Basingstoke.

Jadwa, Ahmed. 2003. "A journey to Basra: Scenes of people and places (2)." *Al Sharq al Ausat*, No. 9025, 14 August, p. 6. Trans. Jack Kalpakian.

Jaffrelot, Christophe. 1996. *The Hindu Nationalist Movement in India.* Viking, Delhi.

Jayaweera, Swarna. 1997. "Women, education and empowerment in Asia." *Gender and Education*, Vol. 9, No. 4, pp.411–424.

Jelin, Elizabeth. 1990. *Women and Social Change in Latin America.* UNRISD/Zed, London and New Jersey.

Jewkes, Rachel, Naeemah Abrahams and Zodumo Mvo. 1998. "Why do nurses abuse patients? Reflections from South African obstetric services." *Social Science and Medicine*, Vol. 47, No. 11, pp.1781–1795.

Jha, J. and R. Subrahmanian. 2004. *Secondary Education in the Indian State of Uttar Pradesh: Gender Dimensions of State Policy and Practice.* Programme on Social Policy and Development, Paper No. forthcoming, UNRISD, Geneva.

Jie, Du. 2004. *Women's Participation in Politics in the Transition to a Market Economy in China: Progress at High Level Politics since 1995.* Background Paper for UNRISD Report on Gender Equality: Striving for Justice in an Unequal World.

Jimenez, M. 2003. "U.S. starting to embrace illegal workers." *Globe and Mail*, Monday 17 November.

Jomo, Kwame Sundaram. 2003. *Globalization, Liberalization and Equitable Development: Lessons from East Asia.* Programme on Overarching Concerns, Paper No. 3, UNRISD, Geneva.

—. 2001. *Globalization, Export-Oriented Industrialization, Female Employment and Equity in East Asia.* UNRISD Programme Papers No. 34, UNRISD, Geneva.

Jordan Department of Statistics (various dates). *Employment and Unemployment Survey*, Jordan Department of Statistics, Amman.

Kabeer, Naila. 2004. "Globalization, labour standards, and women's rights: Dilemmas of collective (in)action in an interdependent world." *Feminist Economics*, Vol. 10, No. 1, pp.3–35.

—. 2003. *Gender Mainstreaming in Poverty Eradication and the Millennium Development Goals. A handbook for Policy Makers and other Stakeholders.* Commonwealth Secretariat, International Development Research Centre (IDRC), Canadian International Development Agency, Ottawa.

—. 2002. *Citizenship and the Boundaries of the Acknowledged Community: Identity, Affiliation and Exclusion.* IDS Working Paper No. 171, IDS, Brighton, UK.

—. 2000. *The Power to Choose: Bangladeshi Women and Labour Market Decisions in London and Dhaka.* Verso, London.

—. 1999. "Resources, agency, achievements: Reflections on the measurement of women's empowerment." *Development and Change*, Vol. 30, No. 3, pp.435–464.

—. 1995. *Necessary, Sufficient or Irrelevant? Women, Wages and Intra-Household Power Relations in Urban Bangladesh.* IDS Working Paper No. 25. IDS, Brighton, UK.

—. 1994. *Reversed Realities: Gender Hierarchies in Development Thought.* Verso, London.

Kabeer, Naila and Simeen Mahmud. 2004. "Globalization, gender and poverty: Bangladesh women workers in export and local markets." *Journal of International Development*, Vol. 16, No. 1 (special issue), pp.93–109.

Kaldor, Mary. 1999. *New and Old Wars: Organized Violence in a Global Era.* Polity, Cambridge.

Kandiyoti, Deniz. 2004. *The Politics of Gender and Reconstruction in Afghanistan.* Background Paper for UNRISD Report on Gender Equality: Striving for Justice in an Unequal World.

—. 2003. "The cry for land: Agrarian reform, gender and land rights in Uzbekistan." *Journal of Agrarian Change*, Vol. 3, No. 1/2, pp.225–257.

Kanji, Nazneen and Carin Vijfhuizen. 2003. *Cracking the Cashew Nut Myth? The Dilemmas of Gendered Policy Research in the Cashew Sector in Mozambique*. Paper presented at Gender Myths and Feminist Fables Workshop, IDS/University of Sussex, Brighton, 2–4 July.

Kanter, R. M. 1977. *Men and Women of the Corporation*. Basic Books, New York.

Kapur, Ratna and Brenda Cossman. 1995. "Communalising gender, engendering community: *Women, legal discourse, and the saffron agenda*." In Tanika Sarkar and Urvashi Butalia (eds.), Women and the Hindu Right: A Collection of Essays, Kali for Women, New Delhi.

Kathlene, Lyn. 1994. "Position power versus gender power: Who holds the floor?" In Georgia Duerst-Lahti and Rita Mae Kelly (eds.), *Gender, Power, Leadership, and Governance*. Ashgate, Ann Arbor, Mich.

Kaushik, P. D. (ed.) 1996. *New Dimensions of Government and Politics of Nepal*. South Asian Publishers, New Delhi.

Keiser, Lael R., Vicky M. Wilkins, Kenneth J. Meier and Catherine Holland. 2002. "Lipstick and logarithms: Gender, institutional context and representative bureaucracy." *American Political Science Review*, Vol. 96, No. 3, pp.553–564.

Kelly, Liz. 2000. "Wars against women: Sexual violence, sexual politics and the militarised state." In Susie Jacobs, Ruth Jacobson and Jennifer Marchbank (eds.), *States of Conflict: Gender, Violence and Resistance*, Zed, London.

Kenworthy, Lane and Melissa Malami. 1999. "Gender inequality in political representation: A worldwide comparative analysis." *Social Forces*, Vol. 78, pp.254–255.

Khadiagala, Lynn. 2001. "The failure of popular justice in Uganda: Local councils and women's property rights." *Development and Change*, Vol. 32, No. 1, pp.55–76.

Khan, Azizur and Carl Riskin. 1998. "Income and inequality in China: Composition, distribution and growth of household income, 1988 to 1995." *China Quarterly*, Vol. 154, pp.221–253.

Khattry, Barsha. 2003. "Trade liberalization and the fiscal squeeze. Implications for public investment." *Development and Change*, Vol. 34, No. 3, pp.401–424.

Khattry, Barsha and J. Mohan Rao. 2002. "Fiscal faux pas?: An analysis of the revenue implications of trade liberalization." *World Development*, Vol. 30, No. 8, pp.1431–1444.

Kiiza, Enid, Winifred Rwe-Beyanga and Agnes Kamya. 2000. "Accounting for gender: Improving Ugandan credit policies, processes and programs." In Dzodzi Tsikata and Joanna Kerr (eds.), *Demanding Dignity: Women Confronting Economic Reforms in Africa*. North–South Institute and Third World Network-Africa, Ottawa.

Kirkpatrick, Colin. 2002. "Finance matters. Financial liberalization: Too much too soon?" *Insights*, No. 40 (March), IDS, Brighton, UK.

Klasen, Stephen and Claudia Wink. 2003. "'Missing women': Revisiting the debate." *Feminist Economics*, Vol. 9, Nos. 2–3, pp.263–299.

Knodel, John, Mark Van Landingham, Chanpen Saengtienchai and Wassana Im-em. 2001. "Older people and AIDS: Quantitative evidence of the impact in Thailand." *Social Science and Medicine*, Vol. 52, No. 9, pp.1313–1327.

Korac, M. 1998. *Linking Arms: Women and War in Post-Yugoslav States*. Life and Peace Institute, Uppsala.

Krug, Etienne G., Linda L. Dahlberg, James A. Mercy, Anthony B. Zwi and Rafael Lozano (eds.). 2002. *World Report on Violence and Health*. World Health Organization (WHO), Geneva.

Kucera, David and William Milberg. 2000. "Gender segregation and gender bias in manufacturing trade expansion: Revisiting the 'Wood asymmetry'." *World Development*, Vol. 28, No. 7, pp.1191–1210.

Kutzin, J. 1994. *Experience with Organizational and Financing Reform of the Health Sector*. SHS Papers No. 8 (SHS/CC/94.3), WHO, Geneva.

Laky, Teréz. 2004. *Gender Equality and Employment in Hungary and in Some Other Eastern European Countries*. Background Paper for UNRISD Report on Gender Equality: Striving for Justice in an Unequal World.

Lan, Pei-Chia. 2003. "Political and social geography of marginal insiders: Migrant domestic workers in Taiwan". *Asian and Pacific Migration Journal*, Vol. 12, Nos. 1–2, pp.99–125.

Lancet, (The). 1995. "Public health impact of Rwandan refugee crisis: What happened in Goma, Zaire in July 1994." The Lancet, Vol. 345, No. 9846 (February), pp.339–344.

Lanjouw, Peter. 2001. "Nonfarm employment and poverty in rural El Salvador." World Development, Vol. 29, No. 3, pp.529–547.

Lastarria-Cornhiel, S. 1997. "Impact of privatisation on gender and property rights in Africa." World Development, Vol. 25, No. 8, pp.1317–1333.

Lazreg, Marnia. 2004. Political Liberalization, Islamism and Feminism in Algeria, Egypt and Jordan. Background Paper for UNRISD Report on Gender Equality: Striving for Justice in an Unequal World.

Lee, Ching Kwan. 2004. Livelihood Struggles and Market Reform: (Un)making Chinese Labour After State Socialism. Background Paper for UNRISD Report on Gender Equality: Striving for Justice in an Unequal World.

Lee, Hye-Kyung. 2003. "Gender, migration and civil activism in South Korea". Asian and Pacific Migration Journal, Vol. 12, Nos. 1–2, pp.127–153.

Legros, Dominique and Vincent Brown. 2001. "Documenting violence against refugees." The Lancet, Vol. 357, No. 9266, pp.1429–1435.

Lewis, J. and J. Giullari. 2004. The Adult Worker Model Family, Gender Equality and Care: The Search for New Policy Principles and the Possibilities and Problems of a Capabilities Approach. Paper prepared for the UNRISD Project on Social Policy and Gender. Mimeo, UNRISD, Geneva.

Li, Zongmin. 2004. Gendered Impacts of Changes in Property Rights to Rural Land in China. Background Paper for UNRISD Report on Gender Equality: Striving for Justice in an Unequal World.

Liebowitz, Debra J. 2004. Women, Gender and the Governance of Globalization: Activists Engagement with International Trade Policy. Paper presented at Globalization and Governance Workshop on Gender, 17–18 September, University of Warwick, UK.

Lim, Joseph Y. 2000. "The effects of the East Asian crisis on the employment of women and men: The Philippine case." World Development, Vol. 28, No. 7, pp.1285–1306.

Lipsky, Michael. 1980. Street-Level Bureaucracy: Dilemmas of the Individual in Public Services. Russell Sage Foundation, New York.

Liu, Zhiqiang. 1998. "Earnings, education, and economic reforms in urban China." Economic Development and Cultural Change, Vol. 46, No. 4, pp.697–725.

Loxley, J. 1997. "International capital markets, the debt crisis and development." In B. Culpeper and F. Stewart (eds.), Global Development Fifty Years after Bretton Woods, Macmillan, Basingstoke.

Luciak, Ilja. 2004. Joining Forces for Democratic Governance: Women's Alliance-Building for Post-War Reconstruction in Central America. Background Paper for UNRISD Report on Gender Equality: Striving for Justice in an Unequal World.

—. 2001. After the Revolution: Gender and Democracy in El Salvador, Nicaragua and Guatemala. Johns Hopkins Press, Baltimore, Md.

Lund, Frances. 2004. Informal Workers' Access to Social Security and Social Protection. Background Paper for UNRISD Report on Gender Equality: Striving for Justice in an Unequal World.

—. 2002. "'Crowding in' care, security and micro-enterprise formation: revisiting the role of the state in poverty reduction, and in development." Journal of International Development, Vol. 14, No. 6, pp.681–694.

Lund, Frances, Jillian Nicholson and Carolyn Skinner. 2000. Street Trading. School of Development Studies, University of Natal, Durban.

Mackintosh, Maureen and Paula Tibandebage. 2004a. Gender and Health Sector Reform: Analytical Perspectives on African Experience. Background Paper for UNRISD Report on Gender Equality: Striving for Justice in an Unequal World.

—. 2004b. "Inequality and redistribution in health care: Analytical issues for developmental social policy." In Thandika Mkandawire (ed.), Social Policy in a Development Context, Palgrave/UNRISD, Basingstoke/Geneva.

Malhotra, A., S.R. Schuler and C. Boender. 2002. *Women's Empowerment as a Variable in International Development.* ICRW Working Paper No. 802, International Centre for Research on Women, Washington, D.C.

Malhotra, Kamal. 2003. *Making Global Trade Work for People.* Earthscan, London and Sterling, Va.

Mamdani, Mahmood. 2001. *When Victims Become Killers: Colonialism, Nativism, and the Genocide in Rwanda.* Princeton University Press, Princeton, N.J.

Manji, Ambreena. 1999. "Imagining women's 'legal' world: Towards a feminist theory of legal pluralism in Africa." *Social and Legal Studies,* Vol. 8, No. 4, pp.435–455.

Mantilla, Julissa. 2003. "Gender in Peru's Truth and Reconciliation Commission." Gender and Development In Brief, *Bridge Bulletin,* No. 13. http://www.bridge.ids.ac.uk/dgb13.html#2, accessed on 30 November 2004.

Massolo, Alejandra. 2004. *Local Governments and Women in Latin America: New Changes and Challenges.* Background Paper for UNRISD Report on Gender Equality: Striving for Justice in an Unequal World.

Matland, R.E. 1999. "The impact of different electoral system on women's representation." In Paloma Saavedra (ed.), *Women: Citizens of Europe: Towards Democratic Parity.* European Commission, Madrid.

Matland, Richard and Donley T. Studlar. 1996. "The contagion of women candidates in single-member district and proportional representation electoral systems: Canada and Norway." *Journal of Politics,* Vol. 58, pp.707–733.

Maurer-Fazio, Margaret and James Hughes. 2002. *The Effects of Market Liberalization on the Relative Earnings of Chinese Women.* WDI Working Paper No. 460, William Davidson Institute at University of Michigan Business School, Michigan.

Maurer-Fazio, Margaret, Thomas G. Rawski and Wei Zhang. 1997. *Gender Wage Gaps in China's Labor Market: Size, Structure, Trends.* Davidson Institute Working Paper Series No. 88, William Davidson Institute at University of Michigan Business School, Michigan.

Mayaram, S. 2000. *Resisting Regimes: Myth, Memory and the Shaping of a Muslim Identity.* Oxford University Press, New Delhi.

Mbatha, M. 2003. *The NGDS Agreement: Its Relevance to Sector Job Summits.* National Labour and Economic Development Institute (NALEDI), Johannesburg.

McAllister, Ian and Donley T. Studlar. 1992. "Gender and representation among legislative candidates in Australia." *Comparative Political Studies,* Vol. 25, No. 3, pp.388–411.

McKay, Susan and Dyan Mazurana. 2004. *Where are the Girls? Girls in Fighting Forces in Northern Uganda,* Sierra Leone and Mozambique. Rights and Democracy, Montreal.

McKinley, Terry. 2004. *Economic Policies for Growth and Poverty Reduction: PRSPs, Neoliberal Conditionalities and "Post Consensus" Alternatives.* Paper presented at International Development Economics Association (IDEAS) International Conference on The Economics of the New Imperialism, INU, New Delhi, 22-24 January.

Meintjes, Sheila. 2003. "The politics of engagement: Women transforming the policy process in South Africa." In Anne Marie Goetz and Shireen Hassim (eds.), *No Shortcuts to Power: African Women in Politics and Policy-Making,* Zed, London.

Menon, Ajit. 2000. *State, Communities and the Forest Question in the Kolli Hills: A Study of the Political Economy of Decentralisation.* Unpublished PhD thesis, Madras Institute of Development Studies, Chennai.

Mensah, K. 2004. *Outmigration of Health Care Staff from Ghana: Extent and Policy Responses.* Paper presented at UNRISD Conference on Commercialization of Health Care: Global and Local Dynamics and Policy Responses, Helsinki.

Mikell, Gwendolyn. 2003. "African feminism: Toward a new politics of representation." In Carole McCann and Seung-Kyung Kim (eds.), *Feminist Theory Reader: Local and Global Perspectives,* Routledge, New York.

Milanovic, Branko. 2003. "The two faces of globalization: Against globalization as we know it." *World Development,* Vol. 31, No. 4, pp.667–683.

Minister of Public Works and Government Services Canada. 2001. *Citizenship and Immigration. Facts and Figures, 2000: Immigration Overview*. Minister of Public Works and Government Services Canada, Ottawa. www.cic.gc.ca/english/pdf/pub/facts2000.pdf, accessed on 12 April 2004.

—. 2000. *Citizenship and Immigration. Facts and Figures, 1999: Immigration Overview*. Minister of Public Works and Government Services Canada, Ottawa. www.cic.gc.ca/english/pdf/pub/facts1999.pdf, accessed on 12 April 2004.

—. 1999b. *Citizenship and Immigration. Facts and Figures, 1998: Immigration Overview*. Minister of Public Works and Government Services Canada, Ottawa. www.cic.gc.ca/english/pdf/pub/facts1998.pdf, accessed on 12 April 2004.

—. 1999a. *Citizenship and Immigration. Citizenship and Immigration Statistics 1996*. Minister of Public Works and Government Services Canada, Ottawa. www.cic.gc.ca/english/pdf/pub/1996stats.pdf, accessed on 12 April 2004.

—. 1998. *Citizenship and Immigration. Citizenship and Immigration Statistics 1995*. Minister of Public Works and Government Services Canada, Ottawa. www.cic.gc.ca/english/pdf/pub/1995stats.pdf, accessed on 12 April 2004.

—. 1997. *Citizenship and Immigration. Citizenship and Immigration Statistics 1994*. Minister of Public Works and Government Services Canada, Ottawa. www.cic.gc.ca/english/pdf/pub/1994stats.pdf, accessed on 12 April 2004.

—. 1994. *Citizenship and Immigration. Immigration Statistics 1992*. Public Works and Government Services Canada, Ottawa. www.cic.gc.ca/english/pdf/pub/1992stats.pdf, accessed on 12 April 2004.

Minister of Supply and Services Canada.1996. *Citizenship and Immigration. Citizenship and Immigration Statistics 1993*. Minister of Supply and Services Canada, Ottawa. www.cic.gc.ca/english/pdf/pub/1993stats.pdf, accessed on 12 April 2004.

—. 1992. *Employment and Immigration. Immigration Statistics 1991*. Minister of Supply and Services Canada, Ottawa. www.cic.gc.ca/english/pdf/pub/1991stats.pdf, accessed on 12 April 2004.

—. 1991. *Employment and Immigration. Immigration Statistics 1990*. Minister of Supply and Services Canada, Ottawa. www.cic.gc.ca/english/pdf/pub/1990stats.pdf, accessed on 12 April 2004.

Ministry of Agriculture Food and Fisheries (MAFF) (Zambia). 1999. *Strategies for Increased Food Security and Rural Incomes in the Isolated Areas of Zambia*. MAFF, Lusaka, Zambia.

Minority Rights Group International. 1997. *War: The Impact on Minority and Indigenous Children*. Minority Rights Group International, London.

Mitra, M. 1989–90. "Women in Santhal society: Women as property; women and property." *Samya Shakti*, Vols. 4/5, pp.213–227.

Mitter, Swasti. 1994. "On organizing women in casualised work: A global overview." In Sheila Rowbotham and Swasti Mitter (eds.), *Dignity and Daily Bread: New Forms of Economic Organizing Among Poor Women in the Third World and the First*, Routledge, London.

Mkandawire, Thandika. 2004 "Good governance: The itinerary of an idea." *Development and Cooperation*, Vol. 31, No. 10, October. http://www.inwent.org/E+Z/content/archive-eng/10-2004/tribune_art1.html, accessed on 30 November 2004.

—. 2002. "The terrible toll of post-colonial 'rebel movements' in Africa: Towards an explanation of the violence against the peasantry." *Journal of Modern African Studies*, Vol. 40, No. 2, pp.181–215.

—. 2001. *Social Policy in a Development Context*. Programme on Social Policy and Development, Paper No. 7, UNRISD, Geneva.

Mody, A. 2003. "It is about equality, not uniformity." *The Hindu*, 10 August.

Moghadam, Valentine. 2004. *Women's Livelihood and Entitlements in the Middle East: What Difference has the Neoliberal Policy Turn Made?* Background Paper for UNRISD Report on Gender Equality: Striving for Justice in an Unequal World.

—. 1998. *Women, Work, and Economic Reform in the Middle East and North Africa*. Lynne Rienner, Boulder, Colo.

Mohanty, Chandra Talpade. 2003. ""Under Western Eyes" revisited: Feminist solidarity through anticapitalist struggle." *Signs*, Vol. 28, No. 2, pp.499–539.

Molyneux, Maxine. 2004. *Poverty Relief Programmes and the "New Social Policy in Latin America": Women and Community Carework.* UNRISD Project on Gender and Social Policy, Mimeo, UNRISD, Geneva.

—. 2002. "Gender and the silences of social capital: Lessons from Latin America." *Development and Change*, Vol. 33, No. 2, pp.167–188.

—. 2001. *Women's Movements in International Perspective: Latin America and Beyond.* Palgrave, Basingstoke.

—. 1994. "Women's rights and the international context: Some reflections on the post-communist states." *Millennium*, Vol. 23, No. 2, pp.287–314.

Molyneux, Maxine and Shahra Razavi (eds.). 2002a. *Gender Justice, Development and Rights.* Oxford University Press, Oxford.

—. 2002b. "Introduction." In Maxine Molyneux and Shahra Razavi (eds.), *Gender Justice, Development and Rights.* Oxford University Press, Oxford.

Montenegro, Claudio and Ricardo Paredes. 1999. *Gender Wage Gap and Discrimination: A Long Term View using Quantile Regressions.* Mimeo, University of Chile, Santiago de Chile.

Moore, H. and M. Vaughan. 1994. *Cutting Down Trees: Gender, Nutrition and Agricultural Change in the Northern Province of Zambia 1980–1990.* James Currey, London.

Morokvasic, Mirjana. 1996. "Entre l'est et l'ouest, des migrations pendulaires." In Mirijana Morokvasic and Hedwig Rudolph (eds.), *Migrants. Nouvelles mobilités en Europe*, L'Harmattan, Paris.

Moyo, Sam. 2002. *Africa's Agrarian Transformation: The Efficacy of the NEPAD Agriculture Strategy.* Mimeo. Council for the Development of Social Science Research in Africa (CODESRIA), Dakar.

Msimang, Sisonke and Cecile Ambert. 2004. *Outputs versus Outcomes: Gender, Culture and HIV/AIDS in Southern Africa.* Background Paper for UNRISD Report on Gender Equality: Striving for Justice in an Unequal World.

Mueller, Carol M. 1988. "The empowerment of women: Polling and the women's voting bloc." In Carol M. Mueller (ed.), *The Politics of the Gender Gap: The Social Construction of Political Influence*, Sage, Newbury Park, Calif.

Mukhopadhyaya, Maitrayee. 1998. *Legally Dispossessed: Gender, Identity and the Process of Law.* Stree, Calcutta.

Mung'ong'o, Claude. 2000. *Market Liberalization in Tanzania: A Review in Relation to Food Security and Sustainable Livelihoods.* Rural Food Security Group, IDS, University of Dar es Salaam.

Murray, C. 1991. *Development Data Constraints and the Human Development Index.* UNRISD Discussion Paper No. 25. UNRISD, Geneva.

Murray, C.J.L., G. King, A.D. Lopez, N. Tomijima and E.G. Krug. 2002. "Armed conflict as a public health problem." *British Medical Journal*, Vol. 324, pp.346–349.

Musse, Fowzia. 2004. "War crimes against women and girls." In Judith Gardner and Judy El Bushra (eds.), *Somalia—The Untold Story: The War through the Eyes of Somali Women*, CIIR and Pluto, London.

Namibian. 2004. *Women's Share in Local Government Up.* http://www.namibian.com.na/2004/may/national/0442622236.html, accessed in May 2004.

Narayan, Jayaprakash, Dhirubhai Sheth, Yogendra Yadav and Madhu Kishwar. 1999. *Enhancing Women's Representation In Legislatures: An Alternative to the Government Bill for Women's Reservation.* Forum for Democratic Reforms, New Delhi and Hyderabad.

National Bank for Agriculture and Rural Development (NABARD). 2004. *SHG-Bank Linkage Programme: Highlights.* NABARD, India. http://www.nabard.org/roles/mcid/highlights.htm, accessed on 30 November 2004.

National Bureau of Statistics (China). 2004. China Statistical Yearbook. China.

National Women's Information Center, Poland (OSKa). 2002. *Participation of Women in Local Government in Poland.* 24 May. http://www.oska.org.pl/english/womeninpoland/local.html, accessed in May 2004.

Naz, Antonia Cristina Corinthia. 2002. "The political participation of women legislators in Congress." *Review of Women's Studies*, Vol. 13, Nos. 1/2, pp.13–48.

Newland, K. 2003. *Migration as a Factor in Development and Poverty Reduction.* Migration Information Source, Migration Policy Institute. www.migrationinformation.org, accessed on 24 July 2003.

Nicolau, J.M. and R.A. Schmitt. 1995. "Sistema eleitoral e sistema partidario." *Lua Nova,* No. 36, pp.129–147.

Nordstrom, Carolyn. 1997. *Girls and Warzones: Troubling Questions.* Life and Peace Institute, Uppsala.

Norris, Pippa. 1996. "Women politicians: Transforming Westminster?" *Parliamentary Affairs,* Vol. 49, pp.89–102.

Norris, Pippa and Joni Lovenduski (eds.). 1993. *Gender and Party Politics.* Sage, London.

Nowrojee, Binaifer. 2004. *"Your Justice is Too Slow": How the ICTR Failed Rwanda's Rape Victims.* Background Paper for UNRISD Report on Gender Equality: Striving for Justice in an Unequal World.

Nussbaum, M. 2000. *Women and Human Development: The Capabilities Approach.* Cambridge University Press, Cambridge.

Nyamu-Musembi, Celestine. 2004. *For or Against Gender Equality? Evaluating the Post Cold-War "Rule of Law" Reforms in Sub-Saharan Africa.* Background Paper for UNRISD Report on Gender Equality: Striving for Justice in an Unequal World.

—. 2002. "Why engage with local norms and institutions? The case of women's property rights in rural Kenya." In A An-Na'im (ed.), *Cultural Transformation and Human Rights in Africa.* Zed, London.

—. 2000. "How should human rights and development respond to cultural legitimisation of gender hierarchy in developing countries?" *Harvard International Law Journal,* Vol. 41, No. 2, pp.381–418.

O'Donnell, G. 1998. "Horizontal accountability in new democracies." *Journal of Democracy,* Vol. 9, No. 3, pp.10–126.

—. 1993. "On the state, democratization and some conceptual problems: A Latin American view with glances at post-communist countries." *World Development,* Vol. 21, No. 8, pp.1355–1369.

Ohnesorge, John K.M. Forthcoming. "Asia's legal systems in the wake of the financial crisis: Can the rule of law carry any of the weight?" In M. Woo-Cumings (ed.), *Neoliberalism and Institutional Reform in East Asia,* UNRISD and Cornell University Press.

Oostendorp, Remco. 2004. *Globalization and the Gender Wage Gap.* World Bank Policy Research Working Paper No. 3256, World Bank, Washington, D.C.

Organization of African Unity (OAU). 2000. *Rwanda: The Preventable Genocide (Report of the International Panel of Eminent Personalities to Investigate the 1994 Genocide in Rwanda and Surrounding Events).* OAU, Addis Ababa.

Organisation of American States (OAS). 2000. *Inter-American Convention on the Prevention, Punishment and Eradication of Violence Against Women.* http://www.oas.org/cim/English/Convention%20Violence%20Against%20Women.htm, accessed on September 2004.

Organization for Economic Co-operation and Development (OECD). 2004a. CRS *Online Database on Aid Activities.* http://www.oecd.org/dataoecd/50/15/5037782.htm, accessed on 11 August 2004.

—. 2004b. *Labour Market Integration Remains Insecure for Foreign and Immigrant Women.* http://www.oecd.org/document/27/0,2340,en_2649_37457_29871963_1_1_1_37457,00.html, accessed on 20 September 2004.

Orloff, Ann Shola. 2002. *Women's Employment and Welfare Regimes: Globalization, Export Orientation and Social Policy in Europe and North America.* Programme on Social Policy and Development, Paper No. 12, UNRISD, Geneva.

Oxfam/IDS. 1999. *Liberalisation and Poverty: Zambia Case Study.* Report to DFID.

Packard, Le Anh Tu. 2004. *Gender Dimensions of Vietnam's Comprehensive Macroeconomic and Structural Reform Policies.* Background Paper for UNRISD Report on Gender Equality: Striving for Justice in an Unequal World.

Paidar, Parvin. 2002. "Encounters between feminism, democracy and reformism in contemporary Iran." In Maxine Molyneux and Shahra Razavi (eds.), *Gender Justice, Development, and Rights,* Oxford University Press, Oxford.

Palma, Gabriel. 2003. *Trade Liberalization in Mexico: Its Impact on Growth, Employment and Wages.* Employment Paper No. 55, Employment Sector, ILO, Geneva.

Pankhurst, D. 1999. "Issues of justice and reconciliation in complex political emergencies: comceptualising reconciliation, justice and peace." *Third World Quarterly* Vol. 20, No. 1, pp.239–256.

Pankhurst, Donna. 2003. "The 'sex war' and other wars: Towards a feminist approach to peace building." *Development in Practice*, Vol. 13, Nos. 2&3, pp.154–177.

—. 2002. "Making a difference? The inclusion of gender into conflict management policies." In Marianne Braig and Wölte Braig (eds.), *Common Ground or Mutual Exclusion?*, Zed, London, pp.129–135.

Pankhurst, Donna and Jenny Pearce. 1997. "Engendering the analysis of conflict: Perspectives from the South." In Haleh Afshar (ed.), *Women and Empowerment: Illustrations from the Third World*, St Martin's Press, New York.

Patnaik, Utsa. 2003. "Global capitalism, deflation and agrarian crisis in developing countries." *Journal of Agrarian Change*, Vol. 3, Nos. 1&2, pp.33–66.

Paus, Eva and Michael Robinson. 1998. *Globalization and Labor: The Impact of Direct Foreign Investment on Real Wage Developments, 1968–1993.* Paper presented at the 21st International Congress of the Latin American Studies Association, Chicago, 24–26 September.

Pearson, Ruth. 2004. "Organizing home-based workers in the global economy: An action-research approach." *Development in Practice*, Vol. 14, Nos. 1&2, pp.136–148.

Penal Reform International. 2000. *Access to Justice in Sub-Saharan Africa: The Role of Traditional and Informal Justice Systems.* Penal Reform International, London.

Persson, T. and G. Tabellini. 1994. "Is inequality harmful to growth? Theory and evidence." *American Economic Review*, Vol. 84, No. 3, pp.600–621.

Petchesky, Rosalind Pollack. 2003. *Global Prescriptions: Gendering Health and Human Rights.* Zed and UNRISD, London and New York.

—. 2000. "Human rights, reproductive health and economic justice: Why they are indivisible." *Reproductive Health Matters*, Vol. 8, No. 15, pp.12–17.

Phillips, Anne. 2002. "Multiculturalism, universalism, and the claims of democracy." In Maxine Molyneux and Shahra Razavi (eds.), *Gender Justice, Development and Rights*, Oxford University Press, Oxford.

Physicians for Human Rights. 2002. *War-Related Sexual Violence in Sierra Leone: A Population-Based Assessment.* A Report by Physicians for Human Rights with the support of UNAMSIL. Physicians for Human Rights, Cambridge, Mass. http://www.phrusa.org/publications/sl_report.html, accessed on 30 November 2004.

Pierson, Ruth Roach. 1989. "Beautiful soul or just warrior: gender and war." *Gender and History*, Vol. 1, No. 1, pp.77–86.

Piper, Nicola. 2004. "Gender and migration policies in Southeast and East Asia: Legal protection and socio-cultural empowerment of unskilled migrant women." *Singapore Journal of Tropical Geography*, Vol. 25, No. 2, pp.216–231.

—. 2003. "Bridging gender, migration and governance: Theoretical possibilities in the Asian context." *Asian and Pacific Migration Journal*, Vol. 12, Nos. 1–2, pp.21–48.

Piper, Nicola and Mina Roces (eds.). 2003. *Wife or Worker? Asian Women and Migration.* Rowman and Littlefield, Lanham, Md. and Oxford.

Platteau, J.P. 1995. *Reforming Land Rights in Sub-Saharan Africa: Issues of Efficiency and Equity.* Discussion Paper No. 60, UNRISD, Geneva.

Polanyi, Karl. 1957. *The Great Transformation: The Political and Economic Origins of Our Time.* Beacon Press, Boston.

Pollert, Anna. 2003. *Interim Report: Gender, Work, and Employment in Ten Candidate Countries of Central Eastern Europe*, Project No. 9285. Manuscript prepared for the European Foundation for the Improvement of Living and Working Conditions, Dublin.

Prakash, K.P. 2002. "International Criminal Court: A review." *Economic and Political Weekly*, pp.4115.

Preston, Rosemary. 1994. "Returning exiles in Namibia since Independence." In Tim Allen and T. Morsink (eds.), *When Refugees Go Home*. UNRISD/James Currey, Geneva/London.

Raghavan, C. 2004. "Groser's 'semantic skills' may decide the July package fate." *North-South Development Monitor* (SUNS), 14 July.

Rajasingham-Senanayake, Darini. 2001. "Ambivalent empowerment: The tragedy of Tamil women in conflict." In Rita Manchanda (ed.), *Women, War and Peace in South Asia*, Sage, New Delhi.

Rama, Martin. n.d. *The Gender Implications of Public Sector Downsizing: The Reform Program of Vietnam*. Mimeo, World Bank, Washington, D.C.

Ramachandran, V. K. and Madhura Swaminathan. Forthcoming. *Institutional Reform and Rural Credit in India, 1969–2003*. Tulika, New Delhi.

Randall, V. 1987. *Women and Politics: An International Perspective*. Macmillan Education, London.

Rao, A., R. Stuart and D. Kelleher. 1999. *Gender at Work: Organizational Change for Equality*. Kumarian Press, West Hartford, Conn.

Rao, Nitya. 1999. "Cycling into the future: A report on women's participation in a literacy campaign in Tamil Nadu, India." *Gender, Technology and Development*, Vol. 3, No. 3, pp.457–474.

Razavi, Shahra. 2000a. "Export-oriented employment, poverty and gender: Contested accounts." In Shahra Razavi (ed.), *Gendered Poverty and Well-Being*, Blackwell, Oxford.

—. (ed.) 2000b. *Gendered Poverty and Well-Being*. Blackwell, Oxford.

Razavi, Shahra and Carol Miller. 1995. *From WID to GAD: Conceptual Shifts in the Women in Development Discourse*. Beijing Occasional Paper No. 1, UNRISD, Geneva.

Reardon, Thomas. 1997. "Using evidence of household income diversification to inform study of the rural non-farm labour market in Africa." *World Development*, Vol. 25, No. 5, pp.735–747.

Recovery of Historical Memory Project at the Human Rights Office (REMHI). 1999. *Guatemala Never Again: Recovery of Historical Memory Project at the Human Rights Office of the Archdiocese of Guatemala*. Orbis Books, New York.

Reddy, Sanjay G. and Thomas W. Pogge. 2003. *How Not to Count the Poor: A Paper Critical of the World Bank's Estimate of Global Income Poverty*, Version 4.5, Institute of Social Analysis, Columbia University, New York.

Rehn, Elisabeth and Ellen Johnson Sirleaf. 2002. *Women, War and Peace: The Independent Experts' Assessment on the Impact of Armed Conflict on Women and Women's Role in Peace-Building*. UNIFEM, New York.

République Algérienne. 2000. *Données Statistiques*, No. 263. Office National des Statistiques, Algeria.

Resources Oriented Development Initiative (RODI) Kenya. 2004. *Agricultural Trade Liberalisation: Its Effect on Women and Food Security in Kenya*. Third World Network Africa, Accra.

Reynolds, A. 1999. *Women in African Legislatures and Executives: The Slow Climb to Power*. EISA, Johannesburg.

Rodrik, D. 2004 *Rethinking Economic Growth in Developing Countries*. Luca d'Agliano Lecture for 2004, Turin, Italy, October.

Rowbotham, Sheila and Swasti Mitter (eds.). 1994. *Dignity and Daily Bread: New Forms of Economic Organising Among Poor Women in the Third World and the First*. Routledge, London.

Roy, A. 2003. *City Requiem, Calcutta: Gender and the Politics of Poverty*. University of Minnesota Press, Minneapolis/London.

Ruggie, John Gerard. 2003 "Taking embedded liberalism global: The corporate connection." In David Held and Mathias Koenig-Archibugi (eds.),*Taming Globalization: Frontiers of Governance*, Polity, Cambridge.

Rupp, L. 1997. *Worlds of Women: The Making of an International Women's Movement*. Princeton University Press, Princeton, N.J.

Rweyemamu, D.C. 2003. *Reforms in the Agricultural Sector: The Tanzanian Experience*. Economic and Social Research Foundation, Dar Es Salaam.

Sacchet, Teresa. 2004. *Political Parties and Gender in Latin America*. Background Paper for UNRISD Report on Gender Equality: Striving for Justice in an Unequal World.

Said, Yahia and Meghnad Desai. 2003. "Trade and global civil society: The anti-capitalist movement revisited." In Mary Kaldor, Helmut Anheier and Marlies Glasius (eds.), *Global Civil Society Yearbook*, Oxford University Press, London.

Saith, Ruhi and Barbara Harriss-White. 1999. "The gender sensitivity of well-being indicators." *Development and Change*, Vol. 30, No. 3, pp.465–498.

Salame, Ghassan (ed.) 1994. *Democracy without Democrats: The Renewal of Politics in the Muslim World*. I.B. Tauris, New York.

Samson, Colin. 2003. *A Way of Life That Does Not Exist: Canada and the Extinguishment of the Innu*. Verso, London.

Samuel, Kumudini. 2004. *Doing Peace Versus Talking Peace Making Visible the Invisible*. Background Paper for UNRISD Report on Gender Equality: Striving for Justice in an Unequal World.

Santiso, Carlos. 2001. "Good governance and aid effectiveness: The World Bank and conditionality." *Georgetown Public Policy Review*, Vol. 7, No. 1, pp.1–22.

Sassen, Saskia, 2000. "Women's burden: counter-geographies of globalization and the feminization of survival." *Journal of International Affairs*, Vol. 53, No. 2, pp.503–524.

Save the Children. 2000. *War Brought Us Here: Report into Children Displaced by War*. Save the Children UK, London.

S.B. Civil Writ Petition No. 5963/1998, 1998. Chaggi Bai – Petitioner vs. State of Rajasthan and Others – Respondents. High court of Judicature for Rajasthan at Jaipur Bench, Jaipur.

Schoeni, Robert F. 1998. "Labor market outcomes of immigrant women in the United States: 1970 to 1990." *International Migration Review*, Vol. 32, No. 1, pp.57–78.

Schuler, Sidney, Syed Hashemi, Ann Riley and Shireen Akhter. 1996. "Credit programs, patriarchy and men's violence against women in rural Bangladesh." *Social Science and Medicine*, Vol. 43, No. 12, pp.1729–1742.

Seguino, S. 2005. "Taking gender differences in bargaining power seriously: Equity, labor standards, and living wages." In Edith Kuiper and Drucilla Barker (eds.), *Feminist Perspectives on Gender and the World Bank*. Routledge, London.

—. 2004. *Gender, Well-Being and Equality: Assessing Status, Progress and the Way Forward*. Background Paper for UNRISD Report on Gender Equality: Striving for Justice in an Unequal World.

—. 2003a. *Is Economic Growth Good for Well-Being? Evidence of Gender Effects in Latin America and the Caribbean*. Background Paper for Center for Global Development, Washington, D.C.

—. 2003b. "Why are women in the Caribbean so much more likely than men to be unemployed?" *Social and Economic Studies*, Vol. 52, No. 4, pp.83–120.

—. 2002. "Gender, quality of life, and growth in Asia 1970 to 1990." *Pacific Review*, Vol. 15, No. 2, pp.245–277.

—. 2000a. "Accounting for gender in Asian economic growth." *Feminist Economics*, Vol. 6, No. 3, pp.22–58.

—. 2000b. "Gender inequality and economic growth: A cross-country analysis." *World Development*, Vol. 28, No. 7, pp.1211–1230.

—. 1997. "Export-led growth and the persistence of gender inequality in the NICs." In J. Rives and M. Yousefi (eds.), *Economic Dimensions of Gender Inequality: A Global Perspective*. Greenwood Press, Westport, Conn.

Selolwane, Onalenna. 2004. *Gendered Spaces in Party Politics in Southern Africa: Progress and Regress since Beijing 1995*. Background Paper for UNRISD Report on Gender Equality: Striving for Justice in an Unequal World.

—. 1999. *Women Running for Political Office: The Launching of the Women Candidates for the 1999 General Elections: Report on the 1999 National Conference on Women in Politics*. Emang Basadi Women's Association, Political Education Programme, Gaborone.

—. 1997. *Report on the National Conference for Women in Politics: Setting an Agenda for Women's Empowerment Towards 1999 and Beyond*. Emang Basadi Women's Association, Political Education Programme, Gaborone.

Sen, Amartya. 1999. *Development as Freedom*. Oxford University Press, Oxford.

—. 1990. "Gender and cooperative conflicts." In Irene Tinker (ed.), *Persistent Inequalities*, Oxford University Press, Oxford.

—. 1989. "Women's survival as a development problem." *Bulletin of the American Academy of Arts and Sciences*, Vol. 43, No. 2, pp.14–29.

—. 1985. *Commodities and Capabilities*. North Holland, Amsterdam.

Sen, Gita. 2004. *Reproductive Rights and Gender Justice in the Neo-Conservative Shadow*. Background paper for UNRISD Report on Gender Equality: Striving for Justice in an Unequal World.

—. 2003. "Feminist politics in a fundamentalist world." In Maitrayee Mukhopadhyay (ed.), *Governing for Equity: Gender, Citizenship and Governance*, Royal Tropical Institute (KIT), Amsterdam.

Sen, Gita and Sonia Correa. 1999. *Gender Justice and Economic Justice: Reflections on the Five-Year Reviews of the UN Conferences of the 1990s*. Paper prepared for UNIFEM in preparation for the Five-Year Reviews of the Beijing Platform of Action.

Sen, Kunal. 2002. *Economic Reforms and Rural Livelihood Diversification in Tanzania*. Working Paper No. 12 (draft). LADDER Project, University of East Anglia, UK. http://www.odg.uea.ac.uk/ladder/, accessed 30 November 2004.

Sender, J. 2002. "Women's struggle to escape rural poverty in South Africa." *Journal of Agrarian Change*, Vol. 2, No. 1, pp.1–49.

Sender, J., C. Oya and C. Cramer. 2004. *Women Working for Wages: Putting Flesh on the Bones of a Rural Labour Market Survey in Mozambique*. Mimeo, School of Oriental and African Studies, University of London.

Shah, S. 2003. *Migration, Sex and Work: Gender and Daily Wage Labour in Mumbai*. Paper presented at International Conference on Gender and Migration in Asia, New Delhi.

Sharoni, Simona. 1995. *Gender and the Israeli-Palestinian Conflict: The Politics of Women's Resistance*. Syracuse University Press, New York

Shumway, J. Matthew and Thomas J. Cooke. 1998. "Gender and ethnic concentration and employment prospects for Mexican-American migrants." *Growth and Change*, Vol. 29, No. 1, pp.23–54.

Sieder, Rachel. 2003. "Renegotiating 'law and order': Judicial reform and citizen responses in post-war Guatemala." *Democratization*, Vol. 10, No. 4, pp.137–160.

Siegemann, Karin Astrid. 2004. *The Agreement on Textiles and Clothing: Potential Effects on Gender Equality in Pakistan*. Mimeo, Sustainable Development Policy Institute (SDPI), Geneva.

Silliman, Jael. 1999. "Expanding civil society, shrinking political spaces: The case of women's non-governmental organizations." In Jael Silliman and Ynestra King (eds.), *Dangerous Intersections: Feminist Perspectives on Population, Environment, and Development*, South End Press, Boston.

Simmons, R.L., J. Beaman, R.D. Conger and W. Chao. 1993. "Stress, support and anti-social behavior traits as determinants of emotional well-being and parenting practices among single mothers." *Journal of Marriage and the Family*, Vol. 55, pp.385–398.

Singh, Ajit. 2002. *Capital Account Liberalization, Free Long-Term Capital Flows, Financial Crises and Economic Development*. Working Paper No. 245, ESRC Centre for Business Research, University of Cambridge, Cambridge.

Singh, Ajit and Ann Zammit. 2000. "International capital flows: Identifying the gender dimension." *World Development*, Vol. 28, No. 7, pp.1249–1268.

Small Arms Survey. 2004. *Small Arms Survey 2004: Rights at Risk*. Oxford University Press, Oxford.

Smart, Carol. 1989. *Feminism and the Power of Law*. Routledge, London and New York.

Sobritchea, Carolyn. 2004. *Filipino Women's Participation in Politics and Governance*. Background Paper for UNRISD Report on Gender Equality: Striving for Justice in an Unequal World.

Solimano, Andre (ed.). 1998. *Social Inequality: Values, Growth, and the State*. University of Michigan Press, Ann Arbor, Mich.

Sørensen, Birgitte. 1998. *Women and Post-Conflict Reconstruction: Issues and Sources.* War-torn Societies Project Occasional Paper No. 3, Programme for Strategic and International Security Studies (PSIS) and UNRISD, Geneva.

South Center. 1997. *Foreign Direct Investment, Development and the New Global Economic Order: A Policy Brief for the South.* South Center, Geneva.

Sow, Fatou. 2004. *Mobilisation politique des femmes en Afrique de l'Ouest (Women's political mobilization in West Africa).* Background Paper for UNRISD Report on Gender Equality: Striving for Justice in an Unequal World.

Special Court for Sierra Leone. 2004. *Trial Chamber Approves New Count of Forced Marriage.* Press Release, Freetown Sierra Leone, 7 May 2004. Press and Public Affairs Office. www.sc-sl.org/Press/pressrelease-050704.html accessed on 24 November 2004

Spees, Pam. 2003. "Women's advocacy in the creation of the International Criminal Court: Changing the landscapes of justice and power." *Signs,* Vol. 28, No. 1, pp.1233–1254.

Spindel, Cheywa, Elisa Levy and Melissa Connor. 2004. *With an End in Sight: Strategies from the UNIFEM Trust Fund to Eliminate Violence Against Women.* UNIFEM, New York.

Spoor, Max. 2002. "Policy regimes and performance of the agricultural sector in Latin America and the Caribbean during the last three decades." *Journal of Agrarian Change,* Vol. 2, No. 3, pp.382–401.

Squires, J. and M. Wickham-Jones. 2001. *Women in Parliament: A Comparative Analysis.* Equal Opportunities Commission, Manchester.

Standing, Guy. 1999. "Global feminisation through flexible labour: A theme revised." *World Development,* Vol. 27, No. 3, pp.583–602.

—. 1997. "Globalization, labour flexibility, and insecurity: the era of market regulation." *European Journal of Industrial Relations,* Vol. 3, No. 1, pp.7–37.

Stasiulis, Daiva K. and Abigail B. Bakan. 2003. *Negotiating Citizenship: Migrant Women in Canada and the Global System.* Palgrave Macmillan, New York.

Statistics Canada. 1996. Public use file of individuals. Statistics Canada, Ottawa.

Staudt, Kathleen. 1995. "The impact of development policies on women." In M. Hay and S. Stichter (eds.), *African Women South of the Sahara,* Longman, Essex.

Steinhilber, Silke. 2004. *The Gender Implications of Pension Reform.* General Remarks and Evidence from Selected Countries. Background Paper for UNRISD Report on Gender Equality: Striving for Justice in an Unequal World.

Stewart, Frances and Valpy Fitzgerald (eds.). 2001. *War and Underdevelopment,* Volume 2. Oxford University Press, Oxford.

Stewart, Frances, Cindy Huang and Michael Wang. 2001. "Internal wars: An overview of the economic and social consequences." In Frances Stewart and Valpy Fitzgerald (eds.), *War and Underdevelopment,* Oxford University Press, Oxford.

Stiglitz, Joseph. 2002. *Globalization and its Discontents.* W.W. Norton, New York.

Stockholm International Peace Research Institute (SIPRI). 2004. *Yearbook 2004: Armaments, Disarmament and International Security.* Oxford University Press, Oxford.

Sunshine for Women. 2004. *Nineteenth-Century Advocates of Political Power for Women (Non-US): Woman Suffrage in Iceland.* http://www.pinn.net/~sunshine/whm2003/iceland.html, accessed on 18 May.

Svara, J. 2003. *Two Decades of Continuity and Change in American City Councils.* Report prepared for National League of Cities, Washington, D.C.

Swamy, Anand, Stephen Knack, Young Lee and Omar Azfar. 2001. "Gender and corruption." *Journal of Development Economics,* Vol. 64, No. 1, pp.25–55.

Tamale, Sylvia. 1999. *When Hens Begin to Crow: Gender and Parliamentary Politics in Uganda.* Westview Press, Boulder, Colo.

Tantiwiramanond, Darunee. 2002. *Situation Analysis of Out-Migration from Thailand and the Role of GOs, NGOs and Academics*. Paper presented at the Conference, Gender, Migration and Governance in Asia, Australian National University, Canberra, 5–6 December.

Teerink, R. 1995. "Migration and its impact on Khandeshi women." In L. Schenk-Sandbergen (ed.), *Women and Seasonal Labour Migration*, Sage, New Delhi.

Tendler, Judith and Sarah Freedheim. 1994. "Trust in a rent-seeking world: Health and environment transformed in northeast Brazil." *World Development*, Vol. 22, No. 12, pp.1771–1792.

Therborn, Göran. 2004. *Between Sex and Power: Family in the World, 1900–2000*. Routledge, London.

Thielemann, Gregory S. and Joseph J. Stewart Jr. 1996. "A demand side perspective on the importance of representative bureaucracy." *Public Administration Review*, Vol. 56 (March/April), pp.768–773.

Third World Network (TWN). 2003. *Developing Countries Prepare for Agriculture Battle at Cancun Ministerial*. Report from Cancun, 9 September 2003. TWN, Penang. http://www.twnside.org.sg/title/update1.htm, accessed on 30 November 2004.

Thomas, S. 1991. "The impact of women on state legislative policies." *Journal of Politics*, Vol. 53, No. 4, pp.958–976.

Tibandebage, Paula. 2004. *Health Sector Reforms and Gender Implications: A Case Study of Mutual Health Insurance Schemes in Tanzania*. UNRISD Research Paper, Project on Gender and Social Policy, UNRISD, Geneva.

Tibandebage, Paula and Maureen Mackintosh. 2002. "Institutional reform and regulatory relationships in a liberalising health care system: A Tanzanian case study." In Judith Heyer, Rosemary Thorp and Frances Stewart (eds.), *Group Behaviour and Development*. Oxford University Press, Oxford.

Times of India. 2003. "Rs. 70 Lakh in Rs 1.3 Cr. just vanishes: The first public hearing of its kind in East Delhi had officials running for cover." Times of India, 24 January.

Tokman, Victor E. 2002. "Jobs and solidarity: Challenges for labour market policy in Latin America." In Evelyne Huber (ed.), *Models of Capitalism: Lessons for Latin America*. Pennsylvania State University Press, University Park PA.

Topalova, Petia. 2003. *Women are Changing Governance in India? The Impact of Female Leadership on household Satisfaction*, Quality of Public Goods and Governance. Mimeo, MIT, Boston.

Traynor, Ian. 2004. How commuters from the hard scrabble margins let the elite live in clover. *Guardian*, 26 April. www.guardian.co.uk/international/story/0,3604,1203336,00.html, accessed on 7 June 2004.

Tremblay, Marion. 1998. "Do female MPs substantively represent women? A study of legislative behaviour in Canada's 35th Parliament." *Canadian Journal of Political Science*, Vol. 31, No. 3, pp.435–465.

Tripp, Aili Mari. 2000. *Women and Politics in Uganda*. James Currey, Oxford.

Truth and Reconciliation Commission for Sierra Leone. 2003. *The Truth and Reconciliation Commission for Sierra Leone*. http://www.sierra-leone.org/trc-trcforsierraleone.html, accessed on 21 July 2004.

Tsikata, Dzodzi. 2004. *Economic Liberalization, the Informalization of Work and Urban Women's Livelihoods in Sub-Saharan Africa since the 1990s*. Background Paper for UNRISD Report on Gender Equality: Striving for Justice in an Unequal World.

—. 2003a. *Reconciling Liberalization, Technicism and Social Equity or How to Put Wheels on a Horse: Ghana's Land Reforms Reviewed*. Mimeo, UNRISD, Geneva.

—. 2003b. "Securing women's interests within land tenure reforms: Recent debates in Tanzania." *Journal of Agrarian Change*, Vol. 3, Nos. 1&2, pp.149–184.

—. 2001. *National Machineries for the Advancement of Women in Africa: Are they Transforming Gender Relations?* Third World Network-Africa, Ghana.

Tsui, Ming. 2002/03. "Managing transition: Unemployment and job hunting in urban China." *Pacific Affairs*, Vol. 75, No. 4, pp.515–534.

Turshen, Meredith and Clotilde Twagiramariya (eds.). 1998. *What Women Do in Wartime: Gender and Conflict in Africa*. Zed, London.

United Cities and Local Governments (UCLG). 2003. *Women's Participation Survey.*

> http://www.cities-localgovernments.org/uclg/admin/survey/scripts/sta_stats_world.asp?L=EN, accessed in May 2004.

United Nations. 2004. *United Nations Common Database* (UNCDB).

> millenniumindicators.un.org/unsd/cdb/cdb_simple_data_extract.asp, accessed on 2 September 2004.

—. 2003. *The World's Women 2000: Trends and Statistics,* Table 6.A. http://unstats.un.org/unsd/demographic/ww2000/tables.htm, accessed in May 2004.

—. 2000a. *Women's Indicators and Statistics Database* (WISTAT). Version 4, CD-ROM. United Nations, New York.

—. 2000b. *The World's Women: Trends and Statistics.* United Nations, New York.

—. 1999. *World Survey on the Role of Women in Development: Globalization, Gender and Work.* United Nations, New York.

—. (1998) Commission for the Status of Women, *Resolution on Women and Armed Conflict.* United Nations, New York.

—. 1997. *Report of Expert Group Meeting on Adolescent Girls and Their Rights.* United Nations, New York.

—. 1996. *Report on the World Conference to Review and Appraise the Achievements of the United Nations Decade for Women: Equality, Development and Peace.* United Nations, New York.

—. 1995a. *Platform for Action, Beijing.* http://www.un.org/womenwatch/daw/beijing/platform/, accessed on 1 December 2004.

—. 1995b. *The World's Women 1995: Trends and Statistics.* United Nations, New York.

—. 1994. *World Survey on the Role of Women in Development.* United Nations, New York.

—. 1990. *The World's Women: Trends and Statistics.* United Nations, New York.

—. 1989. *World Survey on the Role of Women in Development.* United Nations, New York.

—. 1986. *World Survey on the Role of Women in Development.* United Nations, New York.

UNAIDS. 2003. *Progress Report on the Global Response to the HIV/AIDS Epidemic.* UNAIDS, Geneva.

—. 1998. *AIDS and the Military.* UNAIDS, Geneva,

United Nations Children's Fund (UNICEF). 2002. *Situation Analysis and Children and Women in Ghana 2000.* UNICEF, Accra.

—. 1993. *The State of the World's Children.* UNICEF, New York.

UNICEF Innocenti Research Centre. 2001. *Early Marriage: Child Spouses.* Innocenti Digest No. 7. UNICEF, Florence.

United Nations Conference on Trade and Development (UNCTAD). 2004. *UNCTAD Databases.*

> http://www.unctad.org/Templates/Page.asp?intItemID=1888&lang=1, accessed on 30 September 2004.

—. 2002. *The Least Developed Countries Report 2002: Escaping the Poverty Trap.* UNCTAD, Geneva.

—. 1996. *World Investment Report.* UNCTAD, Geneva.

United Nations Department of Economic and Social Affairs (DESA). 2004. *Abortion Policies: A Global Review.* Population Division, United Nations, New York.

—. 2003. *Levels and Trends of International Migration to Selected Countries in Asia.* Population Division, United Nations, New York.

—. 2001. *Demographic Yearbook 2001.* Statistical Office, United Nations, New York.

United Nations Development Fund for Women (UNIFEM). 2004a. *Women, Peace and Security.*

> http://www.womenwarpeace.org/h_index.htm, accessed in July 2004.

—. 2004b. *Gender Profile of the Conflict in Abkhazia.* Women War Peace, UNIFEM.

> http://www.womenwarpeace.org/abkhazia/docs/abkhazia_pfv.pdf, accessed on 15 July 2004.

—. 2002. *Progress of World's Women.* UNIFEM, New York.

—. 2001. *Women's Land and Property Rights in Situations of Conflict and Reconstruction.* UNIFEM, New York.

—. 2000. *Progress of World's Women.* UNIFEM, New York.

United Nations Development Programme (UNDP). 2004. *Human Development Report 2004: Cultural Liberty in Today's Diverse World*. Oxford University Press, Oxford.

—. 2003. *Human Development Report 2003. Millennium Development Goals: A Compact among Nations to End Human Poverty.* Oxford University Press, New York/Oxford.

—. 2002. *Human Development Report 2002: Deepening Democracy in a Fragmented World*. Oxford University Press, Oxford.

—. 1995. *Human Development Report: Gender and Human Development*. Oxford University Press, Oxford.

United Nations Educational, Scientific and Cultural Organization (UNESCO). 2003. *EFA Global Monitoring Report 2003/04. Gender Education for All: The Leap to Equality*. UNESCO, Paris.

United Nations Economic and Social Commission for Western Asia (ESCWA) (2000), *Women and Men in the Arab Region: A Statistical Portrait 2000*. UNESCWA, Beirut.

United Nations Population Fund (UNFPA). 2004a. *Correspondence on Laws Promoting Gender Equality*. UNFPA, Geneva.

—. 2004b. *Investing in People: National Progress in Implementing the ICPD Programme of Action 1994–2004*. UNFPA, New York.

United Nations High Commissioner for Refugees (UNHCR). forthcoming. *2003 Statistical Yearbook*. UNHCR, Geneva.

—. 2004. *2003 Global Refugee Trends: Overview of Refugee Populations, New Arrivals, Durable Solutions, Asylum-Seekers and Other Persons of Concern to UNHCR*. UNHCR, Geneva.

—. 1994. "Women in Somalia". *Refugee Survey Quarterly*, Vol. 13, Nos. 2–3.

United Nations Office for the Coordination of Humanitarian Affairs. 2004. *SOMALIA: MPs Want More Women in New Parliament*. Report of 13 September 2004. http://www.irinnews.org/report.asp?ReportID=43143&SelectRegion=Horn_of_Africa&SelectCountry=SOMALIA, accessed on 15 October 2004.

—. 2003. *SOMALIA: Feature—Women Slowly Making Political Inroads*. Report of 14 July 2003. http://www.irinnews.org/report.asp?ReportID=35364&SelectRegion=Horn_of_Africa&SelectCountry=SOMALIA, accessed on 15 October 2004.

United Nations Research Institute for Social Development (UNRISD). 2004. *Corporate Social Responsibility and Development: Towards a New Agenda?* Conference News, Report of the UNRISD Conference Geneva, 17–18 November 2003. UNRISD, Geneva.

—. 2000. *Visible Hands: Taking Responsibility for Social Development*. UNRISD, Geneva.

—. 1993. *Rebuilding Wartorn Societies: Report of the Workshops on The Challenge of Rebuilding Wartorn Societies and The Social Consequences of the Peace Process in Cambodia*. Paper presented at The Challenge of Rebuilding Wartorn Societies and The Social Consequences of the Peace Process in Cambodia, Geneva, Switzerland, 27–30 April, UNRISD, Geneva.

United Nations Secretary-General. 2004 *Women Peace and Security: Report of the Secretary General to the UN Security Council*, 13 October, S/2004/814. United Nations, New York.

—. 2002. *Women, Peace and Security: Study Submitted by the UN Secretary General, Pursuant to Security Council Resolution 1325/2000*. United Nations, New York.

—. 2000. *Children and Armed Conflict, Report of the Secretary-General to the Security Council*, 19 July, A/55/163-S/2000/712. United Nations, New York.

United Nations Security Council. 2000. *Security Council Resolution 1325/2000*. Adopted by the Security Council at its 4213th meeting, on 31 October 2000. United Nations, Geneva.

United Nations Statistical Division. 2004. *Millennium Indicators Database*. Women in Parliamentary Seats, per cent (Code 1020). http://unstats.un.org/unsd/mi/mi_series_list.asp, accessed in May 2004.

United States Census Bureau. 2000. *1% Census PUMS*. www.ipums.umn.edu, accessed in 2004.

United Nations Treaty Collection. 2001. *Multilateral Treaty Framework: Invitation to Universal Participation,* http://untreaty.un.org/English/TreatyEvent2001/index.htm, accessed on 15 August 2004.

Upham, F. K. Forthcoming. "Ideology, experience and the rule of law in developing societies." In M. Woo-Cumings (ed.), *Neoliberalism and Institutional Reform in East Asia.* UNRISD and Cornell University Press.

Uppsala Conflict Data Program (UCDP) 2004/ International Peace Research Institute (PRIO). *Uppsala Conflict Database.* http://www.pcr.uu.se/database/, accessed on 24 November 2004.

USAID Office of Women in Development. 2000. *Intrastate Conflict and Gender.* Information Bulletin No. 9, USAID, Washington, D.C.

van der Hoeven, Rolph. 2000. *"Assessing Aid" and Global Governance: Why Poverty and Redistribution Objectives Matter.* Employment Paper No. 2000/8, ILO, Geneva.

Van Staveren, Irene. 2002. "Global finance and gender." In Jan-Aart Scholte and Albrecht Schnable (eds.), *Civil Society and Global Finance,* Routledge, London.

Vandemoortele, J. 2002. *Are We Really Reducing Global Poverty?* UNDP Bureau for Development Policy, New York.

Vanderweert, Susan Jenkins. 2001. "Seeking justice for comfort women: Without an international criminal court, suits brought by world war II sex slaves of the Japanese army may find their best hope of success in the US federal courts." *North Carolina Journal of International Law and Commercial Regulation,* Fall, Vol. 121.

Vega, Arturo and Juniata M. Firestone. 1995. "The effects of gender on congressional behaviour and the substantive representation of women." *Legislative Studies Quarterly,* Vol. 20, pp.213–311.

Vijayalakshmi, V. 2002. *Gender, Accountability and Political Representation in Local Government.* Working Paper No. 102, Institute for Social and Economic Change, Bangalore.

Vijayalakshmi, V. and B.K. Chandrashekar. 2001. *Authority, Powerlessness and Dependence: Women and Political Participation.* Working Paper No.16, Institute for Social and Economic Change, Bangalore.

Vivian, Jessica (ed.). 1995. *Adjustment and Social Sector Restructuring.* Frank Cass in association with European Association of Development Research and Training Institutes (EADI)/UNRISD, London and Geneva.

Wade, Robert. 2001. *Is Globalization Making World Income Distribution More Equal?* LSE Development Studies Institute Working Paper Series No. 01-01, London School of Economics, London.

—. 1990. Governing the Market. Princeton University Press, Princeton, N.J.

Walker, Cherryl. 2003. "Piety in the sky? Gender and land reform in South Africa." *Journal of Agrarian Change,* Vol. 3, Nos. 1&2, pp.113–149.

Walraven, G. 1996. "Willingness to pay for district hospital services in rural Tanzania." *Health Policy and Planning,* Vol. 11, No. 4, pp.428–437.

Walsh, Martha. 2004. *Gendering International Justice: Progress and Pitfalls at International Criminal Tribunals.* Background Paper for UNRISD Report on Gender Equality: Striving for Justice in an Unequal World.

—. 2000. *Aftermath: The Role of Women's Organizations in Postconflict Bosnia and Herzegovina.* Working Paper No. 308, July, Center for Development Information and Evaluation, USAID, Washington, D.C.

Ward, Jeanne. 2002. *If Not Now, When? Addressing Gender-Based Violence in Refugee, Internally Displaced and Post-Conflict Settings, A Global Overview.* Reproductive Health Response in Conflict (RHRC) Consortium. http://www.rhrc.org/resources/gbv/ifnotnow.html, accessed on 1 December 2004.

Watson, Carol. 1996. *The Flight Exile and Return of Chadian Refugees: A Case Study with a Special Focus on Women.* UNRISD, Geneva.

Waylen, Georgina. 2000. "Review of Jane S. Jaquette and Sharon L. Wolchik (eds.), *Women and Democracy: Latin America and Central and Eastern Europe* (Baltimore, MD: The Johns Hopkins University Press, 1998)." Journal of Latin American Studies, Vol. 32, No. 1, p. 265.

Weaver, Mary Anne. 2000. "Gandhi's daughters: India's poorest women embark on an epic social experiment." *New Yorker,* 10 January.

Weeks, John. 1998. *Economic Integration in Latin America: Impact on Labour.* Employment and Training Papers No. 18, Employment and Training Department, ILO, Geneva.

Weisbrot, Mark, Dean Baker, Egor Kraev and Judy Chen. 2001. *The Scorecard on Globalization 1980–2000: Twenty Years of Diminished Progress.* Center for Economic and Policy Research, Washington, D.C.

Weldon, S. Laurel. 2004. "The dimensions and policy impact of feminist civil society." *International Feminist Journal of Politics,* Vol. 6, No. 1, pp.1–28.

—. 2002. *Protest, Policy, and the Problem of Violence against Women: A Cross-National Comparison.* University of Pittsburgh Press, Pittsburgh, Pa.

White, Marceline. 2001. "GATS and women." *Foreign Policy in Focus,* Vol. 6, No. 2.

Whitehead, Ann. 2004. *The Gendered Impact of Liberalisation Policies on African Agricultural Economies and Rural Livelihoods.* Background Paper for UNRISD Report on Gender Equality: Striving for Justice in an Unequal World.

—. 2003. *Failing Women, Sustaining Poverty: Gender in Poverty Reduction Strategy Papers.* Paper for Christian Aid and the Gender and Development Network.

—. 2001. *Trade, Trade Liberalisation and Rural Poverty in Low-Income Africa: A Gendered Account.* Background Paper for the UNCTAD 2001 Least Developed Countries Report., UNCTAD, Geneva.

—. 1981. "I'm hungry mum. The politics of domestic budgeting." In C. Young, C. Wolcowitz and C. McCullagh (eds.), *Of Marriage and Market.* Women's Subordination in International Perspective, CSE Books, London.

Whitehead, Ann and Dzodzi Tsikata. 2003. "Policy discourses on women's land rights in sub-Saharan Africa: The implications of the return to the customary." *Journal of Agrarian Change,* Vol. 3, Nos. 1/2, pp.67–112.

Whiteside, M. 2000. *Ganyu Labour in Malawi and its Implications for Livelihood Security Interventions: An analysis of Recent Literature and Implications for Poverty Alleviation.* Network Paper No. 99, Overseas Development Institute (ODI) Agricultural Research and Extension Network, London.

Wilcox, Clyde, Beth Stark and Sue Thomas. 2003. "Popular support for electing women in Eastern Europe." In Richard E. Matland and Kathleen Montgomery (eds.), *Women's Access to Political Power in Post-Communist Europe,* Oxford University Press, Oxford.

Williams, F. 2003. *Rethinking Care in Social Policy.* Paper presented at Annual Conference of the Finnish Social Policy Association.

Williams, Suzanne and Rachal Masika. 2002. *Gender Trafficking and Slavery.* Oxfam, Oxford.

Wold, B. 1997. *Supply Response in a Gender Perspective: The Case of Structural Adjustment in Zambia.* Statistics Norway, Oslo and Zambian Central and Statistical Office, Lusaka.

Women in Black. 2004. *A Short History of Women in Black.* http://www.womeninblack.org/history.html, accessed on 19 July 2004.

Women in Parliament Support Unit. 2001. *Baseline Survey.* Women in Parliament Support Unit, Harare.

Women Living Under Muslim Laws (WLUML). 2004. *Turkey: Turkey Orders Sermons on Women's Rights.* http://www.wluml.org/english/newsfulltxt.shtml?cmd%5B157%5D=x-157-49322%20&cmd%5B189%5D=x-189-49322, accessed on 2 September 2004.

Women's Environment and Development Organization (WEDO). 2003. *Getting the Balance Right in National Parliaments,* Fact Sheet 4. http://www.wedo.org/5050/5050factsheet4.pdf, accessed in May 2004.

—. 2001. *Getting the Balance Right, 50/50 Campaign.* www.wedo.org/balance2.htm, accessed on 21 August 2001.

World Bank. 2004a. *GenderStats.* http://devdata.worldbank.org/genderstats/home.asp, accessed on 1 December 2004.

—. 2004b. *World Development Indicators 2004.* CD-ROM. World Bank, Washington, D.C.

—. 2003a. *World Development Report 2004: Making Services Work for the Poor*. Oxford University Press, New York.

—. 2003b. *World Development Report 2003: Sustainable Development in a Dynamic World*. Oxford University Press, New York.

—. 2002. *World Development Report 2002: Building Institutions for Markets*. Oxford University Press, Oxford and New York.

—. 2001a. *Engendering Development Through Gender Equality in Rights, Resources and Voice*. Oxford University Press, New York.

—. 2001b. *Participatory Approaches in Budgeting and Public Expenditure Management: Case Study 2: Porto Alegre, Brazil*. Participation Sourcebook, World Bank, Washington, D.C.

—. 2001c. *World Development Report 2000/2001: Attacking Poverty*. World Bank, Washington, D.C.

—. 1997. *World Development Report 1997: The State in a Changing World*. World Bank, Washington, D.C.

—. 1995a. *Will Arab Workers Prosper or Be Left Out in the 21st Century?* World Bank, Washington, D.C.

—. 1995b. *World Development Report: Workers in an Integrating World*. Oxford University Press, New York.

—. 1994. *Adjustment in Africa: Reforms, Results and the Road Ahead*. World Bank, Washington, D.C.

—. 1993a. *The East Asian Miracle*. Oxford University Press, New York.

—. 1992. *Governance and Development*. World Bank, Washington, D.C.

—. 1981. *Accelerated Development for Africa: An Agenda for Africa*. World Bank, Washington, D.C.

World Vision International. 1996. *The Effects of Armed Conflict on the Girl Child*. Working Paper No. 23, World Vision International, Geneva.

Wright, Richard and Mark Ellis. 2000. "The ethnic and gender division of labor compared among immigrants to Los Angeles." *International Journal of Urban and Regional Research*, Vol. 24, No. 3, pp.583–600.

Yamanaka, Keiko. 2003. "Feminised migration, community activism and grassroots transnationalisation in Japan". *Asian and Pacific Migration Journal*, Vol. 12, Nos. 1–2, pp.155–187.

Yamanaka, Keiko and Nicola Piper. 2004. *Feminised Cross-Border Migration, Entitlements and Civil Action in East and Southeast Asia*. Background Paper for UNRISD Report on Gender Equality: Striving for Justice in an Unequal World.

Yemen Ministry of Planning & Development. 1998. *Yemen Human Development Report 1998*. Ministry of Planning and Development, Sana'a, Republic of Yemen.

Yoon, Bang-Soon. 2001. "Democratization and gender politics in South Korea." In Rita Mae Kelly, Jane H. Bayes, Mary E. Hawkesworth and Brigitte Young (eds.), *Gender, Globalization, and Democratization*, Rowman and Littlefield, Lanham, Md.

Zammit, Ann. 2003. *Development at Risk: Rethinking UN-Business Partnerships*. South Center and UNRISD, Geneva.

Žarkov, Dubravka, Rada Drezgic and Tanja Djuric-Kuzmanovic. 2004. *Violent Conflicts in the Balkans: Impacts, Responses, Consequences*. Background Paper for UNRISD Report on Gender Equality: Striving for Justice in an Unequal World.

Zhiqin, Shao. 2000. *Women and Social Security: Impact of the Financial Crisis*. Mimeo, Shandong Academy of Social Sciences, China.

Zlotnik. 2003. *The Global Dimension of Female Migration*. Migration Information Source, Washington, D.C. www.migrationinformation.org/Feature/display.cfm?ID=109, accessed on 1 December 2004.

Acronyms

ACFTU	All China Federation of Trade Unions	FMLN	Frente Farabundo Martí para la Liberación Nacional
ACORD	Agency for Co-operation and Research in Development	GASPP	Globalism and Social Policy Programme
ACP	African Caribbean and Pacific	GAWU	General Agricultural Workers' Union
ADB	Asian Development Bank	GDI	Gender Development Index
AIDS	acquired immunodeficiency syndrome	GDP	gross domestic product
ANC	African National Congress	GEM	Gender Empowerment Measure
CBO	community-based organization	GLTF	Gender Land Task Force
CEDA	Committee for Economic Development of Australia	GNI	gross national income
		HDI	Human Development Index
CEDAW	Convention on the Elimination of All Forms of Discrimination against Women	HIV	human immunodeficiency virus
		HVAE	high-value agricultural export crops
CFEMEA	Centro Feminista de Estudos e Assessoria	HWFC	Health Workers for Change
CIIR	Catholic Institute for International Relations	ICC	International Criminal Court
CRC	Convention on the Rights of the Child	ICPD	International Conference on Population and Development
DEVAW	Declaration on the Elimination of Violence Against Women	ICTR	International Criminal Tribunal of Rwanda
		ICTY	International Criminal Tribunal of Yugoslavia
DRC	Democratic Republic of Congo	IDASA	Institute for Democracy in South Africa
ECLAC	Economic Commission for Latin America and the Caribbean	IDEA	Institute for Democracy and Electoral Assistance
ECOSOC	United Nations Economic and Social Council	IDEAS	International Development Economics Associates
EEA	European Economic Area	IDP	internally displaced person
EPW	Economic and Political Weekly	IDS	Institute of Development Studies
ESCWA	Economic and Social Commission for Western Asia	IFI	international financial institution
		IFP	Inkatha Freedom Party
EU	European Union	IIS	Integrated Insurance Scheme
FAO	Food and Agriculture Organization of the United Nations	ILO	International Labour Organization
FDI	foreign direct investment	IMF	International Monetary Fund

IOM	International Organization for Migration		ONUSAL	Observadores de las Naciones Unidas en El Salvador
IPU	Inter-Parliamentary Union			
IRDP	Integrated Rural Development Programme		OSKa	National Women's Information Center
IRI	Islamic Republic of Iran		PR	proportional representation
IT	information technology		PRI	Partido Revolucionario Institucional
IWRC	Iraqi Women's Rights Coalition		PRIO	International Peace Research Institute
LRA	Lord's Resistance Army		PRSP	Poverty Reduction Strategy Paper
LTTE	Liberation Tigers of Tamil Elam		PT	Partido dos Trabalhadores
MAFF	Ministry of Agriculture Food and Fisheries		RAWA	Revolutionary Association of the Women of Afghanistan
MCH	mother and child health			
MDC	Movement for Democratic Change		REMHI	Recovery of Historical Memory Project at the Human Rights Office of the Archdiocese of Guatemala
MENA	Middle East and North Africa			
MFA	Multi-Fibre Agreement			
MHI	mutual health insurance		RODI	Resources Oriented Development Initiative
MNEs	multinational enterprises		RUF	Revolutionary United Front
MP	member of parliament		SERNAM	Servicio Nacional de la Mujer
NABARD	National Bank for Agriculture and Rural Development		SEWA	Self Employed Women's Association
			SEWU	Self Employed Women's Union
NAFTA	North Atlantic Free Trade Agreement		SHG	self-help group
NGO	non-governmental organization		SIGE	Standardized Indicator of Gender Equality
NMA	Naga Mothers' Association		SIPRI	Stockholm International Peace Research Institute
OAP	old age pension			
OAS	Organisation of American States		STI	sexually transmitted infection
OAU	Organization of African Unity		TC	Truth Commission
ODA	Official Development Assistance		TDP	Telugu Desam Party
OECD	Organization for Economic Co-operation and Development		TRC	Truth and Reconciliation Commission
			TWN	Third World Network
OHCHR	Office of the United Nations High Commissioner for Human Rights		UCDP	Uppsala Conflict Data Program
			UCLG	United Cities and Local Governments

UK	United Kingdom	UNSG	United Nations Secretary General
UMASIDA	Umoja wa Matibabu katika Sekta Isiyo Rasmi Dar es Salaam	UPEU	Uganda Public Employees Union
		URNG	Unidad Revolucionaria Nacional Guatemalteca
UN	United Nations	US	United States
UNAIDS	Joint United Nations Programme on HIV/AIDS	USAID	United States Agency for International Development
UNCTAD	United Nations Conference on Trade and Development	USSR	Union of Soviet Socialist Republics
UNDESA	United Nations Department of Economic and Social Affairs	WAC	Women's Agenda for Change
		WDR	World Development Report (of the World Bank)
UNDP	United Nations Development Programme		
UNESCO	United Nations Educational, Scientific and Cultural Organization	WEDO	Women's Environment and Development Organization
UNFPA	United Nations Population Fund	WHO	World Health Organization
UNGA	United Nations General Assembly	WIB	Women in Black
UNGASS	United Nations General Assembly Special Session	WIDER	World Institute for Development Economics Research
UNHCR	United Nations High Commissioner for Refugees	WLUML	Women Living Under Muslim Laws
		WTO	World Trade Organization
UNICEF	United Nations Children's Fund		
UNIFEM	United Nations Development Fund for Women		
UNITA	União Nacional para a Independência Total de Angola		
UNOCHA	United Nations Office for the Coordination of Humanitarian Affairs		
UNRISD	United Nations Research Institute for Social Development		
UNTAC	United Nations Transitional Authority in Cambodia		
UNSC	United Nations Security Council		

Annex:
Geographical groupings

Africa

North Africa
Algeria
Egypt
Libyan Arab Jamahiriya
Morocco
Tunisia
Western Sahara

Sub-Saharan Africa
Angola
Benin
Botswana
Burkina Faso
Burundi
Cameroon
Cape Verde
Central African Republic
Chad
Comoros
Congo
Congo, Democratic Republic of the
    Côte d'Ivoire
Djibouti
Equatorial Guinea
Eritrea
Ethiopia
Gabon

Gambia
Ghana
Guinea
Guinea-Bissau
Kenya
Lesotho
Liberia
Madagascar
Malawi
Mali
Mauritania
Mauritius
Mozambique
Namibia
Niger
Nigeria
Réunion
Rwanda
Sao Tome and Principe
Senegal
Seychelles
Sierra Leone
Somalia
South Africa
Sudan
Swaziland
Tanzania, United Republic of
Togo
Uganda

Zambia
Zimbabwe

Latin America and the Caribbean

Caribbean
Antigua and Barbuda
Aruba
Bahamas
Barbados
Cuba
Dominica
Dominican Republic
Grenada
Guadeloupe
Haiti
Jamaica
Martinique
Netherlands Antilles
Puerto Rico
Saint Kitts and Nevis
Saint Lucia
Saint Vincent and the Grenadines
Trinidad and Tobago
United States Virgin Islands

Central America

Belize

Costa Rica

El Salvador

Guatemala

Honduras

Mexico

Nicaragua

Panama

South America

Argentina

Bolivia

Brazil

Chile

Colombia

Ecuador

French Guiana

Guyana

Paraguay

Peru

Suriname

Uruguay

Venezuela

Asia

East Asia

China

   Hong Kong Special Administrative
      Region of China

   Macao Special Administrative
      Region of China

   Taiwan Province of China

Korea, Democratic People's Republic of

Korea, Republic of

Mongolia

Southeast Asia

Brunei Darussalam

Cambodia

Timor Leste

Indonesia

Lao People's Democratic Republic

Malaysia

Myanmar

Philippines

Singapore

Thailand

Viet Nam

South Asia

Afghanistan

Bangladesh

Bhutan

India

Iran, Islamic Republic of

Maldives

Nepal

Pakistan

Sri Lanka

Central Asia

Kazakhstan

Kyrgyzstan

Tajikistan

Turkmenistan

Uzbekistan

West Asia

Armenia

Azerbaijan

Bahrain

Cyprus

Georgia

Iraq

Israel

Jordan

Kuwait

Lebanon

Occupied Palestinian Territory

Oman

Qatar

Saudi Arabia
Syrian Arab Republic
Turkey
United Arab Emirates
Yemen

Oceania

American Samoa
Fiji
French Polynesia
Guam
Kiribati
Marshall Islands
Micronesia, Federated States of
Nauru
New Caledonia
Palau
Papua New Guinea
Samoa
Solomon Islands
Tonga
Vanuatu

Developed Regions

Eastern Europe
Albania
Belarus
Bosnia and Herzegovina
Bulgaria
Croatia
Czech Republic
Estonia
Hungary
Latvia
Lithuania
Macedonia, The former Yugoslav
    Republic of
Moldova, Republic of
Poland
Romania
Russian Federation
Serbia and Montenegro
Slovakia
Slovenia
Ukraine

Western Europe
Andorra
Austria
Belgium
Denmark

Finland
France
Germany
Greece
Iceland
Ireland
Italy
Liechtenstein
Luxembourg
Malta
Monaco
Netherlands
Norway
Portugal
San Marino
Spain
Sweden
Switzerland
United Kingdom of Great Britain and
    Northern Ireland

Other developed
Australia
Bermuda
Canada
Japan
New Zealand
United States of America

Photo credits

Section 1: © Mark Henley, Panos Pictures
Section 2: © Rohdri Jones, Panos Pictures
Section 3: © Chris Stowers, Panos Pictures
Section 4: © Paul Lowe, Panos Pictures

Printed by Imprimerie Gonnet, France.

UNITED NATIONS RESEARCH INSTITUTE FOR SOCIAL DEVELOPMENT